NAVIGATING THE DIGITAL AGE:
The Definitive Cybersecurity Guide for Directors and Officers

Published by

CAXTON
Business & Legal inc.

Navigating the Digital Age: The Definitive Cybersecurity Guide for Directors and Officers

Publisher: Tim Dempsey

Editor: Matt Rosenquist

Design and Composition: Graphic World, Inc.

Printed and bound in Canada by TC Printing

Navigating the Digital Age: The Definitive Cybersecurity Guide for Directors and Officers
is published by:
Caxton Business & Legal, Inc.
27 North Wacker Drive, Suite 601
Chicago, IL 60606
Phone: +1 312 361 0821
Email: tjd@caxtoninc.com

First published: 2015
ISBN: 978-0-9964982-0-3

Navigating the Digital Age: The Definitive Cybersecurity Guide for Directors and Officers
© October 2015

Cover illustration by Tim Heraldo

DISCLAIMER

Introduction

New York Stock Exchange – Tom Farley, President

No issue today has created more concern within corporate C-suites and boardrooms than cybersecurity risk. With the ability to shatter a company's reputation with their customers and draw criticism from shareholders, lawsuits from affected parties, and attention from the media, the threat of cyber risk is ubiquitous and insidious. No company, region, or industry is immune, which makes the responsibility to oversee, manage, and mitigate cyber risk a top-down priority in every organization.

The New York Stock Exchange has long advocated that exemplary governance and risk oversight is fundamental to the health of individual companies, as well as to the sound operation of our capital markets. In other words, we too take the threat very seriously. Today, managing cybersecurity risk has expanded far beyond the realm of IT; it has become a business continuity necessity to ensure shareholder value remains intact and that privacy and corporate intellectual property is protected. Accordingly, those responsibilities are weighing heavily on corporate executives and directors, making it vital for them to better understand and prepare for the evolving cybersecurity landscape.

Cyber risk ultimately poses a threat to confidence, a foundational aspect of U.S. corporate issuers and markets. We are taking a leadership role on many fronts, such as reducing market fragmentation and complexity, as well as increasing efficiency through the highest levels of intelligence, analytics, and technology. Confidence in the integrity and security of our assets is concurrent with our success—as it is for every other company operating in the public markets today.

Moreover, because the public markets have become increasingly reliant on interdependent technology systems, the threat looms even larger. As we witnessed during the 2008 financial crisis, rarely does any failure happen in a vacuum; therefore, the threat of systemic disruption has taken on an even higher level of prominence and concern among regulators and policymakers worldwide.

It is important that companies remain vigilant, taking steps to proactively and intelligently address cybersecurity risk within their organizations. Beyond the technological solutions developed to defend and combat breaches, we can accomplish even more through better training, awareness, and insight on human behavior. Confidence, after all, is not a measure of technological systems, but of the people who are entrusted to manage them.

With insights from the preeminent authorities on cybersecurity today, this groundbreaking, practical guide to cybersecurity has been developed to reflect a body of knowledge that is unsurpassed on this topic. At the heart of effective risk management must be a thorough understanding of the risks as well as pragmatic solutions. Thank you for your continued partnership with the New York Stock Exchange, and we look forward to continuing to support your requirements in this dynamic landscape.

Foreword

Visa Inc. – Charles W. Scharf, CEO

For years, cybersecurity was an issue that consumers, executive management, and boards of directors took for granted. They were able to do so because the technologists did not. The technologists worked every day to protect their systems from attack, and they were quite effective for many years. We sit here today in a very different position. The threats are bigger than ever before and growing in frequency and severity every day. Cybersecurity is now something everyone needs to think about, whether it's in your personal or professional life. What worked in the past is not enough to protect us in the present and future.

So what has changed?

First of all, the technology platforms of today are bigger targets than ever given the breadth and criticality of items they control. Second, the amount and value of the data that we all produce and store has grown exponentially. The data is a gold mine for criminals. Third, the interconnectedness of the world just makes it easier for more people—regardless of geography—to be able to steal or disrupt. And fourth, the perpetrators are more sophisticated, better organized, better funded, and harder to bring to justice than ever before.

So the problem is different, and what we all do about it is different.

This is not simply an IT issue. It is a business problem of the highest level. Protecting our data and our systems is core to business today. And that means that having an outstanding cybersecurity program also can't detract from our objectives around innovation, speed, and performance.

Security has been a top priority at Visa for decades. It is foundational to delivering our brand promise. To be the *best* way to pay and be paid, we must be the *most secure* way to pay and be paid. We cannot ask people to use our products unless they believe that we are just that. Thus we must guard carefully both the security of our own network and company and the security of the broader payments ecosystem.

There are several elements that we have found to be critical to ensuring an effective security program at Visa.

- Be open and honest about the effectiveness of your security program and regularly share an honest assessment of your security posture with the executive team and board.

We use a data-driven approach that scores our program across five categories: risk intelligence, malware prevention, vulnerability management, identity and access management, and detection and response. Scores move up and down not only as our defenses improve or new vulnerabilities are discovered but also as threats change. The capabilities of the adversaries are growing, and you need a dynamic approach to measurement.

- Invest in security before investing elsewhere. A well-controlled environment gives you the license to do other things. Great and innovative products and services will only help you win if you have a well-protected business.
- Don't leave the details to others. Active, hands-on engagement by the executive team and the board is required. The risk is existential. Nothing is more important. Your involvement will produce better results as well as make sure the whole organization understands just how important the issue is.
- Never think you've done enough. The bad guys are smart and getting smarter. They aren't resting, and they have more resources than ever. Assume they will attack.

Defending against cyberthreats is not something that we can solve for our company in a vacuum. At Visa, we must protect not only our own network but the whole payments ecosystem. This came to life for us in late 2013 when some of the largest U.S. retailers and financial institutions in the U.S. reported data breaches. Tens of millions of consumer

accounts had been compromised—a pivotal moment for our industry.

The losses experienced by our clients, combined with the impact on consumer confidence, galvanized our industry to take actions that, we believe, will have a meaningful and lasting effect on how the world manages sensitive consumer data—not just payments.

We are taking action as an ecosystem, to collaborate and share information across industries and with law enforcement and governments and to develop new technologies that will allow us to prevent attacks and respond to threats in the future.

- Protect payments at physical retailers. Fraudsters have targeted the point-of-sale environment at leading U.S. retailers, capturing consumer account information and forcing the reissuance of millions of payment cards. As an industry we are rapidly introducing EMV (Europay, MasterCard, and Visa) chip payment technology in the United States. Chip-enabled payment cards and terminals work in concert to generate dynamic data with each transaction, rendering the transaction data useless to fraudsters.
- Protect online payments. Consumer purchases online and with mobile devices are growing at a significant rate. In order to prevent cyberattacks and fraudulent use of consumer accounts online, Visa and the global payments industry adopted a new payment standard for online payments. The new standard replaces the 16-digit account number with a digital token that is used to process online payments without exposing consumer account information.
- Collaborate and share information. Sharing threat intelligence is a necessity rather than a "nice to have," allowing merchants, financial institutions, and payment networks like Visa to rapidly detect and respond to cyberattacks. Public and private partnerships are also critical to creating the most robust

community of threat intelligence, so we also work closely with law enforcement and governments. At the heart of Visa's security strategy is the concept of "cyber fusion," which is centered on the principle of shared intelligence—a framework to collect, analyze, and leverage cyberthreat intelligence, internally and externally, to build a better defense for the whole ecosystem.

Championing security is one of Visa's six strategic goals. This is an area where there are no grades—it is pass or fail, and pass is the only option. Cybersecurity needs to be part of the fabric of every company and every industry, integrated into every business process and every employee action. And it begins and ends at the top. It is job number one.

Chm W Sch

TABLE OF CONTENTS

IV: Comprehensive approach to cybersecurity

V. Design best practices

VI. Cybersecurity beyond your network

VII. Incident response

Introductions — The cyberthreat in the digital age

Prevention: Can it be done?

Palo Alto Networks Inc. – Mark McLaughlin, CEO

Frequent headlines announcing the latest cyber breach of a major company, government agency, or organization are the norm today, begging the questions of why and will it ever end?

The reason cybersecurity is ingrained in news cycles, and receives extraordinary investments and focus from businesses and governments around the world, is the growing realization that these breaches are putting our very digital lifestyle at risk. This is not hyperbole. More and more, we live in the digital age, in which things that used to be real and tangible are now machine-generated or only exist as bits and bytes. Consider your bank account and total absence of tangible money or legal tender that underlies it; you trust that the assets exist because you can "see" them when you log in to your account on the financial institution's website. Or the expectation you have that light, water, electricity, and other utility services will work on command, despite your having little to no idea of how the command actually results in the outcome. Or the comfort in assuming that of the 100,000 planes traversing the globe on an average day, all will fly past each other at safe distances and take off and land at proper intervals. Now, imagine that this trust, reliance, and comfort could not be taken for granted any longer and the total chaos that would ensue. This is the digital age; and with all the efficiencies and productivity that has come with it, more and more we trust that it will just "work."

This reliance on digital systems is why the tempo of concern due to cyberattacks is rising so rapidly. Business leaders, government leaders, education leaders, and military leaders know that there is a very fine line separating the smoothly functioning digital society built on trust and the chaotic breakdown in society resulting from the erosion of that trust. And it is eroding quickly. Why is that, and do we have any analogies? And, more importantly, can it be fixed?

■ Machine vs. human

At the heart of the cybersecurity battle is a math problem. It is relatively simple to understand, but hard to correct. One of the negative offshoots of the ever-decreasing cost of computing power is the ability for cyber criminals and adversaries to launch increasingly numerous and sophisticated attacks at lower and lower costs. Today, bad actors without the capability to develop their own tools can use existing malware and exploits that are often free or inexpensive to obtain online. Similarly, advanced hackers, criminal organizations, and nation-states are able to use these widely available tools to launch successful intrusions and obscure their identity. These sophisticated adversaries are also developing and selectively using unique tools that could cause even greater harm. This all adds up to tremendous leverage for the attackers. (See Figure 1.)

In the face of this increasing onslaught in the sheer number of attacks and levels of sophistication, the defender is generally relying on decades-old core security technology, often cobbled together in multiple layers of point products; there is no true visibility of the situation, nor are the point products designed to communicate with each other. As a result, to the extent attacks are detected or lessons are learned from an attack, responses are highly manual in nature. Unfortunately, humans facing off against machines have little to no leverage, and cyber expertise is increasingly hard to come by in the battle for talent. Flipping the cost curve on its head with automation and a next-generation, natively integrated security platform is required if there is any hope of reducing the "breach du jour" headlines. (See Figure 2.)

It is unlikely that the number of attacks will abate over time. On the contrary, there is every reason to expect that their number will continue to grow. In fact, we can also expect that the "attack surface" and potential targets will also continue to grow as we constantly increase the connections of various things to the Internet.

An understandable but untenable response to this daunting threat environment is to assume that prevention is impossible, so we must simply detect and respond to all intrusions. The fundamental problem with this approach is that without significant prevention no combination of people, process, and technology can prioritize and respond to every intrusion that could significantly impact a network and those who rely on it. The math problem is simply insurmountable. Quite simply, detection and response should be supplements to, instead of substitutes for, prevention.

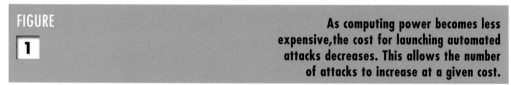

FIGURE

1

As computing power becomes less expensive, the cost for launching automated attacks decreases. This allows the number of attacks to increase at a given cost.

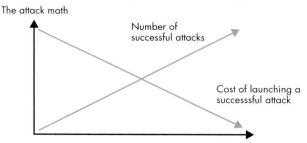

The attack math

Number of successful attacks

Cost of launching a successsful attack

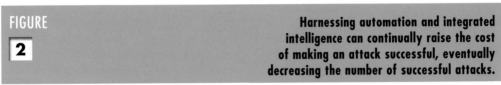

FIGURE 2

Harnessing automation and integrated intelligence can continually raise the cost of making an attack successful, eventually decreasing the number of successful attacks.

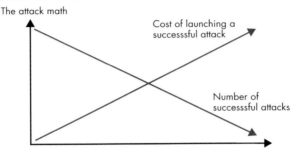

So, the strategy must be to significantly decrease the likelihood, and increase the cost, required for an attacker to perform a *successful* attack. To be more specific, we should not assume that attacks are going away or that all attacks can be stopped. However, we should assume, and be very diligent in ensuring, that the cost of a successful attack can be dramatically increased to the point where the incidence of a successful attack will sharply decline.

When this point is reached, and it will not come overnight, then we will be able to quantify and compartmentalize the risk to something acceptable and understood. It's at that point that cyber risks will be real and persistent but that they will leave the headlines and fade into the background of everyday life, commerce, communications, and interaction. This should be our goal. Not to eliminate all risk, but to reduce it to something that can be compartmentalized. There is a historical analogy to this problem and an approach to solve it.

■ Sputnik analogy

The analogy, which is imperfect but helpful, is the space race. In 1957 the Soviet Union launched Sputnik. The result was panic at the prospect that this technology provided the Soviets with an overwhelming advantage to deliver a nuclear attack across the

U.S. Suddenly, the very way of life in the Western world was deemed, appropriately so, at risk. The comfort and confidence of living in a well-protected and prosperous environment was shattered as citizens lost trust in their ability to follow their daily routines and way of life. It appeared as though there was an insurmountable technological lead, and everywhere people turned there was anxiety and cascading bad news.

In the years immediately following Sputnik, the main focus was on how to survive a post–nuclear-war world. Items like backyard bomb shelters and nonperishable food items were in great demand, and schools were teaching duck-and-cover drills. In other words, people were assuming attacks could not be prevented and were preparing for remediation of their society post-attack.

However, this fatalistic view was temporary. America relied on diplomacy and traditional forms of deterrence while devoting technological innovation and ingenuity to breakthroughs such as NASA's Mercury program. While it took a decade of resources, collaboration, trial, and effort, eventually the Mercury program and succeeding efforts changed the leverage in the equation. The space-based attack risk was not eliminated, but it was compartmentalized to the point of fading into the background as a possible but not probable event. It was at this stage that the panic and confusion receded from the headlines and daily reporting. We will know we are in good shape in the cyber battle when we have reached this point. So, how do we get there?

As with all things in life, ideas and philosophy matter. This is true because if you do not know what you are trying to get done, it's unlikely that you will get it done. In the space race analogy, the philosophy shifted over time from one that primarily assumed an attack was imminent and unstoppable with the majority of planning and resources geared toward life in the post-attack world, to one of prevention where the majority of resources and planning were geared to reduce the probability and effectiveness of an attack.

Importantly, the risk of an attack was not eliminated, but the probability of occurrence and success was reduced by vastly increasing the cost of a successful attack. It was previously noted that no analogy is perfect, so the analogy of "cost" here for space-based attacks and cyberattacks is, of course, measured in different ways. Most notably, cyberthreats are not the sole purview of superpower nations, and the technological innovation most likely to reverse the cost of successful attacks is most likely to come from industry, not governments. However, the principle is the same in that a prevention philosophy is much more likely to result in prevention capabilities being developed, utilized, and continually refined over time.

■ Is prevention possible?

The obvious question then is whether prevention is possible. I think that most security professionals and practitioners would agree that total prevention is not possible. This is disheartening but also no different from any other major risk factor that we have ever dealt with over time. So, the real question is whether prevention is possible to the point where the incidence of successful attacks is reduced to something manageable from a risk perspective. I believe that this is possible over time. In order to achieve this outcome,

it is an imperative that cost leverage is gained in the cyber battle. This leverage can be attained by managing the cyber risk to an organization through the continual improvement and coordination of several key elements: technology, process and people, and intelligence sharing.

Technology

It is very apparent that traditional or legacy security technology is failing at an alarming rate. There are three primary reasons for this:

■ The first is that networks have been built up over a long period of time and often are very complicated in nature, consisting of security technology that has been developed and deployed in a point product, siloed approach. In other words, a security "solution" in traditional network architecture of any size consists of multiple point products from many different vendors all designed to do one specific task, having no ability to inform or collaborate with other products. This means that the security posture of the network is only as "smart" overall as the least smart device or offering. Also, to the extent that any of the thousands of daily threats is successfully detected, protection is highly manual in nature because there is no capability to automatically coordinate or communicate with other capabilities in the network, let alone with other networks not in your organization. That's a real problem because defenders are relying more and more on the least leverageable resource they have—people—to fight machine-generated attacks.

■ Second, these multiple point solutions are often based on decades-old technology, like stateful inspection, which was useful in the late 1990s but is totally incapable of providing security capabilities for today's attack landscape.

■ And third, the concept of a "network" has morphed continues to do so at a rapid pace into something amorphous in nature: the advent of software as a service (SaaS) providers, cloud computing, mobility, the Internet of Things, and other macrotechnology trends that have the impact of security professionals having less and less control over data.

In the face of these challenges, it is critical that a few things are true in the security architecture of the future:

- First is that advanced security systems designed on definitive knowledge of what and who is using the network be deployed. In other words, no guessing.
- Second is that these capabilities be as natively integrated as possible into a platform such that any action by any capability results in an automatic reprogramming of the other capabilities.
- Third is that this platform must also be part of a larger, global ecosystem that enables a constant and near-real-time sharing of attack information that can be used to immediately apply protections preventing other organizations in the ecosystem from falling victim to the same or similar attacks.
- Last is that the security posture is consistent regardless of where data resides or the deployment model of the "network." For example, the advanced integrated security and automated outcomes must be the same whether the network is on premise, in the cloud, or has data stored off the network in third-party applications. Any inconsistency in the security is a vulnerability point as a general matter. And, as a matter of productivity, security should not be holding back high-productivity deployment scenarios based on the cloud, virtualization, SDN, NFV, and other models of the future.

Process and people

Technology alone is not going to solve the problem. It is incumbent upon an executive team to ensure their technical experts are managing cybersecurity risk to the organization. Most of today's top executives did not attain their position due to technological and cybersecurity proficiency. However, all

successful leaders understand the need to assess organizational risk and to allocate resources and effort based on prioritized competing needs. Given the current threat environment and the math behind successful attacks, leaders need to understand both the value and vulnerabilities residing on their networks and prioritize prevention and response efforts accordingly.

Under executive leadership, it is also very important that there is continued improvement in processes used to manage the security of organizations. People must be continually trained on how to identify cyberattacks and on the appropriate steps to take in the event of an attack. Many of the attacks that are being reported today start or end with poor processes or human error. For example, with so much personal information being readily shared on social networking, it is simple for hackers to assemble very accurate profiles of individuals and their positions in companies and launch socially engineered attacks or campaigns. These attacks can be hard to spot in the absence of proper training for individuals, and difficult to control in the absence of good processes and procedures regardless of how good the technology is that is deployed to protect an organization.

A common attack on organizations to defraud large amounts of money via wire transfers counts on busy people being poorly trained and implementing spotty processes. In such an attack, the attacker uses publicly available personal information gleaned off social networking sites to identify an individual who has the authority to issue a wire transfer in a company. Then the attacker uses a phishing attack, a carefully constructed improper email address that looks accurate on a cursory glance, seemingly from this person's manager at the company telling the person to send a wire transfer right away to the following coordinates. If the employee is not trained to look for proper email address configuration, or the company does not have a good process in place to validate wire transfer requests, like requiring two approvals, then this attack often succeeds. It is important that technology, process, and people are coordinated, and that training is done on a regular basis.

Intelligence sharing

Given the increasing number and sophistication of cyberattacks, it is difficult to imagine that any one company or organization will have enough threat intelligence at any one time to be able to defeat the vast majority of attacks. However, it is not hard to imagine that if multiple organizations were sharing what they are seeing from an attack perspective with each other in close to real time, that the combined intelligence would limit successful attacks to a small number of the attempted attacks. This is the outcome we should strive for, as getting to this point would mean that the attackers would need to design and develop unique attacks every single time they want to attack an organization, as opposed to today where they can use variants of an attack again and again against multiple targets. Having to design unique attacks every time would significantly drive up the cost of a successful attack and force attackers to aggregate resources in terms of people and money, which would make them more prone to be visible to defenders, law enforcement, and governments.

The network effect of defense is why there is such a focus and attention on threat intelligence information sharing. It is early days on this front, but all progress is good progress, and, importantly, organizations are now using automated systems to share threat intelligence. At the same time, analytical capabilities are being rapidly developed to make use and sense of all the intelligence in ways that will result in advanced platforms being able to reprogram prevention capabilities in rapid fashion such that connected networks will be constantly updating threat capabilities in an ever-increasing ecosystem. This provides immense leverage in the cybersecurity battle.

■ Conclusion

There is understandable concern and attention on the ever-increasing incidence of cyberattacks. However, if we take a longer view of the threat and adopt a prevention-first mindset, the combination of next-generation technology, improvements in processes and training, and real-time sharing of threat information with platforms that can automatically reconfigure the security posture, can vastly reduce the number of successful attacks and restore the digital trust we all require for our global economy.

2

The three Ts of the cyber economy

The Chertoff Group — Michael Chertoff, Executive Chairman and Former United States Secretary of Homeland Security, and Jim Pflaging, Principal

Thanks to rapid advances in technology and thinking, over the last decade we have seen entire industries and countries reinvented in large part because of the power of the Internet and related innovations. Naturally, these developments created new opportunities and risks, and none is greater than cybersecurity. Today, business leaders, academics, small business owners, and school kids know about hackers, phishing, identify theft, and even "bad actors."

In late 2014, the Sony Pictures Entertainment breach led to debates over data security, free speech, and corporate management as well as the details of celebrity feuds and paychecks. The idea of cybersecurity is rising to the fore of our collective consciousness. Notable cybersecurity breaches, including those at Target, Anthem BlueCross, and the U.S. Office of Personnel Management, have demonstrated that no organization or individual is immune to cyberthreat. In short, the cybersecurity environment has changed dramatically over the past several years, and many of us have struggled to keep up. Many firms now find themselves in an environment where one of their greatest business risks is cyber risk, a risk that has rapidly risen from an afterthought to primary focus.

How do we create more opportunity and a safer world while protecting privacy in an interconnected world? This question is not just for policy makers in government and leaders of global Fortune 500 businesses. It affects the neighborhood small business, the academic community, investors and, of course, our children.

Answering that question requires an understanding of the three Ts—technology, threat, and trust. Why? Because these are big interrelated ideas that have a significant effect on business strategy, policy, and public opinion. For starters, you need to know about the three Ts, think about them, and decide how you are going to embrace the first, deal with the second, and shape the last.

■ Technology

Today we live in a golden age of innovation driven by technologies that dominate headlines—cloud computing, mobility, big data, social media, open source software, virtualization, and, most recently, the Internet of Things. These tectonic shifts allow individuals, government, and companies to innovate and reinvent how they interact with each other. These forces mandate that we redefine what, how, and where we manage any business. We need to challenge core assumptions about markets, company culture, and the art of the possible. The winners will be those who leverage these innovations to reduce costs and deliver better, lower-priced products. Take Table 1 below, for example:

TABLE 1	Market capitalization (or private estimates, USD in millions)	
	3/31/2005	3/31/2015
Amazon	$13,362	$207,275
Apple	$30,580	$752,160
Google	$64,180	$378,892
Uber	N/A	$41,000
AT&T	$78,027	$175,108
Citigroup	$244,346	$165,488
General Electric	$388,007	$274,771
Kodak	$6,067	$794

Sources: Capital IQ, Fortune

It is easy to see the relationship between innovation and valuation. Some companies, such as Kodak, did not react fast enough and lost their market as a result. Others, such as AT&T, have invested heavily in new technology and are thriving. Still, the advantage lies with the firms who not only embraced the Internet but also built their entire business around it: Amazon, Google, and Uber. Finally, there is Apple, which came of age with the Internet and morphed into a wildly successful global leader with the introduction of the iPhone.

There have been applications for these technologies, with significant impact, in a variety of industries. In transportation, Uber is a great example of transforming a pervasive but sedentary sector into a newly reimagined market. Uber used emerging technologies to disrupt seemingly distinct segments such as auto rental and even automotive manufacturing. In the electrical sector, smart meters, transformers, and switches have given utilities greater control over their distribution networks while their customers have gained greater control of their consumption.

However, the golden age of innovation has a dark side. A new class of "bad guys" has emerged and is taking advantage of "holes" in these new technologies and our online behavior to create new risks. This leads us to the second T—Threat.

■ Threat

Lifecycle

It is almost cliché to talk about the pervasiveness and escalating impact of cybersecurity attacks. However, it is useful to provide a map that can help us better understand where we may be heading to help us prepare and to develop more lasting defenses.

Using a simple x-y graph, we can create an instructive map, in which x represents the severity of the impact and y the "actor" or perpetrator. Impact can be divided into the following stages: embarrassment, theft, destruction to a target firm or asset, and widespread destruction. The actors also can be grouped into four escalating stages: individuals, hacktivists, cyber organized crime, and nation-states. See Figure 1. Given the importance of understanding threat, business leaders should understand how the map applies to their business. To aid in this understanding, it is useful to cover a few examples that illustrate various stages of these threats.

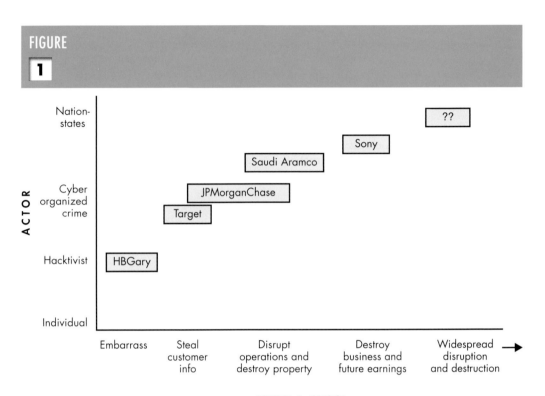

FIGURE 1

INTENT & IMPACT

In 2011, a high-profile attack was undertaken by Anonymous, the prominent "hacktivist" collective, in which it attacked the security services firm HBGary Federal. The attack was precipitated by HBGary's CEO, Aaron Barr, claiming in a *Financial Times* article that his firm had uncovered the identities of Anonymous leaders and planned on releasing these findings at a security conference in San Francisco the following week.[1] Anonymous responded by hacking into HBGary's networks, eventually posting archives of company executives' emails on file-sharing websites, releasing a list of the company's customers, and taking over the firm's website. Although the attack did affect HBGary financially, Anonymous' primary motivation was to embarrass Aaron Barr and HBGary.

More recent attacks have been perpetrated by better-organized criminal gangs and have had a greater impact. For instance, the Target breach, believed to have been the work of criminals operating in Eastern Europe, netted 40 million credit and debit card numbers and 70 million customer records and was largely responsible for the company's 46 percent drop in profit in Q4 of 2013 when compared to 2012.[2] The attack also resulted in a serious decline in the company's stock price and led the company's board to fire their CEO. The attack is estimated to have netted its perpetrators approximately $54 million in profit from the sale of stolen card details on black market sites—quite the motivation for a criminal enterprise.

Another high-profile attack, directed against Sony Pictures Entertainment, is alleged to have been the work of hackers supported by the government of North Korea. The attackers managed to secure not only a copy of *The Interview*, which had offended and motivated the North Korean state, but also a vast trove of data from the corporate network, including the personal and salary details of tens of thousands of employees, internal email traffic, and other highly sensitive information. The attack led the company to delay the release of its big-budget film, and it generated weeks of headlines. The attack also forced the company to take a variety of computer systems offline. Although the long-term impact of the attack is unclear, it has had a dramatic impact on the studio's reputation, stock price, and earnings.

What is next? In the future, we can expect a continued rise in the severity of cyberthreats. Well-financed criminal gangs and well-resourced nation-states appear to be increasingly capable and willing to engage in attacks that cause significant damage.

Boards and risk

After the initial shock of "how is this possible," every business leader has to consider what it means for his or her business. Just a few years ago, many viewed cybersecurity threats as a technical problem best left to the company CIO or CISO. Increasingly, CEOs and boards are coming to the realization cybersecurity threats are a business risk that demands C-level and board scrutiny.

Corporate boards have begun to look at cybersecurity risk in much the same way they would look at other risks to their business, applying risk management frameworks while evaluating the likelihood and impact of cyber risk. Boards also have begun to look at ways to transfer their risk, leading insurance companies to offer cybersecurity insurance products. In their evaluation of cyber risk, companies are also taking a hard look at the second order effects of a cyberattack, notably the ability for a successful attack to undermine customers' trust in the company. A successful attack often leads to the revelation of sensitive, personally identifiable information on customers, eroding consumer confidence in the firm. Many of the commonly understood risk management frameworks and related insurance products now being used recognize this and make it clear that corporate boards must have a thorough understanding of the third T, Trust.

■ Trust

One of the greatest casualties in the ever-increasing torrent of cyberthreats is trust—specifically, the trust consumers have in business, the trust citizens and business have in government, and the trust government has in business. This should be troubling for all corporate executives and government leaders because trust is precious to all relationships and is critical to effective workings of commerce and government. As we know, it takes years to build, but it is easy to lose. For instance, a single data breach can undo years of effort and cause immediate and lasting reputation loss.

Measuring trust

Recent consumer surveys suggest that consumers are tired of dealing with fraudulent charges and are raising their expectations for how their favorite brands and websites protect consumer data and personally identifiable information. In May 2015, Pew Research released a study in which 74 percent of Americans said it was "very important" to be "in control of who can get info about you." Edelman, one of the world's largest public relations firms, does an annual study called The Trust Barometer. The 2015 edition of this survey showed a huge jump in the importance consumers place in privacy of their personal data. The study revealed that 80 percent of consumers, across dozens of countries and industries, listed this as a top issue in evaluating brands they trust. Finally, HyTrust, an emerging technology company, published a study on the impact of a cyber breach on customer loyalty and trust. Of the 2,000 consumers surveyed, 52 percent said a breach would cause them to take their business elsewhere.[3] What business can afford to lose 50 percent of its customers?

What these numbers make clear is that consumers are paying attention to cybersecurity issues and that failure to address these concerns comes at a company's own risk. Recent attacks have served as learning moments for many companies and consumers, allowing them to gain a firmer understanding of just how damaging such an attack can be. However, with this knowledge comes increased expectations for how companies safeguard their data and that of their consumers.

Role of industry

Fortunately, industry is moving in this direction, and many companies have begun to consider cyber risk in their corporate planning. In 2014, the National Association of Corporate Directors issued a call to action, which included five steps that its members should take to ensure their enterprises properly address cyber risk. These include the following:

- Treating cyber risk as an enterprise risk
- Understanding the legal implications of cyber risks
- Discussion of cyber risk at board meetings, giving cyber risk equal footing with other risks
- Requiring management to have a measureable cybersecurity plan
- The development of a plan at the board level on how to address cyber risks, including which risks should be avoided, accepted, mitigated, or transferred via insurance.

Although this guidance is an excellent start, we at The Chertoff Group believe that industry has to go further and move toward a common cyber risk management framework that allows everyone to understand the cyber risks to a business and how the company intends to address them. This model would be a corollary to the General Accepted Accounting Principles (GAAP), the standard accounting guidelines and framework that underlies the financials and planning of almost any business. The emergence of GAAP in the 1950s made it significantly easier for investors, regulators, and other stakeholders to gain a clear understanding of a business and its financials, allowing for comparisons across industries and sectors.

In parallel, banks, insurers, and other providers of risk mitigation are scrambling to develop cyber risk mitigation products. Many of the insurance industry's largest players, including Allstate, Travelers, Marsh, and Tennant, have moved to offer companies cyber insurance products, although the immaturity of the market has created complications for insurers and potential customers. Insurers have had a hard time calculating their risk and thus appropriate premiums for potential customers, while customers have sometimes found their insurance quotes too expensive. Fortunately, time and the accompanying settling of industry standards and actuarial data will help to mature and grow this market.

Role of government

Effective risk management—for governments or private enterprises—starts with an honest understanding of the situation and recognition that information sharing with partners is essential. Information sharing, of course, starts with agreeing on common values, and then trusting vetted, capable, and reliable partners. Information sharing can be, and must be, something that takes place at and across all levels. The Constitution charges the federal government with the responsibility of providing for the defense of the nation while protecting the privacy and civil liberties of our citizens, a difficult balance that requires trust in the government and processes by which we reach that balance.

As we discuss the role of government in information sharing and building trust, we have to acknowledge the impact the Snowden revelations have had on public trust in government. Fundamentally, we have to determine what we want the role of government to be and engage in legal reforms that reflect that role. Laws such as the Computer Fraud and Abuse Act, enacted in 1986 and amended five times since then, and the Electronic Controls Privacy Act (ECPA), which dates to 1986, have to be updated to reflect the significant changes in technology and practice that have occurred since they were envisioned.

Beyond these efforts, we need to establish or reinforce agreed-upon rules and programs for government data collection on citizens and the legal frameworks that manage the transfer of that data between governments for judicial and law enforcement purposes. Importantly, this initiative must provide for mutual accountability for all participants. These initiatives have to lay out clearly the roles of all participants and, in our opinion, reinforce and strengthen the role for NSA in helping this nation deal with the adversaries that are using information technology to harm us.

On the international front, in response to mounting concerns over data privacy, data security and the rise of online surveillance, governments around the world have been seeking to pass new data protection rules. Several governments, including Germany, Indonesia, and Brazil, have considered enacting "data localization" laws that would require the storage, analysis, and processing of citizen and corporate data to occur only within their borders.

However, many of these proposals are likely to impose economic harm and sow seeds of distrust. For example, several of the proposals under consideration would force companies to build servers in locations where the high price of local energy and the lack of trained engineers could translate into higher costs and reduced efficiencies. Furthermore, requiring that data reside in a server based in Germany instead of one in Ireland will do little to prevent spies from accessing that data if they are determined and capable.

So, what should we do? It is critical that policymakers and technology providers work together to develop solutions that keep online services available to all who rely on them. We must develop principles that can serve as a framework for coordinated multilateral action between states and across the public and private sectors. We must be prepared to lead abroad and at home with effective ideas.

Public private partnerships (PPPs) are important pieces of the solution and are good models of trust that we should leverage going forward. First, the formation of Information Sharing and Analysis Centers (ISACs) was a Clinton Administration initiative to build PPPs across critical infrastructure sectors. These sector-by-sector ISACs have proven to be models of trust. The Financial Services ISAC has truly epitomized these ideas and is considered by many to be the leading ISAC in sharing threat information. This model has been replicated in other industries and led President Obama to call for an expansion of the information sharing model to smaller groups of companies through Information Sharing and Analysis Organizations (ISAOs). Another example is a U.S. government-industry initiative to combat botnets, in which the government is working with the Industry Botnet Group to identify botnets and minimize their impacts on personal computers.

■ Technology, threat, and trust in the boardroom

What do the three Ts of the cyber economy mean for you? Here are just a few of the questions every leader has to consider:

- Are we using technology for competitive advantage?
- Are we secure? How do you know? Do we have a framework, a GAAP-equivalent for cyber risk, that gives me the tools to understand and measure risk?
- Are we a good steward of the data we collect about our customers?

Each of us needs answers to these questions. Your response will have a big impact on the future of your organization.

A few years ago, there was a common story in security circles about two types of companies: those who knew they had been hacked and those who had been hacked but did not know it. Going forward, we will talk about companies in terms of who cares about cybersecurity: in some companies, it will be the entire executive suite; in others, it will just be the CISO or CIO. Your company doesn't want to fall into the latter category. Use the three Ts to help your organization manage cyber risk and leverage the fantastic opportunities in this golden age of innovation.

Works Cited

1. *See* Joseph Menn, "Cyberactivists warned of arrest," *The Financial Times*, February 5, 2011, Available at http://www.ft.com/cms/s/0/87dc140e-3099-11e0-9de3-00144feabdc0.html#axzz3cg7emYx4.

2. *See* Maggie McGrath, "Target Profit Falls 46% On Credit Card Breach And The Hits Could Keep On Coming," *Forbes*, February 26, 2014, Available at http://www.forbes.com/sites/maggiemcgrath/2014/02/26/target-profit-falls-46-on-credit-card-breach-and-says-the-hits-could-keep-on-coming/.

3. *See* "Consumers Increasingly Hold Companies Responsible for Loss of Confidential Information, HyTrust Poll Shows," HyTrust, October 1, 2014, Available at http://www.hytrust.com/company/news/press-releases/consumers-increasingly-hold-companies-responsible-loss-confidential-info, Additional survey data available at http://www.hytrust.com/sites/default/files/HyTrust_consumer_poll_results_with_charts2.pdf.

3

Cyber governance best practices

Georgia Institute of Technology, Institute for Information Security & Privacy – Jody R. Westby, Esq., Adjunct Professor

■ The evolution of cybersecurity governance

Corporate governance has evolved as a means of protecting investors through regulation, disclosure, and best practices. The United Nations *Guidance on Good Practices in Corporate Governance Disclosure* noted:

> Where there is a local code on corporate governance, enterprises should follow a "comply or explain" rule whereby they disclose the extent to which they followed the local code's recommendations and explain any deviations. Where there is no local code on corporate governance, companies should follow recognized international good practices.[1]

The Business Roundtable (BRT), one of America's most prominent business associations, has promoted the use of best practices as a governance tool since it published its first *Principles of Corporate Governance* in 2002. In its 2012 update, BRT noted:

> Business Roundtable continues to believe, as we noted in Principles of Corporate Governance (2005), that the United States has the best corporate governance, financial reporting and securities markets systems in the world. These systems work because of the adoption of best practices by public companies within a framework of laws and regulations that establish minimum requirements while affording companies the ability to develop individualized practices that are appropriate for them. Even in the challenging times posed by the ongoing difficult economic environment, corporations have continued to work proactively to refine their governance practices, and develop new practices, as conditions change and "best practices" continue to evolve.[2]

Increases in cybercrime and attacks on corporate systems and data have propelled discussions regarding governance of cyber risks and what exactly boards and senior executives should be doing to properly manage this new risk environment and protect corporate assets. The topic reached a crescendo in May 2014 when the Institutional Shareholder Service (ISS) called for seven of the ten Target board members not to be re-elected on the grounds that the failure of the board's audit and corporate responsibility committees "to ensure appropriate management of these risks set the stage for the data breach, which has resulted in significant losses to the company and its shareholders."[3]

Over the past decade, the concept of cybersecurity governance has evolved from information technology (IT) governance and cybersecurity best practices. The Information Systems Audit and Control Association (ISACA) has been a frontrunner in IT governance best practices with the COBIT (Control Objectives for Information and Related Technology)[4] framework. ISACA founded the IT Governance Institute (ITGI) in 1998 to advance the governance and management of enterprise IT. The ITGI defines IT governance:

> IT governance is the responsibility of the board of directors and executive management. It is an integral part of enterprise governance and consists of the leadership and organisational structures and processes that ensure that the organisation's IT sustains and extends the organisation's strategies and objectives.[5]

Gartner has a similar definition.[6]

■ Cybersecurity program standards and best practices[7]

As IT systems became vulnerable through networking and Internet connectivity, securing these systems became an essential element of IT governance. The first cybersecurity standard was developed by the British Standards Institute in 1995 as BS 7799. Over time, this comprehensive standard proved its worth and ultimately evolved into ISO 17799 and then ISO/IEC 27001.[8] ISO/IEC 27001 is the most accepted cybersecurity standard globally.

Today, the ISO/IEC 27000 series of information security standards is comprised of nearly 30 standards. ISO, of which the American National Standards Institute (ANSI) is the member body representing U.S. interests for the development of international standards, has additional information security standards outside of the 27000 series.[9] ISO information security standards cover a range of topics, such as security controls, risk management, the protection of personally identifiable information (PII) in clouds, and control systems. Additional security standards also have been developed for financial services, business continuity, network security, supplier relationships, digital evidence, and incident response.[10]

The U.S. National Institute of Standards and Technology (NIST) has developed a comprehensive set of cybersecurity guidance and Federal Information Processing Standards (FIPS),[11] including a Framework for Improving Critical Infrastructure Cybersecurity (Framework).[12] The NIST guidance and standards are world-class materials that are publicly available at no charge. NIST recognized existing standards and best practices by mapping the Framework to ISO/IEC 27001 and COBIT.

Other respected cybersecurity standards have been developed for particular purposes, such as the protection of credit card data and electrical grids. The good news is that cybersecurity best practices and standards are harmonized and requirements can be mapped. This is particularly important because as companies buy and sell operating units or subsidiaries or merge, they may have IT systems and documentation based upon several standards or best practices. Thus, the harmonization of standards enables companies to blend IT departments and security programs and continue to measure maturity.

Some companies may need to align with multiple standards. For example, electric transmission and distribution companies will need to meet the North American Electric Reliability Corporation Critical Infrastructure Protection (NERC-CIP) standards, as well as the Payment Card Industry Data Security Standard (PCI DSS) if they take credit cards, and some other broad security program standard, such as ISO/IEC 27001 or NIST for their corporate operations.

Even with harmonization, it is important that companies choose at least one standard to align their cybersecurity program with so progress and security maturity can be measured. In determining which standard to use as a corporate guidepost, organizations should consider the comprehensiveness of the standard. Although standards requirements may be mapped, each standard does not contain the same or equivalent requirements. Thus, it is important to understand the breadth and reach of the standard and to choose one that meets the organization's security and compliance needs.

ISO/IEC 27001, which can be obtained from ANSI at http://webstore.ansi.org, is a comprehensive standard and a good choice for any size of organization because it is respected globally and is the one most commonly mapped against other standards. One should not make the mistake of believing that all standards contain a full set of requirements for an enterprise security program; they do not. Some standards, such as NERC-CIP or PCI, set forth security requirements for a particular purpose but are not adequate for a full corporate security program.

Leading cybersecurity standards and best practices include:

- The International Organization for Standardization (ISO), the information security series, http://www.iso.org/iso/home/search.htm?qt=information+security&published=on&active_tab=standards&sort_by=rel (also available from ANSI at http://www.ansi.org)
- The American National Standards Institute (ANSI)—the U.S. member body to ISO. Copies of all ISO standards can be purchased from ANSI at http://webstore.ansi.org/
- National Institute of Standards and Technology (NIST) Special Publication 800 (SP-800) series and Federal Information Processing Standards (FIPS), http://csrc.nist.gov/publications/index.html
- Information Technology Infrastructure Library (ITIL), http://www.itlibrary.org/.
- International Society of Automation (ISA), https://www.isa.org/templates/two-column.aspx?pageid=131422
- Information Systems Audit and Control Association (ISACA), the Control Objectives for Information and Related Technology (COBIT), http://www.isaca.org/cobit/pages/default.aspx
- Payment Card Industry Security Standards Council (PCI SSC), https://www.pcisecuritystandards.org/
- Information Security Forum (ISF) Standard of Good Practice for Information Security, https://www.securityforum.org/shop/p-71-173
- Carnegie Mellon University's Software Engineering Institute, Operationally Critical Threat, Asset, and Vulnerability Evaluation (OCTAVE), http://www.cert.org/resilience/products-services/octave/
- Health Insurance Portability and Accountability Act (HIPAA) regulations for security programs, http://www.hhs.gov/ocr/privacy/hipaa/administrative/combined/index.html
- North American Electric Reliability Corporation Critical Infrastructure Protection (NERC-CIP), http://www.nerc.com/pa/Stand/Pages/CIPStandards.aspx
- U.S. Nuclear Regulatory Commission, Regulatory Guide 5.71, Cyber Security Programs for Nuclear Facilities, https://scp.nrc.gov/slo/regguide571.pdf

Some information security standards, such as NERC-CIP, U.S. Nuclear Regulatory cybersecurity requirements, PCI standards for credit card data, and HIPAA security requirements are mandatory. Portions of NIST guidance are mandatory for federal government contractors and U.S. government agencies and departments. The remainder of the standards listed are voluntary.

In addition to the leading cybersecurity standards listed in the shaded box, additional standards have been developed for certain industry sectors because they require heightened security protections. For example, ISO/IEC 27015 was developed as additional security requirements for financial organizations; ISO/IEC 27799 was developed for information security in health systems using ISO/IEC 27002 (the controls portion of ISO/IEC 27001); 27011 was developed for telecommunications systems using ISO/IEC 27002; and ISO/IEC 27019 was developed for industrial control system security for the energy utility industry.

The value of using a standard as a guidepost for the development, maintenance, and maturity of a security program is that it sets forth best practices for cybersecurity and is updated as required to meet changing threats, technological innovation, and compliance requirements. Standards also enable boards and senior executives to understand how comprehensive their organization's security program is and provide an objective basis for audits and cybersecurity assessments. Evaluating a cybersecurity program against a leading standard enables an organization to measure progress, assess the effectiveness of controls, identify gaps and deficiencies, and measure program maturity.

■ Cyber governance standards and best practices

Cyber governance standards and best practices have evolved over the past 20 years as companies have increased connectivity to the Internet and networks and as cyberattacks have continued to rise. Directors and officers (D&Os) have a fiduciary duty to protect the organization's assets and the value of the corporation. The increased dependence on IT systems and data in corporate operations necessarily extends this duty to include the protection of the organization's digital assets (data, networks, and software). As a consequence, the governance of cyber risks has become increasingly important for boards of directors and senior management. This includes exercising good risk management, validating the effectiveness of controls, and ensuring compliance requirements are met.

An increase in shareholder derivative suits against D&Os for failure to protect against breaches also has heightened attention on cybersecurity at the board and senior management level. Target was hit with shareholder derivative suits for failure to protect the company and its data from a breach,[13] as was Wyndham Hotels on similar grounds.[14]

In addition, cybersecurity has become an important compliance issue that carries the risk of headlines concerning enforcement actions, investigations, and breaches of personally identifiable information. Several state and federal laws impose privacy and security requirements on targeted industry sectors and types of data. For example, the Gramm-Leach-Bliley Act (GLBA), the Health Insurance Portability and Accountability Act (HIPAA), the Health Information Technology for Economic and Clinical Health Act (HITECH Act), and state breach laws impose specific requirements pertaining to the security and privacy of data and networks.

So, what does cyber governance mean? What actions should board members be taking? Who should be involved—the entire board or just certain committees? Cyber governance means more than D&Os periodically asking interesting questions or receiving reports regarding the company's cybersecurity program. There is now an international standard, ISO/IEC 27014, on the governance of information security, which sets out roles and responsibilities for executive management and boards of directors and is applicable to all types and sizes of organizations.

The standard notes:

[G]overnance of information security provides a powerful link between an organization's governing body, executive management and those responsible for implementing and operating an information security management system. It provides the mandate essential for driving information security initiatives throughout the organization.[15]

The objectives of the standard are to align security program and business objectives and strategies, deliver value to stakeholders and the board, and ensure information risks are adequately managed.[16]

The difference between IT governance and information security governance is that the latter is focused on the confidentiality, integrity, and availability of information, whereas governance of IT is focused on the resources required to acquire, process, store, and disseminate information.[17] ISO/IEC 27014 sets forth six principles as foundation for information security governance:

1. "Establish organization-wide information security": information security activities should encompass the entire organization and consider the business, information security, physical and logical security, and other relevant issues.
2. "Adopt a risk-based approach": governance decisions should be based on the risk thresholds of a company, taking into account competitiveness issues, legal and compliance obligations, reputational risks, business interruption, and financial losses; allocate the resources needed for the risk-based approach.
3. "Set the direction of investment decisions": establish an information security investment strategy that meets business and security requirements; integrate security considerations into existing business and investment processes.
4. "Ensure conformance with internal and external requirements": ensure policies and procedures incorporate legal, regulatory, and contractual obligations; routinely audit such compliance.
5. "Foster a security-positive environment": accommodate human behavior and the needs of users; promote a positive information security environment through training and tone from the top.
6. "Review performance in relation to business outcomes": ensure the security program supports business requirements, review impact of security on business as well as controls.[18]

ISO/IEC 27014 sets forth separate roles and responsibilities for the board and executive management within five processes: Evaluate, Direct, Monitor, Communicate, and Assure. These are set forth in abbreviated form in the following table.[19]

Board of directors	Executive management
Evaluate	
Ensure business initiatives take information security into consideration	Ensure information security supports business objectives
Review reports on information security performance, initiate prioritized actions	Submit new security projects with significant impact for board review
Direct	
Establish risk thresholds of organization	Ensure security and business objectives are aligned
Approve security strategy and overarching policy	Develop security strategy and overarching policy
Allocate adequate resources for security program	Establish a positive culture of cybersecurity

Continued

Board of directors	Executive management
Monitor	
Assess effectiveness of security program	Determine appropriate metrics for security program
Ensure compliance and legal obligations are met	Provide input to board on security performance results, impacts on organization
Evaluate changes to operations, legal frameworks, and impact on information security	Keep board apprised of new developments affecting information security
Communicate	
Report to investors/shareholders on whether information security is adequate for business	Inform board of security issues that require their attention
Provide results of external audits or reviews and identified actions to executive team	Ensure board's actions and decisions regarding security are acted upon
Recognize compliance obligations, business needs, and expectations for information security	
Assure	
Order independent reviews/audits of security program	Support reviews/audits commissioned by board

■ **Beyond ISO/IEC 27014: Other best practices and guidance**

At present, the only guidance NIST has developed that addresses information security governance is its 2006 Special Publication 800-100, *Information Security Handbook: A Guide for Managers*. This publication, however, is written for a federal audience and is more technical than other materials directed toward boards and senior executives.

ISACA's IT Governance Institute updated its *Board Briefing on IT Governance* in 2014,[20] which sets forth an approach similar to ISO/IEC 27014, but is based on ISACA's COBIT best practices. The *Board Briefing* includes questions board members should ask and also checklists, tool kits, roles and responsibilities, and other helpful materials. The *Board Briefing* focuses on five activity areas: Strategic Alignment, Value Delivery, Risk Management, Resource Management, and Performance Measurement. The publication

is IT-focused, however, and does not mention the roles and responsibilities of chief information security officers (CISOs). The separation of the role of the chief information security officer from the chief information officer (CIO) (in other words, not having the CISO report to the CIO), is a best practice that the *Board Briefing* ignores. It assigns all responsibilities to the CIO, IT Strategy Committee, IT Steering Committee, IT Architecture Review Board, and Technology Council. Nevertheless, it is a valuable resource for boards and executive teams seeking to implement good cyber governance practices.

Finally, Carnegie Mellon University's Software Engineering Institute developed the *Governing for Enterprise Security Implementation Guide* in 2007 as a guide for boards and executives on governing enterprise security programs.[21] It is still quite instructive and includes a model organizational structure for cyber governance; composition of a cross-organizational privacy/security committee; sample mission, goals, and objectives for a board Risk Committee; and an explanation of the critical activities in an enterprise security program, including who should lead and be involved in them, and the outputs (artifacts) to be developed. It indicates where the board has a role for governance oversight and sets forth roles and responsibilities for the critical players, as well as shared responsibilities, for the following:

- chief security officer/chief information security officer
- chief privacy officer
- chief information officer
- chief financial officer
- general counsel
- business line executives
- human resources
- public relations
- business managers
- procurement
- operational personnel
- asset owners
- certification authority.

■ Additional considerations in cybersecurity governance

Board structure plays a significant role in cybersecurity governance. A Risk Committee is the best choice for governance of cybersecurity because IT risks must be managed as enterprise risks and integrated into enterprise risk management and planning. Many companies place all oversight for cybersecurity in the board Audit Committee, which can substantially increase the workload of that committee. Placing cyber governance with the Audit Committee also creates segregation of duties issues at the board level because the Audit Committee is auditing the security program, determining remediation measures, and then auditing this work the following year.

One of the most important aspects of cybersecurity governance is the identification of vulnerabilities that could have a material impact on corporate operations and/or bottom line. It is easy for board members to become inundated in technical data and issues and lose sight of the major risks that must be managed. In part, CIOs and CISOs need to develop better executive and board communication skills when reporting on cybersecurity program activities and incidents. Outside experts can also help separate which cybersecurity governance issues should be directed to the executive management team and which are for board consideration.

Once the critical vulnerabilities that require board and executive attention have been identified, the next step is to determine the information flows that are needed to keep the board and senior management informed and enable informed decision-making. These two steps—identification of cyber-related vulnerabilities and associated information flows—should be followed by an analysis of the board's and senior management's roles in incident response and business continuity/disaster recovery.

The Target breach revealed how disastrous it can be when a company's executive team and board are not prepared to manage a major cybersecurity incident. The breach was clever but not terribly difficult to recover from; as ISS pointed out so clearly, it was Target's executive team and board who failed to protect the company's data and ensure a robust incident response plan was in place that involved their participation.

Cybersecurity governance is an area where an independent adviser can provide valuable guidance to a board and executive team by reviewing available reports and assessing the current state of the security program, identifying key vulnerabilities and associated information flows that should be directed to the board, advising on the threat environment, and establishing the proper organizational structures for effective cybersecurity governance. These activities should be undertaken in a collaborative fashion with IT and security leaders and in the spirit of helping them gain visibility and support for security program initiatives.

■ **Dutiful dozen**

There are some actions that boards can take to ensure they are managing cyber risks and meeting their fiduciary duty. Following is a list of a dozen actions that are within best practices, which can be used as a starting point and checklist for governance activities:

A dozen best practices for cyber governance

1. Establish a governance structure with a board Risk Committee and a cross-organizational internal team.
2. Identify the key cyber vulnerabilities associated with the organization's operations.
3. Identify the security program activities over which boards and executives should exercise oversight, and identify the key information flows and reports that will inform board and executives on the management of cyber vulnerabilities and security program activities.
4. Identify legal compliance and financial exposures from IT systems and data.
5. Set the tone from top that privacy and security are high priorities for the organization, and approve top-level policies on acceptable use of technology and compliance with privacy and security policies and procedures.
6. Review the roles and the responsibilities of lead privacy and security personnel, and ensure there is segregation of duties between IT and security functions.
7. Ensure that privacy and security responsibilities are shared, enterprise issues that apply to all personnel.
8. Review and approve annual budgets for security programs.
10. Review annual risk assessments, the maturity of the security program, and support continual improvement.
11. Retain a trusted adviser to independently inform the board on changes in the threat environment, provide assistance on governance issues, and advise on response issues in the event of a major cyber incident.

12. Evaluate the adequacy of cyber insurance against loss valuations and ensure adequate risk strategies are in place for cyber risks.

Many organizations also are struggling with how to integrate cybersecurity into their enterprise risk management process. Most business operations today are dependent upon IT systems and the confidentiality, availability, and integrity of their data. Following are another dozen guiding points on integrating cyber risks into enterprise risk management.:

A dozen best practices for integrating cybersecurity into enterprise risk management

1. Understand the business's strategies, objectives, and needs for IT and data.
2. Inventory assets (data, applications, hardware), assign ownership, classification, and risk categorization.
3. Map legal requirements to data for all jurisdictions.
4. Evaluate the security of vendors, business partners, and supply chain linkages.
5. Align the cybersecurity program with best practices and standards.
6. Ensure controls are determined and metrics identified.
7. Conduct a risk assessment to establish a baseline for cyber risk management.
8. Develop cyber risk strategies (block the risk, cyber insurance, other compensating controls, all of these).
9. Design system architecture to accommodate business goals and objectives, meet security and legal requirements, and detect or prevent unauthorized usage.
10. Use technical tools and services to provide integrated data on threats and attacks.
11. Make cyber training and security compliance part of annual performance reviews for all personnel.
12. Stay abreast of innovation and changes in the threat environment as well as changing operational requirements.

■ Conclusion

Best practices and standards now require boards and senior management to exercise governance over cybersecurity programs and associated risks. Laws such as Gramm-Leach-Bliley, the Health Insurance Portability and Accountability Act, and the Federal Information Security Management Act all require executive oversight of security programs. Each organization's operations, system architecture, policies and procedures, and culture vary, thus, cyber risk management has to be tailored to the organization. Boards should know what standards/best practices their organization is using to implement their security program and determine an approach for their own governance activities. Checklists and the use of ISO/IEC 27014, the ISACA *Board Briefing on IT Governance*, and the Carnegie Mellon University's *Governing for Enterprise Security Implementation Guide* are all useful resources that will help ensure boards are meeting their fiduciary duty and protecting the assets of the organization.

References

1. *Guidance on Good Practices in Corporate Governance Disclosure*, United Nations Conference on Trade and Development (UNCTAD), New York & Geneva, 2006, http://unctad.org/en/docs/iteteb20063_en.pdf.
2. *Principles of Corporate Governance 2012*, Harvard Law School Forum on Corporate Governance and Financial Regulation, Aug. 17, 2012, http://corpgov.law.harvard.edu/2012/08/17/principles-of-corporate-governance-2012/.
4. Elizabeth A. Harris, "Advisory Group Opposes Re-election of Most of Target's Board," *The New York Times*, May 28, 2014, http://www.nytimes.com/2014/05/29/business/advisory-group-opposes-re-election-of-most-of-targets-board.html?_r=0 (quoting ISS report).
4. COBIT is an acronym for Control Objectives for Information and Related Technology. Information on the COBIT 5 framework for the governance and management of enterprise IT is available at http://www.isaca.org/cobit/pages/default.aspx.
5. *Board Briefing on IT Governance*, IT Governance Institute, 2nd ed., 2014 at 10, http://www.isaca.org/restricted/Documents/26904_Board_Briefing_final.pdf.
6. Gartner, IT Glossary, "IT Governance," http://www.gartner.com/it-glossary/it-governance.
7. The term "cybersecurity best practice" may be used interchangeably with "standard" in the cybersecurity context, as the standards embody best practices. The term "standard" is commonly used to refer to mandatory requirements. With respect to cybersecurity programs, however, there is no bright line between best practices and standards. Some standards, such as NERC-CIP and HIPAA, are mandatory for certain organizations, while other standards, such as ISO/IEC, are voluntary. Other standards, such as the Federal Information Processing Standards (FIPS) and NIST guidance (the 800 Special Publication series) are voluntary for some entities and mandatory for others.
8. Wikipedia, "BS 7799," https://en.wikipedia.org/wiki/BS_7799.
9. International Organization for Standardization, Information Security, http://www.iso.org/iso/home/search.htm?qt=information+security&published=on&active_tab=standards&sort_by=rel.
10. Id.
11. National Institute of Standards and Technology, Computer Security Division, Computer Security Resource Center, http://csrc.nist.gov/publications/PubsSPs.html.
12. *Framework for Improving Critical Infrastructure Cybersecurity*, National Institute of Standards and Technology, Version 1.0, Feb. 12, 2014, http://www.nist.gov/cyberframework/upload/cybersecurity-framework-021214.pdf.

13. *See, e.g.*, Kevin LaCroix, "Target Directors and Officers Hit with Derivative Suits Based on Data Breach," Feb. 3, 2014, http://www.dandodiary.com/2014/02/articles/cyber-liability/target-directors-and-officers-hit-with-derivative-suits-based-on-data-breach/.

14. *See, e.g.*, Jon Talotta, Michelle Kisloff, & Christopher Pickens, "Data Breaches Hit the Board Room: How to Address Claims Against Directors & Officers," Hogan & Lovells, Chronicle of Data Protection, Jan. 23, 2015, http://www.hldataprotection.com/2015/01/articles/cybersecurity-data-breaches/data-breaches-hit-the-board-room/.

15. ISO/IEC 27014 (2013), Governance of Information Security, "Summary," http://www.iso.org/iso/home/search.htm?qt=27014&sort=rel&type=simple&published=on.

16. Id. at 4.2. "Objectives."

17. Id. at 4.4. "Relationship."

18. Id. at 5.2. "Principles."

19. Id. at 5.3. "Processes." The full requirements of the standard should be reviewed prior to use by an organization; ISO 27014 is available at http://www.iso.org/iso/home/search.htm?qt=27014&sort=rel&type=simple&published=on.

20. *Board Briefing on IT Governance*, IT Governance Institute, 2nd ed., 2014, http://www.isaca.org/restricted/Documents/26904_Board_Briefing_final.pdf.

21. Jody R. Westby & Julia H. Allen, *Governing for Enterprise Implementation Guide*, Carnegie Mellon University, Software Engineering Institute, 2007, http://globalcyberrisk.com/wp-content/uploads/2012/08/Governing-for-Enterprise-Sec-Impl-Guide.pdf.

4

Investors' perspectives on cyber risks: Implications for boards

**Institutional Shareholder Services Inc. – Patrick McGurn,
ISS Special Counsel and Martha Carter,
ISS Global Head of Research**

Although pundits proclaimed 2014 as the "Year of the Data Breach" and a significant "no" vote at Target's annual meeting put directors on notice that shareholders want to know about potential risks, few 2015 corporate disclosure documents provide evidence that boards increased transparency with respect to cyber oversight. Despite prodding from top regulators and investors' calls for greater transparency, companies continue to fall short on disclosure in their key governance disclosure documents of cybersecurity risks and their board's oversight of them. Equally concerning is the limited information regarding cyber risk oversight provided by boards at a handful of firms that were the targets of 2014's most widely publicized breaches. Boards would benefit from an understanding of investors' perspectives and adoption of best practices in disclosure on cyber risks.

■ Target's breach led to boardroom backlash

Target's high-profile data breach made headlines worldwide. Despite this, neither Target's 2014 proxy statement nor the company's initial annual meeting-related engagement materials discussed in a meaningful way the massive data theft or the board's responses to it. As part of its research process leading up to the annual meeting, Institutional Shareholder Services (ISS) engaged with members of the Target board to learn more about the directors' oversight of cyber risks before and after the breach. In the end, ISS opined in its 2014 annual meeting report on Target that the members of the board's Audit and Corporate Responsibility committees had "failed to provide sufficient oversight of the risks facing the company that potentially led to the data breach." Accordingly, ISS recommended votes against the members of those two board oversight panels. ISS acknowledged the board's actions in the wake of the breach but found that the committees "failed to appropriately implement a risk assessment structure that could have better prepared the company for a data breach."

After investors' concerns emerged before the meeting, the company engaged in a solicitation effort to defend the board's response to the breach. When the votes were tallied, none of the members of Target's audit and governance panels received support from more than 81 percent of the votes cast. Target lead director James A. Johnson received the lowest support—62.9 percent of the votes cast. According to ISS' Voting Analytics database of institutional investors' voting records, governance professionals at funds connected to nearly half of Target's top 10 largest investors cast votes against one or more of the company's directors.

In the direct wake of the 2014 data breach issues and the dearth of proxy-related disclosure on those matters, SEC Commissioner Luis A. Aguilar fired a shot across the bow of boards that lack disclosure. In a June 10, 2014, speech ("Boards of Directors, Corporate Governance and Cyber Risks: Sharpening the Focus") delivered at a New York Stock Exchange (NYSE)–hosted cybersecurity conference, Aguilar said, "[B]oard oversight of cyber-risk management is critical to ensuring that companies are taking adequate steps to prevent, and prepare for, the harms that can result from such attacks. There is no substitution for proper preparation, deliberation, and engagement on cybersecurity issues." Noting the wide damage crater caused by cyber events, Aguilar noted that the boardroom plan should include "whether, and how, the cyber-attack will need to be disclosed internally and externally (both to customers and to investors)."

■ **Shareholders care about breaches**

Are shareholders apathetic about data breaches? Some media reports equate the lack of sharp, downward stock movements in the wake of disclosures of hacks or other data breaches (or quick rebounds from such price drops when they occur) with shareholders' apathy over cybersecurity problems. In a recent *Harvard Business Review* article (*Why Data Breaches Don't Hurt Stock Prices*, March 31, 2015), cybersecurity strategist Elena Kvochko and *New York Times* Chief Technology Officer Rajiv Pant dismiss this easy explanation. They argue that muted stock price reactions to data breaches reflect the absence of timely information and quality tools to price cyber risk: "Shareholders still don't have good metrics, tools, and approaches to measure the impact of cyber attacks on businesses and translate that into a dollar value . . . The long and mid-term effects of lost intellectual property, disclosure of sensitive data, and loss of customer confidence may result in loss of market share, but these effects are difficult to quantify." Faced with this information vacuum, Kvochko and Pant note that "shareholders only react to breach news when it has direct impact on business operations, such as litigation charges (for example, in the case of Target) or results in immediate changes to a company's expected profitability."

Indeed, stock prices may not tell the whole story. Contrary to the conventional wisdom, recent survey data show investors understand the long-term risks stemming from hacks and they may actually shy away from investing in companies with multiple breaches. A recent survey—conducted by FTI Consulting on behalf of consulting giant KPMG LLP—of more than 130 global institutional investors with an estimated $3 trillion under management found that cyber events may affect investors' confidence in the board and demand for the affected companies' shares.

Investors opined that less than half of boards of the companies that they currently invest in have adequate skills to manage rising cyberthreats. They also believe that 43 percent of board members have "unacceptable skills and knowledge to manage innovation and risk in the digital world."

More ominously for boards, four of five investor respondents (79 percent) suggested that they may blacklist stocks of hacked firms. As for a remedy, 86 percent of the surveyed investors told KPMG and FTI that they want to see increases in the time boards spend on addressing cyber risk.

■ Investors raise the bar for disclosure

Insights on the gap between investors' expectations and boardroom practices were gleaned from PwC's juxtaposition of two surveys that it conducted in the summer of 2014, one of 863 directors in PwC's *2014 Annual Corporate Directors Survey,* and the other of institutional investors with more than $11 trillion in aggregate assets under management in PwC's *2014 Investor Survey.*

- Nearly three quarters (74 percent) of investors told PwC that they believe it is important for directors to discuss their company's crisis response plan in the event of a major security breach. Only about half of directors (52 percent) reported having such discussions.
- Roughly three out of four (74 percent) investors urged boards to boost cyber risk disclosures in response to the SEC's guidance, but only 38 percent of directors reported discussing the topic.
- Similarly, 68 percent of investors believe it is important for directors to discuss engaging an outside cybersecurity expert, but only 42 percent of directors had done so.
- Fifty-five percent of investors said it was important for boards to consider designating a chief information security officer, if their companies did not have one in place. Only half as many directors (26 percent) reported that such a personnel move had been discussed in the boardroom.
- Finally, 45 percent of investors believe it is important for directors to discuss the National Institute of Standards and Technology (NIST)/ Department of Homeland Security cybersecurity framework, but only 21 percent of directors reported their boards had done so.

■ ISS policy respondents indicate a disclosure framework

What level of detail do investors expect to see about these issues in disclosures regarding cyberthreats? In 2014, as part of ISS' 2015 policy-formulation process, we asked institutional investors to weigh the factors they assess in reviewing boardroom oversight of risk, including cyberthreats. A majority of the shareholder respondents indicated that the following are all either "very" or "somewhat" important to their voting decisions on individual directors elections:

- role of the company's relevant risk oversight committee(s)
- the board's risk oversight policies and procedures
- directors' oversight actions *prior to* and *subsequent to* the incident(s)
- changes in senior management.

Notably, shareholders do not appear to be looking for scapegoats. Disclosures about boardroom oversight action *subsequent* to an incident drew more demand than firings. An eye-popping 85 percent of the respondents cited such crisis management and "lessons learned" disclosures as "very important." In contrast, only 46 percent of the shareholders indicated that changes in senior management are "very important" to them when it came time to vote on director oversight.

■ 2015 disclosures provide few insights

Despite prodding by the SEC and numerous indications from investors, many boards continue to lack disclosure of cyberthreats in their flagship documents—the proxy statement and the 10-K. Only a handful of the companies that drew widespread coverage of their data breaches during 2014 mention the events in their proxy statements, and many cite materiality concerns to avoid discussing the data breaches in detail in their 10-Ks.

In sharp contrast to the absence of information in Target's 2014 proxy statement, however, another big box retailer provided investors with a window into the board's role in cyber risk oversight in its 2015 proxy materials. Home Depot addressed its 2014 data breach, which affected up to 56 million customers who shopped at the company's stores between April 2014 and September 2014, with a concise (roughly 1000-word) explanation of the steps taken by the board before and after the company's breach.

The proxy statement disclosures include a brief summary of the depth and duration of the breach, an explanation of the board's delegation of oversight responsibility to the audit committee, and an outline of remedial steps that the board took in response to the event.

Notably, Home Depot's disclosures generally align with all the pillars identified by investors in their responses to the ISS policy survey:

First, Home Depot's board details the delegation of risk oversight to the audit committee and describes the directors' relationship with the company's internal audit and compliance team:

> The Audit Committee . . . has primary responsibility for overseeing risks related to information technology and data privacy and security. . . . The Audit Committee stays apprised of significant actual and potential risks faced by the Company in part through review of quarterly reports from our Enterprise Risk Council (the "ERC"). The quarterly ERC reports not only identify the risks faced by the Company, but also identify whether primary oversight of each risk resides with a particular Board committee or the full Board . . . The chair of the ERC, who is also our Vice President of Internal Audit and Corporate Compliance, reports the ERC's risk analyses to senior management regularly and attends each Audit Committee meeting. The chair of the ERC also provides a detailed annual report regarding the Company's risk assessment

and management process to the full Board."

Next, the Home Depot disclosure provides some color on the board's risk oversight policies and procedures:

> For a number of years, IT and data security risks have been included in the risks reviewed on a quarterly basis by the ERC and the Audit Committee and in the annual report to the Board on risk assessment and management. In the last few years, the Audit Committee and/or the full Board have also regularly received detailed reports on IT and data security matters from senior members of our IT and internal audit departments. These reports were given at every quarterly Audit Committee meeting in fiscal 2014, including an additional half-day Audit Committee session devoted exclusively to these matters that was held prior to the discovery of the Data Breach. The topics covered by these reports included risk management strategies, consumer data security, the Company's ongoing risk mitigation activities, and cyber security strategy and governance structure. . . .
>
> To further support our IT and data security efforts, in 2013 the Company enhanced and expanded the Incident Response Team ("IRT") formed several years earlier. The IRT is charged with developing action plans for and responding rapidly to data security situations. . . . The IRT provided daily updates to the Company's senior leadership team, who in turn periodically apprised the Lead Director, the Audit Committee and the full Board, as necessary.

The Home Depot board also highlights its cyber-risk oversight actions prior to the incident:

> Under the Board's and the Audit Committee's leadership and oversight, the Company had taken significant steps

to address evolving privacy and cyber security risks before we became aware of the Data Breach:

- Prior to the Data Breach and in part in reaction to breaches experienced by other companies, we augmented our existing security activities by launching a multi-work stream effort to review and further harden our IT and data security processes and systems. This effort included working extensively with third-party experts and security firms and has been subsequently modified and enhanced based on our learnings from the Data Breach experience.
- In January 2014, as part of the efforts described above, we began a major payment security project to provide enhanced encryption of payment card data at the point of sale in all of our U.S. stores. . . . Upon discovery of the Data Breach, we accelerated completion of the project to September 2014, offering significant new protection for customers. The new security protection takes raw payment card information and scrambles it to make it unreadable to unauthorized users. . . .
- We are rolling out EMV "chip-and-PIN" technology in our U.S. stores, which adds extra layers of payment card protection for customers who use EMV chip-and-PIN enabled cards. . . .

Finally, the Home Depot board discusses the boardroom oversight actions taken subsequent to the incident including changes in senior management:

Following discovery of the Data Breach, in addition to continuing the efforts described above, the Company and the Board took a number of additional actions:

- We formed an internal executive committee, the Data Security and Privacy Governance Committee, to provide further enterprise-wide oversight and governance over data security. This committee reports quarterly to the Audit Committee.
- We are in the process of further augmenting our IT security team, including by adding an officer level Chief Information Security Officer and hiring additional associates focused on IT and data security.
- We are reviewing and enhancing all of our training relating to privacy and data security, and we intend to provide additional annual data security training for all of our associates before the end of Fiscal 2015.
- Our Board, the Audit Committee, and a special committee of the Board have received regular updates regarding the Data Breach. In addition to the IT and data security initiatives described above, the Board, supported by the work of its Audit and Finance Committees, has reviewed and authorized the expenditures associated with a series of capital intensive projects designed to further harden our IT security environment against evolving data security threats.

■ Boards would benefit from engagement and disclosure

Although the good news is that cybersecurity has seemingly come to the forefront for many directors, the bad news is that shareholders are not yet getting the transparency they need to assess the quality of boardroom oversight. The significant "no" vote against the Target board at its 2014 annual meeting, coupled with survey data, show that shareholders are far from apathetic when it comes to assessing cyber risk oversight.

■ Target's lessons learned

In the wake of its challenging 2014 annual meeting, Target hosted calls or held meetings with shareholders representing approximately 41% of shares voted. The majority of these conversations were led by Director Anne Mulcahy. In light of this feedback and with the assistance of a third-party strategy and risk management and regulatory compliance consultant, the board "embarked on a comprehensive review" of risk oversight at the management, board, and committee levels. As a result of this comprehensive review, in January 2015, the Target board "clarified and enhanced" its practices to provide more transparency about how risk oversight is exercised at the board and committee levels. As part of this revamp, the board reallocated and clarified risk oversight responsibilities among the committees, most notably by elevating the risk oversight role of the corporate risk & responsibility committee (formerly known as the corporate responsibility committee).

Examples such as Home Depot and the Target board's 2015 disclosures provide more transparency on risk oversight and are a good framework for other boards to follow. Boards would be wise to raise their games by disclosing more details of their board oversight efforts and engaging with investors when cyber incidents occur, or they may run the risk of a loss of investor confidence.

5

Toward cyber risks measurement

Elena Kvochko, Author, Towards the Quantification of Cyber Threats report; and Danil Kerimi, Director, Center for Global Industries, World Economic Forum

As most companies in the U.S. already use some form of cloud-based solutions, the digital footprint of enterprises is growing, and so are the risks. Technological solutions have always focused on convenience, transparency, and an ever-increasing ability to share information and collaborate, while built-in security hasn't been a priority until recently. Now enterprises are shifting away from this model. Growing privacy and security concerns affect customer perception. According to Deloitte, 80% of customers are aware of recent cyber breaches, and 50% of them are ready to switch brands if they feel their information may be compromised. Experian reported that now cyber breaches are as devastating for the reputation of organizations as environmental disasters and poor customer service.

Most executives recognize that cyber risks are no longer on the horizon but are an imminent cost of doing business. Companies are actively looking for effective mitigation actions. Recent surveys show that cybersecurity is already part of the agenda of 80% of corporate boards (up from around 30% 4 years ago). Companies are adjusting their enterprise risk management frameworks and including cyber risks and accompanying controls as part of the necessary risk management actions. Traditional controls introduced for in-house infrastructure no longer work, as more and more operations are performed in the cloud. Just as in any healthy ecosystem, these environments present great opportunities for stakeholders to interact with each other and with the content, but they also carry inherent risks.

Risk mitigation approaches and technologies lag behind the sophistication of the threat. In fact, our earlier research with the World Economic Forum and McKinsey showed that 90% of executives feel they only have "nascent" and "developing" capabilities to combat cyberthreats. In this situation when cyber breaches have become an inevitable reality of doing business, executives ask themselves, "What does it mean for my business, how probable is it that a devastating breach will happen to us, and how much could it cost us?" Still, very few organizations have developed ways to assess their cyber risk exposure and to quantify them.

In this chapter, we discuss the cyber value-at-risk framework introduced by the Partnering for Cyber Resilience initiative of the World Economic Forum and released at the Annual Summit in Davos in 2015. More than 50 organizations, including Wipro, Deloitte (project advisor), and Aon, have contributed to this effort. The framework laid the foundations for modeling cyber risks and encouraged organizations to take a quantitative approach toward assessing their cyber risks exposure, which could also help make appropriate investment decisions.

We were delighted to see many spin-off projects and initiatives that were initiated as part of this work and hope they will contribute to better risk management tools. Our research showed that the aggregate impact of cybercrime on the global economy can amount to $3 trillion in terms of slow down in digitization and growth and result in the slower adoption of innovation. Multiple other studies showed significant negative impact of cyber breaches. CSIS established that the annual cost of economic espionage reaches $445 billion. Target's breach cost the company more than $140 million, a large portion of which went to cover litigation costs. Interestingly, however, Aon research shows that more than 80% of breaches cost the companies less than $1 million.

■ **Value-at-risk**

How can companies define their risk exposure and the level of investments, as well as priority areas for these investments? To answer this question, we turned to the value-at-risk concept. The concept goes back to the financial services industry and describes the risk appetite and potential losses for a portfolio that an institution will incur over a defined period of time and is expressed in a probability to insure the loss.

In the cyber value-at-risk, we introduced three major pillars, according to which companies can model their risk exposure: existing vulnerabilities, value of the assets, and profile of an attacker. A complete cyber value-at-risk allows us to answer the question: "Given a successful cyberattack, a company will lose not more than X amount of money over period of time with 95% accuracy." The application of these models will depend on particular industries, companies, and available data and should be built for an organization. We discussed specific indicators that can potentially be used to populate the model. Mathematically, these components can be brought together and used to build a stochastic model. For example, vulnerabilities can be measured in the number of existing unpatched vulnerabilities, not up-to-date software, number of successful compromises, or results of internal and external audits. They can be benchmarked against the maturity of existing controls and security of networks, applications, data, etc. The maturity of defending systems has to be benchmarked against the threat environment, hence the profile of an attacker component becomes important. In this model, it would be important to look into their motivations (e.g., financial gain, destruction of assets, espionage), the tools they are using, and the innovative approaches. Because cyber breaches are criminal activity, nontechnical factors, such as behavioral motivations, are to be considered. The component of the value of assets of many organizations is difficult to establish. This includes tangible assets, such as financial flows, infrastructure, and products, and intangible assets, primarily data assets (customer and employee data, business strategies, intellectual property), brand, reputation, and trust of stakeholders. Although cost of business interruption can be qualified easier, the impact on intangible assets is still subject to approximation. The impact of losing these assets can be unnoticed in the short term but may hurt long-term profitability and market leadership of an organization.

The cyber value-at-risk model has a number of limitations, including availability of data, difficulties in calculating probabilities, and applicability across various industries, but it presents a first step and incentives for organizations to move toward quantitative risk management. By publishing the model, we aimed to encourage more industry stakeholders to develop comprehensive quantitative approaches to cyber risks measurement and management. For further examples and information, please refer to Wipro's use of cyber value-at-risk for its clients, Deloitte's continuous development cyber value-at-risk, Rod Becktom's cybervar model, and CXOWare's Cyber Risk application model. The Institute of Risk Management (IRM) announced that it will release a cyber risk quantification framework to help companies assess their cyber risks exposure. The call to action from the Partnering for Cyber Resilience effort was that to develop a unified framework that can be used by industries to reduce uncertainty around cyber risks implications on businesses in the absence of dominant models and frameworks. Aon has defined important ways in which quantification of cyberthreats can lead to better business decisions. First, as the conversation has shifted from technology and information security departments to boardrooms, the question of costs and risks becomes ever more prevalent. It helps show the scale and the impact that cyberthreats can have on financial targets and overall competitiveness of organizations; helps define and narrow down the investments required to mitigate those threats; makes it easy to paint compelling pictures, build scenarios, and make business cases; and helps make a determination whether any parts of the risk can be transferred. Deloitte has put together a comprehensive model for modular approach to cyber risk measurement introducing the following components: probability model ("attractiveness and resilience determine

breach probability distribution"); hacker model (mapping out motivations of adversaries in relation to the organization); attack model (attack types and characteristics); asset and loss model (potential loss given a successful attack); security model (describing organizations' security posture), and company model (modeling organizations' attractiveness as a target). Cyberpoint's Cy-var models looks at "time-dependent valuation of assets" while taking into account an organization's security posture and includes variables such as the values of intellectual property assets, IT security controls in place to protect those assets and other related risks, infrastructure risks, a time horizon, and a probability of an attack.

At the same time, all stakeholders came to agreement that quantifying risks is a challenging task. In a workshop organized together with Deloitte, the World Economic Forum Partnering for Cyber Resilience members defined the attributes of an ideal model of cyber risks quantification: applicability across various industries; ease of interpretation by experts and executives alike; association with real data and measurable security events; scalability across organizations or even across the industry; at the same, not relying on data that are currently absent within most organizations.

Although the cyber value-at-risk framework doesn't specify how to calculate the final number, it presents core components and gives examples of how these components can be quantified. This complete model, however, could be characterized by general applicability across various industries. For it to be effective, it has to be validated by the industry stakeholders. Cyber value-at-risk aimed to bring together "technical, behavioral and economic factors from both internal (enterprise) and external (systemic) perspectives." As a next step, it would be important to understand dependencies between various components in the framework and ways to incorporate these models into existing enterprise risk frameworks. It is important to remember that organizations should be wary of new emerging risks and consider cyber risks in addition to broader technology or operational risks.

Overall, the goal was to help raise awareness of cyber risks as a standing and regular cost of doing business and help find a way to measure and mitigate those risks. This can be done through standardization of various risk factors and indicators into a normal distribution.

The components that we looked at in this chapter help bring together various risk factors via "measures of risk likelihood and impact." To achieve a more granular level of sophistication, quantification and standardization metrics must mature. Some of the main cited obstacles are availability of data to build models, lack of standardized metrics and tools, lack of visibility within enterprise, and inability to collect data and dubbed models internally. The variables and components of the model can be brought together into a stochastic model, which will show the maximum loss given a certain probability over a given period of time. It was discussed that close to real-time sharing of data between organizations could address some of the main challenges of datasets' availability and provide enough data to build models.

Although a silver bullet to achieve cyber resilience doesn't exist, organizations consider comprehensive frameworks for quantifying and mitigating risk factors, including cyber risks. Following this model, companies will assess their assets and existing controls, quantify vulnerabilities, and know their attackers and threats. The most significant challenge so far is the absence of input variables, quality of existing datasets and, following these, no standardized measures to assess cyber risk exposures. Building such a model would require efforts in data classification, encourage a strong organization leadership, process improvement and collaboration, as well improve decision making across various business areas. For example, the car industry, mortgage industry, or most insurances have agreed on a standardized metrics and data collection; the same should happen for cyber risks measurement. Understanding dependencies between these variables and what they mean for various industries should be a subject for cross-industry collaboration so that input variables are unified. The main benefits of this approach are seen in the ability to support decision-making processes, quantify the damage at a more granular level, and define appropriate investments. This would help stimulate the development of risk transfer markets and emergence of secondary risk transfer products to mitigate and distribute the risks. For organizations, the focus will shift from an attacker to assets and how to secure them in such a distributed digital ecosystem, where everything is vulnerable. As more robust quantitative cyber risks models emerge and the industries are moving toward a standardized recognizable model, the confidence of digital ecosystems stakeholders and their ability to make effective decisions will also rise.

Based on *Towards the Quantification of Cyber Threats* report.

6

The evolving cyberthreat and an architecture for addressing it

Internet Security Alliance – Larry Clinton, CEO

According to the Pentagon's 2015 Annual Report, "The military's computer networks can be compromised by low to meddling skilled attacks. Military systems do not have a sufficiently robust security posture to repel sustained attacks. The development of advanced cyber techniques makes it likely that a determined adversary can acquire a foothold in most DOD systems and be in a position to degrade DOD missions when and if they choose."

If the cyber systems of the world's most sophisticated and best funded armed forces can be compromised by "low to meddling skilled attacks," how safe can we expect discount retailers, movie studios, or any other corporate or public systems to be?

That is not even the bad news.

■ Things are getting much worse: Three reasons
1. The system is getting weaker.
The bad news is that the cyber systems that have become the underpinning of virtually all of aspects of life in the digital age are becoming increasing less secure. There are multiple reasons for this distressing trend. First, the system is getting technologically weaker. Virtually no one writes code or develops "apps" from scratch. We are still relying on many of the core protocols designed in the 1970s and 80s. These protocols were designed to be "open," not secure. Now the attacking community is going back through these core elements of the Internet and discovering still new vulnerabilities. So as new functionalities come online, their own vulnerabilities are simply added to the existing and expanding vulnerabilities they are built upon. The reality is that the fabric of the Internet is riddled with holes, and as we continue to stretch that fabric, it is becoming increasingly less secure.

Additionally, vulnerabilities in many open source codes, widely in use for years, are becoming increasingly apparent and being exploited by modern "zero-day" attacks, and the patching system we have relied on to remediate the system can't keep pace. Huge vulnerabilities such as Heartbleed and Shellshock have existed within open source code for years only to be revealed recently when scrutinized by fresh eyes.

Within hours of the Heartbleed vulnerability becoming public in 2014, there was a surge of attackers stepping up to exploit it. The attackers exploiting the vulnerability were much faster than the vendors could patch it. This is a growing trend. In 2014 it took 204 days, 22 days, and 52 days to patch the top three zero-day vulnerabilities. In 2013 it took only four days for patches to arrive. Even more disturbing is that the top five zero-day attacks in 2014 were actively used for a combined 295 days before patches were available.

Moreover, because almost no one builds from scratch anymore, the rate of adoption for open source programming as a core component of new software greatly exceeds the vetting process for many applications. As the code gets altered into new apps, the risks continue to multiply. In 2015 Symantec estimates there are now more than a million malicious apps in existence. In fast-moving, early stage industry, developers have a strong incentive to offer new functionality and features, but data protection and privacy policies tend to be a lesser priority.

The risks created by the core of the system becoming intrinsically weaker is being further magnified by the explosion of access points to the system, many with little or no security built into their development. Some analysts are already asserting that there are more mobile devices than there are people on the earth. If that is not yet literally true, it will shortly be.

It is now common for individuals to have multiple mobile devices and use them interchangeably for work and leisure often without substantial security settings. Although this certainly poses a risk of data being stolen directly from smartphones, the greater concern is that mobile devices are increasingly conduits to the cloud, which holds increasing amounts of valuable data. The number of

new access points to large amounts of data resulting from the explosion in the number of mobile devices vastly increases the challenges to securing cyberspace.

However, the rise in use of mobile devices pales in comparison to the coming Internet of Things (IoT). The IoT, embedded computing devices with Internet connections, embraces a wide range of devices, including home security systems, cars, smart TVs, and security cameras. Like the bring-your-own-device (BYOD) phenomenon, the coming of the IoT further undermines the overall security of the system by dramatically increasing the vectors, making every new employee's internet-connected device, upon upgrade, a potential threat vector.

2. The bad guys are getting better.

Just after the turn of the century, the NSA coined a new term, the "APT," which stood for the *advanced persistent threat*. The APT referred to ultrasophisticated cyberattack methods being practiced by advanced nation-state actors. These attacks were characterized by their targeted nature, often focused on specific people instead of networks, their continued and evolving nature, and their clever social engineering tactics. These were not "hackers" and "script kiddies." These were pros for whom cyberattacks were their day job.

They were also characterized by their ability to compromise virtually any target they selected. APTs routinely compromised all anti-virus intrusion detection and best practices. They made perimeter defense obsolete.

Now these same attack methods, once practiced only by sophisticated nation-states, are widely in use by common criminals. Whereas a few years ago these attacks were confined to nations and the Defense Industrial Complex, they now permeate virtually all economic sectors.

The APT now stands for the *average persistent threat*.

The increasing professionalism and sophistication of the attack community is fueled by the enormous profits cyberattacks are generating—routinely estimated in the hundreds of billions of dollars and growing. It is now apparent that attackers are not going to rely on reusing the same old methods. Instead, like any smart, successful, and growing enterprise, they are investing in R&D and personnel acquisition. They are seeking to grow their business, including finding new vulnerabilities in older infrastructures and thus widening the surface available for attack.

3. The economics of cybersecurity favor the attackers.

Cyberattacks are relatively cheap and easy to access. Virtually anyone can do an Internet search and find vendors to purchase attack methods for a comparatively small investment. The attacker's business plans are expansive with extremely generous profit margins. Multiple reports suggest hundreds of billions of dollars in criminal cyber revenue each year. They can use virtually identical attack methods against multiple targets. The vast interconnection of the system allows attackers to exploit weaker links who have permitted access to more attractive targets, and their "market" is accessible to them worldwide.

Meanwhile, cyber defense tends to be almost inherently a generation behind the attackers, as anticipating the method and point of attack is extremely difficult. From a business investment perspective it is hard to show return on investment (ROI) to attacks that are prevented, making adequate funding a challenge. Moreover, law enforcement is almost nonexistent—we successfully prosecute less than 2% of cyber criminals, so there is little to discourage the attackers from being bold. Furthermore, as we have already illustrated, notwithstanding consumers tend to prefer utility and function over security, which provides a disincentive for investors to enhance devices with added security, which often slows or limits utility.

This little-understood imbalance of the economic incentives is exacerbated by the fact that many of the technologies and business practices that have recently driven corporate growth, innovation, and profitability also undermine cybersecurity.

Technologies such as VOIP or cloud computing bring tremendous cost efficiencies but dramatically complicate security. Efficient, even necessary, business practices such as the use of long supply chains and BYOD are also economically attractive but extremely problematic from a security perspective.

Corporate boards are faced with the conundrum of needing to use technology to grow and maintain their enterprises without risking the corporate crown jewels or hard-won public faith in the bargain. In addition, the fears and potential losses from cyber events tend to be speculative and future oriented, whereas most corporate leaders (as well as the citizen investors who have their 401(k)s tied up in the stock market) tend to make their decisions with an eye toward the next quarter or two.

The national security equation

Finally, from the national security perspective, Internet economics are also complicated. This economic puzzle is important to solve because multiple independent studies indicate that the number one problem with securing critical infrastructure from cyberattack is economic. As the 2014 National Infrastructure Protection Plan makes clear, the public and private sectors have aligned, but not identical, perspective on cybersecurity based on their differing, and legally mandated, roles and obligations.

The private sector is legally required to invest to maximize shareholder value. Although shareholder value is enhanced to some degree by security investment, generally security is considered a cost center in the corporate world. As with most corporate investments, security is a mater of cost benefit for the private sector. What this translates to is that the private sector may legitimately judge that there is a level of security that goes beyond their commercial interest and hence their legally mandated obligation to their shareholders. An example is the common case of pilfering in many retail stores, wherein the owner may be aware that 5% of his inventory is "walking out the back door" every month. The reason he doesn't hire more guards or put up more cameras or other security measures is that the cost benefit presumably suggests it will cost him 6% to do so, and hence the better business decision is to tolerate this level of insecurity.

Government doesn't have that luxury. The government is charged with providing for the common defense. Surely, they have economic considerations with respect to security; however, they are also mandated to a higher level of security largely irrespective of cost to provide for national security, consumer protection, privacy, and other non-economic considerations.

In the Internet space, government and industry are using the same networks. This means the two users of the systems have differing security requirements—both legitimate and backed by lawful authority. Moreover, requiring greater cybersecurity spending, beyond commercial interest as suggested by some, could run afoul of other government interests such as promoting innovation, competitiveness, and job growth in a world economy (presumably not following U.S.-based requirements).

Finally, the presumption that requiring increased security spending by commercial entities up to the government risk tolerance is in the corporate self-interest is complicated by the data that have emerged after highly publicized cyber breaches. One year after the Target breach, which would presumably damage the company's image profitability and reputation, Target's stock price was up 22%, suggesting such predictions were incorrect. Similarly, 6 months after the high-profile cyberattacks on Sony (the second high-profile cyberattack for Sony in a few years), Sony's stock price was up 26%.

■ Some good news: Enlightened policy working in partnership
Traditional regulatory efforts fail
In 2012 President Obama offered a legislative proposal to Congress suggesting that

the Department of Homeland Security (DHS) be given authority to set minimum standards for cybersecurity over the private sector. Subsequently two bills were offered in the Senate, one by the Chairman of the Senate Commerce Committee, Senator Jay Rockefeller (D-WV) with Senator Olympia Snow (R-ME) and separately by Senate Homeland Security Chairman Joe Lieberman (D-CN) and Senator Susan Collins (R-ME). Both bills largely followed the Obama paradigm of DHS setting regulatory mandates for the private sector with substantial penalties available for noncompliance.

Despite strong backing from the Senate Majority Leader Harry Reid and much of the military establishment, the bills could not get out of committee. Even though Reid exercised his parliamentary power to control the Senate agenda, there was not enough support to even get the bills to the floor for consideration, let alone vote on it.

There was certainly industry opposition to these bills, but what killed them was the bipartisan realization that the traditional regulatory model was an ill fit for cybersecurity. Government agencies' ability to craft regulations that could keep up with cyberthreats was highly questionable. Early efforts to apply traditional regulation to cyberspace, such as HIPAA in the health-care industry, had not generated success. Indeed health care is widely considered one of the least cyber secure of all critical infrastructures.

However, with cyber systems becoming increasingly ubiquitous and insecure threatening economic development and national security, there was obvious need for an affirmative and effective approach. The non-regulatory, collaborative model selected largely followed the "social contract" paradigm previously promoted by industry government analysts.

The social contract approach
In 2013 President Obama reversed course 180 degrees. In an executive order on cybersecurity the president abandoned the government-centric regulatory approach

embodied in his previous legislative proposals and the Senate bills. Instead, he suggested a public private partnership—a social contract—that would address the technical as well as economic issues that are precluding the development of a cyber system that can become sustainably secure. In this new partnership, industry and government would work together to identify a framework of standards and practices worthy of industry based on cyber risk assessments conducted by the companies. The president ordered that the framework be voluntary, prioritized, and cost effective. If there were an economic gap between what ought to be done and what would be accomplished through normal market mechanisms, a set of market incentives would be developed to promote voluntary adoption of the framework. Although industry that operates under regulatory systems would remain subject to regulatory authority, no new regulatory authority for cybersecurity would be part of the system. Instead, a partnership system based on voluntary use of consensus standards and practices and reinforced through market incentives would be built.

The cyber social contract model has substantial precedent in the history of infrastructure development in the United States. In the early twentieth century the innovative technologies were telephony and electricity transport. Initially the private companies that provided these technologies, because of natural economies, served primarily high-density and affluent markets. Policy makers of the era quickly realized that there was a broader social good that would be served by having universal service of these services but also realized that building out that infrastructure would be costly and uneconomic either for industry or government.

Instead of government taking over the process or mandating that industry make uneconomic investment, the policy makers designed a modern social contract with industry. If industry would build out the networks and provide universal electric and telephone service at affordable rates, government would guarantee the investment private industry would make in building and providing the service. This agreement ensured enough funds to build, maintain, and upgrade the system plus make a reasonable rate of return on the investment. Thus were born the privately owned public utilities and the rate of return regulation system.

The result was that the U.S. quickly built out the electric and communications systems for the expanding nation, which were generally considered the best in the world. Some have argued this decision was foundational to the U.S.'s rapid expansion and development, which turned it from a relatively minor power in the early part of the twentieth century to the world's dominant superpower less than a generation later.

Although the Obama social contract approach to cybersecurity has different terms than that of previous infrastructure development, the paradigm is similar. Similar modifications of the incentive model are also in use in other areas of the economy, such as environment, agriculture, and transportation, but this is the first application in the cybersecurity field.

Although it is in its formative stages, at this point early indications for the social contract approach are positive. The cybersecurity framework development process conducted by the National Institute of Standards and Technology (NIST) has been completed and received virtually unanimous praise. In an exceedingly rare development, the Obama approach to cybersecurity closely tracks with that outlined by the House Republican Task Force on Cyber Security. Bipartisan bills using liability incentives, instead of government mandates, are moving through Congress, and additional incentive programs are under development.

■ Conclusion

The cybersecurity problem is extremely serious and becoming more so. An inherently insecure system is becoming weaker. The attack community is becoming more sophisticated and enjoys massive economic incentives over the defender community. Traditional government methods to fight criminal activity have not matured to address the threat and may be inappropriate to meet the dynamic nature of this uniquely twenty-first century problem. Fortunately, at least the U.S. government seems to have developed a consensus strategy to better leverage public and private resources to combat cyberthreats without excessively compromising other critical social needs. Although there are some initial signs of progress, the road to creating a sustainably secure cyber system will be long and difficult.

7

Effective cyber risk management: An integrated approach

Former CIO of the U.S. Department of Energy – Robert F. Brese

In its 2015 Data Breach Report, Verizon found that in 60% of the nearly 80,000 security incidents reviewed, including more than 2,000 confirmed data breaches, cyber attackers were able to compromise an organization within minutes. Alarmingly, only about one third of the compromises were discovered within days of their occurrence. This is not good news for C-suites and boardrooms. Data breaches, compromises in which data loss is unknown, denial of service attacks, destructive malware, and other types of cybersecurity incidents can lead to lost revenue, reputation damage, and even lawsuits, as well as short- and long-term liabilities affecting a company's future. Although "getting hacked" may seem, or even be, inevitable, the good news is that by taking an integrated approach to risk management, cybersecurity risk can be effectively managed.

But who is responsible for this integrated approach, and what does it include? Although often the case, managing cybersecurity risk should not be left solely to the chief information officer (CIO) and chief information security officer (CISO). Even though these professionals are capable, only an integrated information (i.e., data), information technology, and business approach will enable a company to effectively manage cybersecurity risk as a component of an organization's overarching enterprise risk program. There is also a movement for board-level involvement and reporting, resulting in a risk to board members' tenure if they are not considered to be sufficiently engaged in the oversight of cybersecurity risk management and incident response. As an example, in 2014, Institutional Shareholders Services (ISS) recommended that shareholders of Target stock vote against all seven of the directors that were on the board at the time of the highly publicized 2013 breach. Although somewhat shocking, it should be inherently obvious that effective cybersecurity risk management is key to meeting the fiduciary responsibilities of corporate officers and the board.

To ensure success, managing cybersecurity risk must be an ongoing and iterative process, not a one-time, infrequent, or check-the-box activity. This area of risk management must grow with the company and change with ever-evolving cyber threats. Data holdings and information technology (IT) systems, and the Internet-connected environment in which they operate, change at a pace that is more rapid than many of the other variables affecting enterprise risk. Not only must the right stakeholders be engaged at the right levels within an organization, but also the right automated tools and processes must be in place to support risk decision making and monitoring.

■ Perfect security is a myth
As in physical security, there is no such thing as perfect IT (cyber) security. All the firewalls, encryption, passwords, and patches available cannot create a zone of absolute safety that enables a company to operate unimpeded and free of concern regarding the cybersecurity threat. However, perfect security is not required, or even desired. The effects of too little security are fairly obvious. However, too much security unnecessarily constricts the business' ability to operate by reducing the effectiveness and efficiency of a customer's access to the company's products and services and unnecessarily constraining internal and business-to-business (B2B) interactions. Effective risk management finds the balance between the needs of the business to operate and the needs and cost of security. In finding this balance, the company will be able to compete successfully in its market while protecting the critical information and assets on which its success relies.

■ Enterprise risk management
Gartner, Inc., the world's leading IT research and advisory company, has found that cybersecurity risk management programs have experienced trouble in scaling with corporate initiatives in mobility, cloud, big data, and collaboration. They also predict that the digital industrial economy, and the Internet of Things (IoT), will result in even greater difficulty. However, attempting to scale cybersecurity risk management in isolation from an organization's enterprise risk program only exposes the organization to greater risk by creating a gap in risk oversight.

Nearly every company has established processes to manage enterprise risk. Larger companies often have a chief risk officer (CRO) or equivalent individual who is independent of the business units and is given the authority and responsibility to manage the enterprise risk processes. Incorporating cybersecurity into the mix of corporately managed risks should be a priority. Some may argue that cybersecurity is too different from the other risks a company faces, such as market risk, credit risk, currency risk, or physical security risk, to be managed in a similar manner. However, although cybersecurity may seem more "technical," the desired outcome of the treatment is the same, that is to eliminate, mitigate, transfer, or accept risk affecting the company's future. One thing is certain: not all cybersecurity risk can be eliminated through controls or transferred through insurance, so residual risk must accepted. Making good decisions requires an integrated, formal approach.

■ The cybersecurity risk management process
There are several key steps that should be taken to effectively integrate cybersecurity risk management into the company's enterprise risk management process. This chapter doesn't attempt to explain the details of any particular process but instead focuses on common attributes that should be used, including risk framing and assessment, controls assessment, risk decision-making, residual risk sign-off, risk monitoring, and accountability. Figure 1 provides a visual of the process. For additional details on approaches to cybersecurity risk management, the National Institute of Standards and Technology (NIST) Computer Security Resource Center (CSRC), international standards organizations, and other industry sources may be consulted.

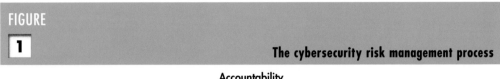

FIGURE

1

The cybersecurity risk management process

Accountability

Risk Framing & Assessment → Controls Assessment → Risk Decision Making → Residual Risk Sign-off → Risk Monitoring

<u>Risk Framing and Assessment:</u> The initial activities in risk management include risk framing and assessment and controls assessment. CIOs and CISOs have been assessing the risk to IT systems for many years and are well informed on the range of cybersecurity threats and vulnerabilities that affect corporate risk. However, the consequences (i.e., business impact) may or may not be well understood, depending on how close the relationship between IT and the line of business leaders has been in the past. The engagement between IT and the line of business owners is crucial and must result in clarity about the type and amount of risk the business is willing to accept with respect to the

confidentiality (preventing unauthorized disclosure);

integrity (preventing unauthorized modification or destruction); and

availability (ensuring data and systems are operational when needed)

of the information and systems on which the business relies. Once IT understands the business owner's risk threshold, the CIO and CISO can begin planning, implementing, and assessing the appropriate security controls.

<u>Controls Assessment:</u> Preparing an appropriate response to risk requires the assessment of potential controls. Controls include all of the tools, tactics, and processes

a company has to avoid, mitigate, share, transfer, or accept risk. This means that corporate structure, training and awareness programs, physical security, and other options should be considered in addition to traditional IT controls. Cyber insurance may also be considered. Again, the CIO and CISO cannot do this alone, and there should be active engagement across all the various business lines, business support, and IT organizations that can contribute to identifying potential controls and the impact they may have on cybersecurity risk.

<u>Risk Decision Making:</u> A crucial element of risk response is the decision-making process. Decisions are made regarding what will be done and what will not be done in response to each risk. A balance must be struck between protecting systems and information and the need to effectively run the business that relies on them. Other factors that should be considered include the amount of risk reduction related to implementation and maintenance costs and the impacts on employee training and certification requirements.

An acceptable course of action is identified and agreed to by the business, and then controls are implemented and initially evaluated for effectiveness. If the controls perform acceptably, then the sign-off and monitoring processes can begin. If not, then a new course of action must be developed, which may require further controls assessment to respond to the risk or even additional framing and assessment to adjust the risk tolerance.

Residual Risk Sign-Off: The sign-off of residual risk closes the decision-making process. This should be the role of the business because it is the operational customer of the risk management process. Additionally, this should be a formal, documented activity. The decisions on how each risk will be treated and/or accepted must be articulated in a manner such that the signatory and reviewers (i.e., regulators, etc.) can clearly understand the risk treatment plan and the residual risk being accepted. Once the residual risk is formally accepted, the system is typically placed into operation. The formal recognition of the residual risk also helps build a culture of risk awareness in the business units.

Risk Monitoring: Monitoring risk is an ongoing process. Each monitoring activity is designed with a purpose, type, and frequency of monitoring. Typically, a risk register has been developed during the risk framing and assessment phase and leveraged throughout all steps of the risk management process. The register also serves as a reference for auditors. The register should contain the risks that matter most and be routinely updated and reviewed with the business over time. If the likelihood or severity of consequences changes, or if other physical or IT environmental factors change, the treatment plan and/or the accepted level of residual risk may require revision. If so, the previous process steps should be revisited. The frequency of review should be in relation to the likelihood and severity of the risk. Because most companies have a large number of systems, each with their own risk register, an automated system is typically used to aid monitoring and review.

Accountability: Last and most important, we have to consider accountability. Accountability is not about who to blame when something goes wrong. As stated earlier, the likelihood of something going wrong is high. Accountability ensures a formal risk management process is followed and that effective decision-making is occurring. One person should be accountable for the risk management process; however, numerous individuals will be responsible or accountable for the various steps, and many more will be consulted and informed along the way. One option to ensure roles and responsibilities are clearly articulated

> A responsibility assignment matrix (RAM), also known as RACI matrix/ 'reisi:/ or ARCI matrix or linear responsibility chart (LRC), describes the participation by various roles in completing tasks or deliverables for a project or business process.

TABLE 1

Process Step	CIO	CISO	LOB	CRO	CEO	Board
Risk Framing and Assessment	A	R	C	C	C	C
Controls Assessment	A	R	C	I	I	I
Risk Decision-Making	C	R	A	C	I	I
Residual Risk Sign-Off	C	R	A	I	I	I
Risk Monitoring	A	R	C	C	I	I
Accountability	R	C	C	A	C	C

is by using a RACI matrix (see insert) to identify which person or organization is responsible, accountable, consulted, or informed. Table 1 provides an example but should be adjusted to align to the enterprise risk management and governance processes of the company.

■ Information supporting cybersecurity risk management

No risk management is a precise science, including cybersecurity risk management. Throughout the risk management process, the information required for success has to be "good enough" to recognize and understand risks to the level necessary to support effective decision-making. Although complex mathematical models may work to manage some risks the company faces, forcibly creating objectivity when little or none exists can actually result in poor or ineffective decisions by creating a focus on the numbers rather than on the meaning of the risk analysis. So, using big bucket approach categories such as low, moderate, and high or unlikely, likely, and very likely may be adequate.

■ Stakeholder engagement

A key success factor of ensuring that fiduciary responsibilities are fulfilled in a company's cybersecurity risk management program is the right level of stakeholder engagement. Leaving the program to the CRO or the CIO alone should not be considered due diligence. Framing and assessing risk requires a clear understanding of corporate risk tolerance. The line of business lead should have the responsibility to sign off on the residual risk, but to make good risk decisions, the perspectives of other individuals and organizations in the company must be consulted and taken into consideration. Depending on the system(s) for which risk is being evaluated, some potential stakeholders include the CIO, CISO, chief financial officer (CFO), legal counsel, and other line of business owners and external partners with supporting or dependent relationships. If there is significant potential to affect the customer experience, there may be a need to conduct user acceptance testing or experience surveys as well.

■ Evaluating maturity of an organization's cybersecurity risk management program

Cybersecurity risk management programs aren't born effective and are not immediately prepared to scale with the business. Equally important as making effective risk management decisions and accepting residual risk is the continuous evaluation of the process itself. Numerous IT, cybersecurity, and business consultants, as well as trade associations have published guidance, checklists, and suggested questions for board members. Although there are many ways for the C-suite and board to stay engaged, a company's cybersecurity risk management program must continuously mature to ensure future success. To understand a program's growing maturity, questions should be focused on evaluating improvements in how well risk is understood and treated, the effectiveness of business leader and general employee participation, how responsive the risk management process is to change, and the capability to effectively respond to an incident.

How consistent is the understanding of the company's tolerance for cybersecurity risk across the C-suite and senior managers? How deep in the organization does this understanding go?

How well do line of business owners understand the cybersecurity risks associated with their business? Are sound and effective risk management and acceptance decisions being made in a timely manner to meet business needs?

How clearly are roles and responsibilities understood, and how well do role owners adhere to and fulfill their responsibilities? Do employees report cybersecurity issues and are they incorporated into the risk monitoring process?

When threats, vulnerabilities, or other conditions change, does the risk management process respond and, when necessary, make sustainable changes to the risk treatment plan?

How effective is the cyber incident response plan? Is it regularly exercised and are lessons learned from exercises and prior incidents leveraged to improve the plan?

■ Effective communications

Long-term effectiveness in cybersecurity risk management requires all employees to fulfill their responsibilities of the security of the organization for which they work. Creating a company culture of cybersecurity risk awareness is critical and is fostered through effective communications. Leadership must understand how risk is being measured across the enterprise, articulate what level is acceptable, and balance the cost they are willing incur for this level of security. Employees must understand the basics of the various cybersecurity threats and vulnerabilities and the importance of their daily decisions and actions as they go about their business. Regular training and awareness activities are essential and can be similar to the "see something, say something" campaigns related to physical security. Additionally, employees must be empowered and rewarded for identifying cybersecurity issues.

Communications are also important to build strong relationships, not only through customer assurances but also with external partners and suppliers. Communicating cybersecurity requirements and expectations to business partners can improve risk decision-making as well as lead to cooperative approaches to mitigating risk. Cybersecurity risks also exist in the supply chain, and communicating cybersecurity requirements and vetting suppliers for certain critical components or services can effectively reduce risk. Had Target, Home Depot, and certain other high-profile cyberattack victims built stronger cybersecurity relationships with external partners, their risk of becoming a victim may have been reduced.

■ Conclusion

C-suites and boards should not fear cybersecurity. By integrating cybersecurity risk management into the enterprise risk management process and by effectively engaging IT and business executives, cybersecurity risk can be understood and managed. Building a risk-aware culture is important to ensuring the quality of the ongoing risk monitoring process. When cyberthreats and vulnerabilities are regularly evaluated, employees are empowered to report issues and business executives are aware of potential impacts to their operations, the company's cybersecurity defenses become more agile and responsive and the overall risk remains under control. Finally, continuous evaluation of the risk management process, including its effectiveness and responsiveness to change and to incidents, is necessary to ensure effectiveness is sustained.

1 Cyber risk and the board of directors

8

The risks to boards of directors and board member obligations

Orrick, Herrington & Sutcliffe LLP – Antony Kim, Partner; Aravind Swaminathan, Partner; and Daniel Dunne, Partner

As cyberattacks and data breaches continue to accelerate in number and frequency, boards of directors are focusing increasingly on the oversight and management of corporate cybersecurity risks. Directors are not the only ones. An array of federal and state enforcement agencies and regulators, most notably the Department of Justice (DOJ), Department of Homeland Security (DHS), Securities and Exchange Commission (SEC), Financial Industry Regulatory Authority (FINRA), and state Attorneys General, among others, identify board involvement in enterprise-wide cybersecurity risk management as a crucial factor in companies' ability to appropriately establish priorities, facilitate adequate resource allocation, and effectively respond to cyberthreats and incidents. As SEC Commissioner Luis A. Aguilar recently noted, "Boards that choose to ignore, or minimize, the importance of cybersecurity responsibility do so at their own peril."[1] Indeed, even apart from the regulators, aggressive plaintiffs' lawyers, and activist shareholders are similarly demanding that boards be held accountable for cybersecurity. Shareholder derivative actions and activist investor campaigns to oust directors are becoming the norm in high-profile security breaches.

Directors have clearly gotten the message. A survey by the NYSE Governance Services (in partnership with a leading cybersecurity firm) found that cybersecurity is discussed at 80% of all board meetings. However, the same survey revealed that only 34% of boards are confident about their respective companies' ability to defend themselves against a cyberattack. More troubling, a June 2015 study by the National Association of Corporate Directors found that only 11% of respondents believed their boards possessed a high level of understanding of the risks associated with cybersecurity.[2] This is a difficult position to be in: aware of the magnitude of the risks at hand but struggling to understand and find solutions to address and mitigate them.

In this chapter, we explore the legal obligations of boards of directors, the risks that boards face in the current cybersecurity landscape, and strategies that boards may consider in mitigating that risk to strengthen the corporation and their standing as dutiful directors.

I. Obligations of Board Members

The term "cybersecurity" generally refers to the technical, physical, administrative, and organizational safeguards that a corporation implements to protect, among other things, "personal information,"[3] trade secrets and other intellectual property, the network and associated assets, or as applicable, "critical infrastructure."[4] This definition alone should leave no doubt that a board of directors' role in protecting the corporation's "crown jewels" is essential to maximizing the interests of the corporation's shareholders.

Generally, directors owe their corporation fiduciary duties of good faith, care, and loyalty, as well as a duty to avoid corporate waste.[3] The specific contours of these duties are controlled by the laws of the state in which the company is incorporated, but the basic principles apply broadly across most jurisdictions (with Delaware corporations law often leading the way). More specifically, directors are obligated to discharge their duties in good faith, with the care an ordinarily prudent person would exercise in the conduct of his or her own business under similar circumstances, and in a manner that the director reasonably believes to be in the best interests of the corporation. To encourage individuals to serve as directors and to free corporate decision making from judicial second-guessing, courts apply the "business judgment rule." In short, courts presume that directors have acted in good faith and with reasonable care after obtaining all material information, unless proved otherwise; a powerful presumption that is difficult for plaintiffs to overcome, and has led to dismissal of many legal challenges to board

action or inaction. To maximize their personal protection, directors must ensure that, if the unthinkable happens and their corporation falls victim to a cybersecurity disaster, they have already taken the steps necessary to preserve this critical defense to personal liability.

In the realm of cybersecurity, the board of directors has "risk oversight" responsibility: the board does not itself *manage* cybersecurity risks; instead, the board oversees the corporate systems that ensure that management is doing so effectively. Generally, directors will be protected by the business judgment rule and will not be liable for a failure of oversight unless there is a "sustained or systemic failure of the board to exercise oversight—such as an utter failure to attempt to assure a reasonable information and reporting system exists." This is known as the *Caremark* test,[5] and there are two recognized ways to fall short: first, the directors intentionally and entirely fail to put *any* reporting and control system in place; or second, if there is a reporting and control system, the directors refuse to monitor it or fail to act on warnings they receive from the system.

The risk that directors will face personal liability is especially high where the board has not engaged in *any* oversight of their corporations' cybersecurity risk. This is a rare case, but other risks are more prevalent. For example, a director may fail to exercise due care if he or she makes a decision to discontinue funding an IT security project without getting any briefing about current cyberthreats the corporation is facing, or worse, after being advised that termination of the project may expose the company to serious threats. If an entirely uninformed or reckless decision to de-fund renders the corporation vulnerable to known or anticipated risks that lead to a breach, the members of the board of directors could be individually liable for breaching their *Caremark* duties.

II. The Personal Liability Risk to Directors

Boards of directors face increasing litigation risk in connection with their responsibilities for cybersecurity oversight, particularly in the form of shareholder derivative litigation, where shareholders sue for breaches of directors' fiduciary duties to the corporation. The rise in shareholder derivative suits coincides with a 2013 Supreme Court decision limiting the viability of class actions that fail to allege a nonspeculative theory of consumer injury resulting from identity theft.[6] Because of a lack of success in consumer class actions, plaintiffs' lawyers have been pivoting to shareholder derivative litigation as another opportunity to profit from massive data breaches.

In the last five years, plaintiffs' lawyers have initiated shareholder derivative litigation against the directors of four corporations that suffered prominent data breaches: Target Corporation, Wyndham Worldwide Corporation, TJX Companies, Inc., and Heartland Payment Systems, Inc. Target, Heartland, and TJX each were the victims of significant cyberattacks that resulted in the theft of approximately 110, 130, and 45 million credit cards, respectively. The Wyndham matter, on the other hand, involved the theft of only approximately 600,000 customer records; however, unlike the other three companies, it was Wyndham's *third* data breach in approximately 24 months that got the company and its directors in hot water. The signs point to Home Depot, Inc., being next in line. A Home Depot shareholder recently brought suit in Delaware seeking to inspect certain corporate books and records. A "books and records demand" is a common predicate for a shareholder derivative action, and this particular shareholder has already indicated that the purpose of her request is to determine whether Home Depot's management breached fiduciary duties by failing to adequately secure payment information on its data systems, allegedly leading to the exposure of up to 56 million customers' payment card information.

Although there is some variation in the derivative claims brought to date, most have focused on two allegations: that the directors breached their fiduciary duties by making a decision that was ill-advised or negligent, or

by failing to act in the face of a reasonably known cybersecurity threat. Recent cases have included allegations that directors:

- failed to implement and monitor an effective cybersecurity program;
- failed to protect company assets and business by recklessly disregarding cyberattack risks and ignoring red flags;
- failed to implement and maintain internal controls to protect customers' or employees' personal or financial information;
- failed to take reasonable steps to timely notify individuals that the company's information security system had been breached;
- caused or allowed the company to disseminate materially false and misleading statements to shareholders (in some instances, in company filings).

Board members may not be protected from liability by the exculpation clauses in their corporate charters. Although virtually all corporate charters exculpate board members from personal liability to the fullest extent of the law, Delaware law, for example, prohibits exculpation for breaches of the duty of loyalty, or breaches of the duty of good faith involving "intentional misconduct" or "knowing violations of law." As a result, because the Delaware Supreme Court has characterized a *Caremark* violation as a breach of the duty of loyalty,[7] exculpation of directors for *Caremark* breaches may be prohibited. In addition, with the myriad of federal and state laws that touch on privacy and security, directors may also lose their immunity based on "knowing violations of law." Given the nature of shareholder allegations in derivative litigation, these are important considerations, and importantly, vary depending on the state of incorporation.

Directors should also be mindful of standard securities fraud claims that can be brought against companies in the wake of a data breach. Securities laws generally prohibit public companies from making material statements of fact that are false or misleading. As companies are being asked more and more questions about data collection and protection practices, directors (and officers) should be careful about statements that are made regarding the company's cybersecurity posture and should focus on tailoring cybersecurity-related risk disclosures in SEC filings to address the specific threats that the company faces.

Cybersecurity disclosures are of keen interest to the SEC, among others. Very recently, the SEC warned companies to use care in making disclosures about data security and breaches and has launched inquiries to examine companies' practices in these areas. The SEC also has begun to demand that directors (and boards) take a more active role in cybersecurity risk oversight.

Litigation is not the only risk that directors face. Activist shareholders—who are also customers/clients of corporations—and proxy advisors are challenging the re-election of directors when they perceive that the board did not do enough to protect the corporation from a cyberattack. The most prominent example took place in connection with Target's data breach. In May 2014, just weeks after Target released its CEO, Institutional Shareholder Services (ISS), a leading proxy advisory firm, urged Target shareholders to seek ouster of seven of Target's ten directors for "not doing enough to ensure Target's systems were fortified against security threats" and for "failure to provide sufficient risk oversight" over cybersecurity.

Thoughtful, well-planned director involvement in cybersecurity oversight, as explained below, is a critical part of a comprehensive program, including indemnification and insurance, to protect directors against personal liability for breaches. Moreover, it can also assist in creating a compelling narrative that is important in brand and reputation management (as well as litigation defense) that the corporation acted responsibly and reasonably (or even more so) in the face of cybersecurity threats.

III. Protecting Boards of Directors

From a litigation perspective, boards of directors can best protect themselves from shareholder derivative claims accusing them of breaching their fiduciary duties by diligently overseeing the company's cybersecurity program and thereby laying the foundation for invoking the business judgment rule. Business judgment rule protection is strengthened by ensuring that board members receive periodic briefings on cybersecurity risk and have access to cyber experts whose expertise and experience the board members can rely on in making decisions about what to do (or not to do) to address cybersecurity risks. Most importantly, directors cannot recklessly ignore the information they receive, but must ensure that management is acting reasonably in response to reported information the board receives about risks and vulnerabilities.

Operationally, a board can exercise its oversight in a number of ways, including by (a) devoting board meeting time to presentations from management responsible for cybersecurity and discussions on the subject, to help the board become better acquainted with the company's cybersecurity posture and risk landscape; (b) directing management to implement a cybersecurity plan that incentivizes management to comply and holds it accountable for violations or noncompliance; (c) monitoring the effectiveness of such plan through internal and/or external controls; and (d) allocating adequate resources to address and remediate identified risks. Boards should invest effort in these actions, on a repeated and consistent basis, and make sure that these actions are clearly documented in board and committee packets, minutes, and reports.

(a) **Awareness.** Boards should consider appointing a chief information security officer (CISO), or similar officer, and meet regularly with that individual and other experts to understand the company's risk landscape, threat actors, and strategies to address that risk. Appointing a CISO has an additional benefit. Reports suggest that companies that have a dedicated CISO detected more security incidents and reported lower average financial losses per incident.[8]

Boards should also task a committee or subcommittee with responsibility for cybersecurity oversight, and devote time to getting updates and reports on cybersecurity from the CISO on a periodic basis. As with audit committees and accountants, boards can improve oversight by recruiting a board member with aptitude for the technical issues that cybersecurity presents, and placing that individual on the committee/subcommittee tasked with responsibility for cybersecurity oversight. Cybersecurity presentations, however, need not be overly technical. Management should use established analytical risk frameworks, such as the National Institute for Standards and Technology "Framework for Improving Critical Infrastructure Cybersecurity," (usually referred to as the "NIST Cybersecurity Framework") to assess and measure the corporation's current cybersecurity posture. These kinds of frameworks are critical tools that have an important role in bridging the communication and expertise gaps between directors and information security professionals and can also help translate cybersecurity program maturity into metrics and relative relationship models that directors are accustomed to using to make informed decisions about risk. It is principally through their use that directors can become sufficiently informed to exercise good business judgment.

(b) **Plan implementation and enforcement.** Boards should require that management implement an enterprise-wide cybersecurity risk management plan and align management's incentives to meet those goals. Although the details of any cybersecurity risk management plan should differ from company to company, the CISO and management should prepare a plan that includes proactive cybersecurity assessments of the company's network and systems, builds employee awareness of cybersecurity risk and requires periodic training, manages engagements with third parties that are granted access to the company's network and information, builds an incident response plan, and conducts simulations or "tabletop" exercises to practice and refine that plan. The board should further consider incentivizing the CISO and management for company compliance with cybersecurity policies and procedures (e.g., bonus allocations for meeting certain benchmarks) and create mechanisms for holding them responsible for noncompliance.

(c) **Monitor compliance.** With an enterprise-wide cybersecurity risk management plan firmly in place, boards of directors should direct that management create internal and external controls to ensure compliance and adherence to that plan. Similar to internal financial controls, boards should direct management to test and certify compliance with cybersecurity policies and procedures. For example, assuming that management establishes a policy that software patches be installed within 30 days of release, management would conduct a patch audit, confirm that all patches have been implemented, and have the CISO certify the results. Alternatively, boards can also retain independent cybersecurity firms that could be engaged by the board to conduct an audit, or validate compliance with cybersecurity policies and procedures, just as they would validate financial results in a financial audit.

(d) **Adequate resource allocation.** With information in hand about what the company's cybersecurity risks are, and an analysis of its current posture, boards should allocate adequate resources to address those risks so that management is appropriately armed and funded to protect the company.

As criminals continue to escalate the cyber-war, boards of directors will increasingly find themselves on the frontlines of regulatory, class plaintiff, and shareholder scrutiny. Directors are well-advised to proactively fulfill their risk oversight functions by driving senior management toward a well-developed and resilient cybersecurity program. In so doing, board members will not only better protect themselves against claims that they failed to discharge their fiduciary duties, but will strengthen their respective organizations' ability to detect, respond, and recover from cybersecurity crises.

Endnotes
1. SEC Commissioner Luis A. Aguilar, Remarks at the N.Y. Stock Exchange, Boards of Directors, Corporate Governance and Cyber-Risks: Sharpening the Focus (June 10, 2014).
2. Press Release, Nat'l Assoc. of Corp. Dir., Only 11% of Corporate Directors Say Boards Have High Level of Cyber-Risk Understanding (June 22, 2015) https://www.nacdonline.org/AboutUs/PressRelease.cfm?ItemNumber=15879.
3. Personal information is defined under a variety of federal and state laws, as well as industry guidelines, but is generally understood to refer to data that may be used to identify a person. For example, state breach notification laws in the U.S. define personal information, in general, as including first name (or first initial) and last name, in combination with any of the following: (a) social security number; (b) driver's license number or

other government-issued identification; (c) financial or credit/debit account number plus any security code necessary to access the account; or (d) health or medical information.
4. Critical infrastructure refers to systems, assets, or services that are so critical that a cyberattack could cause serious harm to our way of life. Presidential Policy Directive 21 (PPD-21) identifies the following 16 critical infrastructure sectors: chemicals, commercial facilities, communications, critical manufacturing, dams, defense industrial base, emergency services, energy, financial services, food and agriculture, government facilities, healthcare and public health, information technology, nuclear, transportation, waste, and wastewater. *See* Critical Infrastructure Sectors, DEPARTMENT OF HOMELAND SECURITY, *available at* http://www.dhs.gov/critical-infrastructure-sector.
5. For Delaware corporations, directors' compliance with their oversight function is analyzed under the test set out in *In re Caremark Int'l, Inc. Derivative Litig.*, 698 A.2d 959 (Del. Ch. 1996).
6. *See Clapper v. Amnesty Int'l USA*, 133 S. Ct. 1138 (2013). Consistent with *Clapper*, most data breach consumer class actions have been dismissed for lack of "standing": the requirement that a plaintiff has suffered a cognizable injury as a result of the defendant's conduct. That has proven challenging for plaintiffs because consumers are generally indemnified by banks against fraudulent charges on stolen credit cards, and many courts have rejected generalized claims of injury in the form of emotional distress or exposure to heighted risk of ID theft or fraud.
7. *Stone v. Ritter*, 911 A.2d 362, 370 (Del. 2006).
8. Ponemon Inst., 2015 Cost of Data Breach Study: Global Analysis (May 2015), http://www-03.ibm.com/security/data-breach/.

9

Where cybersecurity meets corporate securities: The SEC's push to regulate public companies' cyber defenses and disclosures

Fish & Richardson P.C. – Gus P. Coldebella, Principal and Caroline K. Simons, Associate

The risks associated with cyberattacks are a large and growing concern for American companies, no matter the size or the industry. If a company is publicly traded, however, there's a significant additional impetus for executives' cyber focus: the ever-increasing attention the U.S. Securities and Exchange Commission (SEC) pays to cybersecurity issues. The SEC, as one of the newest government players in the cybersecurity space, is flexing its regulatory muscles—including by mandating and scrutinizing cybersecurity risk disclosures, prodding companies to disclose additional information, and launching investigations after a breach comes to light.

This chapter explores the SEC's expanding role as cyber regulator and the growing nexus between cybersecurity and corporate securities. It gives companies a primer on the background and sources of the SEC's cyber authority, discusses tricky disclosure and securities regulation-related issues, and provides a potential framework for companies to think about whether, how, and when they should publicly disclose cybersecurity risks, and—when the inevitable happens—cyberattacks.

■ The SEC's authority to regulate cybersecurity

Generally, a company's duty to disclose material information under U.S. securities laws arises only when a statute or SEC rule requires it, and currently, no existing laws or rules explicitly refer to disclosure of cyber risks or incidents. Even so, the SEC has made it clear that it will use authorities already on the books to promote cybersecurity in public companies. During the SEC's March 2014 "Cybersecurity Roundtable," Chairman Mary Jo White said that, although the SEC's *formal* jurisdiction over cybersecurity is directly focused on the integrity of our market systems, customer data protection, and disclosure of material information, it is incumbent on every government agency to be informed on the full range of cybersecurity risks and actively engage to combat those risks in our respective spheres of responsibility." In other words—formal jurisdiction notwithstanding—the SEC will use every tool it has to combat cyber risks.

To divine the SEC's position on cybersecurity, companies and experienced counsel may look to a patchwork of non-binding staff guidance, SEC officials' speeches, and especially staff comment letters on companies' public filings. Given that cyber disclosures can have an effect on corporate reputations and stock price, give would-be attackers information about vulnerabilities, and trigger shareholder and other litigation and government investigations, companies anguish over exactly when, what, and how much to disclose. To answer these questions, it is crucial to understand the background and contours of existing requirements and the SEC's expectations.

■ History and background of the SEC's cybersecurity oversight

In May 2011, Senator Jay Rockefeller sent a letter to then-SEC Chairman Mary Schapiro urging the SEC to "develop and publish interpretive guidance clarifying existing disclosure requirements pertaining to information security risk." Rockefeller, frustrated with Congress's inability to pass cybersecurity legislation, identified the SEC's control over corporate public disclosure as a vehicle to promote security in the absence of legislation. Five months after the Rockefeller letter, in October 2011, the Division of Corporation Finance (the "Division") issued *CF Disclosure Guidance: Topic No. 2* (the "Guidance"). Even though it's not an SEC rule itself, the Guidance announced the Division's view that—"although no existing disclosure requirement explicitly refers to cybersecurity risks and cyber incidents"—existing SEC rules, such as Regulation S-K, "may impose" obligations to disclose cybersecurity and cyber events in a company's periodic reporting.

■ Contours of the SEC's staff guidance

Taking its cues from Regulation S-K, the Guidance details the key places where cybersecurity disclosures may appear in a company's 10-Ks and 10-Qs. The main focuses are as follows:

■ *Risk factors.* The company's risk factors are the central place for cyber disclosure. If cybersecurity is among the most significant factors making investment in the company risky, the risk factor disclosure should take into account "all available relevant information" from past attacks, the probability of future attacks occurring, the magnitude of the risks—including third-party risk, and the risk of undetected attacks—and the costs of those risks coming to pass, including the potential costs and consequences resulting from misappropriation of IP assets, corruption of data, or operational disruption. The risk factor should also describe relevant insurance coverage.

■ *MD&A.* If the costs or other consequences of a cyberattack represent a material trend, demand, or uncertainty "that is reasonably likely to have a material effect on the registrant's results of operations, liquidity, or financial condition or would cause reported financial information not to be necessarily indicative of future operating results or financial condition," the company should address cybersecurity risks and cyber incidents in its Management's Discussion and Analysis of Financial Condition and Results of Operations (MD&A).

■ *Description of business.* If one or more cyber incidents materially affected the company's products, services, customer or supplier relationships, or competitive conditions, the Guidance suggests disclosure in the "Description of Business" section.

■ *Legal proceedings.* If any litigation arose as a result of a cyber incident, the Guidance suggests disclosure if material.

■ *Financial statements.* If significant costs are associated with cyber preparedness or remediation, they should appear in the company's financial statements.

■ SEC post-guidance practice

Of course, guidance is just guidance unless the SEC, through its actions, gives it teeth. And the SEC has. Under Sarbanes-Oxley, the Division reviews every public company's reports at least once every three years, and the Division has focused intensely on cyber disclosures since the Guidance—especially risk factor disclosures. Responding to a follow-up letter from Senator Rockefeller requesting that the SEC enshrine the Guidance as a formal SEC rule, Schapiro's successor Mary Jo White took pains to stress that active staff review of cybersecurity—using existing disclosure rules—was an SEC priority. In her May 1, 2013 letter, White revealed that the Division had already issued approximately 50 cyber-related comment letters. And many more have been sent since then. Google, Amazon, AIG, Quest Diagnostics, and Citigroup are just some of the scores of public companies that received letters from staff urging enhanced disclosures of their cyber risks. The lessons we can learn from those exchanges are detailed below.

■ Tips for preparing 10-K and 10-Q cyber disclosures

According to a recent survey by Willis, 87% of Fortune 500 companies claim to have complied with the Guidance. The SEC's "enforcement" of it through comment letters has given it the muscle and imprimatur of a rule. Certain noteworthy trends that emerge from these letters follow:

Trend 1: Staff pushes for all cyber incidents to be disclosed—material or not. Materiality is the touchstone of disclosure. Even so, and even though the Guidance calls for disclosure of "cyber incidents... that are individually, or in the aggregate, *material*,"

staff comments have consistently urged companies to disclose past data breaches that are *not* material, even in the face of companies' well-reasoned positions to the contrary. For instance, Amazon resisted disclosing a past cyberattack at its subsidiary Zappos because it said the *entire* Zappos operation was not material to Amazon's consolidated revenues. SEC staff pushed Amazon to disclose it anyway, to place the risk factor "in appropriate context." A version of this comment appears in letter after letter. By first mandating cybersecurity risk factors via the Guidance, and then urging even non-material incidents to be included in those risk factors for "context," the staff appears to be pushing for disclosure of past cyber events notwithstanding materiality.

Trend 2: Staff will research cyber incidents—and ask about them. Division staff is independently monitoring breaches and comparing them with company disclosures. When a breach has been reported by a company or in the press, but there is no concomitant disclosure in the company's filings—especially where the company has already acknowledged susceptibility to attack as a risk factor—the staff will likely notice. Citigroup discovered this when the staff referred to press reports about a 2011 breach that supposedly affected 360,000 credit card accounts and asked why no 10-Q disclosure was made. The staff's practice is to ask for analysis supporting the conclusion that no further disclosure is necessary, including a discussion of materiality from a financial and reputational risk standpoint. Moreover, when a company discloses that a particular kind of potential breach may be material, the staff's comment letter almost always asks the company to disclose whether that kind of breach has already occurred—and if it has, to disclose it, material or not (*see* Trend 1). Taken together, these trends suggest that the SEC may be using its authority to make up for the lack of a federal breach notification law.

Trend 3: Staff is interested not only in the disclosure, but the pre-disclosure process. As Chairman White has stated, even with the absence of a direct law or regulation *directly* compelling companies to adopt strict cybersecurity measure, the SEC is exercising its power to *indirectly* prod companies to analyze and strengthen their cybersecurity programs through issuing disclosure guidance and bringing investigations, enforcement actions, and litigation against companies that fall short. In this way the SEC has taken on a larger mission than simply requiring disclosure—it is using its existing authorities to steer companies to engage in a deep, searching process to evaluate cyber risk. Whether or not you think the SEC is the appropriate regulator of this area, such a searching analysis is important to securing a company's digital assets. Management should engage in and document its analysis of the effects of cyber incidents on the company's operations, with special attention to probability of various types of attacks and their potential cost, from a quantitative and qualitative standpoint. It should do so not just to weather the storm of a possible SEC inquiry, but because such an analysis brings necessary executive-level oversight to a crucial area of enterprise risk.

Trend 4: Third-party risk is on the staff's mind. Staff is encouraging companies to look beyond their four walls to the cyber risk posed by the use of vendors. Staff will ask whether the company's vendors have experienced cyberattacks, and request assessment—and disclosure—if a breach at a third-party vendor could have a material effect on the company. The SEC likely believes that if public companies are required to disclose risks in their supply chain in addition to their own, third-party cybersecurity will improve as a result.

■ **In the heat of battle: 8-K disclosure questions during an attack**

Of course, 10-Ks and 10-Qs are not the only reports public companies produce—certain enumerated material corporate events, such as termination of executive officers or changes in auditors, must be reported on a "current basis" on Form 8-K. However, no currently-existing securities law or rule expressly requires cyberattacks—material or otherwise—to be reported on Form 8-K. Generally, reporting cyber events is entirely voluntary. Companies that do so use Form 8-K's Item 8.01, "Other Events," which is used to voluntarily report events that the company considers to be of importance to investors. Public companies must navigate issues such as materiality, selective disclosure, trading, and effect on stock price, all in an environment where disclosure of a cyber event is almost sure to draw a lawsuit, a government investigation, or other unwanted scrutiny. No one-size-fits-all answer exists—it is almost always a judgment call. In this section, we detail some of the questions and analysis that companies should consider regarding whether to disclose an attack on Form 8-K, and if so, when. One way to think about these questions is outlined in the decision tree on the next page (Figure 1).

Why consider disclosure if you don't have to? Even if no rule mandates disclosure, companies and experienced counsel know that there are frequently upsides to disclosure—especially in a world where securities litigation, derivative suits, and enforcement actions are lurking. Instead of provoking shareholder litigation, might an announcement ward it off? Can an 8-K eliminate a plaintiff's or regulator's argument that an insider traded on the basis on material non-public information? The chart on the next page (Table 1) lays out some of the possible advantages—along with the more well-known disadvantages—that companies should consider.

Is the cyberattack material? The determination of whether a cyber event is material is not clear-cut. First, the Supreme Court has rejected a bright-line, quantitative rule for materiality—instead reaffirming *Basic* v. *Levinson*'s formulation that any nonpublic information that significantly alters the total

FIGURE

1

Fish & Richardson 8-k Disclosure Decision Tree

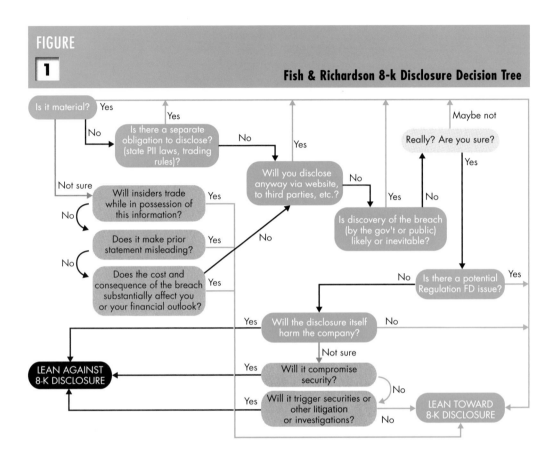

TABLE

1

Fish & Richardson 8-K Pros and Cons Matrix

Pros	Cons
1. May eliminate potential class plaintiffs' argument that information was not known to the market or was not adequately disclosed, cutting off potential securities claims to the date of the 8-K	1. If incident is truly not material and was not going to be discovered, could needlessly cause reputational harm and draw litigation and other unwanted scrutiny
2. May counter allegations that insiders were trading on basis of material nonpublic information about the breach (so long as insider trades happen after 8-K issued)	2. May be seen as concession that incident was material (although companies frequently disavow materiality in 8-K), and even if not material, may make incident seem bigger than it is

Continued

TABLE 1	Pros	Cons
Fish & Richardson 8-K Pros and Cons Matrix	3. Can eliminate a potential Reg FD selective disclosure issue if company has to reveal incident to employees, third parties, others 4. Quick, full disclosure may stave off regulatory scrutiny (but see "Cons") 5. Allows company to own the message, rather than giving control of the message to someone else	3. May trigger stock price drop—and if so, likely to draw shareholder litigation claiming that pre-8-K disclosures were materially misleading 4. Even if no stock price drop, may draw other types of litigation and regulatory scrutiny 5. Could draw other hackers to test company's defenses

mix of information available to shareholders could well be material. Second, even when the scope of an attack has come into focus, the effects of cyberthefts are frequently hard to quantify. Although it is relatively easy for a company to decide to announce a breach of customer personal information (because the breach will likely have to be disclosed under state law and because remediation costs may be significant), what should a company do about, for example, theft of trade secrets, such as source code for a big-selling software product? Without more (such as the thieves' development and marketing of a competing product), such a theft may not have a material effect on the company's financial statements. Adding to the difficult nature of this inquiry: companies must be aware that an initial determination that the event is *not* material—if the event later becomes public—is likely to be critically reexamined with 20/20 hindsight, months or years after the event, by shareholders, plaintiffs' lawyers, regulators, and the press. So careful analysis and documentation of the company's determination are important.

Is there a duty to correct or to update? If the company made public statements about its information systems or other aspects of its operations affected by a cyberattack, and the statements were inaccurate or misleading when made, the company has an obligation to correct the statements—even if it only learned of the inaccuracy afterwards. Failure to comply with this "duty to correct" can provide plaintiffs' lawyers with fodder for a suit alleging that purchasers or sellers relied on the inaccurate statement to their detriment. Moreover, even if the company's forward-looking statements were accurate when made, some courts have found a "duty to update" when circumstances change (such as when an attack happens), and the forward-looking statement becomes inaccurate.

Do you have another legal obligation to disclose? Other disclosure requirements may be at play, such as any state notification laws that require companies to inform affected individuals if their personally identifiable information (PII) was stolen during an attack. If the company is listed on an exchange such as NYSE or NASDAQ, the trading markets themselves may also have rules requiring timely notification of material events. Frankly, it is easier for a company to decide to announce a data breach on Form 8-K—and to accrue the benefits to filing an 8-K—if it is going to disclose for another reason, or already has.

Are you going to disclose anyway? Is the incident likely to become widely known? Absent a mandatory disclosure requirement, a company may still have reasons to disclose the attack to stakeholders. There may be contractual obligations to customers or other third parties to communicate about breaches involving their information. Even without a contractual obligation, a breach may affect a company's vendors, suppliers, or partners, and the company may choose to disclose the incident to them. A sound operating assumption is that once the company discloses an incident to even a single third party, it is likely to become widely known. Thus, the company should have a coordinated, unified disclosure strategy to ensure that all interested parties are informed in a consistent manner, and very close in time. Companies can use affirmative disclosure to mitigate any reputational harm or embarrassment that could arise from having the narrative created on your behalf by the media, security researchers, hackivists, or worse.

Any such disclosure raises potential issues under the SEC's Regulation Fair Disclosure, or Reg FD. Reg FD prohibits companies from selectively disclosing material non-public information to analysts, institutional investors, and certain others without concurrently making widespread public disclosure. Many companies that communicate with third parties—as did J.P. Morgan after its October 2014 breach—will issue a Form 8-K to make sure their communications do not violate Reg FD. It is worth considering whether disclosures on a company's website, or otherwise to customers, vendors, or other parties, trigger a Reg FD requirement.

What to do about trading? Another reason that the materiality determination is a tricky one is that insiders in possession of *material* nonpublic information may not trade while in possession of that information. If there is even a chance that the cyber incident may be material, an early call that a public company general counsel must make is whether to close the trading window for insiders. Even after the incident's details are known, if the company is leaning against declaring the incident material, the question is whether to disclose the incident—material or not—on Form 8-K, so no later allegation of insider trading can stick. (Of course, if the incident is material, no trading by insiders should occur until information about the incident is made public.)

When to disclose? The decision to disclose is only half of the 8-K equation—another question is, when? Target took two months after the world knew of its massive data breach to issue an 8-K; Morningstar, which releases an 8-K regularly on the first Friday of every month, disclosed its 2012 breach a little more than one month after becoming aware of it. Some companies, such as health insurer Anthem, choose instead to wait until the next periodic report. A challenge facing a victim company is to balance the benefits of prompt disclosure against the potential downsides. Because a disclosure should be accurate and not misleading when made, a company should grasp the scope of the cyber incident before disclosing. In a typical breach, however, it is rare for an entity to be able to immediately assess the attack's scope—investigations take time. Therefore, a factor to consider in deciding when to disclose is the pace and progress of the post-breach investigation, which will allow the company to understand the extent of the attack. A company confronts an unenviable disclosure dilemma: disclose based on the state of the world as you know it right now, and later be accused of not telling the whole story? Or disclose when you have a better grasp of what actually happened, but face accusations of allowing earlier (and potentially rosier) cybersecurity disclosures to persist uncorrected? Generally, companies should resist falling into the immediate disclosure trap, because in our experience a cyber incident looks very different at the end of the first week than it does at the end of the first day. Furthermore, the company will not want to have to correct itself after making its cyber disclosure—it will want to get it right the first time.

■ SEC cybersecurity enforcement

The SEC has not yet brought an enforcement action against a public company related to its cybersecurity disclosures. It has, however, opened investigations looking not only into whether companies adequately prepared for and responded to cyber incidents but also as to the sufficiency of their disclosures relating to the breaches. Target's February 2014 Form 8-K filing revealed that the SEC was among the government agencies investigating the 2013 data breach, including "how it occurred, its consequences, and our responses."

With the growing threat of cyberattacks and mounting pressure from Congress and the public, future regulatory and enforcement actions are almost assured. Companies should be prepared for additional scrutiny, review their existing disclosures in light of the Guidance and the SEC's stated priorities, and apply these principles to the public disclosure and related questions that will arise post-breach.

10

A cybersecurity action plan for corporate boards

Internet Security Alliance, NACD – Larry Clinton, CEO of ISA and Ken Daly, President and CEO of NACD

With the majority of cyber networks in the hands of the private sector, and the threats to these systems apparent and growing, organizations need to create an effective method to govern and manage the cyber threat. This responsibility ultimately falls to the corporate board of directors. In fact, the word *cyber* is derived from the same Greek word, *kybernan,* from which the word *govern* also derives.

■ How is cyber risk different from other corporate risks?

Although corporate boards have a long history of managing risks, the digital age may create some unique challenges. To begin with, the nature of corporate asset value has changed significantly in the last 20 years. Eighty percent of the value of Fortune 500 companies now consists of intellectual property (IP) and other intangibles.

With this rapidly expanding "digitalization" of assets comes a corresponding digitalization of corporate risk. However, many of the traditional assumptions and understandings about physical security don't apply to securing digital assets.

First, unlike many corporate risks, such as natural disasters, cybersecurity risks are the product of conscious and often better-resourced attackers, including nation states and state affiliates. This means that the attack methods, like the technology, will change constantly, responding to defensive techniques and often in a highly strategic fashion. This characteristic of cyberattacks means that the risk management system must be a dynamic 24/7/365 flexible process—a full team sport—requiring participation from all corners of the organization rather than being the primary responsibility of any one particular entity.

Second, with many traditional human-based corporate risks, such as criminal activity, companies can plug into a well-defined legal superstructure including enforcement power, which can greatly assist the organization in defending itself. Unfortunately, in the cyber world this system is dramatically underdeveloped. In addition to the major problem of many attackers actually receiving state support, the international criminal legal system has not evolved to the point where there is anything close to the cooperation and coordination generally available in the physical world. As a result, current estimates are that law enforcement is able to apprehend and convict less than 2% of cyber criminals.

Third, corporate cybersecurity is not confined to traditional corporate boundaries. Whereas in the physical world a particularly conscientious organization might be able defend itself by having an especially strong security perimeter, the cyber world is essentially borderless. A fundamental characteristic of cyber systems is that they are interconnected with other, independent systems. For example, the highly publicized breach of Target was accomplished by exploiting vulnerabilities in Target's air conditioner vendor. In another well-publicized case, a well-defended energy installation was compromised by malware placed on the online menu of a Chinese restaurant popular with employees who used it to order lunch. This means that a board must consider not only their "own" security but that of all the entities with whom they interconnect, including vendors, customers, partners, and affiliates.

Fourth, unlike many physical risks, in which the security effort is to create a perimeter around an asset, so many modern corporate assets are in fact digital. Cyber risk must be considered as an integral part of the business process. A good deal of modern corporate growth, innovation, and profitability is inherently tied to digital technology. Rare is the entity that has by now not built the benefits of digitalization into their business plan in many different ways, including online marketing, remote business production, employee use of personal mobile devices, cloud computing, big data, outsourced process, and off-site employment.

However, many digital technologies and business processes that drive business economies come with major cybersecurity risks, which as discussed elsewhere (see Chapter 6), can put the corporation at a long-term catastrophic risk.

This means that cyber risk must be considered not as an addendum to a business process or asset, but as a central feature of the business process. In the modern world, cybersecurity is as central to business decisions as legal and financial considerations. Thus, a board's consideration of fundamental business decisions such as mergers, acquisitions, new product development, partnerships, and marketing must include cybersecurity.

■ Are corporate boards concerned about cybersecurity?

Although some critics have assumed that the publicity from high-profile corporate breaches is prima facie evidence of corporate inattention to cybersecurity, the evidence does not support that proposition.

Corporate spending on cybersecurity has doubled over the past few years and now totals more than $100 billion a year. By comparison, the total annual budget for the U.S. Department of Homeland Security is only about $60 billion—including TSA and immigration—with only $1 billion for cybersecurity. Total U.S. government spending on cybersecurity is generally estimated to be near $16 billion. Moreover, recent surveys indicate cybersecurity now tops the list of issues corporate boards must face—replacing leadership succession, and two thirds of board members are seeking even more time and attention paid to cybersecurity.

Although the data seems to show conclusively that corporate boards are aware of and becoming ever more interested in cybersecurity, the novelty and complexity of the issue has led to a fair amount of uncertainty as to how to approach it.

One recent survey found that despite the "spotlight on cyber security getting brighter" that nearly half of directors had not discussed the company's crisis response plan in the event of a breach, 67% had not discussed the company's cyber insurance coverage, nearly 60% had not discussed engaging an outside cybersecurity expert, more than 60% had not discussed risk disclosures in response to SEC guidance, and slightly more than 20% had discussed the National Institute of Standards and Technology (NIST) cybersecurity framework.

■ A corporate board action plan for cybersecurity

In an effort to fill the gap between awareness and targeted action, The National Association of Corporate Directors (NACD), in conjunction with AIG and the Internet Security Alliance, published their first Cyber Risk Oversight Handbook for corporate boards in June 2014. The handbook was the first private sector document endorsed by the U.S. Department of Homeland Security as well as the International Audit Foundation and is available free of charge either through DHS or NACD. It identified five core principles for corporate boards to enhance their cyber risk oversight.

The five principles can be conceptualized into two categories. Principles 1, 2, and 3 deal with board operations. The final two principles deal with how the board should handle the senior management.

1. Understand that cybersecurity is an enterprise-wide risk management issue.

The board has to oversee management in setting the overall cyber strategy for the organization, including how cybersecurity is understood in terms of the business. It is critical that the board not approach the topic simply by thinking, "What if we have a breach?" Virtually every organization will be successfully breached. The board has to understand the issue is how to manage the risks caused by breaches, not to focus solely on how to prevent them.

One useful metaphor is to think of corporate cybersecurity in a similar fashion to how we think of our own personal health. Obviously, it is impractical to be totally germ free, even as a goal. The goal is to keep your system healthy enough so that you can fight off the germs that will inevitably attack it. When you do get sick, as we all eventually do, you detect and understand the infection promptly and accurately and get access to the appropriate expertise and treatment so that you can return to your normal routine as soon as possible—ideally wiser and stronger.

Thinking of cybersecurity narrowly as an IT issue to be addressed simply with technical solutions is a flawed strategy. The single biggest vulnerability in cyber systems is people. Insiders, whether they are poorly trained, distracted, angry, or corrupted, can compromise many of the most effective technical solutions.

Building on the NACD model, the Institute of Internal Auditors (IIA) extended NACD's principle 1 by commenting that the board should receive an internal annual health check of the organization's cybersecurity program that covers all domains of the organization's cybersecurity, including an assessment of if the enterprise risk levels have improved or deteriorated from year to year, and comments specifically that "Sarbanes-Oxley compliance provides little assurance of an effective security program to manage cyber risks."

2. Directors must understand the legal implications of cyber risk.

The legal situation with respect to cybersecurity is unsettled and quickly evolving. Boards should be mindful of the potential legal risks posed to the corporation and potentially to the directors on an individual or collective basis. For example, high-profile attacks may spawn lawsuits, including shareholder derivative suits alleging that the organization's board neglected its fiduciary duty by failing to take steps to confirm the adequacy of the company's protections against breaches of customer data. To date juries have tended not to find for the plaintiffs in these cases, but that could change with time and boards need to be aware of the risk of court suits.

Prudent steps for directors to take include maintaining records of discussions related to cyber risks at the board and key committee meetings. These records may include updates about specific risk as well as reports about the company's overall security program and how it is addressing these risks. Evidence that board members have sought out specialized training to educate themselves about cyber risk may also be helpful in showing due diligence.

No one standard applies, especially for organizations who do business in multiple jurisdictions. Some countries, including the U.S. have received specific guidance from securities regulators. Many countries have passed a variety of laws, some of which may be confusing or conflicting with mandates in other countries. It is critical that organizations systematically track the evolving laws and regulations in their markets and analyze their legal standing.

Again, building on the NACD model, IIA emphasizes that this legal analysis must be extended to third parties and recommends that the board get a report of all the critical data that are being managed by third-party providers and be sure the organization has appropriate agreements in place, including audits of these providers. The board ought to communicate that a "chain of trust" is expected with these third-party providers that they have similar agreements with their down-stream relationships.

3. Board members need adequate access to cybersecurity expertise.

Most board meetings are incredibly pressed for time, and often there are multiple issues and people who feel they need more board time. Add to this the fact that most acknowledge that directors lack the needed expertise to evaluate cyber risk, and the board is left with the conundrum of how to get enough time to become properly educated to address this serious issue.

One answer is to increase the use of outside experts working directly with the board to provide independent assessments. Indeed,

some boards are now recruiting cyber professionals for board seats to assist in analyzing and judging staff reports. Another technique is to schedule periodic "deep-dives" for the full board. Many organizations have delegated the task to a special committee—often audit but sometimes a risk or even technology committee—although no one approach has been demonstrated clearly superior. A proliferation of committees can exacerbate the board time problem, and due care must be paid to overload any one committee, such as audit, with issues that are not inherently in their expertise lane.

Still another technique is to empower the board with the right questions to ask and require that the outside or internal experts answer the questions in understandable terminology. The NACD Cyber Risk Handbook provides lists of 5 to 10 simple and direct questions for board members covering the key issues such as strategy and operation readiness, situational awareness, incident response, and overall board "cyber literacy."

At minimum, boards can take advantage of the company's ongoing relationships with law enforcement agencies and regularly make adequate time for cybersecurity at board meetings. This may be through interaction with CISOs or as part of the audit or similar committee reports. More appropriately, boards, as discussed above, should integrate these questions into general business discussions.

The final two principles offered by NACD focus on how boards should deal with senior management:

4. Directors need to set an expectation that management have an enterprise-wide cyber risk management framework in place.

It is important that someone be thinking about cybersecurity, from an enterprise-wide perspective (i.e., not just IT) every day. Corporations have introduced a variety of models, chief risk officer, chief financial officer, chief operating officer as well as the more traditional CIO and CISO models. The important aspect to ensure, however, is that the risk management is truly organization wide, including the following steps:

- establish leadership with an individual with cross-departmental expertise
- appoint a cross-organization cyber risk management team including all relevant stakeholders (e.g., IT, HR, compliance, GC, finance, risk)
- meet regularly and report directly to the board
- develop an organization-wide cyber risk management plan with periodic tests reports and refinements. At a more technical level, the Cyber Security Framework developed by the National Institute of Standards and Technologies (NIST) is a useful model.
- develop an independent and adequate budget for the cyber risk management team.

One mechanism to implement the framework is to create a "cybersecurity balance sheet" that identifies, at a high level, the company's cyber assets and liabilities and can provide a scorecard for thinking through management progress in implementing the security system. The balance sheet may begin with identifying the organization's "crown jewels." This is an important exercise because it is simply not cost efficient to protect all data at the maximum level. However, the organization's most valued data must be identified (e.g., IP, patient data, credit card data). Other corporate data can be similarly categorized as to its relative security needs.

The next step is to discuss the strategy for securing data at each level. This strategy generally involves a consideration of people, process, and technology.

At the technology process levels there are a range of options available with good research indicating cost-effective methods to secure lower-level data and thus reserving deployment of more sophisticated, and hence costly, measures to be reserved for the higher valued data.

At the people level, it is important to follow leading practices for managing personnel, especially with respect to hiring and firing. Ongoing cybersecurity training is similarly important and most effective if cybersecurity metrics are fully integrated into employee evaluation and compensation methods.

Of special attention is the inclusion of senior and other executive level personnel who, research has shown, are highly valued targets and often uniquely lax in following through on security protocols.

The asset management process then can be considered in light of the business practices that may create liabilities.

For example, the expansion of the number of access points brought on by the explosion in mobile devices and the emerging "Internet of Things" (connecting cars, security cameras, refrigerators, etc. to the Internet) really increases vulnerability (see Chapter 6).

Still a different type of vulnerability can occur in the merger and acquisition process. Here management may feel pressure to generate value through the merging of highly complex and technical information systems on accelerated pace. In discussions with management, the board must carefully weigh the economics of the IT efficiencies the company seeks with the potential to miss or create vulnerability by accessing a system that is not well enough understood or had its deficiencies mitigated.

5. Based on the plan, management needs to have a method to assess the damage of a cyber event. They need to identify which risks can be avoided, mitigated, accepted, or transferred through insurance.

Organizations must identify for the board which data, and how much, the organization is willing to lose or have compromised. Risk mitigation budgets then must be allocated appropriately between defending against basic and advanced risks.

This principle highlights the need for the "full-team" approach to cybersecurity advocated under principle 4. For example, the marketing department may determine that a particular third-party vendor is ideal for a new product. The CISO may determine that this vendor does not have adequate security. Marketing may, nevertheless, decide it is worth the risk to fulfill the business plan and presumably senior management may support marketing, but condition approval on the ability to transfer some of this additional risk with the purchase of additional insurance.

This is an example of the process proceeding appropriately, wherein cyber risk is integrated into business decisions consistent and managed on the front end consistent with the organization's business plan.

If an organization follows these principles, it should be well on its way to establishing a sustainably secure cyber risk management system.

11

Establishing a board-level cybersecurity review blueprint

Stroz Friedberg LLC — Erin Nealy Cox,
Executive Managing Director

Over the last two years cybersecurity has leaped to the top of the boardroom agenda. If you're like most board members, though, you haven't had enough time to figure out how to think about cybersecurity as part of your fiduciary responsibility, and you're not quite certain yet what questions to ask of management. You may even harbor a secret hope that, like many technology-related issues, cyberthreats will soon be rendered obsolete by relentless advancement.

Don't count on it. Cybersecurity is taking its place among the catalog of enterprise risks that demand boardroom attention for the long term. It comes along with the digital transformation that is sweeping through virtually all industries in the global economy. As businesses "digitize" all aspects of their operations, from customer interactions to partner relationships in their supply chains, entire corporations become electronically exposed—and vulnerable to cyberattack.

Cybersecurity risk is not new. However, in the last two years multiple high-profile attacks have hit brands we all trusted with our personal information, making for big headlines in the media and significant reputational and financial damage for many of the victimized companies. What's more, corporate heads have rolled: CIOs and even CEOs have departed as a direct result of breaches. The ripple effect continues. Cybersecurity legislation is a perennial agenda item for governments and regulators around the world, and shareholder derivative lawsuits have struck the boards of companies hit by high-profile cyberattacks.

Although directors have added cybersecurity enterprise risk to their agendas, there is no standard way for boards to think about cybersecurity, much less time-tested guidelines to help them navigate the issue. This chapter's goal is to help directors evolve their mindsets for thinking about the enterprise risk associated with cybersecurity and provide a simple blueprint to help directors incorporate cybersecurity into the board's overall enterprise risk strategy.

■ Establishing the right blueprint for boardroom cybersecurity review

For boards, cybersecurity is an issue of enterprise risk. As with all enterprise risks, the key focus is mitigation, not prevention. This universally understood enterprise risk guideline is especially helpful in the context of cybersecurity because *no one can prevent all cyber breaches*. Every company is a target, and a sufficiently motivated and well-resourced adversary can and will get into a company's network.

Consequently, terms like "cyber defense" are insufficient descriptors of an effective posture because they evoke the image that corporations can establish an invincible perimeter around their networks to prevent access by bad actors. Today, it's more accurate to think of the board-level cybersecurity review goal as "cyber resilience." The idea behind the cyber resilience mindset is that, because you know network breaches will happen, it is more important to focus on preparing to meet cyberthreats as rapidly as possible and on mitigating the associated risks.

Also important to a board member's cybersecurity mindset is to be free from fear of the technology. Remember, the issue is enterprise risk—not technical solutions. Just as you need not understand internal combustion engine technology to write rules for safe driving, you need not be excluded from the cybersecurity risk discussion based on lack of technology acumen. Although this is liberating, in a sense, there is also a price: directors cannot deny their fiduciary responsibility to oversee cybersecurity risk based on lack of technology acumen.

Given a focus on enterprise risk (not technology) and risk mitigation (not attack prevention), the correct blueprint for cybersecurity review at the board level can best be

expressed through the following three high-level questions:

1. Has your organization appropriately assessed all its cybersecurity-related risks? What reasonable steps have you taken to evaluate those risks?
2. Have you appropriately prioritized your cybersecurity risks, from most critical to noncritical? Are these priorities properly aligned with corporate strategy, other business requirements, and a customized assessment of your organization's cyber vulnerabilities?
3. What actions are you taking to mitigate cybersecurity risks? Do you have a regularly tested, resilience-inspired incident response plan with which to address cyberthreats?

Naturally, these questions are proxies for the industry-specific and/or situation-specific questions particular to each organization that will result in that organization's most productive cybersecurity review. The key to formulating the relevant questions for your organization is to find the right balance between asking enough to achieve the assurance appropriate to board oversight, but not so much that management ends up spinning wheels unnecessarily.

The rest of this chapter is a guide to framing board-level cybersecurity review issues for your organization by exploring meaningful ways to apply these high-level questions in a variety of circumstances and industries. The next step is yours, or your board's: use this blueprint to drive cybersecurity enterprise risk discussions with management, critical stakeholders, and external experts. Doing so will help achieve cyber resilience for your organization.

■ The board's cyber resilience blueprint
Boards are very comfortable managing financial issues and risks. They have audit committees, they have compensation committees, their members include former CFOs (to populate those committees), and they have plenty of experience reviewing financial

statements and analyzing profit and loss. The knowns are known and the unknowns are few, if any.

It is useful to juxtapose this stable, comfortable picture with the state of board-level cybersecurity discussion—that is, you may not yet be certain what questions to ask, or know what to expect from management's responses. To help accelerate you toward the same level of stability and comfort you have managing financial issues, the following board-level cybersecurity review blueprint is organized into six areas:

1. **Inclusive board-level discussion:** empowering all directors to be accountable for cybersecurity
2. **Proactive cyber risk management:** incorporating cybersecurity into all early stage business decisions
3. **Risk-oriented prioritization:** differentiating assets for varying levels of cyber protection
4. **Investment in human defenses:** ensuring the organization's cybersecurity investment goes beyond technical to include awareness, education, and training programs for employees
5. **Assessments of third-party relationships:** limiting cyber exposure through business partners
6. **Incident response policies and procedures:** mitigating potential risks when breaches occur.

1. Inclusive board-level discussion

Given the rapidly growing threat posed by cybercrime and the potentially devastating consequences of a major breach, it is critical that every director have enough of an understanding of cyber risk to be able to take an active part in the board's cybersecurity review process, and that these discussions take place regularly—preferably at every meeting of the board.

A committee responsible for studying cybersecurity risk can cover both of these aspects of participation. With such a committee, someone on the board (i.e., the committee chair) becomes the stakeholder charged with becoming educated about cybersecurity risk and educating the broader group. Although the board will never need to know how to configure a firewall, there is much to learn about the nature of cybersecurity risks, their potential impacts on your organization, and successful mitigation approaches. It may also be appropriate to appoint a director with cybersecurity expertise for this purpose.

Establishing such a committee also fulfills the goal of consistent cybersecurity discussion. The chair can give a report, arrange for reports from the CIO or CISO, or facilitate talks by outside experts on issues around which additional subject matter expertise proves useful. Threat intelligence is an example of an excellent topic for an outside expert because it's not a specialty most organizations have in house or that can be justifiably developed. A person or organization steeped in analyzing the tools, approaches, and behaviors of threat actors can look at your organization's profile and provide customized insight that accelerates the board's cybersecurity education.

To empower all directors to engage in cybersecurity review, board-level discussions should address issues in the enterprise risk language with which boards are already familiar. One requisite, therefore, is that boards not stand for technical jargon. Even reports from the CIO should be delivered in plain language free of specialized terms.

Active inclusion, in sum:
- Establish a cybersecurity risk committee, or add the subject to an existing enterprise risk committee.
- Discuss cybersecurity risk at every board meeting.
- Empower all directors to become educated and comfortable discussing cybersecurity risk.

2. Proactive cyber risk management

It is important to incorporate discussion of cybersecurity risk in all business decisions, from the beginning, because it is much harder and far less effective to consider cybersecurity after the fact. Whether a decision has to do with corporate strategy, new product launches, facilities, customer interaction, M&A, legal or financial issues, management should always proactively consider cybersecurity risk.

As an example, take the white-hot omnichannel marketing trend, which has retailers using mobile technology to collect data from their customers, and then exploiting that knowledge to better target marketing and promotions—sometimes, at the moment a customer walks into the store. Obviously, such retailers are gathering more information about their customers than ever before. How will they protect it? Do the mobile applications that make these approaches possible expose their organizations to new vulnerabilities? No matter how exciting the revenue-driving opportunity, these are questions that retail boards should be asking management as part of the decision to pursue such initiatives. Management should respond with some variation of, "Our software vendor says their security is `X, and in addition, we're doing our own testing to see how vulnerable the software may be before we introduce it to our customers."

Boards should extrapolate the thinking in the above example to all aspects of their business decision-making. To apply proactive thinking to cyber strategy, consider growth through M&A. Boards should think through M&A cybersecurity risks in multiple dimensions. To name three: adding cybersecurity analysis of the target to their diligence process; protecting their M&A process from cyber breaches; and potential cyber exposure resulting from post-deal integration.

In both of these examples, it should be clear how challenging it would be to address cybersecurity concerns after the initiative gets underway.

3. Risk-based prioritization

Everyone's resources are limited. Because there are an infinite number of cybersecurity measures in which a company can invest, the trick is to prioritize such measures based on a customized assessment of the most serious threats facing *your* organization. Such assessments should be approached along two primary dimensions: your organization's most valuable assets and its greatest cyber vulnerabilities.

Often, your most critical assets are obvious: payment card data for a retailer, the script of an upcoming franchise sequel for a movie studio, the source code at the heart of a software company's bestselling product. Every board's cybersecurity review must ask management what measures are being taken to protect a company's most critical assets, beginning with development and on through production and distribution. Beyond the most critical are other assets that require differentiated gradations of protection. Identifying and prioritizing those assets is an information governance challenge, so the board also has to understand the organization's information governance policy and have a sense for the quality of its execution. Has the company identified what are sensitive

---

Proactive cyber risk management, in sum:

- Think about potential cybersecurity risk from the outset of all business initiatives from corporate strategy to new types of customer interaction.
- Think particularly about new kinds of risk associated with emerging digital business initiatives.

data and where they are being held? What data are not sensitive and where are they being held? Are your retention policies ensuring you keep the information that is important and throw away everything else? We've all read headlines about breaches that could have been less sensational if the victims had better retention practices.

The second dimension—your company's cyber vulnerabilities—is where customized threat intelligence plays a role. Analyzing your network for weaknesses, learning where sensitive information is stored and how it is protected, and assessing your environment: the competitiveness of your industry (e.g., how valuable your intellectual property is to others) and the way information flows in concert with business processes (e.g. whether or how you store sensitive information about consumers or clients, what countries you do business in, and what that implies for your security).

The board's cybersecurity review should include discussion of both dimensions, and the issues should be discussed often—these risks are not static. They can vary significantly over time and depend on evolving Internet connectivity and infrastructure complexity.

4. Investment in human defenses

Cyber defense and cyber resilience are as much human matters as they are matters of products and technology configurations. Although security technologies for protection and response are indeed necessary, boards should also ask about enterprise-wide cybersecurity education and awareness. Furthermore, investments in human defenses should be aligned to the insights from customized threat intelligence so they are focused on the 'most valuable/most vulnerable' prioritization discussed in the previous section.

When looking at cybersecurity investment, board reviews should include classic IT spending on systems that authenticate user identity and manage access, as well as compliance with applicable laws and regulations. However, that's just the baseline. Boards need to think further, to issues such as the following:

How well does our IT knowledge/expertise align with the kind of challenges suggested by our threat intelligence reports?

Are we appropriately augmenting our internal staff with outside expertise?

Should we hire "white hat" hackers to attack our networks in search of gaps?

Should we test our employees' anti-phishing awareness/ability?

No matter how well your security technology works, hackers can always go after the weakest link—humans—through a combination of tactics known as social engineering and spear phishing. The only defense against these phenomena is enterprise-wide education. Ongoing education and awareness programs, such as spear phishing training, should be part of the cybersecurity investment. Boards should ask about, support, and ensure these programs are aligned with business requirements.

Risk-based prioritization, in sum:
- Optimize limited resources by prioritizing along two dimensions: what's most valuable and what's most vulnerable.
- Ensure the quality of policies and practices around the organization's approach to information governance so that all assets are protected appropriately.

Human investment, in sum:
Supplement appropriate investment in information security products with continuous enterprise-wide cybersecurity awareness, education, and training programs.

5. Assessments of third-party relationships

Those of us paying close attention to the stories behind 2014's cyber breach headlines know that in many cases the so-called "attack vectors" came through third-party relationships. Bad actors breached a business partner (that likely had weaker security than the intended target) and then used that partner's access credentials to break into the target company.

But this is only one way in which third-party relationships create security vulnerabilities. As business collaboration surges, for example, the amount of confidential, trade secret, and intellectual property information that is being shared among employees of business partners skyrockets. This electronic flow of mission critical information, often across the open Internet, creates an environment ready-made for economic espionage. It used to be such cases were a particular thorn in the side of only a few sectors, such as defense, energy, and technology. Today, all kinds of industries are targeted.

A board's cybersecurity review should include an understanding of how the organization conducts cyber due diligence on third parties. Boards need a clear understanding of the third parties their organizations do business with and must prioritize those relationships in terms of high, medium, and low risk. Once a partner is identified as high risk (e.g., they have access to your corporate network), that partner's own security posture must be understood. How much visibility does your organization have into your vendors' security policies and practices? Do they respond to your security questionnaires? Do you have the right to conduct on-site validations/audits?

Boards also should require IT involvement early in the development of new business partner relationships. That way, information access can be better tuned to the business requirements of the partnership. An HR vendor, for example, may need access to your employee data, but that access may not need to be around the clock. Perhaps it can be controlled and limited to certain times of the month and/or hours of the day to limit risk exposure and enable finely tuned security monitoring.

6. Incident response policies and procedures

Armed with the knowledge that perfect security isn't achievable and breaches are therefore inevitable, boards must ensure their organizations have well-honed policies for cyber incident response, and must test these plans with regular simulation exercises.

Good incident response plans define the roles and responsibilities of the response team (including crisis communications, human resources, legal, IT, etc.) and establish clear initial action items, including notifications to internal and external resources who will lead an investigation or manage communications. Remember, preparing for the worst is not an admission of a weak or vulnerable network. On the other hand, a delayed, bumbling response to a security breach is what often leads to increased data loss, exposure to regulatory action, and reputational damage.

Assessments of third-party relationships, in sum:
Review all business partner relationships for potential cybersecurity vulnerabilities.
Empower IT's involvement earlier in the development of business relationships.

Two key thoughts boards should keep in mind when reviewing incident response plans were noted previously, albeit in a different context. First, it is critical to engage the entire enterprise in your incident response plan. IT security professionals can only do so much if an employee clicks on a spear phisher's link, creating a hole in your network. Employees can be educated to avoid those clicks and incented to be first responders—or, at least, to notice these attempts to breach your company's defenses. Employees are on the front lines of cybersecurity; prompt notice of a breach from an alert employee can often significantly mitigate damage. Second, your organization's cybersecurity risk environment is a dynamic, ever-changing thing. Your incident response plan must be kept up to date and rehearsed continually, taking evolving threat intelligence into account.

Appropriate board-level review questions include the following:

What are the organization's policies and procedures to rapidly identify breaches?

How are all employees empowered to monitor and report/respond?

How are we triaging/escalating once an incident is detected?

How is incident response integrated into IT operations?

What are we doing to align our cyber responses to business requirements and to ensure that all parts of the business understand their roles in the response plan?

How does our response plan match up with our threat intelligence? Are we characterizing our risk in a way that is consistent with most likely attacks?

■ Conclusion: No surprises!

No one likes unpleasant surprises, least of all corporate boards. The goal of a board's cybersecurity review is to avoid being unprepared for a cyber incident. Unfortunately, experience so far suggests that the only companies with truly top-grade, board-level cybersecurity plans are those that have experienced an unpleasant surprise in the form of a bad breach. They felt the pain once and don't ever want to go through it again.

If you follow the board-level cybersecurity review thinking and principles discussed in this chapter, and partner with external experts that bring domain-specific knowledge and skills you may not have in-house, you can avoid surprises and be prepared to meet risk head on. The review approach described in this chapter will enable you to lead your organization's shift from a paradigm of discomfort and uncertainty in the cybersecurity risk realm to one of assurance and comprehensive answers, facilitated by the board's regular cyber risk discussions; from simple perimeter protection to around-the-clock monitoring and universally understood incident response; from lack of cyber risk awareness to enterprise-wide awareness led by top-down C-suite messaging and incentivized employee behavior.

The blueprint presented in this chapter can help ensure you truly have your eye on the cyber risk ball. Obviously, that doesn't mean your company won't be breached. But if—or when—you are, you will be able to handle the event with clear-eyed confidence that the risks have been properly managed.

Incident response, in sum:
- Because breaches will happen, board review must ensure first-class incident response.
- All enterprise employees should be part of the incident response plan.
- Incident response must continually evolve—because threats do.

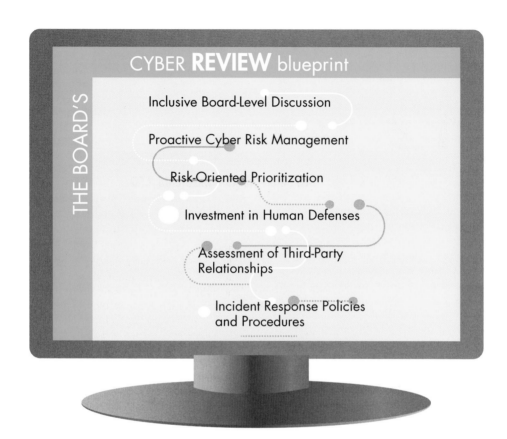

12

Demystifying cybersecurity strategy and reporting: How boards can test assumptions

Dell SecureWorks – Mike Cote, CEO

Cybersecurity is one of those issues that justify the statement, "It's what you don't know that can hurt you." Although board engagement in cybersecurity risk is on the rise, corporate directors continue to struggle with the complexity of the subject matter, making it more difficult for them to assess whether the company's strategy is effective. As one public company director recently stated, "I understand the magnitude of the risk, and I know we have significant resources decked against it, but as a board member how will I know if management has the right measures in place to keep us from being the next story in the news?"

This chapter does not explain how to eliminate the risk of a data breach. In fact, one requirement for being resilient against cyberthreats is to accept that breaches will happen. Nor does this chapter strive to make an expert of the reader. After all, the board's job is to provide reasonable oversight of the risk, not manage it.

What this chapter *does* do is provide boards with a framework of inquiry—elements of a mature security strategy in plain language—to help directors have discussions with management about the company's overall resilience against the threats. By understanding these concepts, directors will have a better context for testing assumptions when management reports on metrics such as the effectiveness of breach prevention, breach frequency, and response time.

■ Background: Who is behind hacking, and why do they do it?

Before delving into the right strategy for cybersecurity, it is helpful for boards to first understand the nature of the threat. Hacking has become a burgeoning global industry that generates billions of dollars in illicit trade annually. It's fueled by a strong reseller's market in which hackers sell stolen data to others who possess the desire but not the tools to harvest valuable intellectual property. It's funded by organized crime and actors within nation-states that not only operate beyond any jurisdiction but also have access to billions of dollars of capital to invest in these criminal operations.

The robust cyber black market offers stolen goods—from credit cards to personal identities—in large quantities at reasonable cost. Sellers also offer money-back guarantees on the quality of their goods. Buyers can obtain tutorials for hacking or for using stolen data, and they can even hire subcontractors to do the dirty work.

It's not always about the money. From attacks based on sectarian hate between nation-states to sabotage from a bitter, laid-off employee, motivations for hacking run deep and wide. Anger about environmental policies and resentment against the excesses of Wall Street are among other examples. Whatever their reasons, hackers are focused on stealing, disrupting, or destroying data every moment of every day. There are thousands of cyber criminals around the globe. They work around the clock, for free or for hire, on speculation or with a known purpose, trying to invent new ways to steal or harm a company. They have the funding and technology to be not only persistent but also highly adaptable, and the barrier to replicating their cyber weapons is low in contrast to the physical world. They have the luxury of always being anonymous, always on offense, and seldom prosecuted.

Companies, on the other hand, are highly visible, and by virtue of being connected to the Internet must operate in an environment where being attacked by hackers is the norm. Companies must prevent, detect, defend against, and take on the threat without the luxury of knowing when they'll be attacked, by whom, or on what front.

A mature cybersecurity strategy prepares for and responds to this challenging environment. Breaking that strategy down into its core elements provides boards with a useful framework for discussing risk assumptions with the chief information security officer.

■ **Elements of a mature security strategy . . . in plain language**

1. *Determine what needs protecting and who holds the keys.*

Companies begin their journey to resiliency by identifying and prioritizing *the assets they must protect.* What do cyber criminals want that they can get from us and why? Do employees handle intellectual property that could make or break us competitively? Do we collect personally identifiable information that cyber criminals could sell to identity thieves? Do we store customer account information? How would someone take command and control of our infrastructure or systems?

It is equally important to know *where* those coveted assets are located. Many boards are surprised to learn that the information security team is fending off hackers across the entire enterprise, even outside it: for example, in a supplier's network, on a home computer, or on an employee's iPad, where he or she just reviewed a proprietary schematic. Hackers are capable of scanning for vulnerabilities wherever someone connects to the Internet, and business leaders must operate under the assumption that even they are a target.

As with sensitive financial information, only those who need access to the assets should have it, and policies should be in place to ensure stringent controls. Administrator passwords are gold to cybercriminals, and increasing the number of people with access to them effectively multiplies the ways that hackers can attack.

2. *Prevention is not an endgame.*

It's tempting to think that we can eliminate breaches if we just put more effort into prevention at the front end, but information security professionals know that eliminating the possibility of a breach is an unrealistic goal in today's environment. Preventative tools such as firewalls play an essential role because they provide the first layer of defense: they 'recognize' and stop the threats we already know about. As we already established, however, hackers are highly adaptive. No one piece of technology can provide a complete defense. A good security program assumes that at some point prevention will fail and the business will have to deal with threats in its network.

Detection then becomes the focus. Companies need the right technology, processes, programs, and staff to help them detect what has happened so that they can find the threat and respond more quickly to contain and eradicate it. The question is not if the hackers will get in but when. Board members may test this assumption by asking their security team, "Do we know if hackers are inside our defenses right now? How do we know when they get in?"

3. *You can't defend with your eyes closed.*

No one wants to be blindsided. If a company's security team can't "see" what is happening on the network and across all of the endpoints such as work stations, point-of-sale terminals, and mobile devices, then the company will have little chance to detect or respond quickly to an attack when prevention fails. Visibility across the enterprise is an essential attribute of the cybersecurity strategy because it helps companies respond to unusual activity more quickly, reducing down time and related costs.

Business leaders should know that having visibility means collecting large amounts of data from all of those places. Unfortunately those data are useless if the security team doesn't have the bandwidth to analyze and act on it. The information security industry has responded to this problem, and services are available to manage the data, do the heavy lifting, and sort out what is actionable. The actionable data can then be fed back to the information security team to more efficiently zero in on the threats that need their immediate attention. Boards may ask if their security team is managing all the data itself, and, if so, does it still have the bandwidth to focus on the actual threats.

4. *Stay a step ahead: The future won't look like the past.*

To stay one step ahead of the threat, an information security program should also be able to predict what the adversary will do next. To make financial predictions, business leaders apply internal and environmental intelligence to test assumptions. In the case of cybersecurity, security teams should apply "threat intelligence," which tells them the intent and capabilities of current, real-world hackers who may want to harm them. Gathered from a company's own environment and often supplemented with much broader environmental intelligence from a third party, threat intelligence can be applied to cybersecurity technologies and human procedures. As a result, the enterprise is able to anticipate the nature of forthcoming attacks and more effectively allocate limited resources to stop them.

Companies with the ability to predict can also defend earlier with less effort and recover faster when a breach occurs. When boards and management discuss metrics like breach frequency, response time, and potential impact, it's helpful to know if the security team is applying threat intelligence to help them make their assumptions.

5. *Educate and train vigilant employees.*

One of the most important defenses against cyberattack is an informed, vigilant employee population. Employees and executives are often targeted with carefully crafted emails designed to be relevant to the employee's personal or work life. In reality, these phishing emails are often loaded with malicious code. One click by a less careful individual can deploy a cyber weapon into the company's network and execute various actions that shut down critical business functions or steal information and accounts. Similar tactics may be used over the phone to get employees to divulge confidential information such as client lists, which can then be paired with other stolen data to complete a set of stolen identities.

The bottom line is that human behavior is equally as important as security technologies in defending against the threat. Boards should know whether employee awareness and training programs are in place and how effective they are. The best programs will simulate how hackers may trick an employee and provide on-the-spot training if the employee falls victim. An open dialog in these cases helps employees and the organization as a whole learn from mistakes. It also builds a culture of security awareness.

6. Organize information security teams for success.

Defending and responding effectively against cyber adversaries also depends on manpower and expertise. Technologies cannot be used to full advantage without highly skilled people to correlate, analyze, prioritize, and turn the data into actionable intelligence that can be used to increase resilience. A properly organized and staffed security team needs people with many different types of expertise and skills. It requires people to deploy the technologies, understand what the threats are, determine what hackers are doing, fix system and software vulnerabilities, and counter active threats. Although these professional capabilities are interdependent, they are not all interchangeable, requiring different training and certifications. Information security leaders also need the management skills to put the right governance processes and procedures in place, advocate for security requirements, and communicate risk to senior management.

Boards are encouraged to inquire as to whether the security team has the bandwidth and manpower to be able to respond and remediate a crisis, as well as to handle day-to-day operations. Security teams should be organized to focus on what matters most—immediate threats—and other resources should be considered where there are gaps.

7. Measure effectiveness, not compliance.

It is impossible for a company to know how effective its security program is against real-world attackers unless it conducts real-world exercises to test its defenses. Compliance frameworks can improve rigor in many areas of cybersecurity, but it is folly to assume that following a compliance mandate (or even passing a compliance inspection) is commensurate with resilience. No matter how well architected a security program is against recommended standards, no two companies' environments are alike.

That's why it is so important to battle-test one's own environment. Network security testing emulates actual hackers using real-life tactics such as phishing to validate how well defenses work against simulated attacks. By learning how hackers penetrate security defenses, companies can determine actual risk and resource cybersecurity operations accordingly. Testing also helps companies meet compliance mandates. Compliance should be a by-product of an effective security program, not the other way around.

8. Emphasize process as much as technology.

Technology is only half the solution to making a company resilient. Breaches can occur as the result of human and process errors throughout the enterprise. Take the example of recent high-profile cases in which weaknesses in a supply chain or a business partner's security allowed hackers to access the parent company's network and do significant damage. Leading practice today is for companies to insist, by contract, that their business partners meet the same security requirements.

However, what if a business line leader fails to insist on contract requirements in the interest of going to market quickly? What happens when business enablement trumps security in the far reaches of the business, where people think, "No harm done"? Adequate checks and balances should be in place to ensure that IT security and business procedures are being executed, and policies should hold relevant business leaders and employees accountable for implementation. How do you know when procedure isn't followed? Real world testing confirms not only the effectiveness of your defenses but also the process, policies, and procedures that keep those defenses in place, operational and optimized for resilience.

■ Summary: A framework for oversight

By the very nature of being connected to the Internet, companies are targeted 24/7, 365 days a year by anonymous, sophisticated hackers who strive to steal from or harm the business and its employees. That ongoing challenge is taking place across the entire enterprise, not just on the network, so it's important to remember that we all play a role in managing the risk: employees, business partners, and even board members. There is no silver bullet piece of technology that will eliminate all danger, and being resilient is just as dependent on people and process as it is on technology. A cybersecurity 'win' in this environment is defined as how effectively and efficiently the company finds and removes threats from its environment and whether it remains fully operational in the process.

Cybersecurity risk is an enterprise risk, not a function of IT. For boards to provide reasonable oversight they'll have to understand what the company is protecting, inquire about how well the company is organized to defend those assets, and explore whether it has the manpower and capabilities to respond and remediate in the event of a breach. Compliance is an important

element of cybersecurity, but it is a by-product of a good program, not the measure of effectiveness. Nor is it a guarantee of security, as illustrated by many recent high-profile breaches in which companies had already met the requirements for one compliance mandate or another.

Difficult decisions about funding can be made more easily by discussing how existing resources are allocated. Many business leaders fear that "we'll never spend enough," but experience shows that a pragmatic approach to funding the security program is to focus on effectiveness and prioritization:

- Determine actual vulnerabilities by regularly testing defenses.
- Detect the perpetrators more quickly by increasing visibility.
- Predict and mitigate risks more quickly and efficiently by applying threat intelligence.
- Apply time, attention, and funding accordingly.

Companies may also want to consider third-party providers to monitor, correlate, and analyze the massive quantity of data that a mature security program generates. This allows valuable, and sometimes scarce, human resources to focus on the actual threats. A reputable third party can also provide the testing that determines effectiveness and be a helpful validator of the program.

Armed with an understanding of what a mature security program looks like and how it plays out across the entire enterprise, boards will be better equipped to discuss the company's current strategy and inquire about assumptions in the metrics.

II Cyber risk corporate
structure

13

The CEO's guide to driving better security by asking the right questions

Palo Alto Networks Inc. – Davis Hake,
Director of Cybersecurity Strategy

I recently met with a chief information officer (CIO) whose chief executive officer (CEO) had just taken a striking and dramatic interest in cybersecurity. He had read an article in the paper about cyberthreats to major corporations and wanted to know what his own company was doing to solve the specific problem described in the article. The CIO was incensed, because the question would inevitably force him to shift priorities for his already overworked team to an issue that had little to no effect on their actual security efforts. There is an old saying in the disaster response community that you shouldn't exchange business cards during an emergency. In essence, you need to familiarize yourself with the risks and relevant people before an emergency so security teams are not blown in different directions depending on the new security scare of the day.

Similarly, CEOs cannot familiarize themselves with cybersecurity narrowly through the lens of a single incident that occurs on their network or with one of their competitors. The danger in responding to a singular event or threat in isolation—or daily incidents we read about in the press—is that this is a reactive approach rather than a holistic, risk-based approach. Cybersecurity is the poster child for this phenomenon. Executives know that there is a newfound focus on cybersecurity at the boardroom level—incidents like Target's 2013 data breach have been a wake-up call for many—but there is often still a severe lack of understanding about the real risks behind the headlines. The statistics also back up the magnitude of these anecdotes.

A recent New York Stock Exchange (NYSE) and Veracode survey looking at boardroom attention to cybersecurity found 80 percent of participants said it is discussed in most or every boardroom meeting. They noted specifically that "responsibility for attacks is being seen as

87 ∎

a broader business issue, signaling a shift AWAY from the chief information security officer (CISO) and the IT security team." Where is this shift moving to? "When a breach does occur, boards are increasingly looking to the CEO and other members of the executive team to step up and take responsibility," said the authors.

Yet despite this shift in perceived responsibility to the executive level, there does not appear to be the same drive to connect technical teams to the board-level focus on concerns about cybersecurity risk. A 2015 Raytheon and Ponemon Institute study of those with the day-to-day technical responsibility for cybersecurity, CIOs, CISOs, and senior IT leaders, found that 66 percent of respondents believe senior leaders don't perceive cybersecurity as a priority. What this means is that while CEOs are increasingly on the hook from their boards for being savvy about cyber risks, many are not yet engaging with the necessary parts of their organization to address cybersecurity issues.

Our hope is that this guide can prime you to ask productive questions that drive better people, processes, and technological change to reduce the risk of successful breaches of your organization. As the CEO, it is your job to balance risk and reward within your company. Cyberthreats are not magic, hackers are not wizards, and the risks to your specific organization from a breach can be managed just like any other risks that you make decisions about every day. In fact, these risks can even be turned into opportunities for new innovation.

But where to begin? You want to avoid causing unnecessary work, but you are required to participate, and often lead, the conversation around addressing cyber risks. When the U.S. Government began working with members of the IT and critical infrastructure industry on a Cybersecurity Framework for improving critical infrastructure cybersecurity, a key point that arose was the need for nontechnical tools that could be used at an executive level. Technical best practices have existed in international standards and government agencies for years, but

common problems such as a lack of investment, absence of high-level strategy, and failure to integrate into business operations still plagued many organizations struggling to address cyberthreats. Seeing this tension in many of the organizations they were briefing on cyberthreats, the U.S. Department of Homeland Security worked with current and former executives to help capture five simple questions that a CEO could ask his or her technical team, which would also drive better security practices. They are:

1. What is the current level and business impact of cyber risks to our company? What is our plan to address identified risks?
2. How is our executive leadership informed about the current level and business impact of cyber risks to our company?
3. How does our cybersecurity program apply industry standards and best practices?
4. How many and what types of cyber incidents do we detect in a normal week? What is the threshold for notifying our executive leadership?
5. How comprehensive is our cyber incident response plan? How often is the plan tested?

The team that coordinated the Cybersecurity Framework also provided key recommendations to leadership, to align their cyber risk policies with these questions. First and foremost, it is critical for CEOs to lead incorporation of their cyber risks into existing risk management efforts. Forget the checklist approach; only you know the specific risk-reward balance for your business, so only you can understand what is most important to your company. It seems simple, but with cybersecurity, the default practice tends to be for organizations to silo considerations about risks into a separate category apart from thinking about their valuable assets. You have to start by identifying what is most critical to protect and work out from there. The process of aligning your core value with your top IT concerns is a journey and is not something that can be solved in one lump investment or board meeting. Just like any risk analysis, it requires serious consideration and thought about what is most important to your core business practices.

Which brings me to the second recommendation to come out of the Cybersecurity Framework effort: don't begin your journey alone! Bring your leadership team, especially your CIO, chief security officer (CSO), and CISO, into the conversation from the start, to help determine how your IT priorities match to your business goals. Building a diverse team that includes other leaders, such as your head of human resources, will help foster a culture that views cyberthreats not as "someone else's problem" but as challenges that should be addressed and dealt with as an entire organization. For example, cyber criminals still continue to successfully use fake emails as a primary method for gaining access to a company's network. Stopping these attacks requires not just a technical solution but also strong training, which is often the responsibility of human resources and not your IT security team.

As more significant challenges arise, and they will do so often and unexpectedly, lean on your leadership team to evaluate problems in relation to the impact to your other business risks. Then let your team address them based on your existing business goals. For example, if you experience a cyber breach or accidental disclosure of sensitive information, a diverse leadership team is incredibly helpful at not just responding to the technical problems but also ensuring other areas such as public image, legal ramifications, and revenue impact are taken into consideration in any mitigation and remediation efforts. It is your job to help frame the problem for your team and provide oversight and guidance, not micromanage a crisis.

As with normal business operations, you should also be asking your team to assist you in day-to-day requirements of your cybersecurity, such as reviewing IT budgets and personnel security policies. None of this is surprising, and you will find that despite not having a cybersecurity background, you will certainly be able to make valuable contributions about which cyber risks are acceptable. You will find situations where the operational priorities that you are responsible for as CEO, outweigh cybersecurity risks. Your perspective on these matters is what makes you core to leading cybersecurity efforts in your organization.

Finally, as with any risk management effort, you must plan for the best but prepare for the worst. Cyberthreats are very real, and advanced hacking tools once available only to nation-states are regularly sold on the online black market. There are technical architectures that can prevent and limit damage done by cyberattacks (see Palo Alto Network's other chapter, "Designing for breach prevention"), but no solution is ever 100 percent. Developing an incident response plan that is coordinated across your enterprise and regularly tested is vital for even the most well-defended organizations. Use your existing risk management practices and your leadership team to identify your most important assets; then plan for what would happen to your company if those assets were shut off or inaccessible for a sustained period of time. Similar to fire drills, regular practice also helps you stay aware of cybersecurity's constantly changing environment and shows a personal interest that will signal the issue's importance throughout your company. There are also excellent chapters in this book to get you started in setting up an incident response plan, and there are many good companies that specialize in the sticky problems of rebuilding your network when you need to call in the cavalry.

While risk management is a strong approach to tackling the challenges of cybersecurity, the bottom line is that it will often require some investment in new people, processes, or technology. A common myth is that security must be a cost center for every organization. This view has plagued IT security experts for years, as their efforts are viewed as drains on resources that would otherwise be bringing in revenue. But as you start to lay out cybersecurity from a risk management perspective, you will be forced to identify your most valuable assets, pressing vulnerabilities, and core motivations. This introspective approach can also drive new ideas applicable to your core business lines. It is imperative that you recognize these innovations and make the right investments to reap both the benefits of better security and new business opportunities.

For example, take a company that wants to enable its sales staff to securely meet with customers face to face away from the office for consultations. Using mobile devices and phones to access internal company data, such as customer accounts, from the field can open serious cyber risks. In this case you could ensure that when purchasing a mobile platform, you also choose a security vendor that can provide mobile device management capabilities. This allows your IT department to secure lost or stolen devices and limit malicious software that could be accidentally downloaded by employees (or often their kids), limiting cyber risks and enabling flexibility of your sales team.

Another great example is the use of software as a service (SaaS) products. You may know these as web-based email or online storage services. They are incredibly popular for their low cost, flexibility, and availability across multiple platforms, but they also exist on servers outside your control and can present a huge risk from users accidentally making company resources available to external parties. There are now innovative solutions that can manage these programs just like any normal application that lives on your network and even block their use for only malicious purposes.

True leadership in any issue doesn't involve simply throwing more money at the problem; you must always balance the risks and rewards of your decisions and investments into a coherent strategy. Cybersecurity is no different. Unfortunately, today's reality is such that cyberthreats will remain an issue of fear for boardrooms in the foreseeable future, leading to default knee-jerk reactions as new threats evolve. Ultimately, we must get to a place where cybersecurity is a normal part of any business's operational plan. With cool-headed, rational leadership, you have the unique ability to help transform this issue in your company from a crisis to an opportunity for real innovation.

14

Establishing the structure, authority, and processes to create an effective program

Coalfire – Larry Jones, CEO and Rick Dakin, CEO (2001-2015)

Cybersecurity program oversight is currently an unsettling process for many C-suites and boardrooms. Establishing structure, authority, and program oversight should be aligned to existing management processes and structure for other critical programs. However, cybersecurity programs remain unsettling. Why?

Simply put, cybersecurity programs address a different type of risk. Typically, the risk that is being addressed includes sophisticated attacks that are intended to interrupt operations or steal sensitive data. In either case, *organizations find themselves under attack*. In the case of Sony, a nation-state attacked the company for the sole purpose of disrupting the distribution of media. In the case of JP Morgan Chase, a highly sophisticated adversary launched a denial of service attack against the service delivery platform to disrupt the flow of transactions. Both cases provide business justification to manage cybersecurity initiatives as a *bet-your-business* type of risk management program.

The connection between the boardroom and those managing the technical infrastructure is critical. However, no board or C-Suite has the skills or knowledge of the threat landscape or technologies involved in cybersecurity programs to flatten the management structure for top to bottom direct management. Each level of the organization must participate in an integrated and collaborative fashion. The structure and risk management responsibilities have been documented many times by well-respected cybersecurity organizations such as the National Institute of Standards and Technology (NIST) in a series of special publications. Coalfire has specifically supported the local adoption and application of these general principles for the electric utility, financial services, health-care, and retail sectors. As a result, this chapter leverages the lessons learned from those previous engagements to provide a condensed but effective approach to cyber risk management and cybersecurity program creation and oversight.

First, the nature of the threat landscape is evolving, while the underlying technology platforms that hold sensitive data are also changing. In this fluid environment, management must create a nimble program of active cyber defenses informed by an iterative risk management process. For the foreseeable future, cybersecurity program oversight will not be one that can be reduced to an annual review process. When cyberattacks go undetected for months and then bring a company to its knees overnight, the level of vigilance and communication is heightened. To be effective, the structure has to be distributed throughout the organization, and risk thresholds have to be set that cause unplanned alerts to drive management action on a regularly scheduled review and ad hoc incident-response basis.

Often the primary risks to cyber assets is a cyberattack. The sophistication and determination of known threat actors drives the executive team to put on war paint and respond in kind. Unlike other enterprise risks that can be managed with traditional controls, cybersecurity requires the mindset of a warrior. Think in terms of Sun Tzu's guiding principles published in 473 BC, *The Art of War*: "we must know ourselves and our enemies and select a strategy to positively influence the outcome of battle. There is no reason to fear the attack but there is reason to be concerned about our readiness to defend ourselves from the attack and respond appropriately."

The most common approach for creating and maintaining an enterprise cybersecurity program follows a five-step risk management process. The process is iterative and constantly informed by new information. I am often asked, "When will the cybersecurity program be completed?" Unfortunately, the answer is never. Cybersecurity has to be viewed as a process and not an end point, the proverbial marathon versus sprint.

Each of the steps in the process requires participation at multiple levels across an organization.

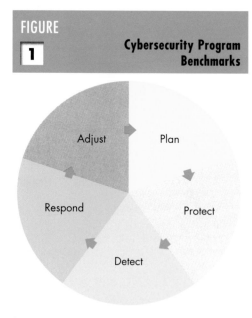

FIGURE 1
Cybersecurity Program Benchmarks

1. Plan
   i. Cyber asset inventory and environment characterization
   ii. Risk assessment and risk management strategy
   iii. Governance and organization structure
2. Protect
   i. Program control design, control selection, and implementation
   ii. Training
   iii. Maintenance
3. Detect
   i. Threat and program effectiveness monitoring and reporting
   ii. Incident alerting and response planning
4. Respond
   i. Event analysis and escalation
   ii. Containment, eradication, and recovery
5. Adjust
   i. Lessons learned and program adjustment
   ii. Communications

The rest of the chapter addresses each step of the cybersecurity program development process and highlights responsibilities for stakeholders throughout the organization.

■ Plan

Cyber asset inventory and environment characterization

In accordance with the principles of Sun Tzu, "know thyself." When cybersecurity programs are managed at only a technical level, the focus of the program is at risk of being misdirected. Sensitive data hosted on an inexpensive platform may bely the true value to the organization. Only senior executives and business unit managers understand the relative importance of specific operations or data.

Simple cybersecurity program designs often include some level of network and data segmentation, encryption, or levels of access. As a senior executive, one of the things you should be asking is if your most important systems and most sensitive data are properly deployed in the protected zones within your system architecture. However, the IT team will never know how to answer that question if senior management (specifically business unit management) does not specifically provide guidance on the relative importance of business functions and their associated systems.

The new generation CIOs and CISOs understand this principle completely, and the best of them have structured the operating environment and security programs to focus on the most important cyber assets. However, to assume all CIOs or CISOs understand this principle of critical asset classification and environment characterization is dangerous, because many do not. The most important part of this discussion is, "Does every business unit manager understand what his or her most critical cyber assets are and where they are deployed?" Even if the CIO and CISO understand the relative priorities, senior executives cannot effectively participate in either cyber risk management or cybersecurity program oversight without first understanding the extent of the environment being protected.

As a quick warning, many of my clients have the false expectation that cybersecurity has become a critical part of the design for new or more modern platforms being purchased from large vendors and hosting providers. This expectation has proven false so

many times that it is more realistic to expect that vendors have done little to inherently protect systems or data in the native design of their systems. In many cases, unless deployed appropriately, new cloud and mobile applications can actually decrease the level of cybersecurity already deployed on legacy systems. It is the responsibility of each executive to fully define his or her operating environment and include critical third parties in the assessment.

Although lack of cybersecurity integration by vendors is not universal, we're seeing some enlightenment in a few security-focused service providers. However, it remains a serious concern for the majority of new system acquisition and support processes, and cybersecurity typically shifts to an add-on feature after procurement of a major new system in many cases. In short, the process of identifying critical cyber assets and the systems that support those assets will remain a key part of the cybersecurity program oversight function for the long term. The process of 'knowing thyself' has been expanded to knowing your partners and vendors and where your sensitive data has been shared or managed by third parties.

The following is a quick test:

- What are your top 3 most important business processes, and what systems support those functions?
- Does the way your CIO answers the previous question match your understanding of critical systems?

Risk assessment and risk management strategy

After a solid understanding of the battlefield is established and executives appreciate the critical cyber assets being protected, an assessment of risk to those cyber assets is critical to the design of the cybersecurity program. The ability to adjust the program to meet the evolving threat landscape and technology architecture shifts is an important component of organizational security maturity. Responsibilities for conducting an effective cyber risk assessment are distributed at three levels, as shown in Figure 2.

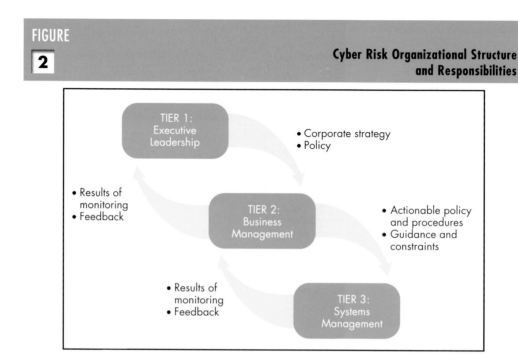

FIGURE 2

Cyber Risk Organizational Structure and Responsibilities

TIER 1: Executive Leadership

- Corporate strategy
- Policy

- Results of monitoring
- Feedback

TIER 2: Business Management

- Actionable policy and procedures
- Guidance and constraints

- Results of monitoring
- Feedback

TIER 3: Systems Management

The primary objective for a risk assessment is to drive selection of adequate and rational controls and then assign responsibilities to manage those controls. During the process the environment will be characterized to bring context and the existing system vulnerabilities, and weaknesses will be evaluated to select controls to offset the probability of compromise during an attack. A comprehensive cybersecurity program addresses administrative, physical, and technical controls as an integrated suite.

Once the inherent threats and vulnerabilities are understood within the context of the impact they could have on the organization, its clients, and partners, senior executives must approve the risk management strategy. Many executives want to see all risk either mitigated or transferred. However, the bulk of companies in critical infrastructure industries end up accepting some level of risk in their strategy. Cost, continuity of operations, or other concerns may drive the formation of the cybersecurity program to mitigate what is reasonable and accept the residual risk. Cybersecurity insurance is becoming an increasingly popular means of transferring risk but comes with the requirement that you understand risk in ways that may not have been previously considered. It is important that the business units and security staff are able to communicate the constraints as well as the risk mitigation alternatives for senior executives to make reasonable decisions on risk management strategies.

Governance and organization structure

The risk assessment management duties and responsibilities are typically allocated in accordance with Table 1.

■ Protect

Program design and implementation

The outcome for any cybersecurity program is the expectation that an organization can defend its critical cyber assets from irreparable damage resulting from a cyberattack. The impact of cyberattack is different for every organization. As a result, the cybersecurity strategy and associated program must be considered against the potential impact.

TABLE 1		Levels of Authority and Responsibility
Executive	**Business Unit**	**Systems Management**

■ Prioritize critical assets
■ Establish risk appetite
■ Approve risk Management strategy
  ■ Mitigate the risk
  ■ Transfer the risk
  ■ Accept the risk
■ Approve the program and policies
■ Assign responsibilities
■ Provide oversight
	■ Define boundaries
	■ Design use case scenarios to understand impact from system attack and compromise
	■ Identify constraints for mitigating all risk
	■ Develop a justified risk management strategy
	■ Identify all required users of systems or delegates to receive data on a "need to know" basis
		■ Recommend technical and physical controls
		■ Identify threats and system vulnerabilities
		■ Evaluate the likelihood and probability of impact for each threat and vulnerability
		■ Estimate the impact on systems and operations from a financial, legal, and regulatory perspective

Although security programs are different for every company, the principles for developing the program are fairly consistent. NIST Special Publication 800-53 has done a good job in describing the selection of controls for high-, medium-, and low-level impacts. Every organization needs access controls, but only those that result in national security impact are realistic candidates for deploying the high-level version of that control. Many executives are "sold" a package of controls because they are used by the NSA, but the question to ask is, "How does the NSA mission relate to our operations?"

As discussed in the risk assessment segment, executives have to define their risk appetite. This is hard during the early days of cybersecurity program development because most of the C-suites have an inherently low risk appetite and do not yet understand the impact of lowering the threshold for control selection. As a result, cybersecurity programs are often a work in process for several years.

Training

The best cybersecurity programs are the ones that staff and partners will actually execute. Contrary to what many vendors and partners will tell you, the magic is not in the security solutions selected. Rather, the magic is in the ability of the organization to manage those solutions to mitigate risks. Because the security skills available in the industry today are low and growing increasingly rare, companies should expect to spend a disproportionate amount of training dollars on cybersecurity.

Maintenance

Anyone working in forensic response will tell you that system compromise and data breach are rarely the result of some sophisticated attack that no one has ever been seen before. The bulk of effective attacks use vulnerabilities that have been known for years. Cross-site scripting, shell or SQL injection, shared administrator accounts, lack of patching, and other standard security hygiene issues are normally the culprits. There are two significant operations that go dramatically underfunded in most organizations: maintenance of systems and security controls, which leaves organizations vulnerable to attack.

■ Detect
Program monitoring and reporting

The days of 'acquire, deploy, and forget' are over. For years, senior executives did not have to participate in cybersecurity program oversight, because a combination of fire-walls, malware protection, and light access controls were adequate to defend against previous generations of relatively static cyberattacks. Today, continuous monitoring is critical to see the evolving threat and technology landscape.

Cybersecurity programs have moved from a period of static defenses to active defenses, and we must become more nimble to successfully protect critical systems and sensitive data. From a military perspective, think of this shift as moving from multiple armored divisions with significant force and firepower protecting cities or regions to the more recent Special Forces mindset, in which quick detection and reaction are the key to success.

In the previous section, we mentioned two areas for increased investment. The second area is to develop cybersecurity programs with a much higher focus on threat intelligence, monitoring, and alerting. This requires new security solutions and specially trained security professionals. The old line of firewalls, malware protection, and access controls are still required, but much more active system patching, vulnerability management, and monitoring are driving modern security programs.

To avoid the perception of negligence, senior executives often reinforce old line security controls that are audited for regulatory compliance. However, focusing only on compliance will not secure an organization. Cyberthreats are ongoing, while compliance is a point-in-time review. What is needed to address increasing cyberthreats is a nimble program that can suffer an intrusion but repel the intruder and recover operations quickly. Just like a good boxer needs to be able to take a punch and stay in the ring, companies today must be able to absorb a cyber punch and keep operating while at the same time mitigating and recovering.

Incident alerting and escalation

Identifying a potential attack is only half the solution. Cybersecurity programs must alert the technology teams and business units to respond appropriately. One potential

response is to take systems off line. Without executive and business unit involvement, a poor decision could be made.

■ Respond

Response capabilities vary after discovery of a cybersecurity incident, and organizations are typically faced with two unappealing options:

1. Pull up the drawbridge and stop the hoards from overrunning the castle.
2. Keep the drawbridge down while trying to figure out where the bad guy is.

The most immediate, and some say rational, response is to "pull up the drawbridge" to eliminate whatever access hackers have. Unfortunately, this alerts the bad guy that you know he's inside, so whatever systems and accounts he may have compromised or whatever backdoors he's created will be unknown.

On the other hand, if a company decides to take option two, to play it low-key and continue with business as usual to determine the scope of the problem, the organization can determine what systems have been compromised, what new privileged accounts have been created, and what back doors may exist. This will give the company a better chance of long-term success in eliminating the breach and repairing lost or damaged information.

One response is not necessarily better than the other, because situations vary. However, these critical decisions must be made almost immediately.

■ Adjust

No program is ever perfect. Continuous monitoring and reporting will enable all three tiers of responsibility to constantly adjust the program and inform the other tiers of actions.

■ Summary

Effective cybersecurity program development and oversight requires executives to implement and manage a distributed process at three levels within an organization: executive level; business unit level; and operational level (Table 2).

TABLE 2	Levels of Authority and Responsibility		
	Executive	Business Unit	Systems Management
Plan	■ Prioritize systems and functions for protection ■ Establish risk appetite	■ Inventory critical systems ■ Risk assessment	■ Select justified controls ■ Develop an architecture to integrate controls ■ Provide periodic updates to executives to help them understand context for the program
Protect	■ Approve cybersecurity program strategy ■ Approve standards and metrics for control oversight ■ Approve policies	■ Train users ■ Enforce controls ■ Design and manage physical and logical controls	■ Design, deploy, and manage technical controls
Detect	■ Receive periodic threat briefings and controls effectiveness reports ■ Receive periodic education on changes to the threat landscape and emerging controls	■ Incident and event reporting form staff, partners and third parties	■ Operate system and control monitoring ■ Actively participate in threat intelligence functions
Respond	■ Lead Incident Response Team	■ Participate in the Incident Response Team	■ Containment ■ Recovery
Adjust	■ Allocate resources for program enhancements	■ Deploy enhanced training ■ Deploy updated administrative and physical controls	■ Provide advice for control enhancements

If Sun Tzu lived today, he would clearly see the nature of current cybersecurity programs and responsibilities and recognize that criticality of executive level management. We have to take a warrior's attitude in developing strategies and programs to be successful in combatting the cybersecurity challenges we face today.

III Cybersecurity legal and regulatory considerations

15

Securing privacy and profit in the era of hyperconnectivity and big data

Booz Allen Hamilton – Bill Stewart, Executive Vice President; Dean Forbes, Senior Associate; Agatha O'Malley, Senior Associate; Jaqueline Cooney, Lead Associate; and Waiching Wong, Associate

Companies increasingly use consumer data, including personal information, to stay competitive; this includes the capability to analyze their customers' demographics and buying habits, predict future behaviors and business trends, and collect and sell data to third-parties. Consumers' willingness to share their data centers on trust, however, and 91% of adults believe that they have lost control over how their personal information is collected and used (2014 Pew Research Center). So how do companies effectively manage consumer data while simultaneously building trust? It has been said that you cannot have good privacy without good security. A first step is to build an effective security program while also better understanding what privacy means and how it can be a strategic business enabler in our era of hyper-connectivity and "big data".

■ Why does this matter? The data economy

The power and insights driven by consumer data has changed the corporate landscape. This has created the

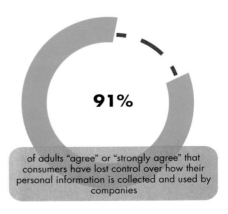

91%

of adults "agree" or "strongly agree" that consumers have lost control over how their personal information is collected and used by companies

data economy—the exchange of digitized information for the purpose of creating insights and value. Companies are building entire businesses around consumer information, including building data-driven products and monetizing data streams. This is a supply-driven push made possible by widespread digitization, ubiquitous data storage, powerful analytics, mobile technology that feeds ever more information into the system, and the Internet of Things. This also has a demand-driven effect as more consumers expect their products to be "smart" and their experiences to be targeted to delight them on an individual basis.

The data economy goes beyond the tech industry. For example, many supermarkets now record what customers buy across their stores and track the purchasing history of loyalty-card members. The most competitive companies will sift through this data for trends and then, through a joint venture, sell the information to the vendors who stock their shelves. Consumer product makers are often willing to purchase this data in order to make more informed decisions about product placement, marketing, and branding.

The enabler of the data economy is data itself. Individuals generate data. They do this every time they "check in" to a location through a mobile app, when they use a loyalty card, when they purchase items online, and when they are tracked through their Internet searches. Companies gain consumers' trust and confidence through transparency about the personal information that they gather, providing consumers control over uses and sharing of such information, and offer fair value in return.

■ **Privacy definitions vary**

"Privacy" may have different meanings to stakeholders due to factors such as the context, prevailing societal norms, and geographical location. There is no consensus definition of privacy, which makes it challenging to discuss, and act upon, a need for privacy. However, an important central concept regarding privacy recurs, which is, the appropriate collection, use, and sharing of personal information to accomplish business tasks. Determining what appropriate and limited means for your customer is key to gaining trust and unlocking the potential of the data economy.

■ **What is personal data?**

Personal information comes in variations such as: (1) self-reported data, or information people volunteer about themselves, such as their email addresses, work and educational history, and age and gender; (2) digital exhaust, such as location data and browsing history, which is created when using mobile devices, web services, or other connected technologies; and (3) profiling data, or personal profiles used to make predictions about individuals' interests and behaviors, which are derived by combining self-reported, digital exhaust, and other data. According to research, people value self-reported data the least and profiling data the most (2015 Harvard Business Review). For many companies, it is that third category of data, used to make predictions about consumer needs, that truly provides the ability to create exciting, thrilling products and experiences. However, that same information is what consumers value the most and seek to protect.

Every minute

Facebook users share nearly 2.5 million pieces of content.

Twitter users tweet nearly 300,000 times.

YouTube users upload 72 hours of new video content.

Amazon generates over $80,000 in online sales.

Privacy is very often conflated with security. While privacy is about the appropriate collection, use, and sharing of personal information, security is about protecting such information from loss, or unintended or unauthorized access, use, or sharing.

■ Privacy and security intersect through breaches

Although privacy and security are two separate concepts, the importance of these two ideas intersect for the consumer if personal information is not safeguarded. In a nutshell, consumers are more likely to buy from companies they believe protect their privacy. Large-scale security breaches, such as the recent theft of credit card information of 56 million Home Depot consumers (2015) and 40 million Target shoppers (2013), provide consumers with plenty to worry about. Breach-weary consumers need to know who to trust with their personal information, to ensure that only the company that they provided the information to can use it. Risk management for data privacy and security of that data should guard against external malicious breaches and inadvertent internal breaches and third-party partner breaches.

■ Privacy is linked to trust — differentiate with it

Trust, and the data that it allows companies to have access to, is a critical strategic asset. Privacy issues that erode trust can dismantle the goodwill that a brand has spent decades building with consumers. Forward-leaning companies are already moving toward proactively gaining the trust of their customers and using that as a differentiator. Learning from its issues with the lack of security on iCloud, Apple now markets all of the privacy features of their products and apps. With an eye toward the desires of its customers, the iPhone's iOS 8 is encrypted by default. This makes all "private" information such as photos, messages, contacts, reminders, and call history inaccessible without a four-digit PIN and numeric password. In 2012 Microsoft launched its "Don't get Scroogled" campaign as a direct attack on its rival, Google, by highlighting that its

Gmail service scans emails in order to target and tailor advertising to the user. In 2013 Microsoft ran TV ads that claim that "your privacy is [Microsoft's] priority."

Companies are also competing to be privacy champions against government surveillance. For the last few years, the Electronic Frontier Foundation has published the "Who Has Your Back" list—highlighting companies with strong privacy best practices, particularly regarding disclosure of consumer information to the government.

■ Challenges and trends
Maintaining compliance

Beyond the moneymaker of the data economy, there is also a need to comply with a swirl of conflicting regulations on privacy. For global companies, this task is made more difficult as privacy regulations vary by region and country. Although international accords often serve as the basis of national laws and policy frameworks,[1] the local variations complicate compliance. For example, the May 2014 ruling of the European Court of Justice on the "right to be forgotten" set a precedent for removing information from search results that are deemed to be no longer relevant or not in the public interest by affirming a ruling by the Spanish Data Protection Agency. Countries across Europe have applied the ruling at a national level, which means that they are not exactly the same.[2] Compliance with this decision has yet to be fully understood. Google has fielded about 120,000 requests for deletions and granted approximately half of them.[3] Compliance is costly and complicated. Beyond technical issues (which were easier to solve), Google's main issue with compliance was administrative—forms needed to be created in many languages, and dozens of lawyers, paralegals, and staff needed to be assembled to review the requests. Issues remain, such as the possibility of removing links from Google.com as well as from country-specific search engines.

Compliance with established laws in the U.S. is often topic- and industry-specific. For example, Congress has passed laws prohibiting the disclosure of medical information (the Health Insurance Portability and Accountability Act), educational records (the Buckley Amendment), and video-store rentals (a law passed in response to revelations about Robert Bork's rentals when he was nominated to the Supreme Court).[4]

Growing data = growing target for hackers

As data availability increases, the attractiveness of datasets for hackers increases as well. Companies in all sectors—health care, retail, finance, government—all have datasets that are attractive to hackers. Just a few of the confirmed cyberattacks that targeted consumer information in 2014 include: eBay, Montana Health Department, P.F. Chang's, Evernote, Feedly, and Domino's Pizza.[5]

Beyond personal information

Personal information (PI) is described in privacy and information security circles as information that can be used on its own or with other information to identify, contact or locate a single person, or to identify an individual in context. With the advent of rich geolocation data, and powerful associative analysis, such as facial recognition, the extent of PI is greatly expanded. Regulations are struggling to keep up with the changes, and companies can maintain consumer confidence by collecting, using, and sharing consumer data with privacy in mind.

■ What to do? Build consumer trust

To unlock the data economy, companies will need to tune in to their customer's needs and move quickly to earn and retain customer trust. Privacy can be a competitive differentiator for your business—and this goes beyond lip service. Appropriate privacy policies are needed internally, this means building privacy considerations into business operations and expected employee

conduct, along with a clearly defined means of enforcement. Externally, this means building privacy considerations into the products and services offered to customers. Some of the ways to do this include the following.

Create easy-to-understand consumer-facing policies

The average website privacy policy averages more than 2,400 words, takes 10 minutes to read, and is written at a university-student reading level.[6] No wonder half of online Americans are not even sure what a privacy policy is.[7] Writing clear, easy-to-understand consumer-facing policies can help you increase the number of people who will actually read them, and you will gain the trust of your consumers. No company has a perfect solution, but many organizations have come closer. Facebook has recently rewritten its privacy policy for simplicity and included step-by-step directions for users.[8] To increase trust, privacy policies should clearly state the following:

1. the personal information that you will collect
2. why data is collected and how it will be used and shared
3. how you will protect the data
4. explanation of consumer benefit from the collection, use, sharing, and analysis of their data.

Additionally, companies should give a clear and easy opt-out at every stage and only use data in the ways stated. To ensure that the data is used in the ways stated, develop clear internal data use and retention guidelines across the entire enterprise, limit internal access to databases, create a procedure for cyberattacks, and link it directly to the consumer privacy policy.

Go "privacy by design"

The concept of "privacy by design" is integrating and promoting privacy requirements and/or best practices into systems, services, products, and business processes at the planning, design, development, and implementation stages, to ensure that businesses meets their customer and employee privacy expectations, and policy and regulatory requirements. The approach is a market differentiator that is intended to reduce privacy and security risks and cost by embedding relevant company policies into such designs. As such, privacy settings are automatically applied to devices and services. Privacy by design and default is recognized by the U.S. Federal Trade Commission as a recommended practice for protecting online privacy, and is considered for inclusion in the European Union's Data Protection Regulation, and was developed by an Ontario Information and Privacy Commissioner.

Communicate your good work

Privacy policies and actions are more than legal disclosure; they are marketing tools. All the actions you take to protect consumers' privacy should be communicated so they know you can be trusted. The Alliance of Automobile Manufacturers, representing companies such as Chrysler, Ford, General Motors, and Toyota, publicly pledged more transparency about how they will safeguard data generated by autonomous vehicle technologies. Many groups have published data principles that communicate how data is gathered, protected, and shared.[9]

■ Conclusion

Our current data economy brings exciting opportunities for companies to grow by enhancing their products and services. These innovations rely on consumers to trust your organization with their personal information.

Building consumer trust includes keeping information safe from hackers, creating easy-to-understand consumer-facing policies, and applying the principle of "privacy by default". Companies that reframe these actions as business enablers instead of business costs will thrive—and find it easier to comply with an increasingly complex web of regulations. Finally, communicating your good work to consumers will elevate the profile of your organization as a trusted partner, and pave the way for future gains.

References
1. https://www.eff.org/issues/international-privacy-standards.
2. http://www.hitc.com/en-gb/2015/07/07/facebook-questions-use-of-right-to-be-forgotten-ruling/.
3. http://www.newyorker.com/magazine/2014/09/29/solace-oblivion.
4. http://www.newyorker.com/magazine/2014/09/29/solace-oblivion.
5. http://www.forbes.com/sites/jaymcgregor/2014/07/28/the-top-5-most-brutal-cyber-attacks-of-2014-so-far/.
6. http://www.computerworld.com/article/2491132/data-privacy/new-software-targets-hard-to-understand-privacy-policies.html.
7. http://www.pewresearch.org/fact-tank/2014/12/04/half-of-americans-dont-know-what-a-privacy-policy-is/.
8. https://www.washingtonpost.com/blogs/the-switch/wp/2014/11/13/facebook-rewrites-its-privacy-policy-so-that-humans-can-understand-it/.
9. https://fortunedotcom.files.wordpress.com/2014/11/privacyandsecurityprinciplesforfarmdata.pdf.

16

Oversight of compliance and control responsibilities

Data Risk Solutions: BuckleySandler LLP & Treliant Risk Advisors LLC – Elizabeth McGinn, Partner; Rena Mears, Managing Director; Stephen Ruckman, Senior Associate; Tihomir Yankov, Associate; and Daniel Goldstein, Senior Director

For too long, cybersecurity has been considered the realm of the Information Technology (IT) Department, with corporate executives assuming that the goal of cybersecurity is simply to make sure IT is secure enough to allow the company to use data reliably to do its business. In today's economy, however, data are not only a tool for doing business but also a core asset of the business itself. The collection, analysis, and sale of rich data about one's products and customers inform decision-making and business strategy and provide a key revenue generator for many companies. Because data are now so valuable, the increasingly pervasive and debilitating nature of cyberthreats poses an existential threat to the company's success. Data's value to cyber criminals also has the attention of federal and state regulators concerned with consumer privacy and safety, posing new legal and compliance challenges.

This is why companies can no longer afford to approach the oversight of cybersecurity as an IT issue. Simply because a cyberthreat's mode of attack usually exploits vulnerabilities in a company's IT infrastructure does not mean that oversight should rest purely with the team that maintains and repairs that infrastructure. Certainly, a secured IT infrastructure is crucial and an important first line of defense. However, the enterprise risk created by cyberthreats requires a holistic approach that considers the management of an entire array of impacts—from reputational to regulatory to financial—that transcend core IT competencies and functions. Because securing today's data is central to securing the company's future, effective oversight of cybersecurity compliance and controls requires leadership from the C-suite and the boardroom.

Critically, this leadership must be coordinated. For a company's cybersecurity compliance and control programs to be effective, efforts must be structured in ways that ensure the board and senior management, including the C-suite, work together to achieve its risk objectives. Each has distinct cybersecurity responsibilities: senior management is responsible for determining relevant cyber-related risks and implementing a compliance program that incorporates appropriate processes and controls to mitigate them, whereas the board is responsible for overseeing the risk identification process and independently evaluating whether the program is designed, implemented, and operating effectively to meet the company's cybersecurity risk mitigation objectives. Meeting these responsibilities well requires a formalized integrated approach to cybersecurity risk evaluation, defined roles and responsibilities, implementation of a program that is supported by the board, clearly articulated by the C-suite, and effectively implemented by operational resources. Disconnect between the board, C-suite, and operations poses as much of a challenge to corporate cybersecurity as cyberthreats themselves.

■ Cybersecurity oversight is risk management oversight

To understand why coordinated C-suite and board oversight of cybersecurity is essential, one must understand cybersecurity as a means of managing and responding to corporate risk. The purpose of risk management in general is to identify and mitigate the risks a company faces to a level acceptable to the enterprise as determined by the board, a level known as a company's "risk appetite." The strategies and objectives for managing risks and responding to threats are articulated in the policies, procedures, and controls of the organization and are the responsibility of senior management.

One significant and growing area of risk for most companies is data risk. Data risk encompasses the risks of financial loss; business or operational disruption; loss or compromise of assets and information; failure to comply with legal, regulatory, or contractual requirements; or damage to the reputation of an organization because of the unauthorized access to or exploitation of data assets. Cybersecurity is the protection of data assets from unauthorized electronic access or exploitation risks through processes designed to prevent, detect, and respond to these risks.[1] Effective oversight of cybersecurity is therefore essential to a company's oversight of risk management.

Two core components of the company's cybersecurity program must be overseen at the highest levels of management: compliance and controls. Compliance here means the company's program for ensuring actual adherence to internal cybersecurity policies as well as external privacy and data protection laws and regulations in the jurisdictions where the company operates. Controls mean the company's systems and processes for protecting its data infrastructure and carrying out incident response. These components should be overseen actively to confirm that compliance and controls are going beyond mechanical application of generic cybersecurity rules and standards, which may just establish a regulatory floor for corporate practices, not a set of industry-leading practices, and which may not be appropriate or relevant to the threat landscape and unique regulatory requirements for the company's industry. Moreover, even industry-leading practices quickly may become dated, because regulators' views on "reasonable" cybersecurity are changing all the time.[2] The legal risks from inattentive oversight are limited only by plaintiffs' imagination and regulators' zeal, and the practical risks are limited only by hackers' ambition and creativity.

From a risk management perspective, the key inquiry revolves around the value of each data asset. For example, data assets whose business usefulness has long passed may still be rich in information that may be embarrassing to the organization if released publicly. So in a way, cybersecurity risks are partially an extension of data retention risks, for what the organization does not have (and has no obligation to keep) cannot be hacked.

Thus, the board and senior management must approach the oversight of cybersecurity compliance and control from a broader risk management vantage point: one that weighs the value of the data as an asset class to the organization, the value that may be assigned by the threat actors who may seek the asset, and the broader impact and costs—including but not limited to legal and compliance costs—stemming from the potential compromise of data.

In this vein, perhaps the board's most critical inquiry to senior management is whether the organization has adopted sufficient processes to inventory and value its various data assets. From a cybersecurity perspective, senior management should then weigh under what circumstances, through what channels, and on what platforms the organization's most critically valued data assets should be made accessible.

■ Board of directors' role in oversight of compliance and controls

Too often, boards have exercised limited oversight of cybersecurity, yet monitoring the management of data risk associated with cybersecurity is part of the board's fiduciary duty to the corporation. The time for the board to begin to play an oversight role is *not* the moment when data actually are put at risk, through a breach or corporate theft; the board must build cybersecurity oversight into its general strategy for overseeing risk management from day one.

Managing the risks associated with cybersecurity compliance and control involves determining one's risk appetite in a variety of areas and requires senior management to make fundamental judgment calls about the design of the control environment, the scope and depth of the compliance program, and the resource allocation for each. The board must be well informed of how the corporate leadership is managing these risks and able to assess the adequacy

of the organization's risk management efforts.

The board also has to be sure to engage in oversight of cybersecurity compliance and controls at all phases of the company's data risk management "lifecycle." See Figure 1.

The lifecycle involves, first, *identification*—looking at the company's cybersecurity risk profile, identifying the key data assets that have to be protected (the "crown jewels"), and determining the applicable laws and regulations governing their protection; next, *design and implementation*—creating and implementing operational controls and compliance processes to manage the risks to those data assets; next, *monitoring*—actively overseeing the compliance processes and controls; next, *evaluation*—evaluating the effectiveness and management of the controls and compliance processes implemented; and finally *reporting and reassessment*—documenting how the controls and compliance processes are working, and reassessing to the extent that there are gaps. The last phase of the lifecycle involves internal reporting on capabilities to respond to threats, external reporting on those capabilities to stakeholders (e.g., SOC 2 reporting), and adjusting management to respond to internal drivers (e.g., business changes) and external drivers (e.g., constantly evolving regulatory requirements and guidance). Strong C-suite supervision and board oversight are needed at every phase.

The oversight and compliance need not rest on the entire board—a standing committee comprising knowledgeable board members, armed with outside expertise where appropriate, often can provide a more focused and better informed oversight. However, whatever oversight activities are undertaken must be documented so that the board can show that it is carrying out its fiduciary duties.

■ Building blocks of effective oversight of cybersecurity compliance

An organization's cybersecurity compliance efforts must support the company's business units and management in their efforts

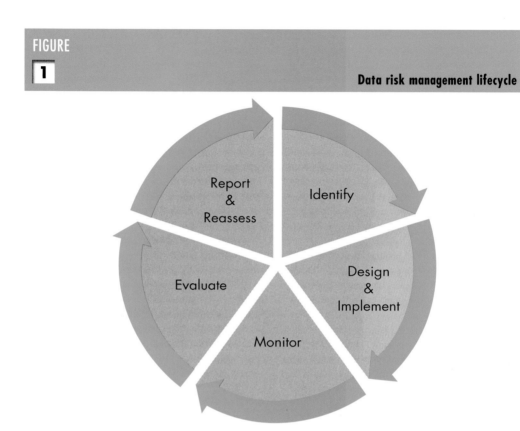

FIGURE 1

Data risk management lifecycle

to achieve compliance with government rules and regulations as well as the organization's internal policies and procedures by (1) identifying risks; (2) preventing risks through the design and implementation of controls; (3) monitoring and reporting on the effectiveness of those controls; (4) resolving compliance difficulties as they occur; and (5) advising and training.[3]

There are several steps the board and C-suite should take to provide effective oversight of the cybersecurity compliance program's execution of all of these functions. First and most important, the C-suite should implement an enterprise-wide approach to compliance risk management. As part of this approach, the organization should create a formalized Cybersecurity Risk Management Plan that is reviewed by the board. If the Plan is developed internally by the corporate leadership, the board should consider obtaining outside review for deficiencies or improvements. A mechanism for periodic updates to the Plan should be included in the Plan; many companies get into trouble with regulators for failing to update their cybersecurity approach as their business model changes or as regulations or enforcement strategies change.

If the company is operating in the United States, the Plan must be neither aspirational nor hyper-specific. An aspirational plan—one that sets out where the organization envisions its cybersecurity program to be at some point in the future—may end up causing the company to look like it is falling short if regulators come calling. Similarly, a hyper-specific Plan may put the company at risk of technical noncompliance. In short, the Cybersecurity Risk Management Plan should match what the company actually does.

Second, the C-suite should extend the enterprise-wide approach to compliance risk management to the company's entire ecosystem—its vendors and other third-party partners (e.g., cloud services providers, outside data processors). This means ensuring that oversight is robust for the corporate vetting of cybersecurity practices at third parties and that the contractual relationships with third parties allow for monitoring and oversight. Many technological innovations are leading companies to outsource aspects of their business involving data, but this comes with risks of the partners not securing data to the degree the company is.

Third, the C-suite should ensure—and the board should monitor—the independence of the cybersecurity compliance team from the company's IT and business units. Given silos that frequently develop around the compliance, IT, and business teams, the C-suite ought to ensure that the compliance team has the resources and skills to independently evaluate the sufficiency of the company's cybersecurity program. If the compliance team is not equipped to understand what technological steps the IT team is or should be taking to advance the organization's cybersecurity, and so defers entirely to their judgment, it may fail to apprehend the compliance implications of the steps ultimately taken.

Of course, independence should not mean isolation. It is critical that these teams can and do speak to each other regularly: compliance risks arise in the IT and business lines, and the compliance team must be involved in assessing those risks. For example, if a new business line involves collection of new pieces of customer data, failure to ensure that data are properly secured and kept private from the start creates compliance risks. Likewise, the IT Department's failure to patch software in a timely manner creates compliance risks. The compliance team must be sufficiently in the loop to ensure steps are being taken to prevent these failures, without being operationally involved in the actual prevention efforts. This can be achieved through

well-developed monitoring and assessment processes that encourage timely internal communication of potential risks to the compliance team.

Fourth, consistent with the risk management lifecycle, the C-suite should make sure it has effective means to test compliance in practice and communicate the results to the board. It is critical for updates to cybersecurity compliance policies to translate actually into updated implementation, and the board must be able to see—and where needed spur—this implementation. (See the next section). The C-suite also has to be able to test to see that cybersecurity compliance is taking root across the company's operations and prevent 'siloing' within business lines or cost centers.

Fifth and finally, the board should make cybersecurity compliance a priority, plain and simple. None of the above measures will be prioritized at the senior management level and below unless they are also the board's priority.

■ Building blocks of effective oversight of cybersecurity controls

Board and C-suite oversight of cybersecurity controls relates to the control of associated enterprise risks: legal, financial, regulatory, and reputational, to name a few. None of these risks can be fully avoided, but effective controls can reduce their impact on the organization, and effective oversight can ensure that these controls are thorough.

One step a board can take to provide effective oversight of cybersecurity controls is to ensure that the controls implemented by the C-suite contain prevention, detection, and rapid remediation components. Many companies focus on prevention and detection, but not remediation, and then are caught off guard when they learn of an intrusion requiring immediate remediation that went undetected. Prevention measures include data inventorying, data loss prevention planning, strong perimeter and internal defenses, and processes for timely patching core software to plug security holes. Many of these are IT measures, but prevention is not limited to IT and includes building a corporate culture that is mindful of data risk, as is discussed more below.

Detection measures include analysis of operational data and anomaly detection as well as systems for logging, monitoring, and testing data moving into and out of the corporate IT environment and across various devices (e.g., from computer to cloud service or external storage devices), where legally permissible. Rapid remediation measures include incident response plans that are rehearsed, implementation of forensic recovery tools, and measures to quickly restore failed systems from back-ups. Boards should recommend appointment of a permanent incident response team—comprising senior management from IT, legal, compliance, vendor management, PR, investor relations, and business lines—to lead the incident response efforts, report incidents and remediation plans to the C-suite and the board, and notify external regulators and customers when necessary.

In line with the previous point, a key step the C-suite should take is to oversee lines of communication among the various parts of the company that either manage or make use of the company's cybersecurity controls. If a business line is experiencing occasional bugs in its online customer order processing, for example, and IT is not informed of the issue in a timely manner, malware may go undetected. If an employee with database access quits and HR does not timely inform IT, then user credentials may remain active long after they should.

Another key step the C-suite can take is to prioritize regular training of employees—at a minimum annually—on cybersecurity threats and how to avoid them. A surprising number of threats can be thwarted by employee education about suspicious emails, strong password practices, and cautious use of personal devices. The more employees at every level learn to treat data as a valuable asset, the more careful they will be. Conversely, no matter how strong a company's cybersecurity controls, it only takes one employee mistake to expose sensitive company data.

As with cybersecurity compliance, for the above measures to be prioritized, they must be a board priority. In this vein, the board should check to see that cybersecurity controls are appropriately funded; none of these controls can be prioritized without adequate funding.

■ Implementation challenges

Even the best designed data security initiatives are prone to failure if not implemented correctly. A common problem that can occur even after apparently successful program implementation is a disconnect between appropriately drafted policies and procedures on the one hand, and operational practices and technology infrastructure on the other (in-house and third party-managed), and a failure of the board to notice.

Cybersecurity policies and procedures are effective only if they are tailored to the company's unique business environment, applicable regulatory requirements, and known security risks. However, too often, boards and C-suite leadership oversee the development and adoption of boilerplate policies and procedures that, although perhaps built on generally appropriate foundations, are either insufficiently customized or implemented inappropriately. The resulting disconnects may lead not only to damaging data breaches and unauthorized disclosure of personal information but also to scrutiny from regulators and actions from the plaintiffs' bar. For example, the Federal Trade Commission (FTC) currently views the disconnects between cybersecurity policies and procedures and their actual implementation as unfair or deceptive trade practices under Section 5 of the FTC Act, and this is a trend that senior executives should expect to continue.

It is critical to the success of a cybersecurity program that the operational uptake of—and ongoing adherence to—program requirements are measured effectively. Monitoring of the program not only enables effective reporting up to the board but also, more importantly, identifies vulnerabilities in the program and areas for improved security. Although evaluating the effectiveness of a cybersecurity program would appear to be a core component of any successful implementation, many organizations fail to adequately address this need, often leading to exploited weaknesses, data breaches, and programmatic failure.

Effective metrics for evaluation can be broken down into several categories to enable more targeted application across the enterprise. Programmatic metrics measure the progress of various organizational components of the information protection program, such as overall program development, implementation, and maintenance (e.g., cybersecurity policies are updated to meet new regulatory requirements). Operational metrics measure the performance of (as the name implies) various operational components of the information protection program; the number of cybersecurity incidents per reporting period is an excellent example. And compliance metrics measure individuals' compliance with program requirements. Such metrics may measure, for example, whether employees are observing required data security protocols when sending sensitive customer information to a third party for processing. In general, the trend for many of these metrics is toward the measurement of outcomes; metrics that demonstrate a company's frequent intrusion detection scanning are not helpful if the outcome is still a high number of intrusions each year.

Regardless of whether your organization is seeking to measure programmatic, operational, or compliance aspects of your cybersecurity program, the metrics that you design must be clearly defined and meaningful and measure progress against a clearly stated objective. A properly implemented metrics program helps leadership ascertain initial uptake and improve the compliance with—and performance of—a well-designed cybersecurity program.

Another challenge for effective implementation of cybersecurity compliance and controls—and one that must be closely monitored by the board—is resource allocation. The recognition of data as a highly valued

business asset is clearly established; its value is verified on a daily basis by those who seek to gain access to business networks and view, remove, or otherwise exploit the data residing there. However, resources allocated to cybersecurity are still frequently an IT line item, rather than an enterprise-wide issue. Businesses operating in this environment of perpetually evolving digital risks must recognize that data security is no longer a cost of doing business; it is a core component of remaining in business. As such, budgets must be allocated appropriately to meet the risks. Budgets vary according to business type, data types and sensitivity, volume of data, sharing with third parties, and any number of other of risk factors that must be considered by the board and executives. The budgeting process has to enable the company to do more than get the right people and processes in place but also to implement technology that truly addresses the security needs of the organization. This process requires commitment from the C-suite and oversight from a board that understands the importance of cybersecurity.

Cybersecurity budgeting also must include dedicated resources for training of personnel. As mentioned above, the human element is frequently the weakest link in an otherwise solid data security program. Staff must have the resources they need to be trained not only to be proactive in taking steps to safeguard data but also to recognize attempts by unauthorized parties trying to gain network access. Phishing, for example, remains a remarkably effective tool for gaining credentials that open a door to the network and the data therein, and inadequate training may increase a company's vulnerability to phishing attacks. Regulators know this and expect board members providing cybersecurity oversight to know, too.

The board and C-suite also must bear in mind that successful initial implementation of a cybersecurity program does not necessarily lead to a cybersecurity program that has longevity. Ongoing success is largely dependent on top-down involvement by the board and active management by the C-suite. The board should be apprised regularly of data security incidents and emerging data risks, as well as changes to the regulatory environment. An actively informed and involved board, working in harmony with the C-suite, enables agile enterprise-wide response to evolving threats and appropriate upkeep and improvement of a robust cybersecurity program.

■ Conclusion

Today's cybersecurity risks affect organizations of all sizes and across industries and lead to not only IT headaches but also headaches for the entire business. Companies are increasingly put into the unenviable position of needing to put up shields against a variety of cyberthreats, knowing that no defense can provide perfect protection. However, the C-suite nevertheless must strive to employ strong cybersecurity compliance and control measures that go beyond mechanical satisfaction of applicable legal rules, and the board has an obligation to

ensure that these measures are being adopted. Only with consistent C-suite involvement and strong board oversight—informed by an understanding of data risk as a central enterprise risk—can cybersecurity challenges be handled effectively.

References

1. *See* NIST, "Framework for Improving Critical Infrastructure Cybersecurity" (2014) (defining "cybersecurity"). Of course there are many definitions of "cybersecurity"; the NIST definition adapted here is just a recent American example.
2. For example, some regulators require certain data to be encrypted while many others do not. *See, e.g.,* 201 Mass. Code Regs. § 1700 (2009).
3. *See* International Compliance Association, "What is Compliance?," available at http://www.int-comp.org/faqs-compliance-regulatory-environment.

17

Risks of disputes and regulatory investigations related to cybersecurity matters

Baker & McKenzie — David Lashway, Partner; John Woods, Partner; Nadia Banno, Counsel, Dispute Resolution; and Brandon H. Graves, Associate

Disputes and regulatory investigations are two of the more important risk categories related to cybersecurity matters. These risk categories can create significant financial exposure, brand risk, and distraction. In the worst case, some of these risks could result in bankruptcy.

The risks related to disputes are traditional (e.g., litigation, arbitration, and negotiation of contract terms) and novel (e.g., data ownership disputes). They arise not only in the context of data breaches but in everyday operations.

Regulatory investigations are another source of risk. This risk is hard to quantify because there is not clear statutory authority for all regulatory investigations begun or threatened. This creates uncertainty for regulated entities. The costs for non-compliance can be extensive, with fines in the millions of dollars and consent decrees authorizing audits for 20 years.

These risks affect businesses even in the absence of a data breach incident. More businesses recognize this fact and are accounting for these risks in all aspects of their businesses. Businesses that attempt to deal with risk related to cybersecurity matters as an afterthought may be left behind.

Many businesses are international in scope and must comply with cybersecurity rules and regulations in a variety of countries. This can create a highest-common-denominator situation: businesses end up attempting to comply with the strictest regime in which they operate.

The dynamic nature of cybersecurity matters makes it impossible to completely enumerate every risk associated with such matters. This chapter provides a short survey of some of the most high-profile risks that all businesses will face in our current economy.

■ Risks of disputes

Businesses have a growing awareness of cybersecurity matters. As a result, cybersecurity matters will increasingly impact traditional business activities, such as contract negotiation.

Plaintiffs also have an increasing awareness of cybersecurity-related causes of action. Courts have been receptive to some of these causes of action and skeptical of others, but plaintiffs continue to make threats in pursuit of a lucrative settlement.

Dispute risks in business activities

Cybersecurity matters will impact every traditional business activity, if they do not already. Two activities, contract negotiation and data processing, are already subject to dispute in many industries.

1. *Contract negotiation.* Contractual parties, especially government agencies, are becoming more sophisticated about requesting provisions related to cybersecurity during contract negotiations. Frequently, these provisions will place additional burdens on the counterparty, leading to disputes during negotiation. Many businesses are also attempting to apply existing contract provisions to cybersecurity matters. When this reinterpretation is put forward in the wake of a security breach, the reinterpretation can lead to costly litigation.

   a) *Flow-down provisions.* Federal agencies, especially the Department of Defense, are including more flow-down provisions related to cybersecurity in their contracts with suppliers. Often, the agency requires its contractors to include these provisions in their contracts with subcontractors and other contractual counterparties. As these flow-down provisions expand through the supply chain, businesses with no direct connection with the federal agency will see requests—or demands—that they comply with provisions drafted without their input.

These provisions can include security standards and breach disclosure requirements. For instance, Defense Federal Acquisition Regulation Supplement (DFARS) 204.7300 requires "adequate security" for all contractors and subcontractors with systems on which controlled technical information is resident on or transits. As with many of these provisions, "adequate security" is not defined with a checklist but as "protective measures that are commensurate with the consequences and probability of loss, misuse, or unauthorized access to, or modification of information."

These same provisions include reporting requirements for both actual and potentially adverse effects on an information system, which is a more stringent requirement than many state data breach requirements.

Compliance with these provisions will be difficult, and the set language created by such provisions prevents businesses from negotiating more concrete terms, forcing businesses to accept uncertainty as a cost of entering into such a contract.

   b) *Liability/indemnity.* Cybersecurity creates risk, and more businesses are looking to affirmatively allocate that risk through contractual terms. Actuaries are still developing tables related to cybersecurity risk (Congress is discussing legislating on this issue), so the allocation of risk in a contract may not be based on methods as rigorous as those in other risk allocations. This will create tension between parties who value the risk differently.

Cybersecurity incidents and the attendant response can be very expensive, with some sources placing the average financial cost of a data breach in the millions of dollars. The allocation of such cost, combined with an increasing chance of an incident triggering these clauses, is an area likely to be subject to dispute both during contract negotiation and in the wake of a breach.

Many contracts already contain liability allocation provisions, but those provisions do not explicitly address cybersecurity matters. In the wake of a cybersecurity incident, interpreting the liability allocation provisions will be a matter of some dispute.

c) *Data security and notification.* Laws, regulations, and political and consumer pressure have increased businesses' focus on the security of consumer data. At the same time, consumer data have become a more valuable commodity. For instance, AT&T and Apple both contested Radio Shack's ability to sell consumer data during Radio Shack's bankruptcy.

Recognizing these trends, businesses are placing more provisions in contracts that dictate security requirements. Because the underlying consumer data are valuable, these provisions may be subject to significant disputes during negotiations. Other businesses are attempting to read existing provisions as covering security requirements and privacy responsibility.

Many businesses that entrust sensitive data to counterparties are including breach notification provisions in contracts. These provisions vary greatly, even within a single industry, and create various thresholds for notification. For instance, some provisions require notification in the event of a breach. Others require notification if there is an indication of a breach. Many victims of a security breach seek to keep the existence of a breach out of the press, which can create tension with notification provisions.

2. *Data ownership/data processing.* Most state breach notification laws differentiate between data owners and data processors, but existing contracts do not always explicitly define these roles. Some businesses have attempted to understand these issues and have asserted ownership (or, in some cases, denied ownership) of data in the absence of a specific ownership allocation. This can lead to disputes in long-standing business relationships. One business may seek to sell information it is collecting while a contractual counterparty is attempting to safeguard the same data. Not all businesses seek to clarify this relationship prior to selling data, which can lead to significant disputes when such sales come to light.

In the context of a data breach

Data breaches expose businesses to many additional disputes. At times, these disputes can be more problematic than the intrusion itself. Contractual counterparties, customers, and other impacted businesses may all seek some compensation in the wake of a data breach. Insurance companies may seek to avoid payment under policies that arguably apply, leading to additional litigation.

1. *Contractual counterparties.* Most contracts have provisions that are either directly or indirectly implicated by a data breach. Some of these provisions are triggered by a breach, such as obligations to notify consumers whose information is exposed. A counterparty may allege that other provisions are broken by an intrusion, such as a requirement to have adequate or reasonable security. Businesses often struggle with whether a particular provision requires notification, either because the provision itself is not clear or because the business believes that the intrusion does not rise to the level contemplated in the contract.

Counterparties may disagree with this interpretation, leading to disputes if the intrusion does come to light.

Notification provisions often have an abbreviated time frame for notification. Attempting to identify and comply with notification provisions of impacted counterparties can create additional stress beyond the already significant stress related to a data breach. Reviewing and attempting to interpret these provisions after an intrusion also creates risk of contractual breach, as a business may not discover the notification provision until after the required time frame has passed.

In the wake of a breach, a victim's security will come under scrutiny, and a contractual counterparty may argue that the security was inadequate under the contract. For instance, in the DFARS provision discussed previously, "adequate security" is ripe for protracted litigation in the wake of a cybersecurity incident. It is difficult to define such terms adequately and still provide flexibility in the face of changing threats.

In some industries, such as those that deal with payment cards, many security requirements are codified and subject to audit. The victim of a data breach may be subject to a more intrusive audit to confirm its security.

Many contracts that involve confidential data have a provision for certifying that the confidential data have been destroyed. A counterparty may rightly inquire how such a certification was made in the wake of a cybersecurity incident.

2. *Customers.* Many intrusions lead to lawsuits by customers, whether they be individual consumers or large businesses. Recent card breaches have resulted in significant class-action litigation, and these cases have received much of the

press, but business customers have also pressed for indemnification in the wake of an intrusion.

Disputes with business partners over data breaches can disrupt normal operations, above and beyond the disruption caused by the data breach itself. The need to resume normal operations can pressure the victim to quickly agree to a settlement.

Customers will often file class actions in the wake of a data breach. Plaintiffs' lawyers are growing more sophisticated in how and where they file these actions. Both individual consumers and financial institutions have filed class actions, and, in some cases, these class actions are consolidated into complicated multidistrict litigation with multiple tracks for the differing plaintiffs. This creates expensive and cumbersome litigation.

3. *Other impacted businesses.* Contractual counterparties are not the only businesses that may sue in the wake of a data breach. Banks that issued cards implicated in Target's data breach are suing Target, even if they lack any traditional relationship to Target. Our more interconnected society has spread the effects of cybersecurity problems, and affected parties are developing more creative methods to file suit against the original victim of the intrusion.

4. *Insurance.* More and more insurance companies are offering cyber policies, and more businesses are attempting to make claims for intrusions under general policies. Insurance companies are, in turn, attempting to limit the scope of coverage. Some insurance companies are denying claims, while others are carefully reviewing invoices for services related to data breaches. The cost to respond to a breach can be expensive, and insurers will continue to dispute claims and charges. In some cases, this will lead to additional litigation after the data breach response is complete.

■ Risks of regulatory investigations

Certain regulators have explicit statutory jurisdiction over cybersecurity matters. Other regulatory agencies do not, but they attempt to regulate such matters under their existing, general jurisdiction. As public and congressional scrutiny of cybersecurity measures increases, regulators will be more aggressive in asserting jurisdiction over their regulated entities' cybersecurity matters.

Federal regulators

1. *Industry regulators.* Traditional regulators have already applied or are planning to apply standards related to cybersecurity matters to their regulated entities. The Federal Financial Institutions Examination Council (FFIEC), the Federal Trade Commission (FTC), the Federal Communications Commission (FCC), the Department of Health and Human Services (HHS), and the Department of Homeland Security (DHS) are some of the regulators that have sought to regulate cybersecurity matters among their regulated entities. In addition, the National Institute of Standards and Technology (NIST) publishes documents that plaintiffs and regulators apply in analyzing a business's cybersecurity.

The FFIEC has been one of the leading regulators with regard to cybersecurity. The FFIEC has had an IT examination handbook for several years and is developing a tool to help financial institutions assess risk. In addition, the FFIEC requires financial institutions to require certain cybersecurity measures of the institutions' third-party service providers, effectively expanding the FFIEC's jurisdiction. The FFIEC has experience in investigating data breaches and imposing punishments based on insufficient security. Other regulators look to the FFIEC's examination handbook to inform their own regulations and investigations.

The FTC has been aggressive in filing administrative complaints against businesses that, in the eyes of the FTC, do not adequately protect sensitive consumer information. The FTC requires, among other things, "reasonable security" but provides no formal definition. This creates uncertainty for businesses seeking to understand their obligations. The FTC is involved in litigation in federal court concerning both its jurisdiction over data security and the standards it applies to businesses. Congress is considering a bill to formalize FTC jurisdiction over data security, which may further empower the FTC.

The FCC's Cybersecurity and Communications Reliability Division works to maintain the reliability of communications infrastructure in the face of various cyberthreats. In 2014 the FCC began imposing substantial fines on wireless carriers for insufficient secured sensitive consumer information.

HHS regulates cybersecurity matters under the Health Insurance Portability and Accountability Act of 1996 (HIPAA). Under this authority, HHS has imposed multimillion-dollar fines for insufficient data security.

DHS is involved in coordinating information sharing, securing critical infrastructure, and protecting federal cybersecurity assets. Currently, its programs for most private businesses are voluntary, but as Congress continues to focus on information sharing as a key component of reducing cybersecurity incidents, plaintiffs and courts will see these programs less as voluntary and more as the minimum standard of care.

NIST publishes an array of standards related to cybersecurity. Although none of these standards are binding on private entities (at least as of publication), they are often cited as what is reasonable security or as industry standard. In addition, plaintiffs and regulators look to NIST standards to inform allegations made in complaints and investigations.

2. *Securities and Exchange Commission.* The Securities and Exchange Commission (SEC), under pressure from Congress, has focused on public statements concerning data breaches. This focus encompasses both disclosures made after breaches and risk factors made in market reports. To date, the SEC has stated that the materiality analysis for data breaches is the same as for other risk factors, but there is little formal notice or adjudication on these statements, creating uncertainty and risk.

The SEC released guidance on cybersecurity risks in 2011. According to the SEC, registrants "should disclose the risk of cyber incidents if these issues are among the most significant factors that make an investment in the company speculative or risky."

The SEC, in conjunction with the Financial Industry Regulatory Authority, has engaged in enforcement actions against the entities they regulate for insufficient security for both customer data and market data.

State regulators

State regulators and attorneys general are also involved in cybersecurity matters; indeed, state attorneys general have been active in investigating data breaches. Each state has a different legal environment concerning data breaches. These attorneys general typically assert jurisdiction when the state's citizens are impacted, potentially exposing a business to an investigation even if the business does not typically operate in the state.

California has generally been the first state to impose data breach notification requirements. California passed its data breach notification law in 2003. In the time since, California has expanded what data are covered by the statute, including most recently usernames and passwords. Most other states have similar statutes.

Several other states, including Vermont, New York, and Michigan, have been particularly active in investigations. For certain larger breaches, some state attorneys general will work together in a coordinated investigation.

■ Conclusion

Cybersecurity matters create extensive risks for business. Foremost among these are risks related to disputes and regulatory investigations. These risks are not fully defined and likely never will be.

18

Legal considerations for cybersecurity insurance

K&L Gates LLP – Roberta D. Anderson, Partner

■ **Legal, regulatory, and additional concerns driving the purchase of cybersecurity insurance**

Legal liability, regulatory and other exposures surrounding cybersecurity and data privacy-related incidents

In addition to a seemingly endless stream of data breaches and other serious cybersecurity and data protection-related incidents, the past several years have seen significantly amplified legal liability surrounding cybersecurity and data privacy, a remarkable proliferation and expansion of cybersecurity and privacy-related laws, and increasingly heightened regulatory scrutiny.

In the wake of a data breach of any consequence, an organization is likely to face myriad different forms of legal and regulatory exposure, including class action litigation, shareholder derivative litigation, regulatory investigation, the costs associated with forensic investigation, notification to persons whose information may have been compromised, credit monitoring, call center services, public relations expenses, and other event management activities.

Beyond third-party liability and event management activities, organizations face substantial first-party losses associated with reputational injury and damage to brand in the wake of a serious breach event. They also face substantial business income loss if an event disrupts normal day-to-day business operations. Even if an organization's own system is not compromised, the organization may suffer significant losses if an incident affects a key vendor, cloud provider, or any key third party in the organization's product and service supply chain. Also at stake is the organization's digital assets, the value of which in some cases may eclipse the value of the organization's other property.

Cybersecurity insurance can play a vital role in an organization's overall strategy to address, mitigate, and maximize protection against the legal and other exposures flowing from data breaches and other serious cybersecurity, privacy, and data protection-related incidents.

In October 2011, in the wake of what it phrased "more frequent and severe cyber incidents," the Securities and Exchange Commission's (SEC's) Division of Corporation Finance issued disclosure guidance on cybersecurity, which advises that companies "should review, on an ongoing basis, the adequacy of their disclosure relating to cybersecurity risks and cyber incidents." The guidance advises that "appropriate disclosures may include," among other things, a "[d]escription of relevant insurance coverage" that the company has in place to address cybersecurity risk.

SEC comments in this area have regularly requested information regarding "whether [the company] ha[s] obtained relevant insurance coverage," as well as "the amount of [the company]'s cyber liability insurance." More recently, the SEC is asking not only whether the company has cybersecurity insurance and how much the company has but also how solid the company's coverage is:

"We note that your network-security insurance coverage is subject to a $10 million deductible. **Please tell us whether this coverage has any other significant limitations**. In addition, please describe for us the 'certain other coverage' that may reduce your exposure to Data Breach losses." (Emphasis added.)

"We note your disclosure that an unauthorized party was able to gain access to your computer network 'in a prior fiscal year.' So that an investor is better able to understand the materiality of this cybersecurity incident, please revise your disclosure to identify when the cyber incident occurred and describe any material costs or consequences to you as a result of the incident. **Please also further describe your cyber security insurance policy, including any material limits on coverage**." (Emphasis added.)

The SEC's guidance provides another compelling reason for publicly traded companies to carefully evaluate their current insurance program and consider purchasing cybersecurity insurance.

■ **The exclusion of cybersecurity and data privacy-related coverage from traditional insurance policies**

In response to decisions upholding coverage for cybersecurity and data privacy-related risks under traditional lines of insurance coverage, such as Commercial General Liability (CGL) coverage, the insurance industry has added various limitations and exclusions to traditional lines of coverage.

By way of example, Insurance Services Office (ISO), the insurance industry organization that develops standard insurance policy language, recently introduced a new series of cybersecurity and data breach exclusionary endorsements to its standard-form CGL policies, which became effective in May 2014. One of the endorsements, entitled "Exclusion - Access Or Disclosure Of Confidential Or Personal Information And Data-Related Liability - Limited Bodily Injury Exception Not Included," adds the following exclusion to the primary CGL policy:

This insurance does not apply to:

p. Access Or Disclosure Of Confidential Or Personal Information And Data-related Liability

Damages arising out of:

(1) Any access to or disclosure of any person's or organization's confidential or personal information, including patents, trade secrets, processing methods, customer lists, financial information, credit card information, health information or any other type of non public information; or

(2) The loss of, loss of use of, damage to, corruption of, inability to access, or inability to manipulate electronic data.

This exclusion applies even if damages are claimed for notification costs, credit monitoring expenses, forensic expenses, public relations expenses or any other loss, cost or expense incurred by you or others arising out of that which is described in Paragraph **(1)** or **(2)** above.

In connection with its filing of the endorsements, ISO stated that "when this endorsement is attached, it will result in a reduction of coverage. . . ."

Although there may be significant potential coverage for cybersecurity and data privacy-related incidents under an organization's traditional insurance policies, including its Directors' and Officers' Liability, Professional Liability, Fiduciary Liability, Crime, CGL, and Commercial Property policies, the new exclusions provide another reason for organizations to carefully consider specialty cybersecurity insurance products.

■ Types of cybersecurity insurance
Established coverages
There are a number of established third-party coverages (i.e., covering an organization's potential liability to third parties) and first-party coverages (e.g., covering the organization's own digital assets and income loss) as summarized in Table 1:

Emerging markets
In addition to the established coverages, three significant emerging markets provide coverage for the following:

- first-party losses involving physical asset damage after an electronic data-related incident
- third-party bodily injury and property damage that may result from an electronic data-related incident

TABLE 1	THIRD-PARTY COVERAGES
Type	**Description**
Privacy liability	Generally covers third-party liability, including defense and judgments or settlements, arising from data breaches, such as the Target breach, and other failures to protect protected and confidential information
Network security liability	Generally covers third-party liability, including defense and judgments or settlements, arising from security threats to networks, e.g., inability to access the insured's network because of a DDoS attack or transmission of malicious code to a third-party network
Regulatory liability	Generally covers amounts payable in connection with administrative or regulatory investigations and proceedings, including regulatory fines and penalties
PCI DSS liability	Generally covers amounts payable in connection with payment card industry demands for assessments, including contractual files and penalties, for alleged noncompliance with PCI Data Security Standards
Media liability	Generally covers third-party liability arising from infringement of copyright or other intellectual property rights and torts such as libel, slander, and defamation, which arise from media-related activities, e.g., broadcasting and advertising

Continued

TABLE	FIRST-PARTY COVERAGES
1 Type	Description
Crisis management	Generally covers "crisis management" expenses that typically follow in the wake of a breach incident, e.g., breach notification costs, credit monitoring, call center services, forensic investigations, and public relations efforts
Network interruption	Generally covers the organization's income loss associated with the interruption of the its business caused by the failure of computer systems/networks
Contingent network interruption	Generally covers the organization's income loss associated with the interruption of the its business caused by the failure of a third-party's computer systems/networks
Digital assets	Generally covers the organization's costs associated with replacing, recreating, restoring, and repairing damaged or destroyed computer programs, software, and electronic data
Extortion	Generally covers losses associated with cyber extortion, e.g., payment of an extortionist's demand to prevent a cybersecurity or data privacy-related incident

- reputational injury resulting from an incident that adversely affects the public perception of the insured organization or its brand.

Because privacy and electronic data-related exclusions continue to make their way into traditional property and liability insurance policies, and given that an organization's largest exposures may flow from reputational injury and brand tarnishment, these emerging coverages will be increasingly valuable.

■ **Strategic tips for purchasing cybersecurity insurance**

Cybersecurity insurance coverage can be extremely valuable, but choosing the right insurance product presents significant challenges. A diverse and growing array of products is in the marketplace, each with its own insurer-drafted terms and conditions that vary dramatically from insurer to insurer— and even between policies underwritten by the same insurer. In addition, the specific needs of different industry sectors, and different organizations within those sectors, are far-reaching and diverse.

Although placing coverage in this dynamic space presents a challenge, it also presents substantial opportunity. The cyber insurance market is extremely competitive, and cyber insurance policies are highly negotiable. This means that the terms of the insurers' off-the-shelf policy forms often can be significantly enhanced and customized to respond to the insured's particular circumstances. Frequently, very significant enhancements can be achieved for no increase in premium.

The following are five strategic tips for purchasing cyber insurance:

Adopt a team approach.
Successful placement of cybersecurity insurance coverage is a collaborative undertaking. Because of the nature of the product and the risks that it is intended to cover, successful placement requires the involvement and input not only of a capable risk management department and a knowledgeable insurance broker but also of in-house legal counsel and IT professionals, resources, and compliance personnel—and experienced insurance coverage counsel.

Understand risk profile and tolerance.

A successful insurance placement is facilitated by having a thorough understanding of an organization's risk profile, including the following:

- the scope and type of data maintained by the company and the location and manner in which, and by whom, such data are used, transmitted, handled, and stored
- the organization's network infrastructure
- the organization's cybersecurity, privacy, and data protection practices
- the organization's state of compliance with regulatory and industry standards
- the use of unencrypted mobile and other portable devices.

Many other factors may warrant consideration. When an organization has a grasp on its risk profile, potential exposure, and risk tolerance, it is well positioned to consider the type and amount of insurance coverage that it needs to adequately respond to identified risks and exposure.

Ask the right questions.

It is important to carefully evaluate the coverage under consideration. Table 2 shows ten of the important questions to ask when considering third-party and first-party cyber insurance.

The list is not exhaustive, and many other questions should be considered, including, for example, the extent to which the policy

TABLE 2

Third-Party	First-Party
Does the policy:	Does the policy:
cover the acts, errors, and omissions of third parties, e.g., vendors, for which the organization may be liable?	cover business income loss resulting from system failures in addition to failures of network security, e.g., any unplanned outages?
cover data in the care, custody, or control of third parties, e.g., cloud providers?	cover business income loss resulting from cloud failure?
cover new and expanding privacy laws and regulations?	cover contingent business income loss resulting from the failure of a third-party network?
cover personally identifiable information in any form, e.g., paper records?	cover data restoration costs?
cover confidential corporate data, e.g., third-party trade secrets?	cover business income loss after a network is up and running, but before business returns to full pre-incident operation?
cover wrongful or unauthorized collection of data?	contain hourly sublimits?
cover regulatory fines and penalties?	contain an hourly "waiting period"?
cover PCI DSS-related liability?	contain a sublimit applicable to the contingent business income coverage?
exclude the acts of "rogue" employees?	exclude loss for power failure or blackout/brownout?
exclude unencrypted devices?	exclude software programs that are unsupported or in a testing stage?

covers, or excludes, cyberterrorism. In all cases, the organization should request a retroactive date of at least 1 year prior to the policy inception, given that advanced attacks go undetected for a median of 229 days.

Beware the fine print.

Like any other insurance policy, cybersecurity insurance policies contain exclusions that may significantly curtail and undermine the purpose of the coverage. Some insurers, for example, may insert exclusions based on purported shortcomings in the insured's security measures. One case recently filed in the California federal court on May 7, 2015, highlights the problems with these types of exclusions. The case is *Columbia Casualty Company v. Cottage Health System*, in which Columbia Casualty, CNA's non-admitted insurer, seeks to avoid coverage under a cybersecurity insurance policy for the defense and settlement of a data breach class action lawsuit and related regulatory investigation. CNA relies principally upon an exclusion, entitled "Failure to Follow Minimum Required Practices," which purports to void coverage if the insured fails to "continuously implement" certain aspects of computer security. These types of broadly worded, open-ended exclusions can be acutely problematic and impracticable. If enforced literally, they may vaporize the coverage that the policy is intended to provide. The good news is that, although certain types of exclusions are unrealistic given the nature of the risk an insured is attempting to insure against, cybersecurity insurance policies are highly negotiable. It is possible to cripple inappropriate exclusions by appropriately curtailing them or to entirely eliminate them—and often this does not cost additional premium.

Pay attention to the application.

CNA in the *Columbia Casualty* case also seeks to deny coverage based upon alleged misrepresentations contained in the insured's insurance application relating to the risk controls. The important takeaway is that cybersecurity insurance applications can, and usually do, contain a myriad of questions concerning an organization's cybersecurity and data protection practices, seeking detailed information surrounding technical, complex subject matter. These questions are often answered by technical specialists who may not appreciate the nuances and idiosyncrasies of insurance coverage law. For these reasons, it is advisable to have insurance coverage counsel involved in the application process.

■ Tips for prevailing in cyber insurance coverage litigation

As CNA's recently filed coverage action in the *Columbia Casualty* case illustrates, cybersecurity insurance coverage disputes and litigation are coming. In the wake of a data breach or other privacy, cybersecurity, or data protection-related incident, organizations should anticipate that their insurer may deny coverage for a resulting claim against the policy.

Before a claim arises, organizations are encouraged to proactively negotiate and place the best possible coverage to decrease the likelihood of a coverage denial. In contrast to many types of commercial insurance policies, cybersecurity policies are extremely negotiable, and the insurer's off-the-shelf forms can usually be significantly negotiated and improved for no increase in premium. A well-drafted policy will reduce the likelihood that an insurer will be able to successfully avoid or limit insurance coverage in the event of a claim.

Even where a solid form is in place, however, and there is a solid claim for coverage under the policy language and applicable law, insurers can and do deny coverage.

When facing coverage litigation, organizations are advised to consider the following five strategies to prevail:

Tell a concise, compelling story.

In complex insurance coverage litigation, there are many moving parts and the issues are typically nuanced and complex. It is critical, however, that these nuanced, complex issues come across to a judge, jury, or arbitrator as simple and straightforward. Getting overly caught up in the weeds of policy interpretive and legal issues, particularly at the outset, risks losing the organization's critical audience and obfuscating a winningly concise, compelling story that is easy to understand, follow, and sympathize with. Boiled down to its essence, the story may be—and in this context often is—something as simple as the following:

"They promised to protect us from a cyber breach if we paid the insurance premium. We paid the premium. They broke their promise."

Place the story in the right context.

It is critical to place the story in the proper context because, unfortunately, many insurers in this space, whether by negligent deficit or deliberate design, are selling products that do not reflect the reality of e-commerce and its risks. Many off-the-shelf cybersecurity insurance policies, for example, limit the scope of coverage to only the insured's own acts and omissions, or only to incidents that affect the insured's network. Others contain broadly worded, open-ended exclusions such as the one at issue in the *Columbia Casualty* case, which, if enforced literally, would largely if not entirely vaporize the coverage ostensibly provided under the policy. These types of exclusions can be acutely problematic and impracticable. A myriad of other traps in cyber insurance policies—even more in those that are not carefully negotiated—may allow insurers to avoid coverage if the language were applied literally.

If the context is carefully framed and explained, however, judges, juries, and arbitrators should be inhospitable to the various "gotcha" traps in these policies. Taking the *Columbia Casualty* case as an example, the insurer, CNA, relies principally upon an exclusion, entitled "Failure to Follow Minimum Required Practices," which purports to void coverage if the insured fails to "continuously implement" certain aspects of computer security. In this context, however, comprising the extremely complex areas of cybersecurity and data protection, any insured can reasonably be expected to make mistakes in implementing security. This reality is, in fact, a principal reason for purchasing cyber liability coverage in the first place. In addition,

CNA represented in its marketing materials that the policy at issue in *Columbia Casualty* offers "*exceptional* first-and third-party cyber liability coverage to address a broad range of exposures," including "security breaches" and "*mistakes*":

> **Cyber liability and CNA NetProtect products**
>
> **CNA NetProtect** fills the gaps by offering exceptional first- and third-party cyber liability coverage to address a broad range of exposures. CNA NetProtect covers insureds for exposures that include security breaches, mistakes, and unauthorized employee acts, virus attacks, hacking, identity theft or private information loss, and infringing or disparaging content. CNA NetProtect coverage is worldwide, claims-made with limits up to $10 million.

It is important to use the discovery phase to fully flesh out the context of the insurance and the entire insurance transaction in addition to the meaning, intent, and interpretation of the policy terms and conditions, claims handling, and other matters depending on the particular circumstances of the coverage action.

Secure the best potential venue and choice of law.

One of the first and most critical decisions that an organization contemplating insurance coverage litigation must make is the appropriate forum for the litigation. This decision, which may be affected by whether the policy contains a forum selection clause, can be critical to potential success, among other reasons because the choice of forum may have a significant impact on the related choice-of-law issue, which in some cases is outcome-determinative. Insurance contracts are interpreted according to state law and the various state courts diverge widely on issues surrounding insurance coverage. Until the governing law applicable to an insurance contract is established, the policy can be, in a figurative and yet a very real sense, a blank piece of paper. The different interpretations given the same language from one state to the next can mean the difference between a coverage victory and a loss. It is therefore critical to undertake a careful choice of law analysis before initiating coverage litigation or selecting a venue or, where the insurer files first, before taking a choice of law position or deciding whether to challenge the insurer's selected forum.

Consider bringing in other carriers.

Often when there is a cybersecurity, privacy, or data protection-related issue, more than one insurance policy may be triggered. For example, a data breach like the Target breach may implicate an organization's cybersecurity insurance, CGL insurance, and Directors' and Officers' Liability insurance. To the extent that insurers on different lines of coverage have denied coverage, it may be beneficial for the organization to have those insurance carriers pointing the finger at each other throughout the insurance coverage proceedings. Again considering the context, a judge, arbitrator, or jury may find it offensive if an organization's CGL insurer is arguing, on the one hand, that a data breach is not covered because of a new exclusion, and the organization's cybersecurity insurer also is arguing that the breach is not covered under the cyber policy that was purchased to fill the "gap" in coverage created by the CGL policy exclusion. Relatedly, it is important to carefully consider the best strategy for pursuing coverage in a manner that will most effectively and efficiently maximize the potentially available coverage across the insured's entire insurance portfolio.

Retain counsel with cybersecurity insurance expertise.

Cybersecurity insurance is unlike any other line of coverage. There is no standardization. Each of the hundreds of products in the marketplace has its own insurer-drafted terms and conditions that vary dramatically from insurer to insurer—and even between policies underwritten by the same insurer. Obtaining coverage litigation counsel with substantial cybersecurity insurance expertise assists an organization on a number of fronts.

Importantly, it will give the organization unique access to compelling arguments based upon the context, history, evolution, and intent of this line of insurance product. Likewise, during the discovery phase, coverage counsel with unique knowledge and experience is positioned to ask for and obtain the particular information and evidence that can make or break the case—and will be able to do so in a relatively efficient, streamlined manner. In addition to creating solid ammunition for trial, effective discovery often leads to successful summary judgment rulings, thereby, at a minimum, streamlining the case in a cost-effective manner and limiting the issues that ultimately go to a jury. Likewise, counsel familiar with all of the many different insurer-drafted forms as they have evolved over time will give the organization key access to arguments based upon obvious and subtle differences between and among the many different policy wordings, including the particular language in the organization's policy. Often in coverage disputes, the multi-million dollar result comes down to a few words, the sequence of a few words, or even the position of a comma or other punctuation.

■ Conclusion

Cyber insurance coverage can be extremely valuable. Although placing coverage in this dynamic space presents challenges, it also presents substantial opportunities. Before a claim arises, organizations are encouraged to proactively negotiate and place the best possible coverage in order to decrease the likelihood of a coverage denial and litigation. In contrast to many other types of commercial insurance policies, cyber insurance policies are extremely negotiable, and the insurers' off-the-shelf forms typically can be significantly negotiated and improved for no increase in premium. A well-drafted policy will reduce the likelihood that an insurer will be able to successfully avoid or limit insurance coverage in the event of a claim. If a claim arises, following sound litigation strategies and refusing to take "no" for an answer will greatly increase the odds of securing valuable coverage.

19

Consumer protection: What is it?

Wilson Elser Moskowitz Edelman & Dicker LLP –
Melissa Ventrone, Partner and Lindsay Nickle, Partner

From a legal perspective, consumer protection is the application of rules and regulations to agencies, businesses, and organizations that require them to protect their customers from intentional and unintentional harm. Instead of *caveat emptor*, or buyer beware, the business entity has a mandate to protect its customers from the bad things that may befall them. In essence, the government has decided it is the business's responsibility to protect the least sophisticated consumers from themselves and what may happen to them.

The intersection of consumer protection and cybersecurity imposes a responsibility on businesses to protect their consumers' information. Unlike many areas of business, when an organization is the victim of a criminal attack, such as being hacked, the business is not considered a victim. Instead, the customers are considered the victims, and the business becomes a potential scapegoat—the target of inquiries, investigations, irate customers, reputational harm, and lost business, even though it was the business that suffered the criminal activity. Leading experts agree that no organization is immune from cyberattacks and that impenetrable data security is not possible. Nevertheless the media and the public continue to vilify and hold businesses responsible for failing to do what experts agree cannot be done.

Consumers demand that organizations safeguard their privacy and protect their information from data breaches; however, those same consumers are impatient and intolerant when security measures slow services or degrade usability. Some may terminate their relationships as a result, jumping ship to underfunded start-ups simply because consumers want what they want, and they want it now.

Adding to the difficulty of trying to balance data privacy and security with innovation and usability, organizations must concurrently maintain compliance with the myriad of state and federal data privacy and security laws, regulations, and guidelines. It would take several books to outline all the laws, regulations, and guidelines that affect consumer protection and cybersecurity. This chapter is designed to provide organizations with an understanding of those laws that have the most significant impact on privacy and security from a consumer protection perspective. There is no better place to start this discussion than by examining the recent activities of the Federal Trade Commission (FTC).

■ Cybersecurity, consumer protection, and the FTC

The FTC has deemed itself the enforcer of data privacy and security, the ultimate authority responsible for protecting consumer privacy and promoting data security in the private sector. In fact, the FTC commonly is considered the most active agency in the world in this area. Although the debate continues on whether the FTC has authority to police data privacy and security under section 5 of the FTC Act, organizations must be aware that the FTC and other regulators are monitoring practices and investigating and enforcing various laws under the guise of privacy and cybersecurity as a consumer protection issue.

The FTC regulates this space under section 5 of the FTC Act, which prohibits unfair or deceptive practices. The FTC may choose to investigate an organization if it believes that the organization has made materially misleading statements or omissions regarding the security provided for consumers' personal data. Further, according to a prepared statement by the FTC, "a company engages in unfair acts or practices if its data security practices cause or are likely to cause substantial injury to consumers that is neither reasonably avoidable by the consumer nor outweighed by countervailing benefits to consumers or to competition."

What does this mean? Well, according to an FTC report, this means that an organization's data security measures must be "reasonable and appropriate in light of the sensitivity and volume of consumer information it holds, the size and complexity of its data operations, and the cost of available tools to improve security and reduce vulnerabilities." In other words, the FTC can choose to investigate an organization simply because the FTC believes the organization is doing a poor job protecting consumers' information. Confused? You are not alone. Frankly, it appears that the FTC views poor cybersecurity practices a bit like courts view pornography—they know it when they see it.

Organizations looking for guidance from the FTC on appropriate security measures to protect consumer information may find themselves twisting in the wind like the last leaf on a tree. The FTC has not issued any detailed guidelines on what constitutes "reasonable security measures." To be fair, the FTC most likely struggles, as do many agencies, with establishing guidelines that are flexible enough to apply to a wide range of organizations in a variety of industries, yet structured enough to set a standard.

The FTC addressed this argument by instructing companies to review its previous consent decrees to identify "reasonable"—or more appropriately, what it considered to be unreasonable—security standards. Thus, in the midst of day-to-day operations, the FTC apparently expects an organization to carefully review a multitude of previous consent decrees to identify what it should be doing to reasonably protect consumers' information.

Organizations can also review a 15-page guide the FTC published in 2011, *Protecting Personal Information: A Guide for Business*. This guide informs organizations that a "sound business plan" is based on five principles:

■ Know what information you have and who has access to the information.

- Keep only that information needed to conduct business.
- Protect the information in your control.
- Properly dispose of information that is no longer needed.
- Prepare a plan for responding to security incidents.

Although this may have been an accurate list in 2011, any company that limits its cybersecurity program to these five principles will quickly discover its inadequacies. The FTC claims to recognize that there is no one-size-fits-all data security program, no program is perfect, and the mere fact that a breach occurs does not mean a company has violated the law.

Organizations must be aware of the FTC's heightened activity in this space. Right now, data privacy and protection of consumer information has the public's attention and is sometimes used as a political platform. Organizations must have an in-depth understanding of their cybersecurity posture, identify key vulnerabilities, and have a plan to either mitigate or remediate problems. Failure to place consumer protection and cybersecurity at the top of its priority list may land an organization in the FTC's crosshairs.

■ Cybersecurity, consumer protection, and the financial industry

As in other industries, cybersecurity and consumer protection in the financial sector are a patchwork of federal statutes, regulations, agencies, and enforcers. There are five federal banking regulatory agencies: the Office of the Comptroller of the Currency (OCC), the Board of Governors of the Federal Reserve System (FRB), the Federal Deposit Insurance Corporation (FDIC), the National Credit Union Administration (NCUA), and the Consumer Financial Protection Bureau (CFPB). A representative from each of them sits on the Federal Financial Institutions Examination Council (FFIEC), which is empowered to set out principles, standards, and forms for the uniformity of the supervision of financial institutions. A top FFIEC priority is the strengthening of cybersecurity in the marketplace, particularly as it pertains to the financial industry and those businesses and organizations that provide services in the financial sector. To that end, in the summer of 2014, the FFIEC completed a cybersecurity assessment involving more than 500 community financial institutions with the goal of determining how prepared those institutions were to mitigate cyber risks. The results are instructive as potential standards for the efforts an organization should take when its operations interact with or are tangential to the financial industry, or simply when a business collects, stores, or shares consumers' private information.

Cyber preparedness—which is the crux of consumer protection—encompasses the following:

- **Risk management and oversight:** Organizations should proactively train employees, allocate resources, and exercise control and supervision of cybersecurity operations. This includes involving upper-level management and boards.
- **Threat intelligence:** A business should undertake processes to educate, identify, and track cyber activities, vulnerabilities, and threats.
- **Cybersecurity controls:** Businesses should implement controls to prevent unauthorized access or exposure of information, to detect attacks or attempts to compromise systems, and to correct known and identified vulnerabilities. As the industry begins to more fully recognize the futility of keeping malicious attackers outside the network perimeter, companies also should implement controls that more quickly identify when malicious activity takes place inside the network.
- **External dependency management:** Organizations should have processes in place to manage vendors and third-party service providers and help ensure that connections to systems are secure, as well as processes to audit and evaluate the third-party's cybersecurity protections.

- **Cyber incident management and resilience:** Organizations should have procedures and processes to detect incidents, respond to those incidents, mitigate the impact of the incidents, document and report on the incidents, and provide for recovery and business continuity.

Within the financial sector, and regarding businesses that interact with the financial sector, these can reasonably be considered the components of due diligence. Efforts to protect consumers from the dangers of the exposure of personal information entrusted to a business involve guiding the organization through these steps on a scale appropriate to the size of the business and the scope of the information involved.

Adding to the complexity of compliance, there are multiple statutes and regulations that expressly require businesses to undertake security measures and notify consumers regarding privacy and information-sharing practices. The Gramm-Leach-Bliley Act (GLBA) and the corresponding regulations adopted to implement its requirements are aimed at protecting consumer interests. Similar to other regulations, businesses are required by the GLBA Safeguard Rule to use "reasonable security measures" to protect consumer information that they collect and store. In the financial services industry, this often includes highly sensitive information, such as Social Security numbers, financial account numbers, and income and credit histories.

Fortunately, the GLBA outlines, at least in some fashion, what constitutes "reasonable security measures." For instance, the GLBA Safeguard Rule requires the development and implementation of a written information security plan. In addition, the Rule requires companies to provide an annual written privacy notice to its customers that clearly, conspicuously, and accurately explains its information-sharing practices and provides customers the right to opt out of the organization's sharing practices. Both of these consumer protections are enforced by the FTC along with several other federal regulatory agencies and state insurance authorities.

Those entities governed by the SEC (Securities and Exchange Commission) and FINRA (Financial Industry Regulatory Authority) are expressly required to develop written identity theft prevention programs and, in the face of a breach, will likely face questions regarding cybersecurity policies and efforts. Further, the regulations imposing these requirements mandate that upper-level management signs off on any written program and participates in its administration. As the goal of these requirements is to protect customer information, an organization should be mindful to design programs that consider the nature of the organization's operations, as well as its size and complexity, so that the plan can be effectively implemented to achieve its desired goals.

The OCC recommends all banks and financial institutions implement incident response and business continuity plans and test those plans regularly. It also sets supervisory expectations about how financial institutions and third-party service providers in the financial sector can and should safeguard sensitive information. The OCC conducts on-site audits of financial institutions and certain third-party service providers to confirm compliance. The OCC also gets involved in the aftermath of cyberattacks to assess the corrective actions that financial institutions take in response. The OCC is vested with the authority to require the banks subject to their regulation and the banks' service providers to take steps to protect systems, prevent loss or theft of sensitive information, and mitigate identity theft.

In 2007, under the terms of the Fair and Accurate Credit Transactions Act, the OCC, FRB, FDIC, NCUA, and FTC issued regulations requiring creditors and financial institutions to develop and implement formal written programs aimed at identifying and preventing identity theft (the Red Flags Rule). Large banks have resident OCC investigators trained to assess cybersecurity issues. Smaller banks face on-site visits every 12 to 18 months. In 2013, the OCC updated its Third-Party Relationship Risk Management Guidance to set out expectations for risk assessment and management of third-party relationships. The senior management and boards of banks retain responsibility for cybersecurity even when third parties are involved. As a result, the OCC mandates comprehensive oversight and management of third-party relationships throughout the life of each relationship. This requires extensive due diligence prior to establishing a relationship, execution of written contracts that should include the right to audit the third party, ongoing monitoring, documentation, and reporting regarding risk management processes, and independent review of processes. Further, the OCC requires that third-party contracts stipulate that the OCC has the authority to examine and regulate the services provided to the bank by the third party.

The financial industry is highly regulated, and its consumer protection and cybersecurity aspects are no exception. Identity theft, at its heart, is a consumer protection issue. Enforceable security guidelines set out by regulators and aimed at the protection of consumer information trickle down to service providers, as the financial institutions are affirmatively charged with managing risks associated with vendors and service providers. The recommendations and requirements of the financial regulators make clear that extensive due diligence, monitoring, planning, and management are required in the quest to take reasonable security measures.

■ Health care, cybersecurity, and consumer protection

Any discussion of consumer protection and cybersecurity must include a discussion of the health care industry. The Health Insurance Portability and Accountability Act of 1996 (HIPAA) governs protected health information (PHI) maintained by various organizations that fall under the jurisdiction of HIPAA (covered entities) and other organizations that may receive health information from covered entities while performing various services. HIPAA is enforced primarily by the U.S. Department of Health and Human Services Office of Civil Rights (OCR). State attorneys general also have the authority to enforce HIPAA.

OCR's authority to enforce HIPAA encompasses covered entities regardless of size and their "business associates," a term that includes first-tier vendors that contract directly with covered entities and all downstream entities that receive PHI in the course of their business. Perhaps the most helpful aspect of HIPAA is that it specifies privacy requirements that covered entities must follow, as well as identifies security elements for covered entities to consider.

The HIPAA Privacy Rule outlines standards for the use and disclosure of all forms of PHI and categorizes PHI into three major "usage" categories: treatment, payment, and health care operations and sets up rules associated with each use. Uses that fall outside of these categories or that do not qualify as any of the exceptions described in the rule require an authorization from the affected individual. Meanwhile, the HIPAA Security Rule establishes standards for preserving the confidentiality, integrity, and availability of electronic PHI. Specifically, the Security Rule requires covered entities to have appropriate administrative, physical, and technical safeguards in place to protect PHI and contains detailed security requirements for protecting PHI. For instance, covered entities must conduct an assessment of the risks to and vulnerabilities of the protected health information. These guidelines provide organizations with concrete examples of steps needed to protect PHI and hence the consumer information in their systems. However, organizations should be aware that compliance with HIPAA is a *minimum* standard. As technology continues to change and develop, circumstances may require organizations to exceed the minimum HIPAA compliance requirements to effectively protect consumer information.

This is an important point, because in addition to OCR, the FTC considers itself empowered to regulate organizations that are covered by HIPAA. According to the FTC, HIPAA does not preempt the FTC's authority to also regulate covered entities. Furthermore, in 2010 the FTC issued the Health Breach Notification Rule, which mandates that entities not covered by HIPAA that experience a breach of a "personal health record" provide notification to the affected consumer.

Covered entities and their business associates must do more than merely "check the box" on cybersecurity compliance. If an organization faces an OCR investigation, it will be required to provide information related to its entire data privacy and security program, not just information related to the "incident" that triggered the investigation. Often, organizations are required to provide evidence of policies and procedures going back several years.

As part of its efforts to enforce compliance with HIPAA, OCR conducted security audits of covered entities in 2011 and 2012, commonly referred to as Phase 1. Although Phase 2 was delayed until OCR implements a web portal that enables covered entities to submit information, in May 2015 OCR began sending the first surveys of Phase 2 audits, so covered entities and their business associates should be prepared for this next phase. Similar to other agencies, OCR intends to audit the cybersecurity practices of the organizations that fall under its jurisdiction. OCR previously announced that it would conduct a pre-audit survey of 800 covered entities and 400 business associates, and from that pool select 350 covered entities and 50 business associates for a full audit.

The audits will take place over three years and will focus on:

- Risk analysis and risk management (the Security Rule)
- Notice of privacy practices and access rights (the Privacy Rule)

- Content and timeliness of breach notification (the Breach Notification Rule).

Phase 2 audits will likely not be as comprehensive as the audits in Phase 1 and will focus on key high-risk areas OCR learned of in its Phase 1 audits.

Health care information is commonly considered the most sensitive and personal information a consumer has, and it therefore deserves increased security controls. This is perhaps recognized by the authority of the state attorneys general to enforce HIPAA, a provision not found in all federal statutes. Numerous states have passed laws specifically intended to protect personal health information, regardless of whether the organization holding such information is considered a "covered entity" under HIPAA. As health care breaches continue to increase in number, organizations should expect greater regulatory scrutiny and activity related to their efforts to protect consumer health information.

■ State laws and regulations

In addition to the federal landscape, businesses should be aware that state laws and regulations affect consumer protection obligations. Various states have laws that affect specific industries and general consumer protection laws that may be implicated in business practices. This is a growing concern with the increase in e-commerce. Businesses that in the past would have limited their footprint to the jurisdiction of a single state now are more likely to encounter customers across state lines. Because the applicability of state laws affecting consumers and because cybersecurity is often triggered by the residence of the consumer, even small businesses can find that they face unexpected multijurisdictional questions.

■ Recommendations and conclusion

Given the wide range of laws, regulations, and guidelines—only a few of which could be covered here—how do organizations begin to navigate these treacherous waters?

Organizations must build privacy and security into their systems, processes, and services from the ground up and from the top down. Education and training for all employees should start on day one and be continuous. The time and effort required to assess cyber risk and understand data is minimal compared with the potential implications of failing to do so. Technology is constantly evolving, which means cybersecurity does as well, and an organization's efforts to protect consumer information must similarly adapt. It is better to have considered a tool and rejected it because it substantially degrades the service offered than to ignore the vulnerability entirely. Organizations must face cybersecurity risks as an enterprise and leverage industry experts to guide them through this quagmire of laws, regulations, and threats.

20

Protecting trade secrets in the age of cyberespionage

Fish & Richardson P.C. – Gus P. Coldebella, Principal

The cybertheft of intellectual property (IP) from U.S. companies has, in the words of former NSA director and Cyber Command chief General Keith Alexander, resulted in the "greatest transfer of wealth in human history." And the data bear that out: by some estimates, the value of IP stolen from U.S. businesses over the Internet alone is $300 billion per year—a whopping 6% of our $5 trillion total intellectual property assets. For certain nations, cyber espionage is a central component of their growth strategies: for example, the Report of the Commission on the Theft of U.S. Intellectual Property (the IP Commission Report) found that "national industrial policy goals in China encourage IP theft, and an extraordinary number of Chinese in business and government entities are engaged in this practice." Cyber espionage of IP assets allows companies and countries to circumvent the expense and hard work of basic research and product development—which could take years or even decades—and instead quickly pursue their economic agendas based on stolen IP, all to the detriment of U.S. businesses, jobs, and economic growth.

On May 1, 2014, a federal grand jury brought criminal charges of hacking, economic espionage, and trade secrets theft against five officers of China's military. The hackers are alleged to have penetrated the networks of important American companies to acquire proprietary and confidential technical and design specifications, manufacturing metrics, attorney-client discussions about upcoming trade litigation, economic strategies, and other forms of sensitive, nonpublic information. What was the object of this indictment? Certainly not to get a conviction: the likelihood of China extraditing the defendants to the U.S. is negligible. Instead, the U.S. used the indictment to transmit two strong signals. First, it sent a message to China: that we are aware of this aberrant behavior—in which a nation-state aims its espionage apparatus not at another country, but at another country's *companies*—and that the

U.S. will expose this misconduct to the world. Second, the indictment sent a message to U.S. companies that, although past breaches and legal and reputational risk may have convinced boards and management to shore up defenses against cyberattacks involving 'personally identifiable information,' or PII, the most sophisticated attackers are interested in other, more mission-critical data on companies' networks—intellectual property. The loss of trade secrets could cause more harm to a company's reputation, value, and future prospects than a PII breach ever could. The U.S. government is signaling that companies should focus on taking immediate, reasonable steps to defend their intellectual property assets.

In a world where countries persistently attack companies and compromise of a company's networks seems inevitable, management may be tempted to throw up their hands and concede defeat. There are, however, important legal and practical reasons to fight. In this chapter, we explore reasonable steps companies can take to prevent the cybertheft of their IP assets, to mitigate the harm of such thefts if they occur, and to challenge competitors that use stolen IP assets to unfairly gain an advantage in the marketplace.

■ Conducting a trade secrets risk analysis

So what types of IP are cyber spies after? Intellectual property has four broad categories: patents, trademarks, copyrights, and trade secrets. A trade secret—according to the Uniform Trade Secrets Act, or UTSA, adopted in some form by 48 states and the District of Columbia—is information that gains its actual or potential economic value from being not generally known and reasonably protected from disclosure. Of the four IP types, only trade secrets maintain their value, and their legal protection as trade secrets, through non-disclosure. If a trade secret is not disclosed, the economic benefit it provides and the legal protection it enjoys can theoretically last forever. If it is disclosed, those advantages can be destroyed. Trade secrets stand apart from other IP, which gains and maintains its legal protection through disclosure: the filing of a patent, the registration of a trademark, and the creation/publication of copyrighted material. Cyberthieves generally set their sights on a company's trade secrets—the one type of IP that is not readily available for the world to see.

Some companies keep their trade secrets offline. Legend has it that one of the most storied trade secrets, the formula for Coca-Cola, is on a handwritten piece of paper in a safe in Coke's Atlanta headquarters. But air-gapped trade secrets are rare in the Internet age. Given this, it is crucial for a company to identify and locate the trade secrets on its networks, and those that are being deposited there in the ordinary course of business. Every company has such mission-critical secrets: design specifications, chemical formulas, computer code, financial algorithms, customer lists, and business plans, to name a few. Finding them is a key, and sometimes overlooked, part of a top-to-bottom network vulnerability analysis. Unless a company knows what trade secrets it has and where they are located, it cannot begin to secure them.

Once a company catalogs its online trade secrets, it should ask several high-level strategic questions: How are they currently safeguarded? Who may access them? What systems are in place to alert the company that the trade secrets have been exfiltrated or altered? These questions and the protective measures developed in response are not only important to thwart cyber attackers—but also help to prevent all types of attempted trade secret theft, whether conducted via the Internet or the old-fashioned way. They also help to best position the company if it brings litigation seeking damages, injunctive relief, or other recompense for the theft. Although the *cyber*theft of trade secrets has not yet yielded many judicial decisions, law books are rife with cases of companies seeking damages resulting from current or former employees spiriting off trade secrets to their next employer or to a competitor. One of the central questions in any such litigation is: did the company make reasonable efforts under the circumstances to protect the secrecy of its confidential information? The reasonable measures identified in these decisions—such as training employees on trade secret protection, requiring employee confidentiality agreements prior to granting access, and revoking access upon termination from the company—apply with equal force in the cyber context, and companies should employ them. Below, we discuss additional cyber-specific protective measures that companies can consider taking.

■ Planning for the worst

Certain adversaries—especially nation-states and state-sponsored groups targeting U.S. trade secrets—are highly skilled, technologically savvy, and persistent. They are not trolling for just any IP, and they will not be put off by even best-in-class technical defenses and move onto the next target when their mission is to steal *your* company's secrets. Even with reasonable defenses in place, companies should assume that an attack will eventually be successful, and that a company's IP and trade secrets may be compromised as a result. One way companies can protect themselves is to consider ways, such as the following suggestions, to reduce the likelihood that even a successful intrusion leads to IP theft.

Access controls and segmentation

Companies should implement access controls on crown jewel data. Although almost every employee requires access to certain parts of the company's network, not all of them need access to files containing trade secrets. Not even all employees that require access to *some* trade secrets need access to *all*. A smart access control system makes it clear that secrets actually are treated as secrets—i.e., only those with a need to know (as opposed to everyone with a network password) are given access to the data.

Another related layer of protection is 'trade secret segmentation,' which, according to John Villasenor in his article *Corporate Cybersecurity Realism* (Aug. 28, 2014), is distributing information "so that no single cybersecurity breach exposes enough of a trade secret to allow the attacker to obtain the full set of information needed to replicate a targeted invention, product, or service." A company can achieve segmentation in two ways detailed by Villasenor: first, by dividing a trade secret into modules, distributing the modules across multiple networks, and ensuring that there is no easy path from one network to the next; and second, once the trade secrets are broken up into modules, by allowing employees access only to the modules that are relevant to them. Some modules can be separated physically and allow nearly no user access. For example, 'negative information'—valuable secrets about what *does not* work and is often the result of meticulous collection of data through extensive, costly research—is not frequently accessed in a company's day-to-day operations and therefore can be segmented and stored in an extremely limited set of locations. Implementing robust access control alongside segmentation makes it more difficult for an adversary to steal a company's crown jewel trade secrets in a single attack, and to 'spearphish' its way into accessing some or all of a company's crown jewel data under the guise of an authorized user.

Monitor data flow, not just authorization

Instead of monitoring only for unauthorized access, companies should flag and investigate instances and activity of high-volume or suspicious data transfers, whether or not the transferor is 'authorized.' Systems that look only for suspicious behavior by unauthorized users can blind the company to critical and common cyberattacks. History shows that trade secret theft frequently is carried out by authorized users—think about a disgruntled employee downloading the master customer list, or the trading algorithm, right before he or she quits to work for a competitor. In another common scenario, when hackers obtain privileged user credentials to infiltrate a company's network, activity that appears attributable to 'Mike in Accounting' may actually be malicious. Systems should be designed to monitor the flow of key data, whether or not it is being accomplished by someone with apparent trust.

Mark and tag secrets

Even in the bygone days of trade secrets on paper, companies knew to clearly mark their secrets with a legend. This accomplished two things: employees would know to handle those secrets consistent with the company's trade secrets policies, and if they were stolen, they could be identified as the company's property. Just like cartographers of old intentionally included fake shortcuts, streets, and even towns to immediately recognize misappropriated copies of their maps, tagging digital assets provides a way to definitively prove that the IP was originally yours. Today, with an array of technological means at hand, companies can do more, including tagging digital IP with code that could, say, render stolen files inoperable. The IP Commission Report correctly recommended that "protection...be undertaken for the files themselves and not just the network, which always has the ability to be compromised." It suggested that:

> Companies should consider marking their electronic files through techniques such as "meta-tagging," "beaconing," and "watermarking." Such tools allow for awareness of whether protected information has left an authorized network and can potentially identify the location of files in the event that they are stolen. Additionally, software can be written that will allow only authorized users to open files containing valuable information. If an unauthorized person accesses the information, a range of actions might then occur. For example, the file could be rendered inaccessible and the unauthorized user's computer could be locked down, with instructions on how to contact law enforcement to get the password needed to unlock the account. (IP Commission Report at 81.)

Collect forensic leads as part of incident response

Of course, executives must make sure that the company has created a robust incident response plan and has practiced and exercised it. Under such a plan, the first call should be to experienced outside counsel, who can hire the forensics and crisis PR teams to investigate and respond to what happened, and who give the results of the investigation the greatest chance of being considered privileged, which is important as the legal and regulatory consequences of breaches continue to grow. It is also important—especially with potential trade secret theft—to preserve all information surrounding the incident in a forensically sound way. For example, collecting and analyzing log information may allow a company to determine what data were lifted and where they were sent, which could be critical in investigations by law enforcement and in post-breach litigation.

■ Taking on the IP thieves and their beneficiaries

Adversaries want to steal your trade secrets for a simple reason: to use, sell, and profit from them. Every IP theft contains the seeds of unfair competition based upon the stolen secrets. Assume the worst has happened, and you begin to see the company's hard work or research emerge in the marketplace, embedded in a competitor's product or across the negotiating table. What options do you have? We discuss five here:

> *Misappropriation of trade secrets.* The victim of trade secret theft may bring an action under state law to enjoin the beneficiary of the theft and recover damages. (There currently is no federal private right of action for misappropriation of trade secrets.) As already discussed, most states have adopted a version of the Uniform Trade Secrets Act, or UTSA. UTSA prevents using a trade secret of another without consent if the defendant employed improper means to appropriate the secret, or "knew or had reason to know that his knowledge of the trade secret was derived from or through a person who had utilized improper means to acquire it." UTSA §§ 1(2)(ii)(A); 1(2)(i). UTSA,

therefore, allows an action against the hacker and the company seeking to benefit from the stolen trade secrets, if the plaintiff can show that the competitor had reason to believe that the data it was using were stolen from someone else's network. The remedies available under UTSA are powerful and encompass damages and injunctive relief. UTSA authorizes a court to award damages for actual loss and unjust enrichment, including multiple damages if the misappropriation was "willful and malicious." UTSA §§ 3(a); 3(b). A court also may enjoin actual or threatened misappropriation or may condition the competitor's future use of the trade secret on payment of a reasonable royalty. UTSA §§ 2(a); 2(b).

Section 337 of the Tariff Act of 1930. To stymie competitors that import their products into the U.S., a potent option is to initiate a process at the International Trade Commission (ITC) under Section 337 of the Tariff Act of 1930. A company may petition the ITC to investigate whether imported goods are the result of "unfair methods of competition"—which includes incorporating stolen trade secrets—so long as the unfairness has the potential to injure or destroy a domestic industry. 19 U.S.C. § 337. Because § 337 investigations are brought against goods, not parties, there is no need to prove that the specific company profiting from the stolen data was actually behind the cyberattack, only that the product was made or developed using misappropriated trade secrets. Even though the ITC cannot award damages under § 337, the remedy it can issue is potent against any company seeking to import misappropriated products in the U.S.: it can issue an order, enforceable by Customs and Border Protection, preventing goods from entering the country and enjoining sale of such products already here.

Although the IP Commission has criticized the § 337 process as too lengthy and bureaucratic, that was in the context of arguing for a quicker method for U.S. companies to seek exclusion. Our experience is that § 337 actions tend to be much quicker than currently available alternatives, including state and federal court litigation. The ITC process offers U.S. companies a powerful weapon against importation of goods containing stolen trade secrets.

Computer Fraud and Abuse Act (CFAA). Under certain circumstances, the CFAA provides a private right of action for companies to bring suit against a party who knowingly and intentionally accesses a protected computer without authorization, obtains information, and causes harm. 18 U.S.C. § 1030(g). The victim may be able to seek damages from not only the individual who accessed the computer and stole the information but also the company profiting from the stolen trade secret so long as the victim can plead and prove that the competitor "conspire[d] to commit" such an offense (18 U.S.C. § 1030[b]).

Call the feds. A company may refer the theft to federal criminal authorities, which can bring charges under 18 U.S.C. §§ 1831-32 for theft of trade secrets and economic espionage. The economic espionage and trade secret theft statutes reach not only parties who steal the trade secret but also anyone who "receives, buys, or possesses a trade secret, knowing the same to have been stolen or appropriated, obtained, or converted without authorization." 18 U.S.C. §§ 1831(a)(3); 1832(a)(3). In addition to imposing hefty fines ($5 million for organizations, unless the theft was intended to benefit a foreign government, in which case it is $10 million), the law also allows judges to force the criminals to forfeit "any property, or proceeds derived from the stolen or misappropriated trade secrets, as well as any property used or intended to be used to help steal trade secrets." 18 U.S.C. §§ 1834, 2323(b).

Of course, there are always pros and cons to be weighed before bringing civil litigation or involving federal law enforcement authorities. For example, law enforcement has a greater array of tools to compel production of evidence quickly, unlike in a civil suit, although a parallel criminal action may affect the company's ability to seek civil discovery if the defendants seek a stay or exercise their Fifth Amendment right not to testify. There are also practical and business considerations that may argue for or against such a suit, including its potential to affect existing or future commercial relationships and continued access to foreign markets.

Future action: Report cyberspies and their beneficiaries under Executive Order 13694. In response to high-profile cyberattacks, the President and the federal government recognized that cyber espionage is a serious threat to the nation's economy and national security but acknowledged that it is not always possible to take criminal or civil action against perpetrators because they are often outside the jurisdictional reach of U.S. courts. For that reason, the U.S. has devised another method for reaching these malefactors, punishing them for their actions, and deterring future attacks. On April 1, 2015, the President signed Executive Order 13694, authorizing the Office of Foreign Assets Control, or OFAC, within the Treasury Department, to (i) identify foreign hackers, the parties who aid them, and the parties who benefit from their activity by using their stolen information to profit and (ii) respond by freezing their

U.S. assets and imposing sanctions. OFAC will add foreign individuals identified as being responsible for, contributing to, complicit in, or profiting from significant malicious cyber-enabled activities to its list of Specially Designated Nationals (SDNs). To earn a spot on the SDN list, the associated attack has to be "reasonably likely to result in, or have materially contributed to, a significant threat to the national security, foreign policy, or economic health or financial stability of the United States." Although OFAC cannot assist a company with recovering lost information or barring products from entering the market, reporting the perpetrators of particularly serious cyberattacks to OFAC can serve as a powerful deterrent. It is important to note that E.O. 13694 is, at the writing of this chapter, so new that OFAC has yet to promulgate final regulations governing the SDN-designation process, so companies should consult with counsel to understand their options once final rules are in place.

■ Conclusion

Trade secrets are high on the list of assets that cyber spies are interested in stealing. Careful planning will help your company do its best to prevent the theft of these valuable assets and to thwart a competitor's attempt to profit from its crimes if an attack is successful. If the worst-case scenario materializes and you discover that your company's IP has been stolen, take immediate steps to engage experienced outside counsel to assess your best options to investigate the breach, recover damages, enjoin unfair competition, and seek justice.

21

Cybersecurity due diligence in M&A transactions: Tips for conducting a robust and meaningful process

Latham & Watkins LLP – Jennifer Archie, Partner

To begin with a tautology, when you buy a company, you buy their data—and the attendant risks to that data. Cybersecurity risks are not limited to consumer-facing businesses, whose recent losses of cardholder or patient data grab news headlines. Indeed, few businesses today have assets and liabilities that are not in some sense data driven. For most business combinations—whether M&A, joint venture, or leveraged buyout—cybersecurity should be a risk category in its own right. Buyers should review not just historic breaches but also cybersecurity risk management. Even though these risks are hard to quantify, the analysis will inform deal terms, deal value, and post-deal indemnity claims.

■ First step: Get an early read on cyber readiness at the engagement stage

Buyers should begin all cybersecurity risk assessments early in the engagement process, with the goal of clearly articulating as early as possible the target company's most important information assets, systems, and business processes. Every target business should be able to readily identify which information technology (IT) systems and data sets are most valuable to the business and explain at a high level how the company protects and exploits them. Even at the earliest stages, the seller should be prepared to identify and discuss the following at a high level:

- What types of information or computer systems and operations are most important to your business? What sensitive types of data do you handle or hold relating to natural persons (which data elements in particular)?
- Where is sensitive information stored?
- How is it protected in transit, at rest, and in motion?
- What are the most concerning threats to information, networks, or systems?

- Have there been prior incidents?
- What is the cybersecurity budget?
- What are your recovery plans if critical information or systems become unavailable?

If the front line deal-facing personnel respond, "I don't know, I'd have to ask," this is a telling and interesting sign that the target company's security management program is likely not well integrated into the senior leadership ranks. Sellers thus should be prepared in early discussions to showcase a sophisticated understanding of data security risks and how those risks may materially affect the company's operations, reputation, and legal risks (or not). A buyer's key diligence objective should be to probe and test whether the target company has implemented a mature risk management organization to evaluate the accuracy of management assurances about lack of historical breaches, payment card industry (PCI) compliance, protections against competitor or insider theft, and business continuity. Too often in hindsight, a target's statements made in diligence turn out to have been good faith impressions, or even merely aspirational or reflective of paper policy, but not operational reality.

Tailor diligence to what types of information are handled and how important is information security to the bottom line

Beyond these general questions, the buyer should directly probe whether the target management has a sophisticated understanding of potential cyber-related liabilities and the regulatory environment. Unlike environmental or traditional fire or natural disaster scenarios, cyberattack-related liabilities are multi-faceted and unique. In some industries—such as energy, transportation, financial institutions, health care, defense contracting, education, and telecommunications—government oversight can be active and intrusive, and the target's subject matter expertise will likely reside within the legal, compliance, and/or IT functions. In other industries, however, exposure to costly

government investigations from the Federal Trade Commission (FTC) or other agencies may be poorly understood. Federal investigations tarnish brands, especially if enforcement results. Investigations are expensive and distracting, and may lead to a sweeping 10- or 20-year permanent injunction dictating how future information security will be managed and monitored. Compliance with such a decree is expensive and limits a company's independence and flexibility in significant ways. After a breach, management is often surprised to learn how persistent and aggressive the FTC or state attorneys general can be, even if the company sees itself as a victim of harm, not a perpetrator of consumer injury. If the target's legal or business representatives are not knowledgeable about the regulatory and enforcement environments, buyers should not place much weight on a seller's lulling statements or assurances that there have been no incidents or that risk of a cyber event is low.

Check for integrated cyber risk awareness and mitigation and a comprehensive security management program

Another sign of a mature security program is a management team with cross-functional awareness on these points at the CEO and board levels, as reflected in board minutes or other documentation. A security program will not be effective if it is a silo inside the IT or information security functions. All substantial stakeholder departments should be involved in cybersecurity risk management, including business unit leaders, legal, internal audit and compliance, finance, human resources, IT, and risk management.

Diligence questionnaires should ask the target company to generally summarize the administrative, technical, and physical information security controls currently in place to safeguard the most critical business data sets. Such controls include technical measures (such as boundary and malware defense, data encryption, intrusion detection systems, anomalous event monitoring, and access controls), administrative measures, and physical security. The company should have a current documented crisis management/ incident response plan in place, including pre-staging of legal and forensic experts and a public relations strategy, all approved by senior management. A seller should specifically inquire about and assess what financial resources are applied to data security, in the context of the target's overall approach to risk containment and specific to its industry. Also, sellers should ask the following to gather detailed information about how the company has organized the management of cybersecurity and risk:

- Is there a single designated person with overall responsibility? To whom does he or she report? (Risk Officer? CTO? CIO? CEO?)
- Describe board oversight. Have directors and senior managers participated in data security training/been involved in the development of data security protocols?
- Does the company have legal counsel regularly advising on data security compliance? Is counsel internal or external, and if external, who?
- How does the company educate and train employees and vendors about company policies, information security risks, and necessary measures to mitigate risk?
- How can employees or members of the public (such as independent security researchers) report potential vulnerabilities/ breaches, including irregular activity or transactions?
- What is the plan to recover should critical or other necessary systems become unavailable? What are the recovery point and recovery time objectives? How have these and other elements of the plan been correlated to business needs?

If the company has in the last year or two completed an internal or external audit or assessment to determine compliance with company security policies and/or external security standards, this should be requested, or at a minimum the target company should report whether all recommendations have been adopted, budgeted and scheduled, or already implemented.

For companies whose vendors hold company-sensitive data or access systems, the company should have implemented—prior to engaging in a business relationship—a formal vendor management program that specifically assesses risk and identifies potential security or data privacy concerns and appropriate remediation next steps. After a decision to engage, the company should mitigate data security risks through written agreements and supervision. These third parties should have data security insurance coverage and/or the agreements should require such a party to defend and indemnify the target company for legal liability arising from any release or disclosure of the information resulting from the negligence of the vendor or other third party. Third-party agreements involving data exchange or access also should articulate breach notification procedures, cooperation levels, information sharing, and expressly assign incident control and reporting responsibilities.

Cloud-based or other software-as-a-solution (SAAS) solutions as well as mobile devices present their own cybersecurity risks and should not be overlooked in diligence. Does the company permit employees to use cloud-based file-sharing services? Does it rely on SAAS solutions for critical or other business needs such as contact relationship management or HR? Email? How are the security and compliance risks presented being managed? Companies that issue or support mobile devices should have policies and procedures in place designed to protect sensitive information in those environments.

Use subject matter experts to assess cyber readiness and liabilities

Given the importance of the above questions, the buyer should pay careful attention to who asks these questions on behalf of the buyer or underwriters, in what settings, and with what time allowances. Put simply, deal teams ideally should embed subject matter experts on the business side, the technical side, and even the legal side early on—to do the following:

- Pose questions orally
- Follow up with document requests
- Assess the documentation
- Conduct on-site testing and analysis where appropriate
- Assess and advise on the maturity and suitability of the program to the underlying data risks
- Review and advise on deal terms or costs to remediate gaps in compliance or risk management.

Very importantly, the deal team also must be nimble and focused upon the specific industry, because cybersecurity risks are highly variable across industry sectors; threats, liabilities, and government expectations for adequate security are evolving constantly. For example, if hackers acquire and then re-sell large databases of cardholder data to identity thieves—as happened to Target and Home Depot—the types of expenses and liabilities a buyer could expect are well documented in SEC filings. Expenditures include the following:

- Costs to investigate, contain, and remediate damaged networks and payment systems and to upgrade security
- Liability to banks, card associations, or payment processors for fines, penalties, or fraudulent charges
- Card reissuance expenses
- Expense of outside legal, technical, and communications advisors.

■ For retail sector, diligence surrounding PCI compliance should seek more than a "yes" or "no" response

Buyers of companies who accept, process, store, or handle cardholder payment data streams of course will want to pay particular attention to compliance with current PCI standards. At Home Depot, for example, an attacker used a vendor's username and password to gain access to Home Depot's network. The attacker then acquired elevated rights that allowed it to navigate portions of the company's systems and to deploy unique, custom-built malware on self-checkout systems to access the payment card information of up to 56 million customers who shopped at U.S. and Canadian stores between April 2014 and September 2014. In fiscal 2014, alone, Home Depot recorded $63 million in pretax expenses related to the data breach, partially offset by $30 million of expected insurance proceeds for costs believed to be reimbursable and probable of recovery under insurance coverage, resulting in pretax net expenses of $33 million.

What this sort of financial and reputational exposure means for M&A diligence within the retail sector is that buyers should devote expert and highly substantive attention to how cardholder data are collected, stored, handled, and secured. Payment processing services are material to all retail businesses, and all payment processing agreements have PCI compliance as a material term. So just as the SEC always wants to know about where that relationship stands in its review of risk factors, buyers too want to pay special attention in this area. If PCI compliance is lacking, the seller should at least be able to disclose a specific remediation timeline and a budgeted plan that is hopefully supervised and accepted by the payment processor.

PCI compliance handled correctly is costly and involves constant adaptation and optimization to new threats and new standards. It is not an annual "check-a-box" process. Within the data security space—as was true for Home Depot, Target, and many others—good business practice assumes that a compromised merchant will have a recent, valid, self-certification or even third-party certification of PCI compliance. However, a buyer should not rely simply on the inclusion of such a report or certificate in a virtual data room. Many a breached retailer has held a current PCI certification. Accordingly, the buyer should always test the security of cardholder data independently, at a process level if necessary. The same security consultants who arrive post-breach to assess root cause and damage can examine card-related data security very meaningfully in the M&A setting, even with only a few days of on-site interviews and document collection. If PCI compliance concerns arise in diligence, deal terms can be arranged that mandate and appropriate funding for third-party independent assessments and implementation of recommendations. Moreover, many retailers now are migrating to new payment systems, and this is a unique technology risk because of the likelihood of delay, interruptions, and budgetary over-runs.

■ **Understand and assess awareness and mitigation of risks of trade secret theft, nation-state espionage, and denial of service attacks**

Beyond payment card security risks, theft of trade secrets by competitors and insiders, state-sponsored espionage that is exploited for economic advantage, and cyberattacks that disable or cripple corporate networks are less publicized but can be equally damaging to a target business. For example, the high-profile, studio-wide cyberattack at Sony Pictures in November 2014 at the hands of a group calling itself #GOP, aka the Guardians of Peace, starkly illustrates the potential to cripple a business. The attack, which the FBI attributed to North Korea, resulted in the theft of terabytes of company internal email and documents, release of unreleased movies to file-sharing networks, deletion of documents from Sony computers, threatening messages to the company and individual employees, theft and apparent exploitation of sensitive human resources data, and a near complete and prolonged disruption of the company's ability to transact business and communicate electronically over its networks and systems. In an interview with CBS News, Sony's outside cyber investigator, Kevin Mandia, disclosed that 3,000 computers and 800 servers were wiped, and 6,000 employees were "given a taste of living offline"—no

email and no way to process employee benefits or time cards (Source: http://www.cbsnews.com/news/north-korean-cyberattack-on-sony-60-minutes/). To add insult to injury, much of the exfiltrated material is now readily available (and free text searchable) on WikiLeaks.

The potential for outright theft of intellectual property by competitors should not be overlooked. In *DuPont v. Kolon* (*United States v. Kolon Industries, Inc. et al.*), for example, the manufacturer of Heracron, a competitor product to DuPont's Kevlar, misappropriated DuPont's confidential information by hiring former DuPont employees as consultants and pressuring them to reveal Kevlar-related trade secrets. DuPont sued the competitor, Kolon, in 2009, and in 2012 the Department of Justice brought criminal trade secret misappropriation charges against Kolon and five of its executives pursuant to 18 U.S.C. § 1832. In light of the parallel charges, Kolon settled, paying $360 million in damages—$85 million in fines and $275 million in restitution. (Source: Department of Justice Office of Public Affairs, http://www.justice.gov/opa/pr/top-executives-kolon-industries-indicted-stealing-dupont-s-kevlar-trade-secrets). To assess these sorts of risks, acquirers should ask:

■ Are there former employees who had access to critical intellectual property or other company confidential information who have recently left for competitors?
■ What agreements are in place to protect the proprietary information they have?

U.S.-based businesses, academic institutions, cleared defense contractors, and government agencies increasingly are targeted for economic espionage and theft of trade secrets by foreign competitors with state sponsorship and backing. In the last fiscal year alone, economic espionage and theft of trade secrets cost the American economy more than $19 billion. According to the FBI, between 2009 and 2013, the number of arrests related to economic espionage and theft of trade secrets—which the FBI's

Economic Espionage Unit oversees—at least doubled, indictments more than tripled, and convictions increased sixfold. These numbers grossly understate the frequency of such attacks or losses. Last year, the United States Department of Justice indicted five Chinese military hackers on charges including computer hacking, identity theft, economic espionage, and trade secret theft from 2006 to 2014. The alleged actions affected six U.S.-based nuclear power, metal, and solar product companies. The indictment, filed May 1, 2014, alleges that the defendants obtained unauthorized access to trade secrets and internal communications of the affected companies for the benefit of Chinese companies, including state-owned enterprises. Some defendants allegedly hacked directly—stealing sensitive, nonpublic, and deliberative emails belonging to senior decision makers, as well as technical specifications, financial information, network credentials, and strategic information in corporate documents and emails—while others offered support through infrastructure management. Charges were brought under 18 U.S.C. §§1028, 1030, 1831, and 1832. (Source: Department of Justice Office of Public Affairs, http://www.justice.gov/opa/pr/us-charges-five-chinese-military-hackers-cyber-espionage-against-us-corporations-and-labor).

Many companies choose not to publicly disclose or discuss these sorts of attacks or disruptions, which may go undiscovered for many months and often years. Even when attacks are discovered, breaches may not be reported to law enforcement or even to affected commercial partners. Questions about historical incidents during due diligence therefore should be open-ended but also very direct:

- Have you suffered thefts of confidential data (wherever stored)?
- Has your network suffered an intrusion?
- Did you retain outside experts to investigate?

- What is known about the attackers and the attack vector?
- What data do you suspect or know were taken?
- How long between the first known intrusion and discovery of the incident?
- Do you suspect or know whether the thief or intruder attempted or made fraudulent or competitive use of exfiltrated data?
- During the past three years, have you experienced an interruption or suspension of your computer system for any reason (not including downtime for planned maintenance) that exceeded four hours?

A buyer should assess a target's measures to prevent and detect insider threats, including whether basic protections are in place to identify and mitigate insider threats, such as the following:

- Pre-employment screening via dynamic interviews, background checks, and reference checking
- Workforce education on warning signs
- Internal network security measures such as website monitoring, blocking access to free (unauthorized) cloud-storage sites such as Dropbox, turning off USB drives
- Automated monitoring of Web, deep Web, or peer-to-peer network searching for leaked data.

Private and state actors have made use of denial of service attacks to disrupt the business of a company that meets with their disapproval (or as an extortion scheme). Material impact on ecommerce, on-line entertainment, email, and other critical systems are the result. An acquirer might reasonably ask:

- Has the target company evaluated its exposure to such attacks?
- What measures does it have in place to defend itself?
- How would it know if such an attack was occurring?
- Have any such attacks occurred?

Assessing cyber insurance

Finally, buyers should evaluate the extent to which cyber risks are mitigated by insurance coverage, including whether enhancements to the cyber program may be available post-closing. Most cyber insurance policies today cover the data breach and privacy crisis management expenses associated with complying with data breach notification laws. Those costs include the costs of expert legal, communications, and forensic advisors, benefits such as credit repair or monitoring to affected individuals, and even costs of responding to government investigations or paying fines. Cyber coverage is also widely available for extortion events, defacement of website, infringement, and network security events, even arising from theft of data on third-party systems or malicious acts by employees. Because of the volatility and variability of the cyber insurance market at this time, buyers should closely examine policies for what is covered, deductibles, coverage periods, and limits. Diligence experts should also evaluate post-closing opportunities to enhance the insurance program if significant unmitigated risks of third-party liabilities or direct expense from an attack have been identified.

Conclusion

If there was ever an era when minimizing or commoditizing assessment of cybersecurity risks in the M&A space was sensible, that time has surely passed. Expertise in assessing data-driven risks should be embedded on the front end of every transaction and tracked throughout the deal, so that deal terms, deal value, and post-closing opportunities to strengthen security can be considered against a fully developed factual picture of the target company's cyber readiness and exposure.

22

International inflection point—companies, governments, and rules of the road

Kaye Scholer LLP – Adam Golodner, Partner

In the attorney general's conference room at the United States Department of Justice is a mural on the ceiling—on one end a heavenly depiction of justice granted, and on the other a depressing tableau of justice denied. These images help remind us that principles matter, choices matter, and in many situations divergent outcomes are possible. We are at this kind of inflection point in global cyber. Technology, software, hardware, and physical and social networks are embedded everywhere today. Into the future the Internet of Things and the Industrial Internet will bring the next wave of global hyper connectedness and drive business innovation, new markets, efficiency, and consumer benefits globally. Every business today is a technology business, and every society increasingly a technology society. We all benefit from it. It is good. The world has changed, but it has also stayed the same.

In some sense, cyber issues are not new. They are the same issues countries and societies have been dealing with for centuries—theft, fraud, vandalism, espionage, and war. Over time, societies have created rules to deal with these domestically and globally. But cyber presents new facts. Activities and incidents happen at machine speed, and distance hardly matters. Masking who you are is easier. Some seemingly anonymous person can reach out and touch you instantaneously from anywhere. The kind of information we collect is quantitatively and qualitatively different than the past. We must appreciate and understand these facts and what they mean.

With a future of embedded everything and hyper connectivity, we have to create acceptable 'rules of the road' that ensure we get the promise of the future, not a world where governments or individuals turn that promise on its head and abuse the very same connectedness. Countries and companies have to define acceptable 'rules of the road' for behavior in cyberspace—what's okay and not okay for governments to do to each other, companies, and individuals in cyberspace. Analogies can and should be made to longstanding principles relating to theft, fraud, vandalism, espionage, and war—and how countries deal with each other on these issues. After all, technology is a tool; we have had tools in the past, and we have applied age-old principles to new tools throughout history. However, the pace of change is accelerating. That means we need to move fast to apply new facts to old principles now and help shape the future. Like the mural on the ceiling on the attorney general's conference room, different future outcomes are possible. What principles and rules will secure goodness into the global technology future? What are the roles of companies, boards of directors, and CEOs in shaping that future? We discuss these questions in this chapter.

There are three areas in which companies and their leaders can help: rules of the road, cyber laws globally, and security *and* privacy.

■ Rules of the road

Cyber is a top issue for the U.S., E.U. Member States, China, India, Russia, Brazil, Australia, and Japan, and the heads of state in each of these countries spend significant time on the issue. For the last three years the U.S. has said that cyber is the number one national security threat to the U.S.—not nuclear, biologic, or chemical, but cyberthreat. All these countries view cyber as a national security and economic security issue. In national security, cyber is both an offensive and a defensive issue. On the offensive side, cyber tools and techniques can be a means of espionage, war, or deterring a threat. On the defensive side, conversely, countries are concerned that companies in critical infrastructure sectors (financial, communications, defense, electric, energy, transportation, health care, chemical, public services) can have their operations affected, data compromised or destroyed, or public safety threatened—in effect, bringing important segments of the economy to a halt.

U.S. policy leaders also are highly concerned about other nation-states stealing core intellectual property, business and deal strategies, and next generation innovation from U.S. companies, with that very same stolen intellectual property being given by the governments that stole it to favored domestic champions for the purpose of competing against that very same victim of the theft. Companies share these concerns. No company wants to have its operations, brand, or competitive advantage undermined or destroyed. Despite these concerns, nation-state, non-nation-state, hacktivist, and criminal activity continues. In fact by all accounts it's increasing in all categories across the governmental and commercial sectors.

Although some policy makers have begun to talk about cyber 'norms,' there has not been sustained multi-lateral head-of-state to head-of-state work to set rules of the road. However, it has to begin. The issues are big enough and complex and significant enough that we have to set the right path now. We can build rules that the majority of the family of nations can agree to and then bring the outliers along. Most commentators are of the view that a formal treaty is premature, if it ever makes sense. This sounds right to me. However, the time is right to up-lever the conversation to the head of state level and convene the heads of state of some core countries (such as U.S., U.K., Germany, France, Sweden, Estonia, India, Brazil, Japan, Korea, Australia, Canada) to start to build out offensive, defensive, law enforcement, and commercial rules of acceptable behavior. Of course, other countries, such as China, could join in short order if it turns out they are in fast agreement, but the work of building out the core should move ahead without waiting for everyone to be on board. An additional benefit of doing this is that it reduces the impulse of countries to complain about the activities of other countries when the activity at issue is one that all countries find to be acceptable, and in the converse, gives weight to complaints about activities outside of the acceptable.

Why should companies care? Why should they be integral to these discussions? First, companies own the enterprise networks and databases in which cyber activity takes place—domestic companies and global companies. Companies own the software, hardware, the information, and the upstream and downstream relationships where this contest takes place. Think of the Internet—every little bit of it is owned by somebody, and the vast majority is owned by public companies globally. Although cyber is the fifth fighting domain (along with land, sea, air, and space), it is the only one owned essentially by private companies. Second, information technology and communications services and products are created and sold by the private sector. If a government acts on those services or products, it acts on services and products with a private sector brand. The same brand used by other companies. Third, the future of the global interoperable, open, secure, network is at stake. Will companies be able to continue to drive innovative business models, or will they be stifled by the rules and activities of governments, hacktivists, and criminals playing in their playing field?

Here are some 'rules of the road' that should be in play. What cyber activity is an act of war? What cyber activity is acceptable espionage? What is cyber vandalism, and what is the appropriate response? What activity by a nation-state is acceptable on a bank, stock exchange, energy, transportation, electric, or life sciences company? What if it's a non-nation-state activity? What action is acceptable to proactively stop a planned cyber activity? What principles should animate the decision to use a cyber tool of war on a target connected to the Internet? Is it OK to deliver cyber means through private networks or technologies? What is an acceptable response to another country's cyber or kinetic act? What are the principles for disclosing or stockpiling zero-day vulnerabilities or interdicting a supply chain? How can we make global assurance methodologies such as the Common Criteria for Information Technology Security Evaluation (Common Criteria) for products even more useful? Should there be requirements for governments to share cyberthreat information with other countries and companies to improve security? What tools in the toolbox are acceptable to curb behavior—prosecution, sanctions, trade, covert action? Is it OK for national security services to steal intellectual property of companies? Is it OK for intelligence services to give it to competitors? What collection of information of or about individual citizens of another country is acceptable or unacceptable? What is the standard? What collection on other governments and their leaders is acceptable?

Most of these questions have some grounding in existing principles and laws, but the cyber facts have to be understood and applied to start to enunciate these rules of the road. Although work has certainly begun on cyber 'norms,' the time is right for taking the work to the next level. Furthermore, because the playing field is made up of private networks and elements of technology services and products, the outcomes should by definition be of interest to companies, CEOs, and boards of directors. Good rules of the road should help build trust in networks and technology globally. So, companies should engage in helping set the global rules of the road today. It affects their future.

■ Cyber laws globally

Given that cyber runs the gamut from national security concerns to consumer protection, and countries around the world have different values and interpretation of what laws protect their country and citizens, it should come as no surprise that companies doing business globally will face a myriad of sometimes divergent laws on a range of cyber topics.

An in-depth review of these laws is beyond the scope of this chapter, but it is important to note the categories in which a company, CEO, general counsel, and perhaps even the board must understand that their activity may trigger a compliance issue or affect their ability to provide a product or service.

With regard to compliance and security, there is a saying that 'compliance does not equal security.' There is no doubt that driving to 'real security' is the goal, and one that will likely get you where you need to be for compliance as well.

Here is a list of categories of laws to be concerned about and a few specific-use cases:

- infrastructure security: voluntary public-private partnerships (U.S., U.K.), regulation of critical infrastructure (China, pending in E.U., pending in Germany), sector-specific regulation (India telecoms, U.S. chemical, Russia strategic industries)
- incident notification: data breach (U.S. in 47 states, E.U. telecoms, pending new E.U. Privacy Directive), SEC disclose material adverse events (U.S. SEC)
- tort, contract, product liability: in the absence of specific regulation, a company must use 'reasonable care' to secure their and third-party data, continue to provide service, build secure products, and protect IP (U.S., E.U., India and for contract, globally)
- board of directors corporate: the board must use its 'business judgment' to secure the assets of the company and provide reasonable security (U.S.)
- acquisition of information by nation-states: lawful intercept telecoms (most countries), requests from non-telecoms by judicial or administrative process (most countries), collection outside of home country (most countries)
- technology controls, national security reviews, and certifications: export control commercial technologies (U.S.), export control of military technologies ITAR (U.S.), certification of IT product (26 countries Common Criteria evaluation, China own requirements, Russia own requirements, Korea pending), import restriction on encryption (China, Russia), in-country use of encryption (China, Russia), national security reviews for M&A (U.S. CFIUS & FCC, China).
- privacy: economy-wide limits on collection and transfer of information about individuals (E.U.), sector specific (U.S. health care HIPAA, financial GLB),

data localization (Russia), U.S.-E.U. Safe Harbor (allowing for transfer of E.U. privacy information to U.S.)
- speech and content: protection (U.S. Constitution), limits (France, Germany, Russia, China)
- consumer protection: unfair or deceptive security practices (U.S. FTC)
- criminal law: laws against hacking (U.S. CFAA, Budapest Convention on Cyber Crime, many countries), mutual legal assistance (MLATs) (U.S. and many countries for cross-border investigation and extradition)
- multilateral agreements: Wassenaar arrangement (obligation to limit export of dual-use technologies, including security), mutual defense treaties (e.g., NATO and Article 5 cyber obligations), WTO and technical barriers to trade agreement (obligation of WTO members to use international standards, including technology), WTO government procurement agreements (many countries, rules opening government procurement markets for foreign tech products).

Over the past decade there have been many skirmishes to try to limit the impact of proposed laws that would splinter the global market for technology products and services and protect the ability of companies to continue to drive innovation in products and services. Particularly in the post-Snowden world, where trust of countries and technologies has been strained, companies must pay particular attention to legislative and regulatory proposals that would undermine the global interoperability or security of the network, or use security as a stalking horse to protect or promote domestic manufacturers.

■ Security and privacy

As technology and economics continues to drive connectivity, cloud, mobility, data analytics, the Internet of Things, and the Industrial Internet, we must deal effectively with security and privacy. It's not just the Snowden effect. People are still working through what they think about security and privacy. Most want both. Some regions have differing views. In the U.S., we limit what the government can do through Constitutional Fourth Amendment restrictions on unreasonable searches and seizures, but we freely give personal information to commercial companies in exchange for free content and other services we like. In Europe, it's the opposite. The E.U. presumptively limits what information relating to individuals the private sector can collect and share but often has minimal legal procedures regulating government activities to collect information about its citizens. China has its own view on national security and information, as does Russia. In any event, companies have an important role to play in the future of the intersection of security and privacy.

Most people talk in terms of balancing security and privacy. This may be a false dichotomy. I think the better approach is to drive to security *and* privacy. Try to get both right. Do what you need to secure a system or crown jewels or an enterprise, and use techniques and technologies that help ensure privacy. I think this is the challenge for the future and likely an area that will spur great innovation. How can we work effectively with anonymized data? How can we implement machine-to-machine anomaly detection without identifying the individual or that a device belongs to a particular individual? How can we manipulate encrypted data at scale? Can we know enough from encrypted data streams across the enterprise or network to understand and stop an exfiltration or an attack? How can we share cyberthreat information that is anonymous and actionable? These are the questions companies can and should ask when providing service, domestically, but particularly globally. There no doubt is competitive advantage in providing solutions that don't raise privacy concerns.

■ Conclusion

Cyber is by definition a global issue for any company, CEO, and board. The company's networks are global, products are global, and adversaries are global. Furthermore, the company must have relationships with governments globally. Many companies are 'global citizens' and have a majority of their sales outside their home country. Where the cyber issue is in the top of the mind in each of the major markets these companies serve and where governments have not yet sorted out acceptable global 'rules of the road,' it is incumbent on company leadership to help figure out what the future is going to look like. Without common ground about what's OK and not OK for governments to do with regard to each other, companies, and citizens, we will face an uncertain technology future. I am optimistic about the future and about the ability to master the cyber issue. However, it will take moving through the problem set. We are at an inflection point— as we continue to embed devices, software, and hardware into everything, we need to have a view, a path, a structure that gives us confidence. Therefore, when we sit down in an office such as the attorney general's or a board of directors and ponder the better and lesser proclivities of mankind, we must be confident we are driving rules-based decisions to the happier side of the ledger—one that ensures we reap the benefits of this terrific, accelerating, age of technology.

23

Managing third-party liability using the SAFETY Act

Pillsbury Winthrop Shaw Pittman LLP – Brian Finch, Partner

One of the most pressing questions directors and officers of publicly listed companies is how to manage third-party liability in the post 9/11 era. In particular, directors and officers continually struggle with the issue of whether 'enough' security measures have been deployed to protect not only corporate assets and employees but also innocent bystanders.

Before 9/11, courts typically would not hold makers of items such as ammonium nitrate fertilizer liable for the misuse of their product by terrorists (finding that such terrorist acts were 'unforeseeable' and that the fertilizer manufacturers did not have a duty to protect the unfortunate victims of the attacks).

Unfortunately, a series of decisions completely changed the legal landscape post 9/11. In one case stemming from the 1993 World Trade Center attack, New York state courts initially held the Port Authority of New York and New Jersey partially liable for the losses suffered by the victims of the 9/11 attacks. In that particular case, the Port Authority was held to a standard in which if it knew or should have been aware of the possibility of a terrorist attack, then it was obligated to take all reasonable measures necessary to mitigate the possibility of said attacks.

Even considering that the decision was ultimately overturned on a technicality (the Port Authority was found to have a unique form of 'sovereign immunity' and therefore could not be held liable under any circumstances), the initial decision set forth a blueprint that other courts are sure to follow in future cases involving terrorist or cyberattacks.

Similarly, claims filed against the manufacturers of airplanes used in the 9/11 attacks were also allowed to proceed, leading to significant costs for those companies. In that instance, a federal court in New York allowed claims alleging that the cockpit doors on planes made by Boeing were negligently designed—thereby allowing terrorists to gain control of the planes—were allowed to proceed. The court's rationale in that case was that a jury could find that Boeing should have foreseen that a terrorist would want to breach the cockpit and hijack the plane, and thus its cockpit doors should have been more strongly designed.

Because those claims were allowed to proceed, Boeing on average paid 2½ times in settlement fees what the plaintiffs (here the families of persons killed in the 9/11 attacks) would have received if they had elected to participate in the 9/11 Victims Compensation Fund.

In light of the above, it is obvious that directors and officers of publicly listed companies must be very concerned about post-attack litigation. Even if a court or jury ultimately finds that there is no culpability on the part of a director, officer, or the company itself, the stark reality is that the legal fight to reach that decision will be expensive and protracted.

So, the key question that directors and officers of publicly listed companies must ask themselves is, 'How do we manage/minimize third-party liability in a post 9/11 world?' Insurance is certainly an option, but obtaining a comprehensive policy can be very expensive, and further coverage is uncertain. Again using 9/11 as an example, many companies paid immense amounts in legal fees to force their insurance carriers to honor terrorism-related claims under the policies they issued.

Understanding the limits of insurance, the question then becomes what other risk mitigation tools exist that could limit by statute or eliminate third-party claims? Based on a review of existing statutes, regulations, and alternative options such as insurance coverage, the best opportunity for limiting liability is the Support Anti-Terrorism By Fostering Effective Technologies Act ('SAFETY Act'). Under the SAFETY Act, 'sellers' of security products or services (a term that also includes companies that develop their own physical or cybersecurity plans and procedures and then uses them only for internal purposes) are eligible to receive liability protections under the SAFETY Act.

In addition, entities that purchase or deploy SAFETY Act approved security products and/or services also will have the benefit of immediate dismissal of third-party liability claims arising out of, related to, or resulting from a declared 'act of terrorism' (a term that encompasses physical or cyber-attacks, regardless of whether there is any motive or intent that could be deemed 'political' in nature).

The reader should remember that at the time of the drafting of this article, no litigation specifically involving the SAFETY Act has occurred, and so there is no established legal precedent interpreting the statute itself. However, the fundamental principles of the SAFETY Act are based on the "government contractor defense," a well-established common law affirmative defense to third-party litigation that has been reviewed and upheld by the U.S. Supreme Court.

Accordingly, this article is based on interpretations of the SAFETY Act, the Final Rule implementing the SAFETY Act, and the underlying theory of the government contractor defense.

■ Background of the SAFETY Act

The SAFETY Act provides extensive liability protections to entities that are awarded either a 'Designation' or a 'Certification' as a Qualified Anti-Terrorism Technology (QATT). Under a 'Designation' award, successful SAFETY Act QATT applications are entitled to a variety of liability protections, including the following:

- All terrorism-related liability claims must be litigated in federal court.
- Punitive damages and pre-judgment interest awards are barred.
- Compensatory damages are capped at an amount agreed to by the Department of Homeland Security (DHS) and the applicant.
- That damage cap will be equal to a set amount of insurance the applicant must carry, and once that insurance cap is

reached no further damages may be awarded in a given year.

- A bar on joint and several liability
- Damages awarded to plaintiffs will be offset by any collateral recoveries they receive (e.g., victims compensation funds, life insurance).

Should the applicant be awarded a 'Certification' under the SAFETY Act for their QATT, all of the liability protections awarded under a 'Designation' are available. In addition, the seller of a QATT will be entitled to an immediate presumption of dismissal of all third-party liability claims arising out of, or related to, the act of terrorism.

This presumption of immunity can be overcome in two ways: (1) by demonstrating that the application was submitted with incorrect information and that that information was provided though fraud or willful misconduct or (2) by showing that the claims asserted by the plaintiff related to a product or service are not encompassed by the QATT definition as written by the Department of Homeland Security. Absent a showing of element, the attack-related claims against the defendant will be immediately dismissed.

For the SAFETY Act protections to be triggered, the Secretary of Homeland Security must declare that an "act of terrorism" has occurred. The definition of an "act of terrorism" is extremely broad, and includes any act that:

(i) is unlawful;

(ii) causes harm to a person, property, or entity, in the United States, or in the case of a domestic United States air carrier or a United States-flag vessel (or a vessel based principally in the United States on which United States income tax is paid and whose insurance coverage is subject to regulation in the United States), in or outside the United States; and

(iii) uses or attempts to use instrumentalities, weapons or other methods designed or intended to cause mass destruction, injury or other

loss to citizens or institutions of the United States.

The Secretary has broad discretion to declare that an event is an "act of terrorism," and once that has been declared, the SAFETY Act statutory protections will be available to the seller of the QATT and others.

A cursory review of this definition reveals that there is no need to divine a motivation for the attack and that the language used can be interpreted to include physical attacks as well as cyberattacks. The only 'intent' that must be demonstrated under the SAFETY Act then is that the attack is intended to cause destruction, injury, or other loss to the U.S. or its interests. This is important to remember because it means that cyberattacks also trigger the protections of the SAFETY Act.

■ SAFETY Act protections available to customers and other entities

One of the most significant additional benefits of the SAFETY Act is that the liability protections awarded to the seller of the QATT flow down to customers, suppliers, subcontractors, vendors, and others who were involved in the development or deployment of the QATT. In other words, when a company buys or otherwise uses a QATT that has been either SAFETY Act 'Designated' or 'Certified,' that customer is entitled to immediate dismissal of claims associated with the use of the approved technology or service and arising out of, related to, or resulting from a declared act of terrorism.

The bases for these expanded protections are clearly set forth in the SAFETY Act statute and in the Final Rule implementing the SAFETY Act. Both are detailed below:

With respect to the protections offered to entities other than the Seller of the QATT, the SAFETY Act statute states as follows:

IN GENERAL.—There shall exist a Federal cause of action for claims arising out of, relating to, or resulting from an act of terrorism when qualified anti-terrorism technologies have been deployed in defense against or response or recovery from such act and such claims result or may result in loss to the Seller. The substantive law for decision in any such action shall be derived from the law, including choice of law principles, of the State in which such acts of terrorism occurred, unless such law is inconsistent with or preempted by Federal law. *Such Federal cause of action shall be brought only for claims for injuries that are proximately caused by sellers that provide qualified anti-terrorism technology to Federal and non-Federal government customers.*

The SAFETY Act statute also reads:

JURISDICTION.—Such appropriate district court of the United States shall have original and exclusive jurisdiction over all actions for any claim for loss of property, personal injury, or death arising out of, relating to, or resulting from an act of terrorism when qualified anti-terrorism technologies have been deployed in defense against or response or recovery from such act and such claims result or may result in loss to the Seller.

The key language, which comes from 6 U.S.C. Section 442(a)(1), states that the claims arising out of, relating to, or resulting from an act of terrorism "shall be brought only for claims for injuries that are proximately caused by sellers that provide qualified anti-terrorism technology to Federal and non-Federal government customers."

Furthermore, in Section 442(a)(2), the SAFETY Act states that U.S. district courts shall have original and exclusive jurisdiction for claims that "result or may result in loss to the seller."

The language in 6 U.S.C. Section 442(a)(1) and (a)(2) reads such that terrorism-related claims that have or could have resulted in a loss to the seller may only be brought in U.S. district courts against the seller. Nothing in the statute would give rise to claims against other parties who use or otherwise participate in the delivery and use of the QATT.

DHS, as set forth in the preamble to the SAFETY Act Final Rule, agrees with this interpretation, stating:

Further, it is clear that the Seller is the only appropriate defendant in this exclusive Federal cause of action. First and foremost, the Act unequivocally states that a "cause of action shall be brought only for claims for injuries that are proximately caused by sellers that provide qualified anti-terrorism technology." Second, if the Seller of the Qualified Anti-Terrorism Technology at issue were not the only defendant, would-be plaintiffs could, in an effort to circumvent the statute, bring claims (arising out of or relating to the performance or non-performance of the Seller's Qualified Anti-Terrorism Technology) against arguably less culpable persons or entities, including but not limited to contractors, subcontractors, suppliers, vendors, and customers of the Seller of the technology.

Because the claims in the cause of action would be predicated on the performance or non-performance of the Seller's Qualified Anti-Terrorism Technology, those persons or entities, in turn, would file a third-party action against the Seller. In such situations, the claims against non-Sellers thus "may result in loss to the Seller" under 863(a)(2). The Department believes Congress did not intend through the Act to increase rather than decrease the amount of litigation arising out of or related to the deployment of Qualified Anti-Terrorism Technology. Rather, Congress balanced the need to provide recovery to plaintiffs against the need to ensure adequate deployment of anti-terrorism technologies by creating a cause of action that provides a certain level of recovery against Sellers, while at the same time protecting others in the supply chain.

Within the Final Rule itself, the Department also stated:

There shall exist only one cause of action for loss of property, personal injury, or death for performance or non-performance of the

Seller's Qualified Anti-Terrorism Technology in relation to an Act of Terrorism. Such cause of action may be brought only against the Seller of the Qualified Anti-Terrorism Technology and may not be brought against the buyers, the buyers' contractors, or downstream users of the Technology, the Seller's suppliers or contractors, or any other person or entity.

Thus, the SAFETY Act statute and the Final Rule implementing the law make it clear that when there is litigation involving a SAFETY Act QATT (whether Designated or Certified) alleging that the QATT was the cause, directly or indirectly, of any alleged losses, the only proper defendant in such litigation is the Seller of the QATT. Customers and others are not proper defendants and are entitled to immediate dismissal, because allowing litigation to proceed against customers would be contrary to the SAFETY Act statute and Congressional intent.

■ Practical application of SAFETY Act protections to limit third-party claims

Considering the above, companies that sell or deploy security QATTs, as well as their customers, are entitled to extensive benefits. Sellers of cybersecurity QATTs are entitled to the broad protections from third-party liability claims offered under a 'Designation' and a 'Certification.'

As explicitly set forth in the SAFETY Act statute and the SAFETY Act Final Rule, the only proper defendant in litigation following an act of terrorism allegedly involving a SAFETY Act Designated and/or Certified QATT is the seller itself. In this case, the 'Seller' would be the security vendor or company that deploys its own internally developed security policies, procedures, or technologies with the QATT being said Certified or Designated security policies, procedures, or even technologies.

The basis for this analysis rests upon the fact that sellers of security QATTs will have received the QATT Designation or Certification, thus conferring upon them specific statutory liability protections.

Further, based on the extensive analysis conducted above regarding the applicability of the SAFETY Act statute and Final Rule, buyers of security QATTs will be considered 'customers' for SAFETY Act purposes, and therefore entitled to immediate dismissal of claims related to an approved security technology or service. Thus, the SAFETY Act can and should serve as an excellent tool to mitigate or eliminate said liability.

Accordingly, sellers and customers of 'QATTs' are entitled to all appropriate protections offered by the SAFETY Act, whether those offered by Designation, the presumption of dismissal offered by Certification, or the flow-down protections offered to customers and others. QATT customers and sellers could still face security-related litigation should the Homeland Security Secretary not declare the attack to be an "act of terrorism" or if the claims do not relate to the QATT as defined by DHS.

■ Conclusion

Entities that are potentially at risk for third-party liability claims after an attack can be materially protected through the SAFETY Act. Users of SAFETY Act-approved security products or services will also receive direct and tangible benefits.

The SAFETY Act provides strong liability protections that will flow down to such customers per the language of the SAFETY Act statute and Final Rule. A wide variety of attacks, products, and services, including cyberattacks and cybersecurity products and services, are covered by the language of the SAFETY Act, and thus, such products and services are also eligible to provide dramatically limited litigation and for such litigation to be limited to 'sellers,' not 'customers.'

Certainly not every attack will result in liability for security vendors or their customers, particularly with respect to third-party liability. Should such liability occur, however, it can be mitigated or eliminated using the SAFETY Act.

Perhaps most importantly for directors and officers of publicly listed companies, the SAFETY Act should always be considered when examining risk mitigation strategies associated with the company's internal security programs (physical and/or cyber) as well as security goods and services purchased from outside vendors. The SAFETY Act offers powerful liability protections and can doubly serve as evidence that the company exercised 'due diligence' and 'reasonable care' when designing and implementing its security programs.

Given the relative paucity of case law defining what constitutes 'adequate' or 'reasonable' security, directors and officers should look to the SAFETY Act as a way to help determine whether their company's security plans and programs could be considered to have achieved those benchmarks. Doing so will not only help improve security but also almost assuredly decrease the company's risk exposure.

24

Combating the insider threat: Reducing security risks from malicious and negligent employees

Littler Mendelson P.C. — Philip L. Gordon, Esq., Co-Chair, Privacy and Background Checks Practice Group

"Edward Snowden," the affair that bears his name demonstrates the extreme damage that a privileged insider can cause, even to an organization with the most sophisticated security technology and one of the largest cyber-security budgets. Although Snowden may have been a contractor, survey after survey demonstrates that employees, whether through negligence or malice, are the most common cause of security incidents. According to the Vormetric Insider Threat Report 2015, 89% of respondents globally stated that their organization was more at risk than ever from the insider threat, and 55% identified employees as the #1 internal threat. PwC's Global State of Information Security 2015 found that current employees are the most frequently cited cause of security incidents, well ahead of contractors, hackers, organized crime, and nation-states.

These studies confirm that there has been no abatement in the insider threat in recent years. Just as PwC's study found in 2015, a 2013 Ponemon Institute study, entitled the "Post-Breach Boom," also reported that negligent and malicious insiders were the cause of 61% of security breaches experienced by respondents, substantially exceeding other causes, such as external attacks and system error or malfunctions.

Employers can take a wide range of relatively low-cost, low-tech steps to reduce the risk of insider threats. These steps track the stages of the employment lifecycle, ranging from pre-employment screening at the outset of the employment relationship to exit interviews when that relationship ends. Between those endpoints, employers can reduce the insider threat by implementing and managing access controls, securing mobile devices (whether employer-owned or personal) used for work, carefully managing remote work, providing effective training, and following a myriad other steps discussed in more detail below.

■ Pre-employment screening and post-hire risk alerts

Effective background screening can eliminate the insider threat before it ever occurs by identifying job applicants who pose a threat to the employer's information assets. Employees responsible for evaluating background reports should be looking not only for prior convictions for identity theft but also for other crimes involving dishonesty, such as fraud and forgery, which indicate an applicant's propensity to misuse information. Employers that rely on staffing companies should consider not hiring temporary workers for positions involving access to sensitive employee, customer, or business data, such as positions in the human resources or R&D departments or those responsible for processing credit card payments. If such hiring is imperative, the employer should impose on the staffing company, by contract, background check criteria for temporary placements that are at least as stringent as the employer's own background check criteria.

Employers should beware that pre-employment screening can itself expose an employer to significant risks. In the past few years, the plaintiffs' class action bar has aggressively pursued employers for alleged violations of the federal Fair Credit Reporting Act (FCRA), which regulates the procurement of background checks from third-party consumer reporting agencies. As of mid-2015, nearly 20 jurisdictions—states, counties, and municipalities—have enacted "ban-the-box" legislation to restrict private employers' inquiries into criminal history. At the same time, the U.S. Equal Employment Opportunity Commission (EEOC) has filed several lawsuits against large employers, alleging that their pre-employment screening practices have a disparate impact on African American and Hispanic job applicants. Consequently, organizations should carefully review their pre-employment screening practices for compliance with the many federal, state, and local laws aimed at helping ex-offenders secure employment.

Employers also should consider whether a one-time, pre-employment background check adequately protects their organization. Currently, the vast majority of employers do not conduct background checks after the job application process has been completed. However, several service providers now offer "risk alerts," either directly to employers or indirectly through the employer's background check vendor. These risk alerts notify the employer and/or the background check vendor of post-hire risk factors available through public records sources, such as pending criminal charges, criminal convictions, and bankruptcies. Employers may consider using such "continuous monitoring" services to help identify employees who become security risks over time.

■ Employee-oriented safeguards for sensitive corporate data

Even employees who have been thoroughly screened and have proven their trustworthiness can expose an organization's sensitive data to loss or theft. Organizations and the employees themselves can take the basic precautions described below to mitigate these risks.

A. Safeguarding electronic data

1. **Access control lists:** Restricting access to information, particularly sensitive customer, employee, and business information, on a need-to-know basis is a fundamental principle of information security. Employees in the accounts payable department, for example, should be barred from accessing human resources information. In addition, access to information by employees with a need to know should be limited to the minimum necessary to perform their job responsibilities. Organizations should implement a process for establishing the access rights of new hires based on their job responsibilities, for modifying access rights when job responsibilities change, and for promptly terminating access rights when the employment relationship ends.

2. **Protecting log-in credentials:** Employees should be regularly reminded of the importance of protecting their log-in credentials. They should be instructed not to share their log-in credentials with anyone. Hackers may pose as IT professionals on the phone or send phishing emails purporting to originate with the employer's IT Department, to trick ("social engineer") employees into revealing log-in credentials. Employees also should be instructed not to write down their log-in credentials and to immediately change their log-in credentials when they suspect the credentials have been compromised. Finally, each employee should be required to acknowledge that only he or she is the authorized person to access and view the organization's information through his or her log-in credentials and is personally responsible for all activity using those log-in credentials.

3. **Screen security:** Employees can reveal sensitive data to "shoulder surfers" in airplanes, at coffee shops, and even at work by failing to adequately protect their computer monitor or screen. Employees should be reminded to position their monitor or screen to reduce the risk of viewing by unauthorized individuals. In locations, such as airplanes, where that may not be possible, employees should use a privacy screen to prevent unauthorized viewing. Regardless of location, employees should activate a password-protected screen saver when they leave their screen unattended.

4. **Mobile device security:** One of the most common causes of security breaches is the exposure of sensitive data through the loss or theft of employees' mobile devices. To reduce this risk, organizations should push security controls to all mobile devices—whether employer-issued or personally owned—that are used for work. These controls should include encryption, password protection, automatic log-out after a short period of inactivity, automatic log-out after a small number of unsuccessful log-in attempts, and remote wipe capability. In addition, employees should be routinely reminded of the need to physically safeguard their mobile device, for example, by not sharing the device with others and by securing the device (for example, in a hotel safe) when the device is left unattended. In addition, employees should be instructed to immediately report the loss or theft of the device to a person or group designated to respond to such reports.

5. **Remote work security:** Corporate spies can tap into unsecured WiFi connections to steal sensitive data. To reduce this risk, employees should be required to use a secure/encrypted connection, such as a virtual private network (VPN), to access the corporate network when working remotely. In addition, employees should generally be required to use that secure remote connection to conduct business involving sensitive data rather than storing the sensitive data on a portable storage medium, such as a thumb drive or a laptop's hard drive. Where local storage is a business imperative (e.g., when work must get done during a long flight), employees should be required to use an encrypted portable storage medium to store sensitive data.

6. **No storage in personal online accounts:** Once an organization's sensitive data move to an employee's personal email or cloud storage account, the organization effectively loses control of the information. Absent the employee's prior written authorization, the email or cloud service provider generally cannot lawfully disclose the organization's data to the organization. At the same time, employees often will hesitate to sign such an authorization out of concern that the employer will gain

access to private information stored in the account, and employees almost always will flatly refuse to sign if they are disgruntled or after they have left the organization. Consequently, employers should unambiguously communicate to their workforce that storage of the organization's sensitive data in a personal online account is prohibited.

B. Safeguarding sensitive data in paper and oral form

1. **Clean desk policy/secure storage:** Whether employees are working at the employer's office or their home office, paper documents containing sensitive data can easily be viewed or stolen by those not authorized to access the information, such as maintenance personnel at the office or those making repairs at the home. Employees should be reminded to secure paper documents containing sensitive data in locked offices, desk drawers, filing cabinets, or storage areas and to remove papers containing sensitive data from their physical desktop when it is unattended.

2. **Beware of printers, scanners, and fax machines:** Office equipment located in unrestricted areas poses a risk to sensitive data in paper form. Employees should be instructed to promptly remove print jobs, scans, and faxes from these machines so that sensitive data cannot be viewed by unauthorized individuals.

3. **Avoid off-site use of paper documents:** Massachusetts General Hospital agreed to pay $1 million to settle alleged HIPAA violations after one of its employees left the medical records of 192 HIV patients on the Boston subway. Organizations can avoid incidents like this by prohibiting employees from taking paper documents with sensitive data off-site unless there is a strong and legitimate business need to do so. Typically, employees will be able to access the same information through a secure remote connection. When there is a business need, employees should be required to keep the paper documents with them at all times or to secure the documents when unattended, just as employees should do with a mobile device.

4. **Require secure disposal of paper documents:** Pharmacies and other health care providers around the country have been the subject of scathing publicity and government investigations after journalists-cum-dumpster-divers discovered unshredded patient records discarded in bulk behind the facility. Whether working from the office or from home, employees should be required to shred paper documents containing sensitive data or to discard them in secure disposal bins.

5. **Private conversations are meant for private places:** In today's world of mobile telephony, employees often can end up discussing sensitive information while walking down the street, riding in public transportation, or sitting in a crowded restaurant. Even when working at the corporate office or the home office, employees must be aware that they are not discussing sensitive data over the phone where unauthorized individuals can overhear them.

■ Employee monitoring

Monitoring technology has become increasingly sophisticated and can now help employers root out the insider threat. For example, recently developed email and Internet monitoring software uses "Big Data" techniques to identify patterns of conduct for the workforce as a whole, for particular groups, or for particular individuals to establish a norm for expected online conduct. When an employee deviates from the norm—for example, by downloading an unusually large number of files to an external storage device or by sending an unusual number of emails to a personal e-mail account—the software alerts the employer of the deviation from the norm, so the employer can investigate further. Employers concerned about the insider threat should consider investing in monitoring software that can perform this type of "user-based analytics."

Employers also should consider installing data loss prevention (DLP) software on their networks. This software flags communications, such as outbound emails containing sensitive data, for further action. For example, DLP software may identify strings of digits resembling Social Security numbers in an outbound email, quarantine the email before it leaves the organization's network, and alert the employer's IT department of a potential data theft.

Although network surveillance software can substantially enhance other information security measures, implementation can pose risks for the organization. Although case law applying the Federal Wiretap Act to real-time email interception is somewhat sparse, the cases suggest that employers who capture email content in real time without robust, prior notice to employees may be exposed to civil lawsuits and even criminal prosecution. Multinational employers face broader, potential exposure for violating local data protection laws, particularly in the European Union. Consequently, employers should conduct a thorough legal review before implementing new monitoring technology.

■ Confidentiality agreements, employee training, and exit interviews

Although many of the safeguards described above may appear to be common sense, they likely will appear to be inconveniences to many employees, especially to the Gen-Y members and Millennials in the workforce for whom the broad disclosure of sensitive information through social media has become natural. Cisco's 2012 Annual Security Report bears this out, reporting that 71% of Gen-Y respondents "do not obey policies" set by corporate IT. Similarly, Absolute Software's 2015 U.S. Mobile Device Security Report found that 25% of Millennials admitted to compromising their organization's IT security as compared to 5% of Baby Boomers. Given this "culture of noncompliance," employers should consider three methods for reminding employees of their responsibilities as stewards of the employer's sensitive data.

First, employers should consider requiring that all new hires whose responsibilities will involve access to sensitive data execute a confidentiality agreement. In addition to identifying those categories of information that employees must keep confidential, the agreement should summarize some of the key steps employees are required to take to preserve confidentiality, require return of the employer's sensitive data upon termination of the employment relationship, and confer on the employer enforcement rights in the event the employee breaches the agreement. Employers should note that several federal regulators, including the Securities & Exchange Commission (SEC), the National Labor Relations Board (NLRB), and the EEOC, have been finding unlawful overly broad confidentiality agreements that effectively restrict employees' rights to engage in legally protected conduct, such as whistle-blowing or discussing the terms and conditions of employment with co-workers. Consequently, any confidentiality agreement should be scrutinized by legal counsel before it is distributed to new hires for signature.

Second, educating employees on information security is critical. Training should address a range of topics, including (a) the employer's legal obligations to safeguard sensitive data, (b) the types of information falling within the scope of this legal duty, (c) the consequences for the employer's bottom line of failing to fulfill those legal obligations, (d) the steps employees can take to help the employer fulfill its legal obligations, and critically (e) the situations that constitute a security incident and to whom the incident should be reported. Training should be recurring and supplemented with periodic security awareness reminders. These reminders could take the form of email, posts on an internal blog, or text messages and can include critical alerts, such as notification of a recent phishing email sent to members of the employer's workforce or warnings against clicking on links or opening attachments that could result in the downloading of malicious code.

Third, employers should consider modifying their exit interview process to specifically address information security. At the exit interview, the employer can accomplish the following:

- provide the employee with a copy of his or her executed confidentiality agreement and remind the employee of his or her ongoing obligation not to disclose the employer's sensitive data to unauthorized third parties;
- obtain the return of all employer-owned computers, mobile devices, and portable storage media on which sensitive data may be stored;
- arrange for the remote wiping, or other removal, of the employer's sensitive data from any of the employee's personal mobile devices allowed to access corporate information systems;
- confirm that the employee has not stored any of the employer's sensitive data in personal email accounts, personal cloud storage accounts, personal external storage media, or anywhere else.

■ HR and in-house employment counsel need a seat at the "information security table"

In many, if not most, organizations, there is a chasm between the Human Resources department and in-house employment counsel, on the one hand, and the groups responsible for information security—the IT Department, the Chief Information Security Officer, and/or the Chief Privacy Officer—on the other. The former group views information security as the sole responsibility of the latter, and the latter group views employees (and employee data) as the sole responsibility of the former.

However, HR professionals and in-house employment counsel can play a critical role in enhancing an organization's information security. They typically are responsible for evaluating whether to reject applicants based on information reported by the employer's pre-employment screening vendor. They routinely train new hires and current employees on a wide range of topics and could easily partner with information security professionals to conduct information security training. They often negotiate contracts with service providers who receive substantial quantities of employees' sensitive data. They regularly receive and investigate complaints of suspected employee misconduct, which may include reports generated by DLP software or other online surveillance software or about employees' otherwise mishandling sensitive data. They also typically are involved in disciplinary decisions, including those based on employees' mishandling of sensitive data.

In sum, by making human resources professionals and in-house employment counsel valued members of the organization's information security team, organizations can significantly enhance the effectiveness of their overall information security program.

IV Comprehensive approach to cybersecurity

25

Developing a cybersecurity strategy: Thrive in an evolving threat environment

Booz Allen Hamilton – Bill Stewart, Executive Vice President; Sedar LaBarre, Vice President; Matt Doan, Senior Associate; and Denis Cosgrove, Senior Associate

The Internet and 'always on' connectivity is transforming how we live, work, and do business. Game-changing technology, powered by our increasingly connected society, offers more efficient workers, new revenue streams, and stronger customer relationships. Technology is not optional; it is a core business enabler. That means it must be protected.

Cybersecurity was once widely considered just another item in a long list of back-office functions. Vulnerability patching? Device configuration? These were IT problems for the IT team to worry about. However, that has changed. A series of high-profile cybersecurity attacks—from Stuxnet to Target—demonstrate that cybersecurity represents a business risk of the highest order. The C-suite and board are taking notice.

However, as cybersecurity makes its way onto the executive agenda, it is simultaneously time to rethink our strategies. The 'Internet of Things' is more than a fad. Suddenly, and increasingly, everything is connected. Business leaders get it: to fend off emerging players and ensure market competitiveness, companies are re-architecting their business models around this concept. It will drive success. It also requires new cybersecurity strategies that take a broader view of risk. Developing strategies that recognize risk beyond back-end IT systems is critical, to include products, customer interfaces, and third-party vendors. Above all, the new challenges in cybersecurity demand an organizational-wide approach to protecting, and ultimately enabling, the business. It is time to cast the net wider, and more effectively, than ever before.

■ The value of getting cybersecurity right

An effective cybersecurity strategy must start with placing it in the context of the business—what your company uniquely provides as products or services really determines how to approach the challenge. For old-school IT security hands, this is a different way of thinking. It means getting out of the IT back office and learning the nuances of what makes the business go. Take the view of the CEO and board. It isn't just that it is the right thing to do or because compliance matters. There are more meaningful answers to uncover.

The right cybersecurity strategy is guided by two related considerations: (1) 'How does cybersecurity enable the business?' and (2) 'How does cyber risk affect the business?' From this perspective, cybersecurity breaks out of its technical box and IT jargon. It focuses on competitive advantage, and it positions cybersecurity as an enabler and guarantor of the core business, whatever business you're in. If done right, cybersecurity helps drive a consistent, high-quality customer experience.

■ It takes an enterprise

A cybersecurity strategy grounded in your unique business ecosystem will quickly reveal what must be protected. Enterprise IT still matters; it moves, analyzes, and stores so much of your business-critical data. However, a cybersecurity strategy must now go further. Your industry should shape the fine-tuning of the scope here, but we can boil the components of your ecosystem 'map' down into several key features:

1. **Enterprise IT:** the back-end technology infrastructure that facilitates company-wide communications; processes, stores corporate, and transfers data; and enables workforce mobility
2. **Supply chain:** the flow of materials and components (hardware and software) through inbound channels to the enterprise, where they are then operationalized or used in the development of products and services

3. **Product/service development:** the research, design, testing, and manufacturing environments for your products and services
4. **Customer experience:** the operational realms where customers use and interact with your products or services
5. **External influencers:** all external entities that affect how you guide your business to include regulators, law enforcement, media, competitors, and customers.

A cybersecurity strategy at this scale requires enterprise-wide collaboration. It will take the whole organization to manage cyber risk, so it is imperative to cast a wide net and include representatives from across business units in strategy formulation discussions. It requires a multidisciplinary team effort to develop a security strategy that reflects the scale and complexity of the business challenge.

■ Elements of cyber strategy at scale

Building a cybersecurity strategy can seem overwhelming, but it doesn't have to be. Start with a vision, understand the risk, identify controls, and build organizational capacity. Every element builds on each other.

1. **Set a vision:** It all starts with a creative vision. It's critical to paint a high-level landscape of the future that portrays how cybersecurity is intertwined with the most critical parts of your business. Think about the how value is created within your company. Is it a cutting-edge product? Is it by delivering world-class customer service? Craft a short story on how cyber protects and enables that.
2. **Sharpen your priorities:** You have limited resources, just like every other company. You can't protect everything, so you better be certain you're focusing on the most critical business assets. The first step is to figure out what your company determines to be its 'crown jewels.' Once you've defined what truly matters, it's time you evaluate how exposed—or at-risk—these assets are. That will give

you a basis for right-sizing your security program around these assets.

3. **Build the right team:** Once you define what matters and how much security makes sense, think about the people. What does your direct and extended workforce have to look like to be uniquely successfully at your company? These days, you can't get by with your security program being filled with technologist majority. Time to weave in an accompanying set of skill sets that will help you propel you to success, to include organizational change management, crisis management, third-party risk management, and strategic communications.

4. **Enhance your controls:** This is largely about scope. With your company's quickly expanding 'map,' you'll need to adopt new methods for treating risk. For example, if you deliver a 'connected' product to consumers, you'll have to ensure strong embedded device security, as well as protections over the airwaves. Without this, your brand could be at stake. Fortunately there's a great deal of momentum in the world today, with new methodologies, technologies, and skill sets continuously being developed to meet the challenge of today's expanding cyberattack surface.

5. **Monitor the threat:** Unfortunately, cybersecurity isn't only about reducing risk behind your firewalls. It must also include maintaining awareness of the threat landscape—external and internal. Because the threat is always changing and always determined, you have to take on that same adaptive mindset. Whether that's employing strong monitoring and detection capabilities, consuming threat intelligence feeds, or participating in an industry-level information sharing forum, there many avenues that you should strongly consider using.

6. **Plan for contingencies:** No one can ever be 100% secure, so it's vital to have a strong incident response capability in place to manage the ensuing events when something happens, because something

undesirable will most certainly happen. Incident response is more than just having the right technology capabilities in place, such as forensics and malware analysis. In fact, real success in cyber incident response usually comes down to the people aspect. How plugged in are you with your company's legal, privacy, communications, and customer sales units? They are all critical to success; and with this expanded scope of players, you can imagine how a cyber matter can quickly rise to become a top-line business matter.

7. **Transform the culture:** The best organizations out there today do this well. Because people are the core of your business, it comes down to them 'buying in' to cybersecurity as something that they care about. From your dedicated cyber workforce, to business unit leaders, to those that manage your company's supply chain, you'll need all hands on deck, each doing their part in advocating for and implementing cybersecurity measures. A security organization can make this easier by finding ways to make cyber relevant for each part of the business by sharing innovations that excite and enable the business.

■ Bringing the strategy to life

Perhaps the best measure of an effective cybersecurity strategy is its ability to be implemented and make a visible change in how the business is operated. With a strategy in hand, the next move is to build momentum with 'quick wins' while investing in long-term capability development.

The first step is to use your strategy's risk framework to assess where you must apply new or enhanced controls. Look broadly. The biggest cybersecurity challenges may not be where your organization usually expects to see them. There are multiple ways to assess how well the organization is performing, including workshops, external assessments, tabletop exercises, or war games.

To appropriately assess the organization, you need to know what 'good' looks like.

This is different for each organization and industry, but relying on industry benchmarks and existing standards/frameworks (e.g., NIST Cyber Framework) is a good place to get a quick read on your maturity. However, don't adopt these standards blindly; figure out what's applicable to your needs and what's relevant for your organization.

Once you've assessed your priorities and set a maturity target, the next move is to build a roadmap that pairs 'quick wins' with more strategic and enduring capabilities. Right away, you'll want to ensure that you are doing the basic blocking and tackling of cybersecurity. Many call this instilling proper 'cyber hygiene,' or putting a foundational layer of protections and capabilities in place. Once you've gained a solid foothold, time to take the next step, such as establishing predictive intelligence mechanisms that help you anticipate the next threat, instead of reacting to it when it hits.

Perhaps the best way—and the biggest challenge—to bringing your strategy to life is to remember it isn't policy or technology that matters most, but people. Once you've embraced this idea and put the person at the center of all of your decisions, you can really start to envision what it'll take for cybersecurity 'change' to happen in your organization.

■ What getting it right looks like

It is easier to write about the concepts of a good cyber strategy than it is to deliver one for your organization. However, getting cybersecurity right for the organization has benefits far beyond IT. A strong cyber strategy drives security capability development and ultimately has the power to transform the business into a more successful one. An effective cyber strategy looks different depending on the industry and individual business, but they all share some key features.

It's driven from the top. First, a strong cyber strategy won't be locked away in a file cabinet, buried in a hard drive, or lost in the cloud. Instead, it will be part of your organization's core message, and it will feel alive. That tone will be set from the top, with senior executives explaining how cyber will drive the future success of the business.

It's at the beginning of every new story. Whether you're designing a new product or launching into a fresh multinational joint venture, cyber is a conversation that will always take place. Requirements are built in from the beginning and brought to life as the venture evolves. Remember, it's always easier and cheaper to implement cyber earlier rather than later in the lifecycle.

Cyber is communicated in simple business language. Don't be paralyzed by those who only want to 'speak geek.' Simple, easy-to-understand logic should prevail when communicating how cybersecurity is enabling your business.

You've established a predictive edge. If you've evolved your strategy in a disciplined manner, some really amazing things start to come to life. One powerful aspect is that you're using multiple sources of intelligence to understand the world around you, and you are able to anticipate the adversary's next move. Sometimes this can feel like playing a fun video game, but it could really mean saving the lifeblood of your business.

The puzzle pieces come together. With all that you've invested in cybersecurity, the real payoff comes when you see the component elements work in harmony as a system. A unified construct that links constituent technologies, processes, and people together will prove highly effective in monitoring and responding to events and engaging the broader business ecosystem to get things done.

You play a role in the community. Cybersecurity is not something you should attempt alone as an organization. The complexity of vulnerability and the highly resourced threats today are simply overwhelming for any one entity. Cybersecurity requires the power of community, new ideas, and security capabilities coming to life. When successful, your organization is an active part of key dialogues with industry and government. Threat intelligence and best practices are shared two ways, but more importantly, you integrate into the fabric of a very important and very valuable community.

'Change agents' are swarming. You'll need these thought leaders to move across all elements of the business to shift mindsets and anchor new behaviors. These advocates help spread the cybersecurity vision broadly and provide 'on the ground' feedback to make your security strategy stronger.

Security is now embedded across your ecosystem. You've taken a long, hard look at the 'map' of your business, and you now understand all the points where cybersecurity must play a part. Success at this point means that you've carefully and deliberately initiated dialogue and worked with different elements of the business to embed security in places beyond Enterprise IT and extended it into broader touchpoints across the external world.

Your enterprise embraces it. From senior leadership to customer-facing sales teams, cybersecurity is integrated as part of your cultural DNA. You hear about it all the time, and you see how it's factored into all major business decisions. Your organization has evolved to the point where your organization is now living the principles of good cybersecurity without even thinking about it.

26

Designing a Cyber Fusion Center: A unified approach with diverse capabilities

Booz Allen Hamilton – Bill Stewart, Executive Vice President; Jason Escaravage, Vice President; Ernie Anderson, Principal; and Christian Paredes, Associate

Since the early 2000s, organizations have focused cybersecurity efforts around a preventative, "defense-in-depth" approach. The multiple layers of security are intended to thwart attackers; this trend has become known as the "moat-and-castle" defense: higher walls, a deeper moat, and other fortifications to deter or prevent the enemy from breaching the castle grounds.

Within the past several years, high-profile breaches across the financial, government, retail, health-care, defense, and technology sectors have spotlighted the need for a better incident response (IR) capability to detect, contain, and remediate threats. These breaches are evidence that prevention alone is no longer a sufficient approach. However, many organizations lack a mature IR capability and end up spending millions of dollars to outsource IR services. Furthermore, once the incident is remediated, organizations are still left wondering how to effectively secure themselves for the highest return on investment (ROI).

Prevention remains a critical component of an effective security program. And organizations are increasingly investing in native detection and response capabilities, or a Security Operations Center (SOC). But the people, processes, and technologies that are the backbone of SOC must be integrated within one Cyber Fusion Center (CFC) that also combines functions such as Cyber Threat Intelligence (CTI), Red Teaming, and Attack Surface Reduction (ASR).

The Cyber Fusion Center. The CFC is a comprehensive, integrated approach to security. The CFC mission is to protect the business—its assets, people, clients, and reputation—so that it can thrive and operate without costly disruptions.

The CFC approach does not guarantee that there will be no security incidents; this is an impossible feat. Rather, it ensures that all security efforts are coordinated efficiently by leveraging the benefits of proximity (either physical or logical) and easy communication between security teams.

The CFC is designed to integrate key security functions into a single unit without stovepipes or prohibitive bureaucracy:

- Security Operations Center (SOC): the heart of the CFC and the first line of an organization's defense responsible for detecting, responding to, containing, and remediating threats, as well as proactively identifying malicious activity. The SOC is also home to Threat Defense Operations (TDO), the dedicated "hunting" arm of security and intelligence operations responsible for actioning intelligence, conducting in-depth malware analysis, and continually building and improving prevention and detection methods.
- Cyber Threat Intelligence (CTI): the "forward observers" responsible for identifying threats to the organization and disseminating timely, relevant, and actionable reporting to the SOC, C-Suite, and other stakeholders.
- Red Team: the "attackers" who simulate the tactics, techniques, and procedures (TTP) of threats relevant to your organization. The Red Team will continually "stress test" your SOC, driving improvements in detection, response, and SOC analyst threat understanding.
- Attack Surface Reduction (ASR): the proactive defense group responsible for identifying and mitigating vulnerabilities, unnecessary assets, and nonessential services. More than just patch management, optimized ASR teams focus on continually improving an organization's hardening and deployment procedures to eliminate vulnerabilities before systems go live.

By integrating these functions, the CFC aims to break down communication barriers, centralize threat knowledge and analysis, unify the organization's security strategy, and ultimately maximize the value of investments in cybersecurity.

Although the security functions that make up the CFC are not new, the CFC approach represents a complex interaction between the security teams with multiple "touch points," parallel workflows, and constant feedback mechanisms. With the right design and implementation considerations organizations can:

- increase operational effectiveness by orchestrating the security functions and information flow from threat intelligence, through security and IT operations
- improve security readiness by enabling stronger detection mechanisms and awareness of threats
- accelerate security maturation by reducing the costs associated with coordinating complex security functions across multiple teams.

The CFC is distinguished not by its individual parts but by the integration and interdependencies across its functions. More than just a security approach, the CFC is a security mind-set that organizations can implement to better secure themselves, protect their customers, and reduce costly business disruptions.

■ Building a robust SOC to detect and respond to threats

Organizations are quickly recognizing the need to detect and respond to a variety of threats; simply blocking threats isn't enough. The Security Operations Center (SOC) is the organization's first line of defense against all forms of threats and is the heart of the CFC. The SOC will handle any suspected malicious activity and work closely with the other teams in the CFC. A well-designed and maintained SOC will focus on gaining efficiencies though continuous analyst training and mentoring, and constant evaluation of the organization's security technologies.

A tiered SOC structure. The SOC can be designed around a simple detect, identify, and mitigate model. Analysts at various tiers investigate malicious activity (aka alerts or events) with these three stages in mind: Tier 1 analysts are charged with classifying the severity of the event and correlating the event with any historical activity. If necessary, Tier 1 analysts will escalate incidents to Tier 2 and 3 analysts, who will conduct in-depth investigations and perform root-cause analysis to determine what happened.

Threat Defense Operations (TDO). Additionally, specialized analysts within the SOC—Threat Defense Operations (TDO) analysts—are responsible for creating detection logic in the form of signatures, rules, and custom queries based on CTI-provided threat intelligence. TDO engineers deploy the detection logic to a range of devices, appliances, tools, and sensors that make up an organization's security stack. The rules, signatures, and queries create a threat-based preventative sensor network that generates network and host-based alerts that Tier 1–3 analysts in the SOC respond to.

TDO analysts will then fine-tune their detection logic based on SOC feedback, creating an efficient CFC that won't waste time investigating false alarms. The TDO team is also responsible for providing in-depth malware analysis that yields valuable technical intelligence (TECHINT) that can be used in detection logic and further enriched by CTI.

Managing all the security alerts (aka "alert fatigue"). This process—building detection solutions and then identifying and mitigating threats—is where many organizations struggle. Oftentimes, implementation of efficient and effective SOC processes are stifled by an overwhelming number of consoles, alerts, threat feeds, and tools that prohibit seamless workflows for analysts. While security managers should continually identify potential feeds and technologies to invest in, their impact on the SOC analyst should always be a primary consideration:

- How many new alerts will this technology or new data feed produce?
- Who will tune the technology to limit the number of false positives it produces?
- Is the technology filling a gap in detection capabilities or adding on to existing capabilities?
- How does the introduction of this new technology affect the SOC workflow?

The main point to remember is that more technology, tools, and threat feeds do not necessarily enable your SOC to operate more efficiently. Designs that emphasize smooth

Capabilities	Description
Enable Detection	"Operationlize" threat intelligence to enable automated detection and manual analysis within and across prevention and detection technology
Identify Threats	First-level responder responsible for detecting and assessing cybersecurity threats and incidents across the environment
Mitigate Threats	Conducts in-depth analyses of security incidents with specific ability to identify Indicators of Compromise, perform root-cause analysis, and execute containment strategies

Manage
- Shift Leader Oversight
- Case Mgt. Tracking Tool
- 24/7 Structure

Standardize
- Formal Shift Change Process
- Process and Procedures Documentation
- Business Process Reengineering

Measure
- Case Mgt. Dashboard
- Monitor, Detect, and Contain Metrics
- Real-Time Improvements

workflows and "painless" methods of data collection (e.g., analysts do not need to contact other teams to access certain data) are more likely to succeed than those that prioritize technology. Organizations should focus on technology that enables SOC investigators to spend less time collecting data and more time investigating the root cause of the activity they've been alerted to.

Implementing 24/7 operations and managing investigations. Design and implementation should focus on standardizing daily operations, case management, and methods of "measuring success." Modern-day threats necessitate that SOCs operate 24/7, 365 days a year, requiring well-thought-out shift schedules and defined roles. Leaders with managerial and technical experience can aid in workflow management and provide analyst training.

Having a well-integrated, easy-to-use case-management system that doesn't get in the way of investigations and seamlessly interacts with other SOC tools is key. This tool ideally provides metrics on how effectively your SOC monitors, detects, and contains cases and will allow an organization to identify gaps in people, processes, and technologies.

Standardizing your standard operating procedures. Successful implementation also demands accurate and up-to-date documentation. This includes documentation on network architecture, standardized operating procedures (SOPs), and point-of-contact lists. If the SOC is considered the "heart" of the CFC, then SOPs act as its beat, guiding analysts in situations ranging from collecting forensic evidence to stopping data exfiltration.

These procedures change as new technology and organizational structures are implemented. Many organizations fail to update, train, and test their staff and leaders on SOPs, hurting their response times and containment metrics.

The bottom line. The SOC provides core security functions within the CFC and can achieve efficiencies through close integration with other teams such as CTI and TDO.

Instead of looking to new technology first, successful organizations will constantly evaluate their security posture and frequently train their analysts on how to react to new threats. Organizations must carefully consider how new technology and tools will impact the analysts' workflow and their ability to detect and respond to threats while focusing on processes and procedures.

■ Using Cyber Threat Intelligence to anticipate threats

Cyber Threat Intelligence (CTI) has become the security buzzword of 2015. Many products and services claim to provide threat intelligence and promise to prevent a major incident. As this term has saturated the market and security circles, the true meaning and value of threat intelligence has become clouded. As a result, the usefulness of threat intelligence is, in some cases, dismissed.

However, true threat intelligence is incredibly powerful—it can serve as a force-multiplier for your CFC, helping to improve awareness of threats and offering the means by which these threats could be prevented or detected.

So what is threat intelligence? First, and most important, only humans can produce threat intelligence through focused research, a synthesis of multiple sources (aka "all-source analysis"), and clear, concise communication that explains the relevance of threats to your organization. Generally, threat intelligence feeds will not provide much intelligence value unless they are thoroughly vetted by human analysts first; feeds are more likely to generate false alarms than to indicate malicious activity. Additionally, good threat intelligence will be implemented in a way that demonstrates the following characteristics:

Cyber Threat Intelligence is timely. Cyber intelligence addresses an impending threat to the business environment. Receiving that intelligence before the threat is realized is crucial to the organization. Dissemination of strategic and tactical intelligence, including indicators of compromise (IOCs), can take the form of indications and warning (warning of an imminent threat), daily or weekly reports (highlights on relevant threats), and executive briefs (assessments on major and specific cyber issues for C-suite stakeholders). Depending on the audience, other technical or nontechnical reports can also be produced.

Cyber Threat Intelligence is relevant. For many organizations thresholds for relevancy are tricky to define, especially when media reports constantly warn about a range of threats. A cyber breach in a distant industry—even a major one—may not concern you as much as a breach within your own sector; a vulnerability in a technology platform you don't use is obviously less important than a potential zero-day vulnerability in your enterprise-enabling platform. Relevant threat intelligence produces valuable insights on not only issues occurring in the global business environment but also on specific issues within your industry and related to your IT environment. Even further, it strives to give you unique insight into specific adversaries targeting your organization or peers, by assessing their intentions and capabilities.

Cyber Threat Intelligence is actionable. Actionable threat intelligence is created when analysts filter through large volumes of data and information (from human sources, technical feeds, criminal forums, etc.), analyze why specific pieces of information are relevant to your organization, and communicate how that information can be used by various stakeholders. C-suite executives need strategic "big picture" intelligence to inform business decisions such as risks associated with an increasingly global IT footprint. On the other hand, your SOC, TDO, and ASR teams need tactical and technical intelligence to support current investigations, create detection logic, and prepare for potential attacks. Technical intelligence will also be used to determine if certain malicious actions or indicators have already been present on your network.

Strategic and tactical threat intelligence. Today's corporate leaders face a serious challenge in that it is not always possible to accurately predict a cyberattack or its effects.

Oftentimes, business decisions have to be made without all the information. An understanding of the threat landscape can help to make these business decisions, however. For example, attacks on organizations in related industries can serve as an indication that your business might soon be targeted (or has already been targeted).

Although the SOC team is your organization's first line of defense, it can operate more effectively and efficiently with the support of CTI. Your security team will handle a wide array of potential threats and must be able to quickly triage events, determine the threat level, and mitigate incidents. CTI can help SOC analysts to prioritize these alerts, can aid in investigations, and can help SOC analysts attribute malicious activity to specific threats or threat groups. Over time, by leveraging technical intelligence the SOC will develop a stronger understanding of the threats they face, enabling them to act more quickly. The TDO component of SOC will also closely coordinate with CTI to conduct analysis and develop creative detection mechanisms.

The bottom line. Real, human-developed Cyber Threat Intelligence will enable your organization to pre-empt threats, assess risk, and take appropriate defensive actions. Benefits such as avoiding the cost of postevent recovery and remediation, and preventing the theft, destruction, and public release of critical data, make Cyber Threat Intelligence critical to your organization.

■ **Conducting Red Team exercises to "stress-test" and strengthen your Cyber Fusion Center**

A fundamental question for every business is: Will your cybersecurity organization be ready when an attack comes? An important means of assessing and "stress-testing" your CFC is to actively attack it. Through coordinated Red Team exercises, your CFC personnel can learn to detect and respond to a variety of threats.

Simulate threat actors' TTP. Red Team operations will ideally be designed to simulate the tactics, techniques, and procedures of threats that your CTI team has assessed to be a risk to your organization. Your SOC could also be a valuable source of input as you determine how to implement your Red Team operations. What types of threats does your SOC regularly observe? More important, what types of threats does your SOC typically not see? Does your SOC find that there are gaps in detection? What does your SOC think they detect/mitigate well and is worth testing? Where does your SOC have limited detect/mitigate capabilities?

It is the Red Team's responsibility to test these questions and the limits of your SOC and broader CFC. For example, if it is known that the SOC rarely encounters web shells— a type of malware installed on web servers— your Red Team may choose to directly attack a web server.

An important aspect of a Red Team operation is that only select leaders are aware of operations (often referred to as the "white team"), adding to the realism of the event. This implementation allows those who are aware to observe the event as it unfolds, particularly how teams interact with each other, how information is passed along, how stakeholders are engaged, and how the teams handle a variety of attack scenarios. These leaders can also help to scope Red Team activities to ensure no critical data or operations are actually compromised or exposed. (Remember to loop in the legal department prior to the exercise as well.)

After-action improvements. The end result of a Red Team activity should be valuable insight your security team can use to improve its capabilities. For example, during a web server attack exercise, the CFC will need to evaluate how it handled the incident. At what point did the SOC detect the attack? Are there changes that could be made in how security tools are configured to improve future detection of this type of attack? These sample questions frame the improvements that can be implemented within the cybersecurity organization.

The nature of the Red Team's operations means that communication between the SOC and Red Team can sometimes be strained—no SOC likes to lose, and oftentimes the Red Team has the advantage. This can make after-action review of an incident stressful for both teams. However, a healthy, competitive relationship between the SOC and Red Team can foster improvements in the CFC, particularly in detection and response capabilities. Although the SOC and Red Team functions contrast, their missions are the same: to protect the organization and improve its security capabilities.

Implementation of Red Team operations should therefore emphasize the interdependency between the SOC and Red Team mission. The Red Team should assist the SOC during remediation efforts to ensure any uncovered vulnerabilities are no longer susceptible to exploitation.

The bottom line. Fundamentally, Red Team design and implementation takes a human-centric approach. The benefits of placing your "attackers" in close (physical or logical) proximity to your SOC analysts cannot be understated. SOC analysts learn to develop an appreciation for the fact that they are fighting people who make decisions to achieve an objective—it's not just about the malware.

■ Reducing your organization's attack surface

Efforts to protect your organization will be significantly diminished if your IT systems have easily exploitable vulnerabilities, unnecessary services, and nonessential assets. On the other hand, shutting down all protocols, services, and data resources is not a viable option. Thus, the goal of Attack Surface Reduction (ASR) is to close all but the required doors to your technical infrastructure and limit access to those doors through monitoring, vulnerability assessment/mitigation, and access control.

The ASR team is dedicated to identifying, reducing, and managing critical vulnerabilities, services, and assets, while also focusing on preventing the introduction of vulnerabilities via improved hardening procedures.

Understanding and prioritizing your "attack surface." Implementing ASR is all about identifying and understanding your most critical business applications and services—the "crown jewels"—including their functions, supporting infrastructure, scope, and inherent vulnerabilities. This process entails a series of vulnerability scans, security documentation review, architecture assessments, host discovery scans, nonintrusive penetration tests, and targeted interviews with IT personnel.

Next, the ASR team should prioritize each asset, considering their critical value to operations and the ability for the most relevant threat actors—as assessed by your CTI team—to leverage these assets in an intrusion. In addition, the impact of these attacks must be considered. The assets that are most likely to be the victim of a high-impact attack or leveraged in a high-impact attack (such as Adobe Flash) should receive the highest priority, most robust security controls, and attention from the CFC.

More than just patch management. While vulnerability and patch management is a core ASR function, achieving a vulnerability-free organization is not a realistic goal. Vulnerabilities must be identified and managed appropriately—keeping a focus on preventing and quickly responding to the most critical. Continually improving deployment and hardening procedures, especially for publicly facing services and services that may permit attackers to access high-trust zones, is a critical ASR process for facilitating preventive measure and effective mitigation timing.

As such, the ASR function should be ongoing. ASR closely collaborates with other CFC functions, especially CTI and TDO, which can develop rules to detect exploitation of new vulnerabilities. For example, CTI may become aware of new vulnerabilities that threat actors are leveraging. ASR will work with CTI to prioritize the most relevant vulnerabilities based on reports of their exploitation "in the wild."

A highly technical function that demands strong human analysis. Maintaining complete asset awareness is increasingly difficult in today's dynamic business environment.

Organizations require continuous scans and costly-to-maintain configuration management databases (CMDB) to track and ensure the attack surface hasn't expanded beyond the organization's acceptable risk level. And, new exposures often emerge throughout the course of normal business as new IT systems are introduced or upgraded.

While there are many technologies available to aid organizations in managing vulnerabilities and assets, human analysts can leverage contextual understanding of vulnerabilities and the attack surface in ways that scanning software cannot provide.

Experienced ASR security professionals—who possess a deep understanding of network engineering, IT concepts, and security—are able to synthesize disparate pieces of information that can point to a previously undetected or contextually important attack vector.

The bottom line. Attack Surface Reduction enables organizations to proactively reduce security vulnerability-related risk prior to implementation and to mitigate existing and other inevitable risks. Importantly, the ASR function is designed so that humans complement the technology to minimize the attack surface to an optimized level that balances security risks and day-to-day realities of enterprise business operations.

■ **Cyber Fusion Center attention**
The seemingly endless string of breaches across major U.S. sectors—finance, technology, manufacturing, and others—leaves C-suite executives wondering, "Will we be next?" or even, "Have we already been breached?" New tools, technologies, and data sources may help in preventing an attack, but threat actors are clearly capable of scaling the castle walls, or forging the castle moat. Yet by developing a Cyber Fusion Center, organizations develop the speed, collaboration, coordination, information flows, and C-suite awareness necessary to not only survive but thrive.

V Design best practices

27

What are they after? A threat-based approach to cybersecurity risk management

Intercontinental Exchange & New York Stock Exchange – Jerry Perullo, CISO

Given finite resources and the ongoing threat of the "next big hack," cybersecurity is not the place to let a thousand flowers bloom. How does a governance body that is balancing this complex topic with so many other complex risks pick the right questions to ask? The spectrum of popular guidance ranges from an end-to-end program that generates hundreds of inspection points to a kneejerk reaction to the latest headlines. Distilling the truly critical areas of focus requires a balanced approach that is well served by beginning with the end in mind and asking, "What are they really after?"

Traditional guidance has centered security program construction and audit on comprehensive standards-based frameworks. Although the popularity of specific standards has waxed and waned, general principles have revolved around identifying assets, establishing a risk management program around those assets, and establishing preventative, detective, and corrective controls to protect those assets. There is nothing wrong with this recipe at the tactical level. In fact, boards should expect a continuous program cadence around this type of strategy and expect to see third-party auditors, customers, vendors, and regulators use this approach in examination. Controls should be mapped to an established framework and any gaps or vulnerabilities identified. The challenge, however, is that this produces a massive corpus of focus areas and controls that cannot be digested in a single targeted governance session. And finally, it does not produce a ready answer to the top board concern: "How could we be hacked?"

Likewise, reacting to headlines and rushing to establish the controls and technology cited in the latest news story will divert all resources to someone else's vulnerability, whereas yours may be very different. Simply asking, "Could what happened last week happen to us?" may at best result in a false sense of confidence or a mad dash to address a gap that isn't relevant to your organization. Vendors cannot be faulted for preying on this tendency, and the result is a barrage of solutions to the last headline's problems: "You desperately need encryption." "You need behavioral technology to baseline administrator activity and to alert unusual access times or locations." "You need to give up on securing everything and only focus on the critical assets." "You need stronger passwords." All of these solutions have their place, but if they are not responsive to the threats facing your business, they may cause more distraction than protection based on your unique requirements.

Identifying a relevant and reasonable agenda for a governance session requires a targeted and balanced approach. Let us group the major cyber headlines of the last decade into several large categories. With a finite grouping of threats, we can begin to model what each threat would look like to your organization, which leads to an assessment of likelihood and impact. With this picture of viable threats, the board can hone in on specific questions that will produce the most value. By all means, all of the threats listed below should receive treatment in some capacity in any cybersecurity plan, but prioritizing which are most relevant to your organization will expose the most valuable areas to explore with limited time. Further, identifying business practices that expose you to a particular threat category may lead you to reconsider them in light of new costs that were not included in previous assessments. The calculus around maintaining a lower profile or outsourcing targeted data may change when you factor in cybersecurity risk.

■ Threat category 1: Data theft

Do you manage assets that can be easily monetized? Credit numbers and social security numbers—in bulk—are the drivers behind many newsworthy breaches. Criminals have established the proper fencing operations and can justify enormous risk and effort to capture millions of card numbers or pieces of personally identifiable information (PII) that

allow identity theft. Capturing 100 or 1000 is not, however, alluring enough. Do you have bulk card or PII data? Card processors, retail institutions, and health-care providers are clear targets for this type of penetration. If this is your world, the major breaches of the day serve as case studies. Lessons learned in these areas lead to an emphasis on the following questions:

- Do we know all the places where these sensitive data live, and have we limited it to the smallest set of systems possible (ring-fencing)?
- Is access to the systems housing this data tightly controlled, audited, and alarmed, including via asset-based controls?
- Is this data encrypted in a manner that would thwart some of the specific tactics observed in major breaches?

If you do not hold easily monetized data, these questions may not be the right place to start. Again, this does not mean that data theft is acceptable in any organization. Confidential email, intellectual property, customer login credentials, and trade secrets are some of the many examples of data we must protect. Close examination often shows that ring-fencing, asset-focused controls, encryption, and other concentrations born of the rash of recent card and PII breaches may not be appropriate for more common and less frequently targeted data, however. If the data you are protecting are much more valuable to you than to an assailant, traditional controls such as company-wide access control, permission reviews, and identity management are probably the right emphasis and should not be neglected in pursuit of stopping a phantom menace.

■ Threat category 2: Activism

Is your organization the target of frequent protest or activism? Perhaps the issue is climate change. Perhaps it is labor relations. Perhaps you are caught up in the storm of anti-capitalism, anti-pharma, anti-farming, or simply high profile. You may or may not know if there are groups with an ideological motivation to put a black eye on your business. Cyber opens up a whole new realm of ways for people to accomplish this, and often with anonymity. When attacks fall into this category, the most likely impact is an action that can be touted in public. This usually means one of two things: Denial of Service (DoS) or defacement. The former category will attempt to demonstrate your powerlessness by rendering a component of your business unavailable to your customers or the general public. Although attacking customer access or more internalized systems may be more damaging in reality, remember that the goal is to make a splash on a big stage with minimal effort or exposure. More often than not, that means attacking your public website. The same target (plus social media accounts) is most common for defacement attacks. The only thing more satisfying to an activist than rendering your service unavailable is replacing it with a pointed message. High-profile attacks in this category include the near-incessant Distributed Denial of Service (DDoS) attacks against major banks, particularly those with names evoking western countries. Targets of defacement include Twitter and Facebook profiles of targeted companies and government entities. If this type of threat is likely to be pointed at your organization, good questions to ask include the following:

- Can we sustain a DDoS attack on the order of magnitude recently observed in the wild?
- If we have a DDoS mitigation plan, how long would it take to activate during an attack? Is an outage for this duration acceptable, or would it be considered a failure in the public eye?
- Are we continuously scanning our primary website(s) for common vulnerabilities that may allow unauthorized changes?
- If our website were defaced, how long would it take to restore?
- Are credentials to official company social media accounts tightly controlled by a group outside marketing that is more security conscious?

If this type of threat is not applicable to your organization, focusing controls and review on mitigating such attacks may not be the best allocation of resources.

■ **Threat category 3: Sabotage**

Are you a provider of critical infrastructure? Do you or your key executives issue politically charged statements publicly? Would the interruption of your business further an extremist objective? Although these threats require more sophisticated tactics and more time to perpetrate, they often bring highly motivated and coordinated threat actors. Adversary objectives in this area usually go well beyond website attacks. Physical control systems, data integrity, or even the functionality of employee workstations may be the target in this type of attack. Although there are many vectors for this type of attack and several are often used in conjunction, a common theme quickly becomes targeting employees individually. Social engineering and phishing preys on common habits and assumptions to dupe people into disclosing a password, clicking a malicious web link, or opening an attachment. These attacks can be the most difficult to defend against, but their reliance on persistent access and a longer lifecycle to build towards the final goal makes detective and corrective controls more valuable and decreases reliance on absolute prevention. Additionally, the actors involved and potential impact to national interests likely make mitigation assistance available to you if you focus on detection and have the right contacts in place. Good questions to ask if you are at risk of this category of attack include the following (and employees includes contractors and vendors):

- Do individual employees recognize the importance of their role in securing the organization and what an attack may look like?
- Are employees routinely reporting suspicious activity?
- Are employees educated and incentivized to act responsibly with regard to cyber?

- Are systems detecting suspicious employee behavior that may indicate credentials under the control of an outsider?
- Has contact been established with incident response firms and law enforcement, and could they quickly be mobilized if a compromise is detected?

■ Threat category 4: Fraud

Do you operate a system that makes or processes payments? Although any pay-for-service you offer may be the target of someone looking for a free ride, nothing attracts the sophisticated criminal element like cash. If you offer the ability to move money, you should have a focus here. Although fraud is certainly not a new challenge, Internet connectivity has certainly brought it to new levels. If this is relevant to your organization, you have likely been dealing with the ramifications long before cyber considerations were added. The following questions, however, may be helpful to ensure cybersecurity efforts are aligned with traditional fraud protections:

- Have we deployed and enforced two-factor authentication such as text messages, mobile phone apps, or physical tokens to require our customers to have more than a username or password to authenticate?
- Are we using adaptive authentication to identify suspicious locations, access times, or transaction patterns in addition to classic credentials?
- Are we tracking and trending the sources, frequency, and value of losses?
- Are we working closely with peer institutions and competitors to share threat intelligence and identify common patterns we should detect and/or block?

■ Threat category 5: Commoditized hacking

Although specialized threats are associated with specific targets, all organizations have exposure to the most common family of commoditized threats. These threats are opportunistic and warrant different controls than advanced threats. At a minimum, automated attacks look to procure access to your IT environment so that your computing resources can be made available for more nefarious aims. Even if you do not host critical infrastructure or easily monetized data, commodity threats look to compromise your computers so that they can be used as agents of more sophisticated attacks. Malware looks to enlist your computing, storage, and bandwidth to help criminals blast out junk email, store pirated media, or contribute to a Denial of Service attack. Attackers in this category do not care (or often know) if your computers belong to a financial services firm, manufacturer, university, home network, or hospital. Protecting your organization from these common attacks requires being less exposed than the next target. Ask yourself:

- Have we identified a role in our organization that is responsible for cybersecurity?
- Are only absolutely required services exposed to the Internet?
- Are PCs and email servers protected from common viruses and malware in an automated fashion?
- Does our corporate email employ controls to filter out the most common virus and spam campaigns?
- Does our corporate Internet access incorporate controls to block access to malicious websites?

One special form of opportunistic attack involves ransom. Some malware encrypts the content of infected computers so that it becomes unavailable until a payment is made. This type of attack can be crippling. In addition to the preventative controls outlined above, you should ask the following:

- Are our file servers backed up and tested regularly, and could we recover quickly if all current data were unavailable?
- Have we, via policy and practice, established the principle that PCs and laptops are disposable, that data on these

devices should not be relied upon, and that network storage should be used to house any critical data?

■ Conclusion

Although cybersecurity is a relatively new field, it has already grown into an expansive area requiring monitoring and controls around mission critical infrastructure and data. Attention to governance has ramped up dramatically in a short period, and it can be difficult to sift through the advice of experts. Investing time in analyzing threats and identifying what assets adversaries are truly after is a critical first step in establishing an effective governance policy around cybersecurity.

28

Breaking the status quo: Designing for breach prevention

Palo Alto Networks Inc.

■ **Today's reality and commoditization of threats**

The statistics regarding the success of advanced cyberthreats paint a very grim picture. The increasing speed at which new security threats appear, and the growing sophistication of criminal hackers' techniques, make fighting cybercrime a constant challenge. A recent study by Cyber Edge found that 71 percent of the security professionals polled said their networks had experienced a breach, up significantly from the previous year (62 percent). And half of those respondents felt that a successful cyberattack against their network was likely in the next 12 months, compared to just 39 percent in 2013.

Unfortunately, there isn't a week that goes by these days when we aren't learning about some new data breach. To say that keeping up with attackers' evolving techniques and advanced threats is difficult is an understatement. These attacks come from multiple angles, through the edge of the network and directly at the users of our digital infrastructure. Not only are they more targeted in nature, the mechanisms that attackers use increasingly utilize a growing pool of software vulnerabilities. Some vulnerabilities are known only to the attacker, referred to as zero-days. Others are known to the general public but have yet to be fixed by the software vendor. A fact attackers are very much aware of.

Additionally, new attack methods and malware are shared readily on the black market, each more sophisticated than the last. The cat-and-mouse game between attackers and defending organizations is no longer a competition. Attackers have not only pulled ahead, they've gained so much distance that most security teams have given up on the notion that they can prevent an attack and are instead pouring investment into trying to quickly detect attacks, and defining incident response plans rather than trying to stop them. Why? Because legacy security offerings consist of a set of highly disjointed technologies that only allow detection of attacks once they are already on the network or endpoint.

Organizations cannot hire their way out of this problem by throwing more people at navigating a legacy architecture or making up for the inherent gaps between the siloed technologies. Instead, organizations should be considering next-generation technology that natively integrates security to deliver automated results, preventing attackers from achieving their ultimate objectives. Given the sheer volume and complexity of threats, it's important to use automation to accelerate detection *and* prevention without the reliance on a security middleman.

Despite the growing cybersecurity challenge we are all facing, we cannot give up on our digital infrastructure. Customers are becoming more and more reliant on the Internet and our networks to do business and access commercial services. They use these systems because of the trust they place in them. This trust underpins everything they do online and extends to an organization's brand and place in the market. Legacy security approaches that focus only on detection and remediation, or rely on a series of disjointed tools, abandon this trust and can introduce significant risk by failing to consider how to prevent cyberattacks in the first place.

A new approach is needed in order to prevent modern cyberattacks. This new approach must account for the realities that today's attacks are not only multidimensional in nature but also use an increasingly sophisticated set of techniques that are constantly in a state of change. As these techniques evolve, the risk of breach increases, and, as we all know, an organization is only as strong as its weakest entry point. Therefore, an effective strategy must work to disrupt an attack at multiple points, including:

- developing a Zero Trust security posture that focuses on only allowing legitimate users and applications, as opposed to trying to block everyone and everything that is bad

- blocking the different techniques attackers might use to evade detection and establish command-and-control channels
- preventing installation of malware—including unknown and polymorphic malware
- blocking the different techniques that attackers must follow in order to exploit a software vulnerability
- closely monitoring and controlling data traffic within the organization to protect against the unabated lateral movement when legitimate identities are hijacked.

■ Cyberattack lifecycle

Despite the headlines, successful cyberattacks are not inevitable, nor do they happen by magic. Often it is a 'window' that is left open or a 'bag' that is not screened that lets an attacker slip into a network undetected. After they are inside a network, attackers will sit and wait, patiently planning their next move, until they are sure they can reach their objective. Much like a game of chess, it is only at the end of a long and logical series of steps that they will try to act. Knowing the playbook of a cyberattack can help us disrupt and prevent not just well-understood attacks but also highly sophisticated new attacks used by advanced actors.

Despite different tools, tactics, and procedures used by an attacker, there are certain high-level steps in the attack lifecycle that most cyberattacks have in common. Traditional approaches to security focus on installing a feature to disrupt only one point along this lifecycle. This approach often comes from the fact that different parts of an IT security team have different objectives: network administrators care about connectivity and the firewall, info security analysts care about analytics, and so forth. They seldom have to really work together in a coordinated manner because this approach was previously useful at stopping low-level threats that involved opportunistic targeting, such as the infamous email scam from a foreign prince needing to transfer $1 million to the U.S.

However, today's attacks have become more and more sophisticated as advanced tools have proliferated and as effective attack strategies have been developed and shared among criminal and nation-state adversaries. These attacks are often called advanced persistent threats (APTs), so named because they use advanced tools and persistently target an organization again and again until they get in. They are patient and stealthy, preferring to forego a quick boom and bust for a longer payoff of high-value information.

While APTs used to be the domain of nation-state espionage, today organizations large and small face these high-level threats from actors seeking to steal sensitive intellectual property and financial information, disrupt digital systems, or cause embarrassment. It is against these patient and persistent advanced adversaries that traditional single-point approaches fail. However, by targeting every step of an attacker's playbook, it is possible to architect a solution that offers much greater odds at stopping the attacks before they can reach their objective. At the very least, putting preventative measures in place that take the complete lifecycle into consideration will raise the cost for the attacker, potentially forcing him to look elsewhere for an easier victim. Let's take a look at the steps an attacker goes through to get into and out of a network.

Advice along the cyberattack lifecycle

Reconnaissance. Just like burglars and thieves, advanced attackers carefully plan their attacks. They research, identify, and select targets, oftentimes using phishing tactics or extracting public information from an employee's public online profile or from corporate websites. These criminals also scan for network vulnerabilities and services or applications they can exploit.

- Even job websites can be a gold mine of information. If you are looking to hire a new engineer who is familiar with a certain security product, an attacker can deduce what you are using to protect your network and will know where common gaps are in your security.
- You can't stop all reconnaissance activity, but you certainly shouldn't make it any easier for the attacker! People and processes are just as important to security as technology. Good training and strong security practices will help limit reconnaissance and harden your security profile. You should be aware of what your adversary can learn from your corporate website and ensure that members of your organization with high-level access receive training to be security conscious.
- Finally, there are many services that offer advanced 'red-team' exercises to help you identify weaknesses in your security posture. These simple steps can also put in place policy 'trip wires' that can alert you to unusual activity that may indicate an advanced actor is interested in you.

Weaponization and delivery. As we move to the next stage of the cyberattack lifecycle, technology becomes even more critical to preventing advanced threats. The hacker must choose his method for gaining access onto your network. This access can be digital, or even physical, but is primarily intended to gain a foothold from which to plan the assault and achieve the attacker's objectives.

Spear phishing

- With the information gained from their reconnaissance, the attackers have to determine which methods they must use to penetrate your network. They often choose to embed intruder code within seemingly innocuous files like a PDF document or email message. They may also seek to use highly targeted attacks to catch specific interests of an individual.

Continued

Advice along the cyberattack lifecycle—cont'd

- Spear phishing is by far the most commonly used tactic because it's simple and effective. An attacker will use information gathered during the reconnaissance phase to craft an email with a malicious attachment for a specific user he believes has access to sensitive credentials or information.
- Many organizations have begun training their employees to spot these attacks by sending test emails that can track who opens them. Over time they can see which departments continually fall for these attacks and target training there.
- However, we are all conditioned to read emails and open attachments if they seem relevant to our positions. Even with the best training, a well-crafted spear phishing email that appears to come from a family member, friend, or boss can trick the most seasoned security veteran. It's vital to ensure that you have technical security measures as well to mitigate any malicious malware that might ride email into your networks.

Watering hole

- Another approach to gaining access is known as watering hole attacks. In this method the attacker will set up a fake website that downloads malicious code to any visitor, then direct their victims to it. When a user visits the website, a software exploitation kit installs malware on the victim's computer, which then reports back to the attacker so he knows who he's infected and can access their system to steal data.
- Watering hole attacks are harder to pull off because they require compromising a separate web server, but they can be very effective if a company is watching for malicious files in email. Traditional security products do not always prevent their users from visiting malicious websites. However, advanced approaches will filter known malicious addresses to keep users from becoming a victims of a 'drive-by download.'

Exploitation. Once attackers gain access 'inside' an organization, they can activate attack code on the victim's computer (also known as a 'host') and ultimately take full control.

- To gain full control over a victim, specialized programs exploit vulnerabilities in existing software to install themselves as legitimate users. Vulnerabilities are usually old bugs that were not caught during the original writing of the code. Sometimes they are known bugs that have not been repaired, or 'patched'; sometimes they are as of yet unknown to anyone except the attacker. These unknown vulnerabilities are called zero-days because they are not found by the victim until the first day he realizes he has been penetrated by an attacker.
- As noted earlier, zero-days are the most nefarious of threats. Luckily, true zero-days are also the most rare. When they are used, however, it generally means that no one else is protected from them. Because no one is patched for it, if an attacker moves quickly, he can take advantage of the same vulnerability on many, many systems.
- If you can't catch an unknown threat, you can at least prevent an attacker from using that vulnerability to cause damage. Because attackers have similar goals, such as stealing or damaging important files, there are only so many techniques they can use after they have penetrated a system to achieve their end goals. Advanced security software will hunt for malware that uses zero-days by searching for and stopping common techniques attackers use after they have gained access to your network.

Advice along the cyberattack lifecycle—cont'd

- Common vulnerabilities are being found and fixed every day. Your organization should also have a process in place to regularly update and patch all your software and hardware. However, sometimes these new versions and updates can cause existing systems to malfunction. This will often leave IT teams hesitant to update systems until a new patch can be tested and can cause delays that leave you with vulnerabilities known to the entire world. While you should always lean toward patching and updating as soon as possible, the balance of security and operability must be viewed through your own business risk management practices.

Installation. As a first order of business, advanced attackers will seek to establish themselves as securely and quietly as possible across your network.

- They do this by taking advantage of the trust of the digital systems they are working in. Often an attacker will make himself an administrator on a computer and then try to infect other users in order to steal their digital identities. He will play this game of laterally escalating access privileges to gain a higher and higher level of control of your systems. Along the way the attacker will also open backdoors that allow him to connect back into your network even if he is eventually caught and shut out. This is why it can be especially difficult to fully remove an advanced actor from a network.
- It seems strange, but many of the tools attackers use can be found freely online or for sale on the Internet. Tools are viewed just like a hammer and nails, where on the one hand security professionals use them to test systems and build stronger security, but on the other hand they can be used as weapons. These 'off-the-shelf' security tools, while highly capable, can often be found by traditional security methods such as antivirus software.
- However, more advanced actors will build their own custom tools, such as remote access tools (RATs), that are undetectable by antivirus software. In fact, some tools commonly shut off antivirus software as one of the first steps of installation. These tools require a larger investment from the attacker and will primarily be designed to gain a foothold as a seemingly legitimate user on the network. From there the attacker can act like a normal employee and use authorized applications such as file-sharing software or internal email to cause mischief.

Command and control. Gaining a foothold in a network is of no use to attackers if they can't control their attack.

- An advanced actor knows that he is likely to be discovered at some point and must be ready to improvise by hiding and running from security teams or software. To do this, an attacker establishes a command-and-control channel back through the Internet to a specific server so he can communicate and pass data back and forth between infected devices and his server.
- The most commonly used channel for attackers to communicate to their tools is through regular Internet traffic (using hypertext transfer protocol, or HTTP). Usually their communications will pass through defenses of traditional security tools as they blend in with the large volume of traffic from legitimate users.
- The attacker's tools will periodically phone home, typically referred to as beaconing, to obtain the next set of commands. Beacons can also contain reconnaissance information from the compromised target, such as the operating system configuration, software versions, and the identity of users who are logged on to the network. In very complicated networks, this information can allow an attacker to quietly burrow deeper and deeper. Clever malware also moves beyond simple requests for command and control and tries to emulate human behavior by using email or social networking applications to receive its attacker commands.

Continued

Advice along the cyberattack lifecycle—cont'd

- If you treat your network with zero trust, as though it might already be breached, you can start to lock down unnecessary pathways for attackers to communicate and move around. Segmenting networks and building internal controls on applications can act like a firebreak, keeping an attacker from spreading to other parts of your network.

Actions on the objective. Attackers may have many different motivations for breaching your network, and it's not always for profit. Their reasons could be data exfiltration, defacement of web property, or even destruction of critical infrastructure.

- The most common goals of attackers often involve finding and exfiltrating your data without getting caught. During this late stage, the work is usually done by an active person issuing commands to his tools on your network. He has a goal and a script that is followed in a complex process that may last days, weeks, or months, but ends with all your sensitive data slipping through a backdoor in your network.

- This is one of the most difficult steps to stop, as an active person can improvise and adapt to your security response efforts. While it may seem counterintuitive, it's important to respond with patience when trying to stop an active intruder. A common tactic of advanced attackers when they are caught is to 'smash and grab'; this means they will forget about remaining quiet and do whatever they can to achieve their objectives, potentially damaging your systems in the process. They can also choose to slip deeper into your systems, burrowing in and waiting to reuse one of their backdoors to gain entry after you believe you have patched all your vulnerabilities. For these reasons, it is critical to have a response plan in place ahead of time so that the adversary doesn't detect signs of panic and get tipped off. If you can discover the attacker before he realizes he is caught, you can work to clean up his tools, while closing doors and windows he may have used to get in.

- A strong response plan will also help you prepare in advance for any mitigation efforts needed, including the vital step of external relations if it becomes public that you have had an incident. Depending on the data that was accessed or stolen, you may have regulatory or legal reporting requirements that you will need to be prepared to deal with. Even if the attacker is not successful at actually taking data, these requirements may still be in place as in many cases you may not be able to determine if data was stolen, exposed, or remained untouched.

Trying to stop an advanced adversary at only one point in this lifecycle is an exercise in futility. Just like a network has vulnerabilities and weaknesses, so too does the attacker. He will reuse tactics, techniques, and procedures on multiple victims, establishing patterns that can be recognized, studied, and exploited. But to gain this leverage, a new approach to security is needed.

■ Why legacy approaches fail

Most security architectures today resemble a set of siloed organizations, processes, and technical infrastructure. They have largely been assembled like a manufacturing production line, where a series of security events roll down a conveyor belt of individual point products, while different staff members perform their individual duties. This has been the traditional approach to security, and historically we've been able to use it to fend off low-level threats. However, these architectures are beginning to show their weaknesses as attackers have learned to slip between silos. Today we see how costly legacy systems can be both in their inability to prevent targeted attacks and in their unnecessary expense to the organization.

One of the primary strategic failures of traditional security architectures is their reactive approach. Following the assembly-line model, security teams work to read data logs about events that happened to their network in the past. Since most of these teams operate in a siloed manner, these log files are routinely examined in isolation from other critical teams and thus lack important context that can be used to quickly detect and prevent an attack. Relying on a human in the middle of a network's defenses is too slow to be effective against advanced, automated hacking tools and creative attackers.

A secondary strategic failure is a lack of attention toward 'proactive prevention.' Organizations often don't do enough to reduce their attack surface, allowing certain classes of applications that are unnecessary for their business and leaving doors open on their network by using port-based policies.

This essentially allows adversaries to distribute malware and steal intellectual property through basic applications into which they have little or no visibility. We must break away from the traditional approach to security that has proven ineffective at stopping advanced attacks time and time again.

Over the last several years in particular, there has been a dramatic evolution in both the attackers and the techniques they use. By many estimates cybercrime is now a nearly half-trillion-dollar industry, and like any industry, opportunity fuels more investment and innovation. The best way to get an industry to collapse in on itself is to take away that potential for profit. Therefore, we must make it so unbelievably hard for cyber criminals to achieve their objectives that their only option is to invest more and more resources to stage a successful attack, to the point that it becomes unprofitable.

Tenets of a traditional security architecture

Limited visibility. You can't secure what you can't see. Traditional sensors only seek out what they know to be bad, rather than inspect all traffic to only allow what is good. Your security architecture must eliminate blind spots by having the ability to see all applications, users, and content across all ports and protocols (the doors and windows of your network) even if they are encrypted. It must also have the ability to see and prevent new, targeted attacks that are utilizing threats that have never been seen before, such as malware and zero-day vulnerability exploits.

Lacking correlation. If attacks are multidimensional, your defense must be as well. Today's attackers shift techniques while they are working their way into a network in order to step over traps laid by them for traditional defenses. In order to find the clues they leave behind, your architecture must act like a system of systems where individual technologies work in concert to identify and then automatically prevent attacks. Correlating sensors and protection makes each element within the system smarter. For example, if a thief has hit multiple houses using the same techniques, you will need to adjust your burglar alarm for those techniques. In cyberspace, however, this process can be automated to increase the speed of detection and prevention.

Manual response. With attacks evolving at a rapid pace, it's critical that we wean ourselves from relying on the 'man in the middle.' Systems focused on detection often throw up mountains of alerts and warnings for low-threat items, overwhelming your IT security team. An advanced security architecture must employ a system of automation that's constantly learning and applying new defenses without a requirement for any manual intervention. It must weed out the congestion automatically, handling 99 percent of low-level threats so you can focus your team's attention on the 1 percent of the highest priority incidents.

Stopping today's advanced threats lies in turning the economics of our reality on its head by preventing threats in multiple places at each step of the cyberattack lifecycle. This requires creating an architecture that can detect attacks at every point around and within a network, closing any gaps and preventing them from successfully launching in the first place.

■ Prevention architecture

No organization today is immune to cyberattacks. Cyber criminals are ramping up activity across the globe and utilizing new methods to evade traditional security measures. An effective security architecture must not only prevent threats from entering and damaging the network but also take full advantage of knowledge about threats in other security communities. Traditional solutions typically focus on a single threat vector across a specific section of the organization. This lack of visibility is leaving multiple areas vulnerable to attack. In addition, these legacy solutions are made up of a 'patchwork' of point products that make it very difficult to coordinate and share intelligence among the various devices.

As a result, security teams are forced to invest more and more time and money in detection and remediation efforts, under the assumption that prevention is a lost battle. These efforts require a time-consuming process of piecing together evidence from different devices, combing through them to discover unknown threats, and then manually creating and deploying protections. By the time this happens—often days or weeks later—it's too late because minutes or hours are all an attacker needs to accomplish his or her end goal. This Band-Aid approach doesn't fix the fundamental problem of accounting for the new threat landscape.

While nothing will stop every attack, designing a security architecture with a prevention mindset (and following some of the risk management best practices outlined in our chapter, "The CEO's guide to driving better security by asking the right questions") can make cybersecurity a business enabler. By preventing damage to networks and theft of sensitive information, vital IT resources, people, and time are freed up to tackle core business functions. In order to shift from a 'detect and remediate' stature to preventing attacks, business leaders need to consider three cybersecurity imperatives:

1. Process: organize to reduce your attack surface.
   - Modern networks can be a rat's nest of systems and users cobbled together from mergers, legacy architectures, and prior acquisitions. This confusion leaves many points of entry for attackers to slip in unnoticed and reside on your network for months or even years. A critical step to preventing advanced cyberattacks is to know your network better than the attacker does. To do this you must work at simplifying your architecture down to manageable pieces that can be controlled, watched, and defended.
   - A key step in reducing your attack surface is to only allow network traffic and communications that are required to operate your business by utilizing technology that understands the applications, users, and content transiting your network. This seems to be common sense that any unknown traffic could also be hiding malicious activity, but often when organizations take a deep look at their traffic, they find high-risk applications that they had no idea were running on their network. Legacy approaches often only search to block what is bad, rather than allowing only what is good. This approach is also known as 'white listing' and will immediately reduce the scope of your security challenge by eliminating opportunities for malware to get into your network.
   - Another step to reducing your attack surface is to segment important components of your networks, such as data centers. As described earlier, advanced actors often seek to break

into a less secure part of the network and then move laterally into more sensitive areas. By segmenting the most vital parts of a network from email or customer-facing systems, you will be building in firebreaks that can prevent the spread of a breach.

- You also can't neglect to secure the endpoint or individual user. This is the final battlefield. Originally, anti-virus software contained signatures for malicious software and could, thus, catch most major infections from common threats because it knew what to look for. However, as we learned earlier, today's attacks can include unknown malware or exploits that are essentially invisible to antivirus software. This has led to a massive decline in the effectiveness of traditional antivirus products and a rise in a new way of thinking about endpoint protection. Rather than looking for something that can't be seen, you can reduce the endpoint attack surface by preventing the type of actions taken by exploits and malware. Stopping the type of malicious activity associated with an attack is much more effective than hunting for an attack that, by nature, is stealthy and hidden.
- Finally, it seems simplistic, but as you make investments to re-architect your network and reduce your attack surface, you have to use all those investments to their fullest. Purchasing next-generation technology is useless if you don't turn it on and configure it properly. Establishing a process for staying up to date on your security investments is one of the most critical habits to form.

2. Technology: integrate and automate controls to disrupt the cyberattack lifecycle.
- Don't use yesterday's technology to address today's and tomorrow's security challenges. As noted earlier, legacy security approaches offer individual products to be bolted on for single-feature solutions. This leaves gaps that can be broken by new methods of attack, leaving your organization at

risk. However, by using an integrated cybersecurity platform that protects across your entire enterprise, your defenses can work together to identify and close gaps that would be exploited by an attacker. Communication is key to any strong defense. If your products can't share information on what they are seeing, there is no chance to pick up clues that might aid in preventing an advanced attack.
- The next step is automating prevention measures. Humans have proven time and again that we are the weakest link in security. Advanced actors are faster, more persistent, and stealthier than manual response efforts. It just takes one overlooked log file or one missed security alert to bring down an entire organization. However, if you have an integrated platform that communicates visibility across your defenses, it can also automatically act on new threats, preventing what is malicious and Indeterminate what is unknown.
- Integration should also enable your organization's agility and innovation. Business doesn't stop at the elevator, as employees take laptops to work from home or use their personal mobile devices to access your corporate cloud on the road. As your data moves to enable your workforce, security should go with it. Choose a platform compatible with newer technologies such as mobile, cloud, and network virtualization.

3. People: participate in a community that shares cyberthreat information.
- End users cannot be relied upon to identify every malicious URL or phishing attack. Organizations must educate their constituents about what they can do on their part to stop cyberattacks. However, beyond education, to protect against today's truly advanced cyberthreats, we must utilize the global community to combine threat intelligence from a variety of sources to help 'connect the dots.' Real-time, global intelligence feeds help security teams keep pace with

threat actors and easily identify new security events.

- As attackers move from target to target, they leave digital fingerprints in the form of their tactics, techniques, and procedures. By analyzing this evidence and then sharing it, threat intelligence from other organizations can quickly inoculate you from new attacks as bad guys seek to move between organizations and even industries. Combined with an integrated platform that can act automatically on this intelligence, you can rapidly distribute warnings and make it impossible for attackers to strike twice. The network effect from vendors with large customer bases is extremely powerful as it builds a security ecosystem, which can organically respond to new threats.
- Many organizations are even coming together to share threats as an entire sector. Recent policy from the U.S. Government has made it easier to collaborate and share cyberthreat information between companies and work together to identify and stop advanced cyber actors.

The most significant way to fill in all the gaps and truly protect an organization from advanced and targeted threats is to implement an integrated and extensible security platform that can prevent even the most challenging unknown threats across the entire attack lifecycle. An IT architecture must remain secure while also providing business flexibility and enabling applications needed to run day-to-day operations. Stopping even the most advanced attacks is possible, but we have to begin with a prevention mindset.

Conclusion: Cybersecurity as a business enabler

Traditionally, IT security has been seen by most organizations as a cost center, requiring continued expenses but not bringing in any revenue. The attention and resources devoted to it are often the bare minimum to meet regulatory requirements or mandatory certifications. IT security personnel are often drafted from projects that support core business operations to work in the 'dark corners' of network security with a gloomy future of scanning thousands of false alarms, updating old software, and, of course, getting blamed for the inevitable cyber incidents that are usually caused by larger organizational problems. This sad tale is a reality for a shocking number of organizations; it not only guarantees failure, it ensures lost opportunity for innovation that comes from having a strong security posture.

Adopting a prevention philosophy helps create strategies for better security and maximizes the value of an organization's actions and resources. Viewing cybersecurity as a business enabler helps drive appropriate resource allocation by returning value to the business based on new opportunities that would not have been available without the level of trust afforded by a prevention architecture.

Take the case of the IT security team. When an organization decides to take their security more seriously, usually after a cyber incident, one of the first things they do is dump more people into IT security positions. While trained security experts are a boon for any organization, the architecture they are working in can have them needlessly chasing cycles of work, wasting budget by hunting for cyber needles in digital haystacks of alarms, and manually remediating countless vulnerabilities. Employing a prevention architecture that automates protection capabilities and shares threat intelligence using an integrated platform means that security teams can operate much more efficiently and effectively. Their time is an organization's money, and it's imperative to ensure that personnel working on core IT functions that keep business operations running are not being wasted on outdated security practices.

Strong cybersecurity can also open new opportunities by making organizations more flexible and resilient. Today's workforce is constantly connected to the Internet at home, on the road, and at their desk. Users move between applications and devices seamlessly and expect that their actions will translate between these different environments. However, this traditionally has not been the case. Threats from third-party applications, unsecured cloud environments, and infected personal mobile devices have become so prevalent that many traditional security products will either block them completely or just assume that they cannot be protected. This old way of doing business doesn't match the reality of today's workers, who are expected to be more agile and mobile than ever before. Architecting a network to wrap these devices and third-party services into an existing security platform ensures that data will remain secure as workers go out to meet with customers in the field and expand business beyond its office walls.

The security field is stuck today with few answers to increasingly challenging problems.

If organizations continue to view investments in cybersecurity simply as cost centers to be solved by bolting on legacy technology, we will all continue to suffer the consequences. Our most valuable data and the keys to vital pieces of infrastructure will walk out the door in the hands of cyber criminals, while the trust we have built between our customers and our systems continues to degrade. This will happen time and time again until we are forced to change and narrow the way we use digital systems in our everyday lives. This must not become the reality for the entire community that receives such unimaginable benefits from the Internet. By adopting a prevention mindset it is possible to change the status quo and take back the control and trust in systems that enable critical business operations. Planning for disaster is always a smart move, but preparing for failure will accomplish just that.

Cybersecurity glossary

Advanced persistent threat (APT): An adversary that possesses sophisticated levels of expertise and significant resources that allow it to create opportunities to achieve its objectives by using multiple attack vectors (e.g., cyber, physical, and deception). http://niccs.us-cert.gov/glossary

Attack surface: An information system's characteristics that permit an adversary to probe, attack, or maintain presence in the information system. http://niccs.us-cert.gov/glossary

Antivirus software: A program that monitors a computer or network to detect or identify major types of malicious code and to prevent or contain malware incidents, sometimes by removing or neutralizing the malicious code. http://niccs.us-cert.gov/glossary

Command-and-control channel: Data link for an attacker to communicate with his malicious software installed on a victim's system.

Data exfiltration: After an attacker has found sensitive data that he is targeting, he will attempt to package this data and remove it silently from a victim's system.

Endpoint: Specific parts of an IT infrastructure that users interact with directly, such as workstations or mobile devices.

Exploit: A technique to breach the security of a network or information system in violation of security policy. http://niccs.us-cert.gov/glossary

Hypertext transfer protocol (HTTP): Technical rules for transferring data over the Internet. Web browsers use HTTP, and the encrypted variant HTTPS, to allow users to interact directly with websites in a secure manner.

Malware: Software that compromises the operation of a system by performing an unauthorized function or process. http://niccs.us-cert.gov/glossary

Network: Joined pieces of an IT infrastructure that transfer and route data to and from endpoints and other networks.

Polymorphic malware: Malicious software that is designed to continuously change its appearance, allowing it to evade legacy security detection technology such as antivirus software.

Continued

Cybersecurity glossary—cont'd

Port-based security: Stateful inspection firewalls block any Internet traffic coming into or out of a network on a specific line of communication, called a port. However, modern applications use different ports, and malicious software can change the port it uses.

Remote access tools (RATs): Malicious software that allows an attacker to control a system where he is not physically present. These functions in IT systems also exist for legitimate uses, such as support functions.

Zero-day: A software vulnerability that is unknown to the public but is used by an attacker to gain access and control of a network or system.

VI Cybersecurity beyond your network

29

Supply chain as an attack chain

Booz Allen Hamilton – Bill Stewart, Executive Vice President; Tony Gaidhane, Senior Associate; and Laura Eise, Lead Associate

The supply chain ecosystem reaches farther and wider than ever before. The growing range of suppliers provides significant competitive advantages for companies that strategically and securely source from this global network. Yet this complex footprint comes with an equally complex range of cyberthreats, and the majority of organizations do not realize the breadth and depth of these challenges. However, hackers are well aware of existing supply chain vulnerabilities and are moving aggressively to take advantage of these exposures.

Threat actors typically target organizations' supply chains through two vectors: the first type of attack is known as "adversarial supply chain operations to," or "ASCO To," and the second is known "adversarial supply chain operations through," or "ASCO Through" (Figure 1). In an ASCO To attack, your organization is the direct target. In the latter, the adversary uses your supply chain as a means to target one of your customers. Although the intent is different, both have the potential for devastating impact to your revenue, reputation, and end consumer.

To compound this issue, today's attackers are often well funded and extremely organized. These attackers have the resources, skills, and patience to conduct sophisticated attacks on your supply chain. For example, a supply chain cyber adversary may clandestinely intercept delivery of your products and switch cyber sensitive components with a malware-infused copycat. These attacks are often so sophisticated that the end users may not realize that they did not receive the original version.

Nation-states, hacktivists, organized criminal groups, and lone wolves are constantly scanning supply chains

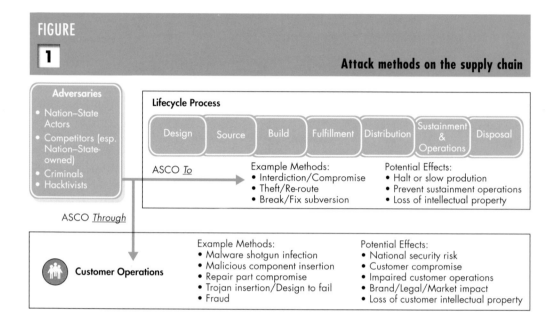

FIGURE 1 — Attack methods on the supply chain

for weak points, and the impact of this attention has the potential to reverberate well beyond your supply chain. You inherit the risks of your suppliers. If one of your suppliers lacks security controls, you may absorb their vulnerabilities. This is particularly true if you do not comprehensively test their components during your acceptance process; once you accept their product, you accept the risks of being attacked or passing along an attack to your customers. In the event that a cyberattack occurs, you own the impacts as well. This includes brand damage, operational stoppage, legal exposure, canceled sales, and government sanctions.

■ **Dangerous combination of hidden risks and higher expectations**

Tackling cybersecurity risk in supply chain may feel like you are trapped between a virtual rock and a hard place. As companies drive to increase supply chain flexibility at the lowest overall cost, sourcing decisions expose them to the vulnerabilities of suppliers and all of their successive networks of suppliers. This ever-evolving cybersecurity threat in the multi-layered supply chain presents a number of challenges when managing cybersecurity. See Figure 2.

Supply chain traditionally has been seen as part of internal operations; it is something that happens behind the scenes for your customers. In the past, customers did not care where you made your products or how you sourced them as long as you delivered them on time, at the appropriate cost, and in good condition. However, this is all changing. Companies and governments around the world are realizing that the supply chain is an ideal way for attackers to quietly infiltrate their networks and infect a system well before customers place an order. Companies, large and small, have to begin looking at supply chain security as part of their overall supply chain risk management process.

By prioritizing supply chain cybersecurity, you are well on your way to tackling this complex issue. You have an opportunity to mitigate cyber risk and transform your supply chain risk management capability into a competitive advantage to inform your broader business.

■ **Increasing expectations**

The U.S. government has been a force for driving higher-level visibility and controls across the supply chain. As the future progresses,

FIGURE 2

Cybersecurity challenges in the supply chain

Lack of Visibility

Limited visibility across the supply chain regarding exposure and controls

Dynamic Threat

The evolving capabilities of well-resourced and determined adversaries means that "point in time" solutions are insufficient.

External Dependencies

Companies cannot ensure part integrity on their own—they will need participation from suppliers and other business partners.

Cross-Functional Challenge

Requires change and collaboration from various internal business functions to collectively manage cyber risk throughout the supply chain

Decision Making

Increased information requires new strategic and tactical decision-making processes.

insurance companies will be an even larger driver for increasing supply chain standards. Business continuity policies are in place to address threats that disrupt the supply chain. Companies with weak supply chain cyber security policies and procedures could find their insurers raising their premiums or excluding claims in case of a breach. The next wave of standards could take shape with requiring you to maintain a list of all cyber sensitive supply chain components as well as develop comprehensive risk frameworks to classify, prioritize, and proactively manage the sourcing of each of those components. You need to proactively get ahead of these standards. Prove to the government, insurers, and your customers that you have a strong supply chain cyber cybersecurity capability.

It is not just the U.S. federal government that is raising the stakes. Many clients also are demanding to know more about the supply chain. Private sector clients are realizing that securing high assurance services on an untrusted hardware platform is the same as building a fort on a foundation of shifting sand. They want to know the depth of visibility into the components and services of products, and they want to be reassured that there are controls in place to manage a robust supply chain cybersecurity program. As with the government, many of these requests and requirements are at an all-time high and will become more sophisticated and comprehensive only during the next several years. If you are their supplier, they know that you are only as trustworthy as your supply chain.

■ How to create both a secure and compliant capability

Complying with standards and guidelines is not enough for securing all of the factors you need to comprehensively increase your security posture. Although standards strive to create consistency among cybersecurity programs, the fundamental truth is that there is no formula for security. Standards and frameworks can help identify the landscape of potential areas to address and may let you set a minimum level of performance, but that's it. You must move beyond merely striving to be compliant rather than noncompliant. Supply chain cybersecurity is more than an IT problem. If not used in the appropriate context, standards can be a generic solution to a highly individualized problem set. Supply chain risk is tied intimately to your business strategy and operations, and it must be tailored to your organization.

Rather than focusing on a standard, look at your program with a maturity lens. Understand the various degrees of risk you face. Then, within a well-established structure, decide where you need to invest and develop. It is up to you to prioritize the control areas to address. Focus on your current maturity in those areas and what you must do to increase your maturity. Focusing on your maturity provides you with an opportunity to identify where your program stands today, where it must be in the future, and how to get there. A maturity approach is not "one size fits all." Special considerations for your organization could necessitate that your approach be different than that of a competitor. Using a maturity model also allows you to answer the questions that are not yet asked by compliance while aligning your supply chain to your business strategy. It allows you to focus on increasing your overall security and to stay ahead of the curve.

■ Where do I start?

Developing a robust supply chain cybersecurity program is complex, but that doesn't mean your approach has to be. It requires a risk-based prioritization approach to changes in policy, supplier contracts, resource allocation, and investment. Most companies do not have the appetite or the budget for wholesale, drastic changes. If you are like most organizations, you face the dilemma of not knowing where to begin.

So the best place to start is to get your arms around what has to be done.

1. Conduct a maturity assessment and build a roadmap.
   Your organization needs a plan for the path forward in securing your supply chain. Before you transition to developing a roadmap, you must begin with a maturity assessment. Supply chain cybersecurity program maturity assessments are simply gap analyses between how well your program operates today compared with how it should operate in a target state. To evaluate this, you must identify the key controls that apply to supply chain risk management—either controls you already use as part of your corporate cybersecurity program or controls that may be more unique to supply chain. Even if you use existing controls, you should modify them to apply to your supply chain operations.

Maturity Assessment Tip

The set of controls you select for your maturity assessment should incorporate the compliance standards that customers might use as part of their Request for Proposal requirements (e.g., NIST SP 800-161). You likely will cover more controls than these standards, but mapping them will allow you to kill two birds with one stone.

Five Common Early Wins

Below are five common ways you can gain early traction with your supply chain cybersecurity program:
- Integrate/enhance component tracking
- Include cyber in your supply chain risk management framework
- Enhance acceptance testing
- Conduct supply chain vulnerability penetration testing
- Enhance monitoring of supplier network access points

Next, identify key objectives for each control you plan to evaluate. Threat intelligence, for example, may have data collection, analysis, and distribution as key control objectives. For each objective, define a scale as well as the key characteristics for each step in that scale. Taking the threat intelligence example, a low maturity rating for data collection could be the ad hoc collection of threat data via unstructured sources, such as email. A higher maturity implementation of data collection would be a comprehensive ingestion of multiple formal data feeds that can be analyzed automatically and efficiently.

Next, conduct a baseline assessment of your current state—an honest assessment, backed by examples. This will help you surface risks associated with each control. After the baseline, define the target state for each control. The target state should be a balance between high effectiveness and practical costs, keeping in mind that not all controls need the highest level of maturity. Comparing the target state with the baseline provides you the gap you need to address.

The outcome of your maturity assessment will be a robust roadmap designed to transform your supply chain cybersecurity program. This equates to quick wins and key priorities for your organization. It should also help address the key requirements your customers demand.

2. Identify key risks throughout your supply chain lifecycle.
   Breaking down your supply chain lifecycle into discrete phases can help you identify key risks for each phase. Each phase presents its own vulnerabilities and risks. For example, during the distribution phase, threat actors can intercept

physical deliveries of products, place malware in cyber sensitive components, and allow the shipments to continue to end customers. As you identify risks for each phase, you have to assess the likelihood and impact of each risk. This prioritized list becomes your risk agenda and helps determine what to address first to enhance your supply chain cybersecurity program.

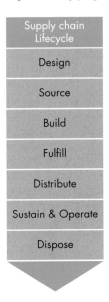

3. Decompose your key product lines.
   To assess the visibility, control, and risks in your supply chain, select a few key product lines and decompose them into their cyber sensitive components. Then see how much information you can collect on their manufacturing sources, acceptance testing, suppliers, and intended customers. You will likely find that your internal systems and policies are prohibiting you from this level of visibility; however, it is this level of visibility that customers will be demanding in

the future, if not already. Once you can obtain this kind of visibility, you can then assess the processes, controls, and risks associated with those cyber sensitive components.

■ **Supply chain cybersecurity as a differentiator**
The risks and expectations of your supply chain cybersecurity are increasing as threats become more sophisticated and customers' expectations rise. As you inherit the vulnerabilities from your suppliers and the risks of your customers, you have to be more aware of how your supply chain can become an attack chain. Compliance is not enough; you must develop a robust maturity model to help identify your vulnerabilities and develop a roadmap to reduce your risks.

Companies that are able to effectively manage their supply chain risks will have the advantage in the market. Understanding how to identify risk and then effectively manage those risks will allow you to be in greater control of your supply chain. A robust supply chain cyber risk management program will allow you to close vulnerabilities, making you less of a target for attackers while helping you meet and even shape your customer expectations. The trust in your brand and the quality of your product depend on the strength of your supply chain cybersecurity.

Creating the right balance of security and resilience in your supply chain will allow you to build a foundationally stronger supply chain cybersecurity program. This not only will differentiate you from your competitors but also will allow you to better understand the opportunities and advantages that are key to your success.

30

Managing risk associated with third-party outsourcing

*Covington & Burling LLP – David N. Fagan, Partner;
Nigel L. Howard, Partner; Kurt Wimmer, Partner; Elizabeth H.
Canter, Associate; and Patrick Redmon, Summer Associate*

■ Third-party outsourcing and cybersecurity risk

Businesses increasingly work with third parties in ways that can render otherwise well-guarded data vulnerable to attack or accidental disclosure. These third parties can include technology service providers; other major business function vendors, such as payroll, insurance, and benefits companies; and accounting and finance, advertising, delivery and lettershop, legal, and other consulting services.

Many of these commercial relationships require sensitive information—whether the business' own confidential business information or the personal information of its employees or customers—to be shared with, or stored by, the third parties. Such relationships also may entail third-party access to a company's networks. There is, in turn, an inherent risk in the third-party services: they can create new avenues of attack against a company's data or its systems and networks—and those avenues require appropriate mitigation.

Perhaps no data security breach highlighted this risk more than the incident incurred by Target. That incident began not with a direct attack on the Target network but with a phishing attack on a Pennsylvania HVAC contractor that had access to Target's external billing and project management portals. The HVAC contractor depended on a free version of consumer anti-malware software that allegedly failed to provide real-time protection. Once the phishing campaign succeeded in installing key-logging malware, the hackers obtained the HVAC contractor's credentials to Target's external billing and project management systems and from there infiltrated Target's internal network, eventually reaching Target's customer databases and point-of-sale systems.

The results of the Target breach are well known: the personal information of up to 70 million customers was compromised, and about 40 million customers had their credit or debit card information stolen. By the end of 2014, the costs to Target from the breach had exceeded $150 million. These costs include the litigation and settlement expenses resulting from lawsuits brought by consumers and credit card issuers. Further, in the quarter in which the data breach occurred, Target's year-over-year earnings plummeted 46 percent. Ultimately, in the aftermath of the breach, Target's CEO resigned.

The Target breach was not an isolated incident. In 2014, a Ponemon Institute survey found that in 20 percent of data breaches, a failure to properly vet a third party contributed to the breach. Even more troubling, 40 percent of the respondents to another Ponemon survey named third-party access to or management of sensitive data as one of the top two barriers to improving cybersecurity. Further, the Ponemon Institute's 2015 U.S. Cost of Data Breach Study reports that third-party involvement in a data breach increased the per capita cost of data breaches more than any other factor. However, despite the cybersecurity risks posed by third-party service providers, many companies fail to systematically address such risks. Only 52 percent of companies surveyed in a 2014 Ponemon Institute report have a program in place to systematically manage third-party cybersecurity risk.

■ Legal risks

Although there are many commercial and other reasons to adopt strong third-party risk management processes, a variety of legal frameworks require the management of third-party risk. Examples of such statutory or regulatory requirements include the following:

- the Interagency Guidelines Establishing Information Security Standards that implement Section 501 of the Gramm-Leach-Bliley Act and require financial institutions to engage in due diligence in the selection of service providers, to use contractual provisions to manage third-party risk, and, in some cases, to monitor service providers on an ongoing basis (e.g., 12 C.F.R. Pt. 225, App. F at III.D. [2012])
- the HIPAA Privacy Rule, requiring specific contractual provisions in dealing with business associates who handle protected health information, 45 C.F.R. §164.502(e) (2014)
- state regulations, such as the Massachusetts Standards for the Protection of Personal Information, requiring reasonable steps in selecting third parties and the use of contractual provisions to require their compliance with Massachusetts law, 201 Mass Code Regs. 17.03(2)(f).

In addition, the Federal Trade Commission has applied its authority under Section 5 of the FTC Act, 15 U.S.C. §45 (governing unfair acts and deceptive trade practices) to apply to cybersecurity and data security, and has taken action against companies that fail to take "reasonable steps to select and retain service providers capable of appropriately safeguarding personal information" a de facto regulatory requirement. See, for example, GMR Transcription Servs., Inc., F.T.C. Docket No. C–4482, File No. 122–3095, 2014 WL 4252393 (Aug. 14, 2014).

■ Sources of third-party cybersecurity risk

The cybersecurity and privacy risks generated by third-party engagements include the following:

- breaches of personal data—whether the personal data of customers or employees—and the attendant regulatory obligations (e.g., notification requirements), as well as legal liability, as in the Target breach
- breaches of a business's proprietary data, including the following:
  - competitively sensitive data, privileged information, attorney work product, and trade secrets
  - business partner data resulting in obligations to notify business partners

as well as potential contractual liability to them
- data that result in financial harm to the company, such as bank account information
- other confidential, market moving insider information in the hands of third parties such as investment bankers, consultants, and lawyers, such as information regarding nonpublic M&A activity, clinical trial results, or regulatory approvals
- the introduction into internal networks of viruses or other malicious code, as in the Dairy Queen attack, in which vendor credentials were used to gain access to internal networks and eventually install malware targeting point-of-sale systems
- the introduction of other vulnerabilities to IT systems, for instance, by the use of vulnerable third-party applications or code, as occurred in the Heartbleed OpenSSL exploit that potentially exposed the data transmitted to and from secure web servers
- misuse and secondary use of company data such as for direct marketing or data mining for the benefit of the vendor
- "fourth-party" risk, that is, the third-party cybersecurity risks introduced by a vendor's relationships with its own third-party service providers and vendors
- potential director or management liability for breach of fiduciary duty in the exercise of cybersecurity oversight.

To help manage this array of risks effectively, companies may consider whether they have appropriate procedures in place to evaluate and monitor individual vendors, as well as a program to manage and monitor third-party relationships.

■ Engagement-level management of third-party cybersecurity risk
The appropriate measures needed to scrutinize and monitor third-party service providers will depend to a large extent upon

the sophistication of the vendor and the nature of the IT systems and data at issue. Nonetheless, three elements are common to all third-party risk management:

1. due diligence prior to entering an engagement
2. contractual commitments and legal risk management
3. ongoing monitoring and oversight.

■ Pre-engagement due diligence
A critical element of managing third-party risk is the assessment of the third party's own security practices and posture before any contract is signed. Such diligence is crucial for the identification and evaluation of risks, and, in turn, can ensure that such risks are mitigated before the engagement, including through the use of contractual provisions. The actual evaluation may be more ad hoc (i.e., conversations with key business or technology stakeholders) or formal (i.e., through a questionnaire or even on-site assessment), and the extent of an evaluation may depend on various factors in the prospective relationship, including, for example, whether the service provider will have access to the company's IT systems, the nature of the information that it may access, and whether it will store such information.

Depending on the extent of the relationship and information that may be accessed by the vendor, the following areas of inquiry may be necessary to inform a cybersecurity diligence assessment:

- whether and how often the vendor has experienced cybersecurity incidents in the past, the severity of those incidents, and the quality of the vendor's response
- whether the vendor maintains cybersecurity policies, such as whether the vendor has a written security policy or plan
- organizational considerations, such as whether the vendor maintains sufficient and appropriately trained personnel to

protect the data and/or service at issue and respond to incidents

- human resources practices, particularly background screening of employees, cybersecurity training, and the handling of terminations
- access controls, particularly whether controls are in place that restrict access to information and uniquely identify users such that access attempts can be monitored and reviewed
- encryption practices, including whether information is encrypted at rest, whether information transmitted to or from the vendor is properly encrypted, and whether cryptographic keys are properly managed
- evaluation of in what country any data will be stored
- the vendor's policies regarding the secondary use of customer data, and whether IT systems are created in such a way as to respect limitations on secondary use
- physical security, including resilience and disaster recovery functions and the use of personnel and technology to prevent unauthorized physical access to facilities
- back-up and recovery practices
- change control management, including protocols on the installation of and execution of software
- system acquisition, development, and maintenance to manage risk from software development or the deployment of new software or hardware
- risk management of the vendor's own third-party vendors
- incident response plans, including whether evidence of an incident is collected and retained so as to be presentable to a court and whether the vendor periodically tests its response capabilities
- whether the vendor conducts regular, independent audits of its privacy and information security practices

■ Contractual risk and negotiation

In addition to evaluating third parties on the basis of their cybersecurity practices, another important risk mitigation tool is the actual contractual language. As with other areas, contractual requirements can be an effective way to allocate risk and responsibility for potential breaches of cybersecurity, including the investigation and remediation of such incidents. Commonly negotiated terms include the following:

- a requirement that the vendor have a written information security program that complies with applicable law or other regulatory or industry standards
- limits and conditions on the use of subcontractors and other third-party service providers
- restrictions on secondary use of data, including making clear that the customer remains the owner of any data transmitted to the vendor and any derivatives of that data
- mandatory and timely notification in case of a security incident
- rights to audit or otherwise monitor the vendor's compliance with the terms of the contract
- in case of a breach, a requirement that the vendor take on reasonable measures to correct its security processes and take any necessary remediation steps
- provisions ensuring an orderly transition to in-house systems or another third party in case of the termination of the relationship.

In addition to such terms, indemnification clauses can be used to shift the risk of data breach onto the third party and to incentivize healthy security practices. To accompany an indemnification clause, it sometimes can be desirable to draft clauses that define when the entity is or is not liable, on which party the burden of proof falls, and how root-cause analysis should be conducted. To ensure capacity to take on the financial costs of a breach, third parties are frequently required to obtain a cybersecurity insurance policy.

From the business's perspective a third-party vendor should be fully responsible for any liability for data breaches that occur while the data are under the vendor's control. However, vendors often push for caps on their cybersecurity liability. To guide negotiations as to appropriate caps on liability, consider the type of data processed or accessed by the third party (e.g., how sensitive is it, does it relate to employees, consumers, or is it not personally identifying information), the volume of records to be handled by the third party, the ability for the customer to implement security controls such as encryption, the nature and extent of the third-party promises on cybersecurity, and the brand and reputation of the third party with respect to data security. Based on those inputs, a company can then consider the potential losses and sources of third-party liability to evaluate what constitutes an acceptable level of risk in terms of exclusions for indemnifications and caps on liability. A business also may consider offsetting any contractual concessions with corresponding increases in their own cybersecurity insurance coverage.

■ Ongoing monitoring and oversight

Ongoing monitoring and oversight of third-party service providers is essential given the rapidly changing landscape of cybersecurity threats. Whereas due diligence provides a snapshot of a third party's cybersecurity stance at a specific point in time, continual monitoring and the right to such monitoring are necessary to help ensure that the third party responds and adapts to secure its systems against new threats. Over the life of the relationship, periodic checks, including on-site reviews of vendor, can be important oversight mechanisms. Other monitoring requirements include access to timely and accurate records and reports of the third-party provider's cybersecurity posture.

Although relatively uncommon outside of certain regulated industries, such as the financial and health-care industries, provisions in vendor contracts for regular security audits by an independent third party provide a robust but intrusive form of periodic monitoring. However, it is not always possible to obtain audit rights from a vendor. Alternatively, the vendor could be required to provide up-to-date certifications of compliance with industry standards or regular, third-party audit reports. In addition, to manage fourth-party risk, vendors could be required to perform initial and periodic assessments of their own service providers and vendors if they will be handling sensitive information. If, in the course of an audit, vulnerabilities are identified or practices are found that are not in compliance with industry practices or regulatory requirements, the vendor may be required to notify the customer and correct any outstanding issues in a timely fashion.

As part of ongoing monitoring of vendor cybersecurity, it is useful if the contract with a third-party service provider also includes notification and remediation provisions if the vendor becomes aware of deficiencies in its cybersecurity posture. In addition, as part of the remedies, the outsourcing party may seek the right to terminate the agreement immediately and to receive a pro rata refund of any fees paid or payable. In addition to contractual provisions dealing with the termination, contingency plans to facilitate an orderly end to the third-party relationship and a smooth transition to an in-house solution or another a third-party provider may prove useful.

■ Conclusion

The measures described above—diligence, contractual terms, and continued monitoring and oversight—are critical elements of a comprehensive cybersecurity program that includes managing third-party relationships. To effectuate these elements, in turn, it often is helpful to have standardized processes and documentation.

Examples include standardized diligence checklists and questionnaires, template contract addendums addressing cybersecurity issues, and standardized schedules for audits and other forms of monitoring. Because there is no one-size-fits-all approach that is appropriate for every vendor, it is appropriate to implement a tiered approach that scales due diligence, contractual obligations, and oversight processes according to the nature and extent of the cybersecurity risks presented by the vendor relationship. In all events, it is important that organizations periodically review their processes for evaluating and overseeing third-party relationships to ensure that such processes are periodically updated and appropriately tailored to address new and emerging threats.

31

A new look at an old threat in cyberspace: The insider

Delta Risk LLC – Thomas Fuhrman, President

" *The first thing that business leaders should do about the insider threat is to take it seriously.*"

People are, without doubt, the most consequential part of cybersecurity. They design the hardware, write the software, build the systems, configure and manage the boxes, install the software patches, and, obviously, use the computers. At every point in cyberspace, people create vulnerabilities. Whether they realize it, people are a major security risk. The insider threat, however, is not just a product of conscientious but fallible humans: the dark side of human nature is also in play. The idea of the 'enemy within' is as old as the hills, and its cyber equivalent is too.

The insider threat to computer systems and networks has been a recognized reality for decades. It was a topic in 1970 in the landmark report by the RAND Corporation, *Security Controls for Computer Systems*, and its roots go back even further. However, since 2013 when defense computer systems contractor Edward Snowden—an insider—carried out one of the largest and most significant unauthorized disclosures of classified government information in U.S. history, the issue was brought home to business executives. They realized, "If that can happen to the National Security Agency, it can happen to me."

■ What's new with the insider threat?

In this, the post-Snowden era, the potential impact of the insider has become a much more tangible issue to companies and organizations of every kind. However, although this heightened awareness is new, there are also other recent developments that make the current insider threat challenge more difficult than ever. Key among such developments are the following:

■ the vast amount of vital business and personal data that is online

- the migration of data outside the security perimeter of the enterprise through the widespread adoption of cloud-based services, increased outsourcing, increasingly Internet-enabled supply chain operations, and the ubiquity of mobile communications and computing devices in the 'bring your own device' (BYOD) environment
- the increase in the marketability of sensitive, personal, proprietary, or confidential data through global cyber crime syndicates and hacker networks.

These developments in combination invest more power—and risk—in the individual insider and make 'keeping a secret while selectively sharing it' a harder problem than ever.

From a cyber perspective, the insider is the person who the enterprise has entrusted to access and operate with the company's data and information resources in the routine course of business. Anyone who has legitimate (or 'authorized') access to the information and the business systems, databases, email, or other information resources of the enterprise is an insider.

In many companies today, a large number of legitimate insiders are not actually employees. This group includes former employees, contractors, business partners, vendors, suppliers, and others such as cloud service providers and business application hosting services that have been granted access to corporate enterprise networks. Evidence indicates that the access privileges of such non-employee insiders are difficult to manage and thus more easily exploited. In the large data breach at The Home Depot in 2014, for example, the hackers entered the corporate network through a vendor's legitimate access credentials.

Can employees and other insiders be trusted? The answer, of course, is mostly yes. It has to be. Business runs on human capital. Without trustworthy insiders, the organization cannot function. However, the residual 'no' is a cause for serious concern. Seen in this light the question is more about setting the limits of trust at the right level. Better ways

to efficiently screen potential employees, manage access rights, enforce obligations, detect malicious tendencies and behaviors, and implement security controls are needed.

The insider threat is usually thought of as having two types: the malicious insider and the unwitting insider. Although these two types of insider are very different in motivations and objectives, they can have similar ruinous effects on the organization.

- *The malicious insider.* The malicious insider is the 'spy' or 'traitor' who represents the insider cyberthreat at its most basic. This rogue employee, at most a small percentage of the workforce (Spectorsoft reports that an estimated 10 percent of employees account for 95 percent of incidents), uses her or his legitimate access to a company's information resources to *deliberately* harm the organization.

Malicious insiders know about the organization's information, its systems, its structure and people, and its internal operations. They have access to the enterprise network from inside the perimeter defenses. They can do damage such as stealing data, disabling systems, and installing viruses or malware. Those with privileged access can do even more, such as disabling accounts, destroying backups, changing configuration files, and more. Those without privileged access can sometimes get it through insider trickery, bypassing authentication processes or gaining access through the credentials of others. Snowden himself reportedly persuaded colleagues to share passwords with him to get access beyond what he was already allowed.

A fundamental and important point to recognize is that the insider as a malicious threat is not limited to the cyber and information systems realm. Other targets and methods are possible, including physical theft, destruction, or violence, coercion and extortion, or other non-cyber actions. This fact has a direct bearing on the approaches available to prevent, detect, and act against malicious or potentially malicious insiders.

The psychology of the malicious insider is a defined field of study. In short, an insider can become a threat for many reasons—including for example, anger as a result of workplace conflicts or disputes, fear of termination, dissatisfaction with workplace policies, ideology, or financial need.

- *The unwitting insider.* Almost anyone can fall into the category of unwitting insider threat agent, including senior executives. As a threat actor, the unwitting insider unintentionally and unknowingly makes security blunders that expose the enterprise to serious cyber risks.

Because the pool of potential unwitting actors is so large and their behaviors are unintentional and hard to predict, the unwitting insider is one of the most dangerous weak points in the entire enterprise.

One group of insiders who can pose a major threat are those who have a lax attitude about security. These attitudes are not always obvious. Security awareness campaigns are so commonplace now that just about everyone exercises at least some caution in online activities. At the same time, though, we can also observe that a certain insouciance about the risks in cyberspace has crept into the behavior of many people. The same person who would refrain from using the word 'password' as a password or from writing it on a sticky note to place on the computer monitor may think nothing of other poor security practices.

Today's culture, for example, seems to encourage the melding of personal and professional pursuits. People have become so accustomed to online life—being always connected, using multiple computing platforms, putting their 'whole life' (as they say) on their smartphones, or posting photos and personal information on social websites—that it appears many have become unconcerned about the associated security and privacy risks. Users sometimes bring such personal Internet habits into the workplace, often paradoxically because of their zeal to do their jobs. They may insert a thumb drive into a corporate machine to transfer a file. ("I needed to work on the file—what was I supposed to do?") They could sync a personal smartphone to a corporate computer. ("What's wrong with that?") They may drop a proprietary document into a public cloud. ("I need to work on it while I travel.") The list continues. All of these actions and many others like them by the unwitting insider create serious enterprise security risks.

The single most common security weakness of most people is a susceptibility to phishing attacks. Phishing is a form of 'social engineering' that has the goal of getting information such as usernames, passwords, or credit card numbers. Phishing usually starts with a fraudulent email message (although other mechanisms are also used) that appears to be from a legitimate or known source. The message may contain an attachment that, if opened, installs malware on the victim's computer, or the message may direct the user to a website that is also designed to look legitimate, even familiar, to the target victim. This bogus website prompts the user to enter information such as log-in credentials or account numbers. If the user's suspicions have not been aroused, she or he may enter the requested data—and gotcha!—the hacker has succeeded in capturing information that can be used for access later. Alternatively or in addition, the bogus website may push out a virus, remote access software, key-logging software, or other malware. Very often phishing is the start of a chain of exploits that leads to a very serious breach. The Verizon 2015 Data Breach Investigations Report (DBIR) states that more than 75% of malware installs were the result of unwitting users clicking on attachments or web links contained in emails.

Phishing also is used in a more focused way that targets specific people—frequently senior executives or people in the organization who have privileged access to information resources. The hacker will mine the Internet for personal information on the target, information that only the target would know, names and contact information of colleagues, web browsing and purchase history, non-business activities and community involvement, even writing styles to zoom in on that specific person. When such information is used in a phishing email, the look and feel, the text, and the context of the message can appear unexceptional and entirely authentic. If this were a game it would be unfair. The target frequently falls for the scheme.

Like the poor soul who sends money to the Nigerian prince or the person who invests in shares of the Brooklyn Bridge, the unwitting person can easily be taken in by a well-designed phishing ploy. However, whether the result of inadvertent or deliberate acts, the impact to the organization can be the same—financial loss, compromise of intellectual property, theft of customer personal information and credit card data, and reputational harm or loss of competitive position.

This highlights a third and more sinister type of 'insider' that must also be considered—the malicious outsider posing as an insider. Such actors explicitly seek to exploit insiders by appropriating their credentials and moving unnoticed within the network.

Figure 1 illustrates the categories of the insider threat, along with typical motivations and potential impacts.

FIGURE 1

Insider threat actors and their effects

Threat Actors	Motivations	Methods	Results
Unwitting insider	• Efficiency and convenience • Customer service • 'Getting the job done'	• Move sensitive internal data to a public cloud • Lose a laptop • Use a memory stick to import or export data • Mix company data with personal data on moblie devices	**Cyber Incident** **Examples** • Theft of sensitive information (e.g., personally identifiable information, intellectual property, proprietary information) • Financial fraud or theft • Insertion of malware and/or establishing a long-term presence in the network for repeat action • Damaged or destroyed information resources • Sabotaged product (the merchandise produced by the enterprise) • Reputation harm and customer alienation; loss of revenue
Malicious insider	• Financial gain • Do harm to the company • Advance an ideology or other personal agenda	• Use legitimate access for illegitimate purposes	
Malicious outsider posing as an insider	• Financial gain—obtain sensistive data that can be monetized • Fraud or theft of money • Do harm to the company • Advance an ideology or other personal agenda	• Exploit the access of a legitimate user • Bypass security controls on privilege escalation and lateral movement throughout the network to get to key systems for exfiltration and/or insertion of malware	

All insider threats can have the same outcomes

■ *The outsider posing as an insider.* This type of insider is not an insider in the true sense, but rather an imposter who uses the legitimate credentials of others to access the network in ways the real user would not. This actor seeks to get legitimate credentials using a variety of tactics and techniques. He then uses these acquired credentials to access password files, directories and access control lists, and other network resources—which is made easier if the credentials are already those of a system administrator or other privileged user.

As described above, the unwitting insider is very commonly exploited by sophisticated hackers as a soft point of entry for advanced attacks. Elaborate penetration techniques are hardly needed when a relatively simple phishing email is likely to serve the purpose. Upon achieving initial access, the hacker may try to move laterally within the network or to escalate access privileges to implant advanced malware deeply in the network fabric. Phishing is the dominant mechanism used today to penetrate networks by even the most sophisticated hackers because it has a high success rate for very low cost.

Other social engineering tactics include in-person deceit, such as impersonating someone in authority, pretending to represent the Help Desk, asking someone for assistance, or claiming to have left an access badge inside the restricted area of a facility. It can be a particularly effective tactic because people usually try to be courteous and helpful.

Hackers have tricks other than social engineering to obtain the access they desire. Most of the time, though, social engineering can be found somewhere along the attack chain because it is a powerful and efficient way of getting past perimeter defenses. The sophistication we hear about in reports of state-sponsored espionage, hacker networks, and organized

cybercrime is exhibited in the tradecraft that is applied once the initial breach is achieved.

The outsider-posing-as-insider is not interested in impersonating a particular person other than to use the person's network or system credentials. Through password cracking and other techniques, a hacker can exploit the credentials of more than one authorized user or administrator in the course of an attack. Unlike the true insider, the only observables that the outsider leaves are those network footprints and fingerprints that may show up in system logs or the actual malware code or other digital fragments they leave behind.

■ The dimensions of the insider threat

The insider threat is easy to understand in concept but very hard to quantify in practice. How big of a threat is it? Hard data and statistics on the frequency of occurrence and the impact of insider threats have historically been elusive and remain so. Lack of detection and discovery of insider events, and an unwillingness to share or report them, are two of the primary reasons for the paucity of data. Nevertheless, recent insider threat surveys and breach data analyses are consistent in their main findings, including the following:

■ There has been an increase in insider threat events in the last few years.
■ Most organizations do not have adequate controls in place to prevent or thwart insider attacks.
■ Insider attacks are believed to be more difficult to detect than external attacks.
■ Third parties and other non-employee insiders represent a major risk, and insufficient attention is devoted to managing them. Most contracts and service level agreements with external vendors, suppliers, and business partners do not include robust security provisions.
■ Insider policy violations and inappropriate activity are often discovered only during

examination of user devices after individuals have left the organization.

- Most incidents are handled internally with no legal nor law enforcement action.

■ What to do

The first thing that business leaders should do about the insider threat is to take it seriously. Although there is widespread recognition that the threat is very serious, in most sectors there is insufficient follow-through to build the threat-specific plans, organizational structures, and controls to deal with it. What is needed is a comprehensive approach that addresses and leverages the unique aspects of the insider threat. Technology by itself is not the answer; the critical human dimension of the insider threat must also be addressed.

A comprehensive approach would include the following:

- *Establishing a threat-aware culture of institutional integrity and personal reliability.* Company culture is a product of many factors, but one of the most decisive is the behavior of senior leadership and the values they model. A culture of institutional integrity and personal reliability is conducive to success in almost any enterprise. Factors for achieving this include the following:
  - Create an environment in which self-directed employee actions reflect a high degree of institutional integrity and personal reliability.
  - Articulate clear expectations in an enterprise Acceptable Use Policy governing IT resources. This should be a formal signed agreement between the company and each employee and external party who has access to the enterprise IT resources or facilities.
  - Create a safe environment in which to self-report accidental actions that jeopardize security. Removing the stigma of having inadvertently committed a security violation can help minimize impact and help everyone learn.

- Provide regular insider threat awareness training as well as realistic phishing training exercises. An organized phishing awareness exercise program can raise the company's standard of performance in this critical area.
- Establish a set of institutional values reflecting the desired culture, select leaders based on their adherence to these values, and include demonstration of these values as an item on employee performance assessments.
- *Building a multi-disciplinary program.* Establish an executive committee to manage an integrated multidisciplinary program designed to deter, prevent, detect, and respond to insider threats and to limit their impact. The program should have the active participation of the functional organizations across the business such as Risk, IT, Cybersecurity, Physical Security, Human Resources, Fraud, and General Counsel, as well as company-specific verticals (manufacturing, operations, etc.).

The program should include the following:
  - creation and oversight of policies related to the management of insider risk
  - regularized workflow, processes, and meetings to actively and collectively review threat intelligence, the internal threat landscape, internal indicators of risk, insider events, sponsored activities, and trends from each subdiscipline
  - implementation and oversight of personnel reliability processes from pre-employment background checks to off-boarding procedures to assess and act upon personnel security risks, behavioral risk indicators, and individual vulnerability to compromise
  - decision-making authority pertaining to the integration of programs within each vertical, the aggregation of insider risk data across the verticals, and the corporate response to insider events

- definition of requirements for employee training and awareness of insider threats and prevention measures.
■ *Building and operating security controls.* Many of the security controls that already exist (or should exist) within the enterprise can be effective in detecting, preventing, or mitigating the results of insider threat activity. Key technical controls include the following:
  - access controls, particularly for privileged users (those with administrative authority)
  - data protection, including encryption, data loss prevention technology, data backups, and exfiltration monitoring
  - configuration management and secure configurations
  - vulnerability and patch management
  - internal network segmentation.
■ *Monitoring and detecting insider behavior.* The program should seek to prevent insider attacks by capturing observable indicators of potential activity before insiders act. Intelligence on the insider threat generally comes from within the enterprise through either technical data or behavioral indicators:
  - *Technical.* The most significant sources of cyber-related technical intelligence are the real-time alerts and outputs of security appliances, network- and host-based sensors, and data loss prevention tools, as well as the network- and system-level logs that are generated automatically (if so configured) throughout the enterprise. In most enterprises these sources provide so much data that managing and effectively integrating it with operations become serious challenges. In addition, the volume of data drives a need for storage that can become acute depending on policy decisions regarding what logs are maintained and for how long.
  Insider threat-tracking tools in use today, such as data loss prevention, threat intelligence, and security information and event management

(SIEM) systems, pinpoint potentially illicit activities by identifying anomalies in a person's IT resource and data access patterns.
  - *Non-technical.* Unique to the insider threat is the availability of a large amount of relevant non-technical behavioral observables. Integrating operational intelligence information at the intersection of cybersecurity, fraud detection, and physical security can yield critical insights about potential insider threats.
  - Examples of non-technical cyber data include the following:
    ■ email behavior: volume, content, and addressees; presence and type of attachments
    ■ workday activities: patterns of on/off duty time, including weekdays, weekends, and holidays; location
    ■ job performance: performance reviews, productivity, and time accountability
    ■ indicators of affiliation: degree of participation in company-sponsored activities; indications of discontent through online behavior and social media usage.

Analysis of this type of data through automated and manual processes can identify patterns of behavior that indicate at-risk employees or imminent insider attacks. There may also be value in integrating external threat intelligence for factors that could influence at-risk insiders.

It is important that the company's legal counsel advise the executive committee on informing employees of ongoing monitoring and how the data will be used. Oversight by the executive committee is essential to ensure it is operated within the bounds of policy.

■ *Having a plan.* The executive committee should develop a detailed (though confidential) action plan for what to do in the event of actual or suspected insider misbehavior or law-breaking. The plan should describe how and when to contact law enforcement and other authorities regarding insider threats or actions. It should provide a framework of possible legal remedies to pursue in the event of an insider attack. This action plan should be tested on a regular basis through scenario-based exercises involving the company officials who would actually be involved if a real event were to occur.

- *Evolving the approach.* The executive committee should refine the program as the organization matures in the use of this capability within the specific business environment.
- *Not 'going it alone.'* The executive committee should take advantage of the many resources available for planning

and conducting operations pertaining to the insider threat. Proven approaches and practices for addressing this threat are available, allowing the company to build on the learnings of other organizations. (See inset box.)

■ Summing up

Companies often declare that people are their greatest asset. Surely the human resource is what propels a company forward. However, the insider threat will always be present. Commitment, loyalty, and general affiliation with the organization cannot be taken for granted. Personal ethics and allegiance to the employer collide with the chance for selfish gains in those who have become security risks or who are vulnerable to compromise. With legitimate

Resources

The following resources can help enterprises deal with the insider threat. Each provides a wealth of information on proven approaches and practices that companies can build upon.

- **Insider Risk Evaluation and Audit Tool.** This tool is designed to help the user gauge an organization's relative vulnerability to insider threats and adverse behavior including espionage against the U.S., theft of intangible assets or intellectual property, sabotage or attacks against networks or information systems, theft or embezzlement, illegal export of critical technology, and domestic terrorism or collaboration with foreign terrorist groups.
  The tool can be used for a number of purposes, including self-audit of an organization's current defenses against insider abuse, the development of a strategic risk mitigation plan, and employee training and awareness.
  http://www.dhra.mil/perserec/products.html#InsiderRisk

- **CERT Insider Threat Center**. Since 2001, the CERT Insider Threat Center has conducted empirical research and analysis to develop and transition socio-technical solutions to combat insider cyberthreats. Partnering with the U.S. Department of Defense, the U.S. Department of Homeland Security, the U.S. Secret Service, other federal agencies, the intelligence community, private industry, academia, and the vendor community, the CERT Insider Threat Center is positioned as a trusted broker that can provide short-term assistance to organizations and conduct ongoing research.
  https://www.cert.org/insider-threat/

- **Federal Bureau of Investigation**. *The Insider Threat: An introduction to detecting and deterring an insider spy.*
  This brochure provides an introduction for managers and security personnel on how to detect an insider threat and provides tips on how to safeguard trade secrets.
  https://www.fbi.gov/about-us/investigate/counterintelligence/the-insider-threat

authorization to access company and information resources, a rogue insider can do tremendous harm to the company. The effects of an insider attack can be felt as financial loss, erosion of competitive position, brand degradation, customer alienation, and more. The Snowden disclosures of 2013 have, at least for now, sensitized business leaders to the grave risks posed by the insider threat.

The unwitting insider is the equal of the malicious insider in potential damaging impact. A momentary and unintentional lapse in vigilance regarding security threats can be all it takes for a major compromise to occur. Insiders are also the target for carefully scripted phishing tactics; the insider who innocently clicks a link in an email may enable damage to the company well beyond her or his pay grade.

However, there is much that the organization's executive leadership can do to mitigate the insider threat, including establishing the right culture, implementing security controls, conducting ongoing monitoring and detection efforts, and being ready to respond quickly if indicators point to a likely insider threat. The following box summarizes the actions that are recommended here.

Summary of actions to address the insider threat

1. Establish a culture of threat awareness, institutional integrity, and personal reliability
   - Provide regular insider threat awareness training as well as realistic phishing training exercises.
   - Articulate clear expectations in an enterprise Acceptable Use Policy governing IT resources.
   - Create a safe environment in which to self-report accidental actions that jeopardize security.

2. Build a multi-disciplinary program to deter, prevent, detect, and respond to insider threats and to limit their impact.

3. Build and operate security controls designed to mitigate the insider risk.

4. Monitor insider behavior:
   - multiple interdisciplinary dimensions
   - draw on outside resources
   - look inside the network for observables of potential insider threat activity

5. Have a plan for what to do in the event of actual or suspected insider malfeasance
   - Know how and when to contact law enforcement and other authorities regarding insider threats.
   - Explore legal remedies.

6. Be ready to develop your approach as conditions continue to change.

7. Don't 'go at it alone.' There are many resources available for planning and ongoing operations. Best practices can be implemented based on another organization's learning curve.

32

The Internet of Things

The Chertoff Group – Mark Weatherford, Principal

In the time it takes you to read this sentence—about eight seconds—approximately 150 new devices will have been added to the Internet of Things (IoT). That's 61,500 new devices per hour, 1.5 million per day. There are currently about 7.4 billion devices connected to the IoT, more than there are human beings on the planet. By 2020, according to Gartner, there will be 26 billion. Cisco puts the number at 50 billion, and Morgan Stanley says it will be 75 billion. By any estimation, it will be a lot more devices than are in existence today.

People are beginning to notice this phenomenal rate of growth, and some companies are seeing incredible economic opportunities. However, the fact that the field has grown so quickly and so dynamically means that some of the lessons we've learned in the past about security and privacy are not being employed—in the interest of first-to-market opportunities—and the lack of oversight has many wondering about the unknown unknowns.

These three definitions together provide a starting point for understanding the IoT and its implications for our future:

- In the physical sense, the IoT is all of those billions of devices, installed on apparel, appliances, machines, vehicles, electronics—most of them incorporating sensors to gather bits of data and then sharing that information via the Internet through central servers. The concept of the IoT was introduced in 1999 and evolved from the Machine-to-Machine (M2M) technology that originated in the 1980s, in which computer processors communicated with each other over networks. The major difference is that most of the new devices cannot be considered processors but rather sensors and relays that simply facilitate the aggregation of data. Analogous to the shift to "cloud" computing, it may be useful to consider this new data-generating aspect as "the fog."

CYBERSECURITY BEYOND YOUR NETWORK

The two concepts—the IoT and M2M—are now poised for complete integration, in what is termed convergence, as we move into technology's future. Keep in mind that in that future, anything that can be connected *will be connected*. Christian Byrnes, a managing vice president at Gartner, says that "The Internet of Things brings a major addition to the responsibilities of cybersecurity: safety. IoT includes the final convergence of physical and information security practices. As such, CIOs and CISOs will face the possibility of their failures being the direct cause of death. Confidentiality, Integrity and Availability will be remembered as 'the good old days.'"

- The IoT can also be thought of as just the collected data. With billions of connected devices, all contributing information around the clock, it's more data about more machines, operations, and people than has ever been collected before—more in the past year than perhaps has been recorded in all of human history, and certainly more than was imagined possible just a few years ago. The intelligent management and implementation of that data make it possible to do such things as navigate a driverless car through city traffic, monitor a person's anatomical signals and take action to manage his or her health, monitor the movement and health of livestock, provide global tracking and communications, manage energy use in buildings, and even operate sophisticated industrial equipment from remote locations. Our intelligence and industrial abilities in the era of the IoT will be limited only by our imaginations; we will have the data we need to accomplish almost anything we can envision.
- In the philosophical sense, the IoT is also part of a movement. It's been evolving for more than a century, from our first ability to communicate with each other instantaneously by radio. The early days of the Information Age quickly showed us how important data gathering could be to the success of an operation. The IoT

is, in that existential meaning, the latest iteration of communication technology. Of course, as soon as we developed the ability to send information over great distances in just seconds, some people began to look for ways to capture that information from sources other than their own. Early twentieth century wartime code breakers monitoring the enemy's radio communications often are mentioned as the first hackers.

The last aspect of the IoT should cause the most concern. As technology has become ever more sophisticated in its march toward providing greater capabilities for private enterprise, governments, and the people they serve, so have the tools and strategies of the people who would access and use the information for more malicious purposes. The lack of recognition about the seriousness of this threat to companies and governments leads to a lack of security sufficient to defend against attacks.

■ IoT benefits

According to John Chambers, CEO of Cisco Systems Inc., the Internet of Everything (which includes the IoT plus the actual networks that support and transmit the data these devices generate) could be worth $14.4 trillion in revenue, plus another $4.6 trillion in savings to industry and government. That's $19 trillion, greater than the GDP of many countries. The benefits the IoT provides can be seen in every area that relies on technology, as well as many that traditionally have not. A few examples:

- The amount of municipal solid waste generated around the world is expected to reach 2.2 billion tons annually by 2025, almost double the amount recorded in 2012. The cost of handling this waste will be about $375.5 billion per year. However, by changing the traffic patterns of garbage trucks and installing sensors in garbage cans to identify when they are full and should be picked up, U.S. cities alone can

■ 230

save $10 billion in waste management costs.

- Unscheduled maintenance events are responsible for about 10 percent of all flight cancellations and delays in commercial aviation, costing $8 billion per year. According to Marco Annunziata, chief economist at General Electric, preventive maintenance systems can allow airplanes, while in flight, to communicate with technicians on the ground so that when the plane lands, the technicians already know what needs attention. These systems are self-learning and can predict issues that a human operator may never see, helping prevent more than 60,000 delays and cancellations every year.
- On the personal scale there's Amazon's Dash button. The idea is a perfect example of how the IoT works at the micro level. The buttons are simple wireless devices with the logos of consumables manufacturers, about the size and shape of a thumb drive. A Dash button for a detergent could be attached to a washing machine. When the supply of detergent is low, the consumer need only press the button, and another bottle is ordered through Amazon Prime. Amazon and other developers are also working on IoT devices that sense when the supply of a consumable is low, and order the item automatically, without the consumer even being aware of the act.

◼ IoT privacy issues

One of the keys to IoT advancements, of course, is the interconnectivity of information sources and their recipients. The information is often used in the commercial realm for monetization strategies, and by the government to target security threats, each of which leads inevitably to concerns about privacy. In many cases when human beings are the sources of this information, they do not even know they are acting as such. Virtually every site a person visits on the Internet in return gathers information about that person, from data stored on the computer being used (such as location and

personal information) to data entered actively during the site visit. In addition, most transactions a person conducts while out in the world have the potential to be recorded and added to databases, and these transactions, when merged with other collected information, can be interpreted using computer algorithms. Even when the data are anonymized, many people believe their privacy is violated by such usage. In his book *Future Crimes*, Mark Goodman writes, "Data brokers get their information from our Internet service providers, credit card issuers, mobile phone companies, banks, credit bureaus, pharmacies, departments of motor vehicles, grocery stores, and increasingly, our online activities. All the data we give away on a daily basis for free to our social networks . . . are tagged, geo-coded, and sorted for resale to advertisers and marketers."

- For example, in a well-publicized case from 2012, mega-retailer Target analyzed purchasing records to predict when women may be pregnant and even when they were due. The company then mailed pregnancy-related coupons to the women's addresses. The program came to national attention when a high school student received the coupons at her family's home, alerting her father to her condition. Although embarrassing for the young woman, Target's use of the information gathered was legal under the Fair Credit Reporting Act, which allows "first parties" to perform in-house analytics on collected data.
- During the Women's Mini Marathon held in Dublin, Ireland, last year, Symantec security researcher Candid Wueest stood on the street and stealthily monitored data from the activity trackers worn by hundreds of runners. The data included everything from their names and addresses to the type of device they were wearing and the passwords for those devices.
- In a 2013 case, a British man discovered that his LG smart TV was clandestinely

transmitting viewing information back to the South Korean manufacturer, as well as reporting the contents of devices, such as a USB drive, that were connected to the TV. LG claimed the information was used, as in the Target case, "to deliver more relevant advertisements and to offer recommendations to viewers based on what other LG smart TV owners are watching." However, the man, an IT consultant, discovered that the TV transmitted the information whether the system setting for "collection of watching info" was set to *on* or *off*.

According to a report on privacy and security released by the Federal Trade Commission in January of 2015, one company that makes an IoT home automation product indicated that fewer than 10,000 households can "generate 150 million discrete data points a day," or approximately one data point every six seconds for each household. Another participant in the report noted that "existing smartphone sensors can be used to infer a user's mood; stress levels; personality type; bipolar disorder; demographics (e.g., gender, marital status, job status, age); smoking habits; overall well-being; progression of Parkinson's disease; sleep patterns; happiness; levels of exercise; and types of physical activity or movement." Such "sensitive behavior patterns could be used in unauthorized ways or by unauthorized individuals."

■ IoT security issues

The IoT is subject to the same security risks as traditional computer systems, but the issues, unfortunately, don't stop there. Like any storage aspect of the Internet, security vulnerabilities can be exploited to compromise sensitive information. Rick Dakin, CEO of Coalfire in Boulder, Colorado, says that "while headlines about cybersecurity usually focus on the changing threat landscape, a greater concern is the evolving technology landscape. Most people rapidly connect unsafe devices to their networks with no thought to security, and the Internet of Things will accelerate the contamination of

our networks." As connectivity grows exponentially, so do the possibilities for security breaches. Any device in the IoT that stores information, whether it contains Internet or TV viewing preferences, credit card numbers, health information, etc., can become a target. The proliferation of devices that are part of the IoT means that the number of access points to a system is limitless.

Don't think that just because a device has a limited function—such as a smart lightbulb, a FitBit, a smart toilet, or a thermostat—that it holds no attractiveness for hackers. Put enough of these connected devices together and cyber criminals can create a botnet, a network of processors that can be used to facilitate large, repetitive tasks, such as generating passcode possibilities.

Also of great concern is the potential to cause physical damage and harm to individuals and property. The FTC report contains claims by company researchers of the ability to hack into a self-driving automobile's built-in telematics unit and control the vehicle's engine and braking. Another claim involves the ability to access computerized health equipment and change the settings so that they are harmful to the patient. Through the medical device hijack attack vector (MEDJACK), the TrapX Labs security team has identified that in many cases, medical devices themselves are the key entry points for health-care network attacks. Devices as diverse as diagnostic equipment such as CT scanners and MRI machines, life support equipment including medical ventilators and dialysis machines, and even medical lasers and LASIK surgical machines are typically delivered to medical facilities wide open for attacks that can compromise device readings and operations, not to mention putting people's health and lives at risk.

A recent Hewlett-Packard report noted that 70 percent of IoT devices contain security vulnerabilities. Some of these weaknesses pertain to the current differences in communication standards, as developers seek to make their devices compatible with all types of systems—an aspect of the convergence factor mentioned earlier. Although many companies are working on standardization protocols, the issue will not go away anytime soon. Sensitive commercial, industrial, and government information is at risk, and that risk will likely grow as the IoT develops, before measures sufficient to mitigate that risk propagate. As Rod Beckstrom, the former CEO of ICANN, said in his Beckstrom's Law:

- If it's connected to the Internet it's *hackable*.
- Everything is being connected to the Internet.
- Therefore, everything is *hackable*.

Putting all the security aspects together, as some cyber criminals apparently already have, and the risks that accompany the growth of the IoT can seem frightening. Hackers have become so sophisticated in their tactics that some are creating databases from the information gathered in previous attacks, which can enable them to defeat common security measures. For example, in the successful breach of more than 100,000 taxpayer returns filed electronically with the IRS in 2014, the attackers were able to correctly answer security questions that the taxpayers themselves had selected, simply by cross-referencing information collected in previous breaches of other organizations' information.

Put a nation-state or other global entity behind such efforts, and the risks to sensitive information in the IoT mount exponentially. In commerce, as well as in politics and war, entities make decisions based on what they believe is in their best interests. This is especially true in the case of state and large non-state actors. It's helpful to think of their efforts to infiltrate technological and security information not so much as instigated by an evil intent or ideology, but as motivated by the survival and practical success of their entity—the concept of realpolitik updated for the twenty-first century. They have a vested interest in hacking information systems that goes far beyond simple greed. It means they are unfazed by potential punishments or repercussions and have the willingness to commit resources and effort towards their

goals because the payoffs, if they are successful, are huge—such as global economic or even military dominance. Looking at the situation in this way helps validate the actual threat these actors represent and can in turn stimulate companies and governments to mount a more adequate defense.

■ Addressing the issues

The U.S. Congress, since 2012, has proposed more than 100 pieces of legislation related to Internet security and privacy. Only a couple were actually signed into law, but continuing security incidents, such as the breach of Sony's network and subsequent hostage-taking of one of its movies, have created greater awareness of security issues that will surely prompt more attempts at legislation and regulation. In fact, as of this writing, at least 10 pieces of legislation are being considered on Capitol Hill. In its report, the FTC endorsed strong, flexible, and technology-neutral general legislation but added that IoT-specific legislation would be premature, as the field is still in its early stages of development. They would prefer to see industry adopt self-regulatory practices.

At the corporate or company level, though, there is much decision makers can do now to address security and privacy concerns. Much of that involves adopting a forward-thinking attitude about the IoT and its role.

- First is to understand that the IoT is not a possibility or a projection of the future—it is a reality. It is here now and will only continue to grow and affect every facet of our world.
- The IoT carries with it many risks and challenges; it's the companies and organizations that address those issues head on that will survive. Conventional approaches to network security will likely have to be rethought.
- Companies and organizations should stay up to date with evolving vulnerability assessments and advancements in security solutions. This also applies to

administrators and executives, who should become fluent in the language that describes IoT capabilities, trends, and risks so that they can make more relevant and responsive decisions for their shareholders and customers. Administrators should attend conferences and industry events when possible as well.

- Standardization of security protocols in the IoT space must be made an industry-wide priority.
- When breaches to networks do occur, it's important to notify consumers quickly so that they can protect themselves from the misuse of their data.
- Such breaches should also prompt industry-coordinated action to address the vulnerabilities exposed and propagate industry standards.
- Companies can give themselves some degree of protection also by entering into legal agreements with IoT vendors to provide adequate, tested, and updated security measures and to guard against the unauthorized access of sensitive information.

Remember that IoT security is not a battle that can be won and left behind. It is a war that will be fought for the foreseeable future—the proverbial marathon versus a sprint.

Keep in mind also that the IoT challenges we face mean a tremendous opportunity for fresh thinking. The future of the Internet, which carries with it the future of our world, is ours for the making. If you've read Isaac Asimov, you know that he was visionary about the future of technology. In his science fiction composed in the 1940s, he wrote, "No sensible decision can be made any longer without taking into account not only the world as it is, but the world as it will be." That realization is more important now than ever before because someday soon we'll almost certainly ask why things aren't connected to the Internet rather than why they are connected.

VII Incident response

33

Working with law enforcement in cyber investigations

U.S. Department of Justice – CCIPS Cybersecurity Unit

The decision to call law enforcement, or to respond to a law enforcement inquiry, during a cyber incident can be a harrowing moment for a company's executives and board members. Fear of losing control of key systems, of the investigation's course, or over sensitive company information are often given as reasons for caution or even to forego cooperation altogether. However, working with law enforcement need not be fearsome. With early planning, clear communications, and an understanding of law enforcement's roles and responsibilities, law enforcement and private companies can partner successfully on cyber investigations.

■ Law enforcement's role in cyber investigations

Law enforcement's roles and responsibilities in a cyber incident vary depending on the nature of the incident, the suspected perpetrators, and the desires of the victim. Although every investigation is different, law enforcement agencies working on cyber investigations are trained to understand company concerns and to incorporate their needs into the investigation's goals. Although a primary law enforcement goal is to protect public safety and national security, agencies have evolved to do this in a way that does not cause further harm to the victims of a cyberattack.

■ Why work with law enforcement?

The first question that may come to mind in the hours after a cyber incident is why a company should work with law enforcement at all. After all, it introduces another source of management challenges to an already difficult working environment. However, working with law enforcement can have significant benefits:

- Agencies can compel third parties to disclose data (such as connection logs) necessary to understanding how the incident took place, which can help a company better protect itself.

- Investigators can work with foreign counterparts to obtain assistance that may be otherwise impossible.
- Early reporting to and cooperation with law enforcement will likely be favorably considered when a company's response is subsequently examined by regulators, shareholders, the public, and other outside parties.
- Law enforcement may be able to secure brief delays in breach reporting requirements so that they can pursue active leads.
- A successful prosecution prevents the criminal from causing further damage and may deter others from trying.
- Information shared with investigators may help protect other victims, or even other parts of the same organization, from further loss and damage.

Effective partnership with law enforcement can be built into an overall response plan, especially when companies understand law enforcement's priorities and responsibilities.

■ Law enforcement's priorities and responsibilities

Law enforcement agencies, including the FBI and the U.S. Secret Service, prioritize conducting cyber investigations in ways that limit disruptions to a victim company's normal operations. They work cooperatively and discreetly with victims, and they employ investigative measures that avoid computer downtime or displacement of a company's employees. If they must use an investigative measure likely to inconvenience a victim, they try to minimize the duration and scope of the disruption.

Law enforcement agencies also conduct their investigations with discretion and work with a victim company to avoid unwarranted disclosure of information. They attempt to coordinate statements to the news media concerning the incident with a victim company to ensure that information harmful to a company's interests is not needlessly disclosed

and work with companies on timing. Law enforcement also has tools, including obtaining judicial protective orders, that can protect sensitive information from disclosure during investigations and prosecutions.

If an investigation is successful and an indictment is contemplated, prosecutors will consider victims among other factors when making charging decisions. If a particular charge would place sensitive company information at risk, for example, prosecutors may seek protections from the court or, if appropriate, use alternative charges that can reduce that risk, while still serving the overall interests of justice.

Sometimes, the best available course of action in a cyber investigation may not be pursuing an arrest of the perpetrator but rather disrupting the threat in some other way. For example, law enforcement has used combinations of civil and criminal tools to disrupt attacks from 'botnets' designed to steal financial information from companies and individuals. In other cases, pursuing the financial or technical infrastructure of a criminal organization will be the most effective strategy. Other tools may be available to the government that work best in a particular case. Whatever path is chosen, law enforcement's aim is to consult regularly with victims to ensure that the path chosen advances, rather than harms, the interests of the victim as well as the public.

■ Best practices for preparing for work with law enforcement

Preparing to work with law enforcement is an essential part of incident planning. The full scope of such preparation goes beyond what this chapter can cover. The CCIPS Cybersecurity Unit has published a short guide entitled *Best Practices for Victim Response and Reporting of Cyber Incidents*, which covers this topic in greater detail. Some of the recommended preparations include the following:

- *Implement appropriate technology, services, and authorizations.* Investigations will be severely hampered if a business lacks key information needed for law enforcement to develop and pursue leads early. Ensure that intrusion detection systems and network logging tools are in place, as well as the banners and other legal authorizations necessary to use them.

- *Identify the information, services, or systems that are most essential to your business operations.* Knowing and communicating this information to law enforcement early in an investigation will be crucial to prioritizing early investigative steps.
- *Determine who will work with law enforcement.* Law enforcement may need essential information about your systems and what you have learned about the attack to pursue ephemeral leads. Designating a person or group as a principal liaison to law enforcement will ease this process and allow others in your company to focus on other immediate priorities. This person or group should be authorized to gather necessary information and communicate it to law enforcement agents.
- *Ensure that legal counsel are familiar with key legal and technology issues.* Cyber investigations often raise difficult legal issues relating to privacy and monitoring. Legal counsel who are familiar with your systems and with legal principles in this area will be able to navigate these issues with law enforcement counsel more quickly. These counsel can work with your company's law enforcement liaison to ensure that information is collected and transferred lawfully and appropriately.

Calling authorities for assistance

Optimally, your first contact with law enforcement will not be in the throes of a crisis. Companies should establish relationships with their local federal law enforcement offices before they suffer a cyber incident. Having a point-of-contact and a pre-existing relationship with law enforcement facilitates any subsequent interaction that may occur if an organization needs to enlist law enforcement's assistance. It also helps establish the trusted relationship that

cultivates information sharing that helps victims and law enforcement.

Law enforcement agencies, including the FBI and U.S. Secret Service, have established regular outreach channels for companies that may be victims of cyberattacks. These include the following:

- FBI Infragard chapters and Cyber Task Forces in each of their 56 field offices
- U.S. Secret Service's Electronic Crimes Task Forces
- Computer Hacking and Intellectual Property coordinators and National Security Cyber Specialists in every U.S. Attorney's Office

Incorporating these resources into your planning can pay dividends in the hours after you discover that you may be a victim of an attack.

Victims may wonder which law enforcement agency is best to call when they face a cyberattack. Although agencies have different areas of expertise, they work together to ensure that there is 'no wrong door' for victims. As agencies follow leads and develop information about the likely attacker, they understand and can bring together expertise from across the government to ensure that the investigation is pursued aggressively using all appropriate tools.

What to expect when law enforcement knocks on your door

Often, a company will not be the first to know that they have been the victim of an intrusion or attack. Law enforcement may discover additional victims as they investigate an intrusion into a single entity. When this happens, agencies typically reach out to these additional victims directly.

A primary goal in such contacts is to ensure that additional victims get the information necessary to mitigate harms and secure their systems. At the same time, understanding the victim's business, the information that it processes, and its relationship with other entities can help agencies better understand the relationship among a series of thefts and the possible motivations for a given cyberthreat.

Cyber intrusions are rarely isolated to a single victim, and law enforcement collects examples of common techniques and practices from cyberthreats that can assist victims in securing their systems. For example, knowing that a particular group of criminals enters systems through a common vulnerability but once inside patches the original vulnerability while introducing several more can be crucial information for victims. By the same token, knowing that a group is focused on a specific version of a common software package or is targeting a particular industry can help law enforcement narrow down a list of possible perpetrators.

■ Realities of cybercrime investigations

Not surprisingly, the realities of cyber investigations differ from their portrayals in movies and television. Agents are rarely, if ever, able to trace an intrusion in progress instantly, nor do they often identify a perpetrator from halfway around the world quickly. Instead, such investigations often require painstaking assessment of historical log files, a long-term understanding of key motivations of likely attackers, and collection of evidence using exacting legal processes.

■ Cooperation with law enforcement in the investigation

Robust cooperation with law enforcement in the early hours and days of an investigation is essential to success. Agents likely will have many questions about the intrusions and the overall configuration of the system. Beginning from the time the intrusion is discovered, companies should make an initial assessment of the scope of the damage, take steps to minimize continuing damage, and begin preserving existing logs and keeping an ongoing written record of steps undertaken. Such documentation is often essential to understanding the scope of the intrusion at the inception; it can also be essential much later in the prosecution, as companies assess

damage and response costs for loss and restitution purposes.

When contacting law enforcement or communicating within the company, companies should avoid using systems suspected in the compromise. Such actions may provide a key tip to attackers that they have been discovered. To the extent possible, companies should use trusted accounts and systems for communication about the incident and be wary of attempts to gather information about the investigation via 'social engineering.'

■ Network forensics and tracing

One way that law enforcement conducts investigations is through network forensics and tracing. Although it is occasionally possible to follow a "hot lead" when an attack is ongoing, investigations more often depend on a careful examination of network logs. Because company systems are often complex and interrelated, investigators must consult with the system administrators who are experts on critical systems to identify where information necessary to developing leads will be stored. Such consultations can prove difficult if all system personnel are working intently on rebuilding security or restoring critical systems.

Companies can help with this by reserving a few experts whose job it is to work with law enforcement and to identify critical logs and other information that can be used to identify leads for law enforcement. These experts will be particularly important if the threat is believed to be an insider who has stolen trade secrets or other sensitive information, because the most important evidence is likely to be on internal systems.

■ Working with outside counsel and private forensic firms

Companies experiencing a severe cyber incident often turn to outside legal counsel and private forensic firms to assist them. Such entities can provide substantial support and expertise, based upon their experience assisting other victims, and can guide companies through difficult legal and technical issues relating to system monitoring, response options, and breach notification. Having ready access to advice from lawyers well acquainted with cyber incident response can speed decision-making and help ensure that a victim organization's incident response activities remain on firm legal footing.

An additional benefit is that legal and forensic firms often have established connections with law enforcement agencies and are familiar with the information that they will likely seek and understand the cyberthreats that they are investigating. Far from a replacement for law enforcement, these entities are often a crucial link between law enforcement and victims.

■ International issues

Because of the unbounded nature of computer networks and hence of cyberthreats, cyber investigations often cross international borders. A prime advantage of working with law enforcement on a cyberthreat investigation is that it has the tools and capabilities to broaden an investigation to include foreign partners and collect foreign evidence.

U.S. law enforcement agencies recognize the international opportunities and challenges and so have worked to build investigative and prosecution capabilities around the world. The U.S. and other countries have entered into international treaties, most prominently the *Budapest Convention on Cybercrime*, to ensure that there is an adequate legal foundation for investigations into cyberthreats. Investigative agencies have trained cyber agents who regularly work alongside their foreign counterparts on investigations.

Many times, direct police-to-police international cooperation will be the fastest way to get information necessary to advance an investigation. More formal processes, such as Mutual Legal Assistance requests, are used when evidence needs to be in a form usable in prosecutions. Although they are often slower than direct assistance, they provide an internationally recognized means for exchanging evidence.

If a suspect is identified overseas, law enforcement has a range of options to obtain justice for the victim. Extraditing the suspect to face charges in the U.S. is a traditional means, but the process can be lengthy, and many countries refuse to extradite their own nationals. In such cases, prosecutors in the U.S. may work with their counterparts abroad to ensure an appropriate prosecution in the suspect's home country. Other options may be available depending on the case. Because these choices often implicate victim interests, prosecutors frequently consult with victims before undertaking major international investigative steps.

■ Victim rights and expectations

Victims of cyber incidents—including corporate victims—have established rights under federal law. The specific victim rights and the responsibilities of prosecutors and law enforcement are described in the *Attorney General Guidelines for Victim and Witness Assistance* (2012), which is available on the Department of Justice's public website. Victim rights typically attach at the time that charges are filed, and include the following:

- the right to notice of public hearings in the prosecution
- the right to be reasonably heard at such hearings
- the reasonable right to confer with the attorney for the government
- the right to full and timely restitution as provided in law.

Beyond these mandatory rights, investigators and prosecutors in cyber cases strive to ensure cooperation with and support to the victim, to pass key information back to victims to support their security and recovery efforts, and to work to ensure that the victim is not further harmed by the investigation and prosecution.

Although law enforcement cannot disclose every aspect of an ongoing investigation, especially when such sharing may implicate other victims, companies should expect that law enforcement will communicate with them regularly. Information flow should not be a "one-way street" to law enforcement.

■ Legal considerations when working closely with law enforcement

As useful as it can be to cooperate with law enforcement, it is also crucial that companies understand and delineate their role in the investigation and exercise care before they take on roles that may effectively make them agents of law enforcement. For example, companies are generally permitted under U.S. law to monitor their own systems to protect their rights and property. Usually, that information can be shared with law enforcement once they arrive on scene. If law enforcement begins directing the response, however, different authorities and limitations typically apply.

The law relating to law enforcement monitoring is complex and goes beyond what can be discussed in this chapter. In general, companies should carefully delineate between actions undertaken by the provider for its own purposes and those undertaken at law enforcement's behest. If possible, companies should set out the facts and their understandings relating to such monitoring in writing shared with the investigating agency. More information on this topic can be found in Chapter 4 of the Department of Justice's manual *Searching and Seizing Computers and Obtaining Electronic Evidence in Criminal Investigations*, which is available from the Department's website. In addition, a sample letter relating to company monitoring that can be used by company counsel is included as Appendix G of that manual.

■ Active defense, hacking back, and potential liabilities

Companies undergoing a cyber attack may be tempted to "hack back" and attempt to access or impair another system that appears to be involved in a cyber intrusion or attack. Although that temptation is certainly understandable in the heat of an incident, doing so is often illegal under U.S. and foreign laws and could result in civil or even criminal liability. Many intrusions and attacks are launched from already compromised systems, precisely to confuse the identity of the true actor. Consequently, hacking back may damage or impair another innocent victim's system rather than that of the intruder.

This does not mean, however, that companies cannot engage in "active defense" within their own systems. For example, reacting to cyberattacks by changing network configurations or establishing "sandboxes," in which companies place realistic but false data to distract intruders from more sensitive data are active steps that can be taken to help defend systems. Law enforcement agencies can help identify other proactive steps that companies may be able to undertake to protect their systems.

■ Conclusion

Effective cybersecurity and cyber investigations are essential to protecting company assets and public safety in our increasingly networked world. A close and respectful partnership between companies and law enforcement when cyberattacks occur is an important aspect of both. Planning for such cooperation in advance and carefully delineating the roles played by company representatives, law enforcement, and outside experts greatly enhances the likelihood of success.

34

Planning, preparation, and testing for an enterprise-wide incident response

Booz Allen Hamilton – Jason Escaravage, Vice President; Anthony Harris, Senior Associate; James Perry, Senior Associate; and Katie Stefanich, Lead Associate

Cyber incident management is happening at your organization right now. In fact, it's happening every day, all day. Sometimes a cyber breach requires very little response; for example, it may be a benign attempt by a curious but harmless hacker to see if your network can be accessed. For large companies, this kind of attack can happen hundreds of times in a week. You probably never even hear about it from your IT department because those small incidents aren't worth your attention. They are easily eradicated; usually, just deleting the malicious email is enough, so they hardly cause any irreparable harm.

But what happens when it is a not-so-small breach? What happens when your intellectual property is stolen, or your employees' personal records are exposed? What if your e-commerce website goes down for a day? Those incidents you *will* hear about, and that moment is not the time to figure out what to do.

Of course, every situation has its own nuance, but at a foundational level, every organization, regardless of size, geographical location, or industry must have an incident management plan. One that includes participation from organizations and staff throughout the enterprise.

Effective cyber incident management happens in phases; it is not just about a response. Planning and preparing, or "steady-state" activities are just as important, if not more important than responding to a breach. To truly be ready for any kind of cyber incident, organizations need C-level support for smooth incident management coordination. This is supported by a plan that is thorough, easy to understand, and widely tested.

Fill in the blank: During a major cyber breach, the first thing I do is _____

HINT: The answer is *not* to wait for instruction from the IT department.
If you can't answer, imagine whether your legal department could. How about HR department? Or corporate communications team or VP of sales? They all should; they're all impacted by cyber incidents, so they have a role to play.

This chapter will focus on the following:

- incident response responsibility for the C-Suite and the business
- key considerations for cyber incident management plans
- testing a plan
- enabling plan adoption across the enterprise

■ Incident response for the C-Suite and beyond

Cyber incident response is often thought of as an IT department function. This assumption could be a costly mistake. Businesses in their entirety are connected to the Internet. As such, a cyber breach can happen anywhere within the business, ranging in severity, complexity, and impact. Relying on the IT department alone to be ready for any manifestation of a cyber incident would be an unfair if not impossible expectation.

IT security, typically led by a chief information security officer (CISO), needs to be empowered by the C-Suite so they can coordinate cyber incident response activity among all the impacted organizations and staff—this requires the facilitation of good working relationships during non-crisis times. One way to do this is for the CISO and the CEO to connect on cybersecurity trends frequently. The CISO has responsibility for assembling the right team, making sure the right technology architecture is in place, and for reporting cybersecurity issues upward. In a show of partnership, C-level leadership should enable the CISO to improve the organization's incident management capability.

The C-suite must understand and enforce organization-wide roles in cyber incident management. Everyone—corporate communications, legal, business unit leaders, and so on—has a role to play. They may not even know it—so it is important for leadership to stress their responsibility in these efforts.

In addition to collaborating with the CISO and truly understanding the incident management capability, stay on top of current cyber risks. They change all the time—phishing becomes spear-phishing becomes pharming, for example. Not only that, some are exclusive to certain industries. Product security risks vary from retail. Retail varies from automotive. However, one thing is certain—all parts of the business have evolving cyber risks. By staying on top of cyber risks, you can incorporate them as part of your enterprise-wide risk management strategy. Which would do the most harm? Which are most likely? Anticipating and preparing for all kinds of cyberthreats doesn't mean sitting on edge all the time. It requires simple demonstration of good steady-state behavior—which is the first phase of any incident management lifecycle, so a key section of an incident management plan.

■ Putting together the cyber incident management plan

Cyber incident management is constant; it happens in phases, and an actual incident lifecycle is only one part of it.

Shown in Figure 1 is a full lifecycle for incident management.

If you are starting from scratch, the National Institute of Standards and Technology (NIST) Cybersecurity Framework is a good reference point. It was created in collaboration between public sector and private industry.

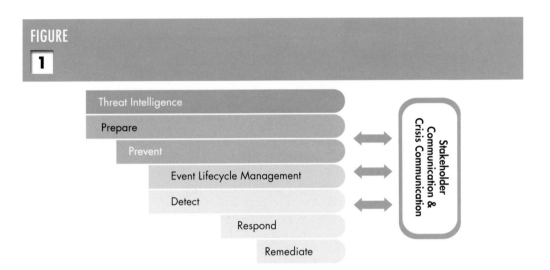

FIGURE
1

There is a caveat, however: incident management lifecycles do not fit neatly into a calendar. They overlap, phases are repeated, and truly, "Preparation" and "Prevention," or steady-state activities are happening all the time, even in the midst of an incident.

When the steady-state activities are done well, it makes an organization resilient and better able to bounce back after a breach occurs.

■ Elements of planning

A good cyber incident management plan considers the whole enterprise, and it considers more than just the technical aspects of incident response. When planning for cyber incident management, responsibilities and activities can be organized and integrated by three categories: people, process, and technology (Table 1).

Each of these things should be considered in the context of your organizational philosophy to risk management. Policies that help mitigate risk—such as acceptable use policies and data handling policies—can be used as governing authority for cyber incident management planning.

Although an incident management plan starts with the CISO, the rest of the business units should follow suit. Drafting an initial plan requires substantial effort to integrate how people, process, and technology work together in harmony across the whole enterprise. And, once the plan is created, it requires consistent support from the C-level to ensure adherence by the whole organization. The plans must be tested and updated frequently to make sure they keep up with changes in threats, tools, and resources.

■ Testing the plan

Short of being the victim of an actual intrusion, testing your incident response program is paramount to understanding how well your business would fair during a real incident. Many organizations pay for expensive tools, documentation, and consultation but are unable to replicate any of their strategies because they are not prepared to use them. Executives should understand that an incident response program with an always vigilant, always ready team is the greatest defense to a cyber intrusion and will reduce risk and increase confidence.

Assessing an organization's incident response program can provide a clear vision into their future, showing would happen if a cyberattack occurred and delivering insight into what works and what does not. There are several benefits to testing an organization's incident response plan:

| TABLE
 | | |
People	Process	Technology
■ In the main incident management plan, consider how the incident management team is structured and staffed. Is it composed of people already in your IT department or are there some roles that need to be filled? Staff should have the mix of skills necessary to orchestrate the strategic and technical sides of an incident response.	■ An incident management plan should include a process and procedure for every phase of the incident management lifecycle.	■ Technology aids the incident response process—from vulnerability intake to understanding the security controls on your electronic assets to facilitating quick communication. At a basic level, there should be automated process for incident handling—if your organization is still using manual incident tracking systems, you are overdue for a technology investment.
■ Consider also the touchpoints from the IT department into the rest of the organization. Make sure you know who will provide you with the information you need to make critical decisions in the midst of an incident. ■ Finally, keep in mind the partnerships internal and external— such as vendors and media—to the organization that must be built prior to an incident that would enable the smooth coordination of incident response.	■ The plan should be supported by runbooks, which are tactical guides that address specific incident scenarios most likely to affect your business. Make sure the processes are updated per a determined frequency to reflect evolving cyberthreats.	■ Threat and vulnerability detection technology can mitigate the impacts of a cyber breach. Beyond basic, more sophisticated data analytics tools provide complex, customized statistics that can help measure the business impact of a breach, among other capabilities.

Steady-state activities should be the heftiest part of your plan.
Your IT department is always monitoring your network, but you'd be surprised how often organizational cybersecurity relies on the human eye and manual processes. Your IT team could use your support to enhance their capability, for example:
- Automated tool development
- Asset management
- Threat detection ability
- Trend analysis
- Wargaming and tabletop exercises

- Keeping the program relevant and at the forefront of cybersecurity: reducing risk and increasing executive confidence
- Understanding current knowledge and tool gaps
- Increasing work performance and efficiency to reduce cost and time spent resolving an incident.

■ **Testing methods**

Testing entails far more than just making sure employees are trained on tools and procedures, they have to be able to detect, contain, and remediate active incidents—real or fictional—and the only way to do that is by managing realistic situations. There are a variety of ways to provide scenarios that can test an organization's incident response program.

Using a "red team," or a group whose purpose is to simulate a cyber adversary, is a way to covertly test the response to an actual adversary. Only employees with a need to know will be aware of a red team's activities, so to the organization's incident responders, the scenario is treated like an actual incident (without the loss of capital). Results from these exercises can be shared with executives, providing an overview of strengths and weaknesses to tweak the program and try again.

Engaging specialized third parties to review an incident response program can validate program elements. It's often said that a second set of eyes can find flaws in a document that the author overlooked. This same

strategy can apply to an incident response program. Although many organizations have plenty of documentation surrounding their program, they sometimes rarely review or update it. The cybersecurity landscape changes every day, which leaves an under-reviewed program in an incomplete state, becoming more irrelevant as time passes. Employing specialized third parties to review an organization's program on a regular basis can assist in maintaining an up-to-date, risk-averse program.

Strategic simulations, also known as war games, can simulate numerous possible situations in which their program will be applied. These scenarios ask participants to use their current technological and process knowledge to solve situations ranging from the exfiltration of organizational intellectual property to a large phishing campaign requesting employee information, to an enterprise-wide denial of service—halting productivity, sales, or transactions. War games also help an organization to craft scenarios in which teams that do not typically communicate with one another have to cooperate to solve problems. This is especially helpful when senior leadership is involved—it helps illustrate major decision points and clarifies the business impact of various cyber breach scenarios.

Although developing, preparing, and implementing the incident response plan is essential, making sure all of that work is functional and as efficient as possible is vital to having a successful incident response program. By implementing tests such as red team exercises, war games, and regular reviews, an organization can understand what may happen if they are an unfortunate victim of a cyberattack and, maybe, through solutions implemented through test findings, prevent a real incident.

■ Internal and external communications planning

Once the plans have been written and tested, it's important to keep up momentum and continued awareness about cyber risks. Just as the IT department is constantly engaged in cyber incident management, so too must the staff throughout the organization—albeit with regard to their own personal role.

Enlist the help of your corporate communications department to help with cybersecurity awareness messaging that is tailored for all staff. Messaging should help employees stay attuned to cyberthreats that could affect them, as well as how they can play a part in keeping the organization secure. Keep in mind that "cyber" may not resonate with staff outside the IT department, which

is why corporate communications can help craft the appropriate messaging.

In addition to internal messaging, make sure cyber incidents are incorporated into the organization's crisis communications capability. Just as corporate communications would be on hand to protect the brand's image during an emergency, they should similarly have a crisis communications plan for a cyber incident. As a part of that, ensure that the right spokespersons are media trained prior to an incident.

■ The inevitable cyber breach

It's hard to estimate the cost of a cyber incident. Undoubtedly, the longer that business operations are affected—production is stalled, websites are down, IP is stolen, and so on—the cost climbs higher and higher. Having a plan that is pervasive enterprise-wide that uses a tested, all-staff approach can help resolve cyber incidents quicker. Given that cyberthreats are present all the time, an incident is all but inevitable. Fortunately, incident response planning can mitigate the impacts of such an event.

35

Detection, analysis, and understanding of threat vectors

Fidelis Cybersecurity – Jim Jaeger, Chief Cyber Strategist

Rapidly evolving cyberthreat landscape

Cybersecurity and cyberattacks are no longer emerging issues. Over the past three to five years, the complexity of cyberthreats has increased dramatically, and the nature of cyberattacks has evolved from the theft of financial data and intellectual property to include recent destructive attacks. Organizations now face increasingly sophisticated attacks from adversaries using multiple threat vectors and cunning strategies to penetrate the security perimeter.

Although the 2008 TJX data breach has long been assumed to be the turning point in board of directors' awareness of cybersecurity, it took the 2013 Target breach to have an impact on the boards' agenda. Faced with the possibility of loss of data and intellectual property, decreased shareholder value, regulatory inquiries and litigations, and damaged reputations, boards are realizing that cybersecurity is no longer just an IT issue but one of strategic risk.

Corporate directors understand that they must become more involved in addressing cyber risks; however, cybersecurity is a new and highly technical area that leaves many corporate boards uncertain as to how to proceed. Research from the Ponemon Institute reveals that 67 percent of board members have only some knowledge (41 percent) or minimal to no knowledge about cybersecurity (26 percent). Although board members realize that they need to invest in cybersecurity, such a lack of knowledge is affecting their ability to respond to cybersecurity risk and provide proper oversight.

Understand the adversaries

Cybercrime is big business, and sophisticated cyber criminals are playing for high stakes. However, motivations among the groups may differ:

- Hacktivists often seek to damage the reputation of an organization and cause disruptions.

- Organized cyber criminals include international crime syndicates targeting organizations largely in the financial services and retail industries for financial gain. Although there are a number of players, this arena is dominated by loosely knit teams of attackers located in Eastern Europe.
- State-sponsored espionage threat actors deploy targeted malware in stealthy, multi-stage attacks, sometimes called advanced persistent threats (APT), targeting intellectual property. At risk is anything that may be of value, including business plans and contracts; trading algorithms; product designs and business processes; trade secrets; client data; lists of employees, customers, and suppliers; and even employee log-on credentials.

As attackers have sharpened their skills and expanded their techniques over the last couple of years, organizations are now facing a new challenge. Cybercrime has advanced to include cyber warfare and cyber terrorism as nation-state actors have moved from disruptive to destructive attacks.

Experts predict that cyberattacks will intensify as cyber criminals accelerate their activities. Organizations face a world of continuous compromise. It is no longer a question of whether the company will be breached, but when. Ponemon research, however, shows that board members generally lack knowledge about cybersecurity breach activity within their organizations. One in five, for example, was unaware if the organization had been breached in the recent past.

Although larger organizations are generally able to recover from a significant breach, providing that negligence is not a factor and excessive liability is avoided, sustaining operations over the course of two or more

Blurring lines of attack

It used to be that the tactics employed by Eastern European cyber criminals were relatively unique compared with those used by hackers deploying state-sponsored APT attacks to target intellectual property. Cybercrime experts are now seeing a blurring of the lines of attack, which has caused some forensics teams to misidentify the adversary. For example, researchers from two forensics firms investigated an attack on a global credit card processor for two months without success, convinced that it was an APT attack. It wasn't until the firm brought in a new forensics team that they were able to identify the attack as originating from Eastern Europe and stop the breach.

Corporate espionage leads to company downfall

Cyberattacks aimed at stealing intellectual property can put a company out of business. A classic example involves Nortel, a telecommunications giant that was the victim of a decade-long low and slow attack wherein hackers used seven stolen passwords to extract research, business plans, technical papers, corporate emails, and other sensitive data. The attack was discovered by an employee who noticed unusual downloads that appeared to have been made by a senior executive. The company changed the compromised passwords but did little else beyond conducting a six-month investigation that yielded nothing. In the following years, the company reportedly ignored recommendations to improve network security. Analysts speculate that the extensive cyberattacks on the technology company ultimately contributed to its downfall. The company continued to lose ground to overseas competitors and ultimately declared bankruptcy.

extended breaches would be considered a huge challenge. Clearly, cybersecurity has become an increasingly challenging risk that demands both corporate management and board attention. To provide the proper risk oversight, the C-level leaders and board members are advised to work closely with IT security leaders to examine the threat environment and how adversaries are attacking peer organizations.

■ Understand the threat vectors

The fast pace of cloud, mobile, virtualization, and emerging technologies present opportunities to gain operational efficiencies, deploy innovative business models, and create new markets. However, as companies increasingly digitize valuable assets and move operations online, the risk of cyberthreats grows even greater. In today's digital world, employees are increasingly interconnected and leverage a variety of mobile devices, applications, and cloud platforms to conduct business in the office, at home, and "on-the-go." Mobile applications, email, WiFi networks, and social media sites are just some of the vulnerable access points that attackers seek to exploit.

Not only are employees increasingly interconnected, but organizations are as well. Boards and corporate management must consider the extended attack surface and the potential security risks associated with third parties such as suppliers, transaction processors, affiliates, and even customers. Not to be overlooked are law firm partners, as they hold data relating to an organization's confidential operations and trade secrets.

Internal employees present at least as big an exposure for companies as do external attacks. There is increasing recognition that the activity of employees with privileged access and administrative rights must be monitored, controlled, and audited. Part of the concern is not necessarily that the employees go rogue and become insider threats, which certainly has to be considered, but that hackers target the credentials of system administrators because they grant unfettered system access. To guard against the use of compromised credentials, organizations should implement the concept of least privilege for employee digital rights, especially for those with administrative rights.

Determined attackers use a variety of approaches to exploit system vulnerabilities and penetrate virtually all of a company's perimeter defense systems. Threat vectors used to compromise an organization can include network intrusions, compromised websites and web applications, malware, targeted "spear phishing" and other email attacks, Trojans, zero-day exploits, social engineering tactics, and privilege misuse. This dynamic nature of the cyberthreats presents ongoing challenges to companies and boards as every possible threat vector must be addressed.

■ Detect advanced threats

Like any business risk, cybersecurity risk must be calculated and then mitigated through the use of specific types of controls, such as firewall, antivirus, intrusion detection, and other similar solutions. However, no network is so secure that hackers won't

Questions to ask about risk

- Who are our most likely intruders?
- What is the biggest weakness in our IT systems?
- What are our most critical and valued data assets? Where are they located?
- Do we consider external and internal threats when planning cybersecurity programs?
- Do our vendor partners have adequate security measures? Do we have sufficient contractual clauses regarding such security?
- What are best practices for cybersecurity? Where do our practices differ?
- Have we created an incident response plan?

find their way in. Once in, they can go for months, even years, without detection. Because deeply embedded hackers can be extremely difficult to eradicate, the challenge is to detect these threats as soon as possible. Unfortunately, organizations are hard pressed to match resources with cyber criminals. Similar to a game of "whack-a-mole," once organizations get on top of one type of attack, the cyber criminals simply evolve their tactics.

A solid cybersecurity governance program is vital to getting ahead of cybercrime. Unfortunately, there is a gap in the perception of governance effectiveness between board members and security professionals.

Ponemon research indicates that 59 percent of board members believe the corporations' cybersecurity governance practices are very effective, whereas only 18 percent of security professionals believe so. This gap in perspective has to be closed if organizations are to improve their ability to face increasingly stealthy and sophisticated cyber risks.

■ **Robust, constant monitoring is key to detection**
The saying, "You don't know what you don't know" is especially true in cybersecurity. Robust, constant network monitoring is vital to uncovering threats. Any number of solutions are available that enable organizations to monitor network activity. Because the volume of network traffic combined with increasingly complex networks defies manual threat analysis, many organizations often rely

on the automated threat-detection capabilities of numerous disparate solutions. However, this overreliance on technology alone to address security threats can cause organizations to lose sight of the bigger threat picture.

Organizations also jeopardize their ability to detect advanced threats through a failure to fully integrate the security solutions into the entire network defense infrastructure. Often security technologies are deployed with default settings, resulting in many false-positive alerts. Many times organizations overlook the human element. Organizations can't depend on technology alone to defend networks. Detecting advanced threats requires a risk management program that includes technology, people, and processes. Board members should ensure that security budgets include funding for security experts who can understand the risk, interpret the alerts, and act on the intelligence.

■ **Anticipate attacks**
Today's threat actors conduct detailed reconnaissance and develop custom malware in an effort to penetrate networks. It's difficult to know when an attack will happen. A dynamic threat intelligence capability helps to ensure that organizations can anticipate breaches before they occur and adjust their defensive strategies.

Widespread sharing of threat intelligence among security professionals can empower organizations to detect threats more efficiently and effectively and avoid

Dismissed security alerts lead to massive breach

A large retailer became the victim of a major data breach. The retailer had invested hundreds of millions of dollars in data security, had a robust monitoring system in place, and had been certified as PCI compliant. Despite the investment, the company failed to completely deploy and tune the monitoring system. The system could have been configured to remove malware automatically, but because the software was new and untested, the feature was deactivated. A small amount of hacker activity was surfaced to the security team, evaluated, and acted on; however, the team determined it didn't warrant further investigation. Several subsequent alerts were either ignored or lost in the noise of hundreds of false-positive alerts. It wasn't until the Department of Justice warned the company about suspicious activity that the retailer began investigating the activity.

cyber attacks. At one end of the threat intelligence spectrum are indicators of compromise (IOC). Integrated from several sources and typically shared through an automated, continuous, real-time threat intelligence data stream, IOCs provide information on malicious code and malicious web pages that hackers are using.

At the other end of the threat intelligence spectrum are threat advisories, which provide big picture analysis of current security issues posing risks to enterprises. Such advisories typically feature an overview of the threat, a risk assessment, indicators, and mitigation strategies.

■ Build board cyber literacy

As boards become more involved in cybersecurity, they should address cybersecurity risk as they would other types of business risk. To be effective in leading their organizations with the right knowledge, oversight, and actions, boards need a base level of understanding of cybersecurity risks facing the organization. However, organizations are challenged with what is the best way to build this board cyber literacy.

Many boards already have some form of oversight when it comes to cyber exposure, generally in the audit committee or risk committees specifically tasked with enterprise IT security and emerging risks. To gain a deeper understanding of the relevant issues surrounding cyber risk, some organizations are adding cyber expertise directly to the board via the recruitment of new directors. However, because nominating and governance committees must balance many factors in filling board vacancies, there is a concern that it may take a long time for boards to achieve the proper board composition.

In addition to board composition, directors point to a lack of available time on the agenda to discuss cybersecurity as a roadblock in becoming cyber literate. Although board members are not expected to be cybersecurity experts, they need access to expertise to help inform boardroom discussions. Ways to bring knowledgeable perspectives on cybersecurity matters into the boardroom include the following:

- Periodic briefings from in-house specialists
- "Deep dive" briefings from third-party experts, including cybersecurity firms, government agencies, and industry associations
- Guidance from the board's existing external auditors and outside counsel, who will have a multi-client and industry-wide perspective on cyber risk trends and how the organizations' cyber defense program compares with others in the industry
- Director education programs, whether provided in house or externally
- Periodic exercise of the incident response plan to include board members.

■ Empower the chief information security officer

Boards have a responsibility to manage cyber risks as thoroughly as possible. One critical element in providing effective oversight is to empower the chief information security officer (CISO) to drive security throughout the organization. In many organizations the CISO's role is subordinate to that of the chief information officer (CIO). Directors should be mindful that the agenda of the CIO is sometimes in conflict with that of the CISO. Whereas the CISO is focused on data and network security, the CIO is focused on supporting business processes with applications and networks that have high availability.

Recognizing that business strategies that lack a security component increase vulnerabilities and place the organization at risk, the CISO must have a strong, independent voice within the organization. To accomplish this, the board must ensure that the CISO is reporting at the appropriate levels within the organization. Although there is no single right answer, the trend has been to migrate reporting lines to other officers, including the general counsel, the chief operating officer, the chief risk officer, or

Questions to ask about cyber literacy and CISO empowerment

- Are we considering cybersecurity aspects of our major business decisions, such as mergers and acquisitions, partnerships, and new product launches?
- Are we allocating enough time for cybersecurity on the board agenda?
- Are we continuously monitoring and regularly reporting on governance compliance, maturity level, progress of information security, and data privacy projects and activities, as well as the status of incidents, risks, and issues within the organization? Are they used for active oversight?
- Do we have clear lines of accountability and responsibility for cybersecurity?
- Is the information security management function organizationally positioned at the appropriate level to effectively implement policies?
- Is the cybersecurity budget adequate? Are we investing enough so that we are not an easy target for a determined hacker?

even the chief executive officer, depending on the industry, size, and scope of the company, and the organization's dependency on technology.

■ Conclusion

The threat landscape is rapidly evolving as well-funded cyber criminals continue to launch increasingly sophisticated attacks through multiple threat vectors. Cybersecurity will continue to pose a serious risk that will demand corporate management and board attention and oversight. Boards that fail to actively measure and continuously monitor cybersecurity as part of the organization's strategy will leave their firms open to significant financial, reputational, and competitive risk.

The overwhelming number of cyber incidents has forced board members to become more involved in cybersecurity, which is as it should be. However, to be effective, much education is still needed. Board members don't need to be cyber experts, but they should have a thorough knowledge of the risks their organization faces and provide the support needed to the IT security professionals to protect against those risks.

36

Forensic remediation

Fidelis Cybersecurity – Jim Jaeger, Chief Cyber Strategist and Ryan Vela, Regional Director, Northeastern North America Cybersecurity Services

When a data breach occurs, directors and C-level executives must be ready with an incident response and remediation plan to minimize the damage, limit the company's liability and exposure, and help the company resume normal operations as quickly as possible. Incident response preparedness, however, varies greatly. Although some organizations are well prepared, sometimes even companies that have invested millions of dollars on preventive and detection systems fall short in responding to and remediating data breaches. Frequently, it's because the organization hasn't fully developed the relationships and processes necessary for rapid and coordinated response.

Companies that have been compromised must act quickly to investigate and remediate the breach while preserving all electronic evidence. Ascertaining what data were lost, destroyed, or stolen is paramount because it enables companies to determine their risk exposure and potential liability. Beyond digital forensic preservation, investigation, and containment, the complexities of breach remediation require notification of a broad range of third parties and engagement with law enforcement. By engaging breach resolution experts that provide forensics services, litigation support, and crisis communications, organizations can more effectively combat today's sophisticated cyberthreats.

■ Assemble a cross-functional response team

Effective investigation and remediation of a data breach requires an understanding of the cyber adversary and specialized forensic skills that most IT staffs lack. When a company that does not have its own internal security team experiences a cyberattack, it is vital that the firm hire experts who are experienced in digital forensics, incident response, and remediation. Engaging an independent and impartial breach response firm:

- provides the technological expertise and industry knowledge to fully remediate the incident
- ensures integrity in incident response and creates a defensible record of investigation and remediation
- enables the organization to maintain and secure attorney-client privilege for the reports and other investigative documents.

Breach response also requires that an organization have a well-prepared internal incident response team. Companies that suffer a breach without having established such a team often waste valuable time trying to get organized and assign responsibilities, stalling the breach remediation process. The team should include representatives from IT, security, legal, compliance, communications, risk management, and affected business units. In addition, it is important to involve a member from the executive leadership team to ensure that business considerations are addressed and to maintain the remediation momentum by ensuring rapid approval on courses of action when needed.

■ Engage outside legal counsel

The legal ramifications of a data breach can be devastating, ranging from litigation and regulatory investigations to civil liabilities effects that may include shareholder and customer-driven lawsuits. Because inside counsel lacks the specialized cyber expertise that is needed for effective breach response, it's vital that an organization identify, vet, and retain outside counsel that has the ability to respond on a moment's notice. The benefits of outside counsel include the following:

- **specialized skillsets:** cyberattack investigations require a team of lawyers with regulatory, data-breach response, privacy, litigation, and eDiscovery expertise; outside counsel brings the

specialized skills and credentials that internal teams lack
- **law enforcement liaison:** serves as liaison with law enforcement, such as the Secret Service, Federal Bureau of Investigation, and Department of Justice
- **attorney-client privilege:** engaging outside counsel secures the privilege needed to protect internal communications from discovery by any opposing party during pretrial investigation and from being used as evidence in a trial; also, invoked privilege allows the forensic company to report breach results directly to the law firm
- **leadership advice:** leadership of any organization falling victim to a data breach instinctively seeks to minimize costs and take shortcuts in incident response; by quarterbacking the investigation and remediation, outside counsel often proves invaluable in providing a strategy and helping C-level leadership and directors to hold themselves to the course of action.

■ Control breach communications

Ultimately, all communications about the breach have the potential to leave an organization open to legal liability. Outside breach counsel should therefore oversee all breach communications. This includes facilitating conversations between members of the incident response team and organizing external communications.

Internally, getting the right information to the right people at the right time can make or break breach incident response efforts. When members of the response team are working with incomplete, inaccurate, or different sets of information, it can lead to costly inefficiencies, delays, and errors in breach response. Outside counsel is well positioned to know the types of conversations that must happen between incident response team members to keep efforts on track. Similarly, breach counsel knows what hazards are likely to arise with external communications.

It is also vital that organizations engage a crisis communications firm to handle all external communications. Because such

Vetted investigation report vital to external communications

When faced with a data breach, the instinct is often to go public as quickly as possible to get ahead of the situation. However, to avoid public announcements backfiring and making an already bad situation worse, leadership would do well to wait for confirmation of breach status from the incident response team. On occasion, they even get to give their client good news. Case-in-point is a large blood donor system involving multiple hospitals and universities. The organization was maintaining a database of 90,000 donors when it noticed indications of hacker activity in the network.

Already under media pressure for physical loss of sensitive data, leadership was understandably concerned about reducing negative publicity by being proactive in its communications. They agreed to give the response team the time needed to conduct an investigation, and fortunately so. It was determined that the indicators were actually false-positive alerts. By synching the communication cycle with the progress of the investigation, the organization was able to avoid falsely alerting 90,000 donors that their data was at risk.

communications have either positive or negative lingering effects, it's important that all communications be carefully composed and carry the right tone.

Just as important, there is nothing worse than having to publically recant information. In deciding whether to release a statement, organizations should consider the following:

- **Is there accurate information to report?** Executives, feeling pressure to go public, may disclose key facts only to retract the statement at a later date. Waiting until a report from an external forensic response firm has been reviewed can help organizations maintain accurate communications.
- **Is disclosure within a specific timeframe required?** Timing of disclosures often is dictated by statutory and regulatory requirements. Several state breach laws, for example, require notification upon discovery or without reasonable delay. Here, outside counsel often can be invaluable in providing justification to delay an announcement until the facts are solid.
- **Has the incident been leaked?** However it occurs, leaks by journalists or postings in the blogosphere can accelerate a company's disclosure timeline. It is critical that firms experiencing a breach

prepare and pre-coordinate a contingency announcement in case their hand is forced. Crisis communications firms also have the media relationships that can enable the rapid response necessary in these situations.

■ **Partner with law enforcement and seek their assistance**

Seeking assistance from law enforcement can be extremely valuable in data breach investigations because these agencies are continuously following the digital trail of cybercrime. Law enforcement can play a vital role in providing indicators of compromise (IOCs) observed in similar breaches that may be linked, thus providing the incident response and forensic team with key data to search for and fill in missing pieces in the breach investigation. Attributing a single breach to a specific attacker or hacker organization is often difficult, but when you look at the IOCs provided by law enforcement across multiple hacks, this task often becomes much easier.

Involving law enforcement is also prudent in that cyber criminals routinely hide behind borders, and bringing them to justice remains a challenge. The U.S. government is increasingly partnering with foreign governments and international law enforcement agencies in efforts to prosecute malware creators and

Collaboration with law enforcement takes down hacking ring

Monday mornings can hit hard for many people, but for a major payments processor, one particular Monday morning packed a punch. In a brazen move, a global network of thieves had breached the processor's network. As a result of the hack, the gang was able to generate debit cards and crack the ATM PIN codes. Once that was done, the gang withdrew millions of dollars over the weekend.

By acting on information provided by the FBI, the forensic team was able to uncover additional details about the breach and advance the investigation to the point of identifying the culprits. Through cooperation from various law enforcement agencies worldwide, the investigation broke the sophisticated computer hacking ring and, for the first time, resulted in a Russian court convicting hackers for cybercrimes committed in the United States via the Internet.

those who are engaged in cybercrime. If there is any indication that the investigation may have an international aspect, federal law enforcement may be able to expedite the investigation. Law enforcement's expertise in gathering evidence and conducting forensic analysis can be leveraged to ensure that the data can be used in future court proceedings. Also, in some cases, organizations may be able to delay notification requirements if it would impede or interfere with a law enforcement investigation.

■ Alert industry regulators

Threat actors are neither attacking one institution at a time, nor are they quickly changing their methods. They often use the same techniques on multiple institutions in multiple sectors. With the increasing number of data breaches comes a renewed push for the sharing of cyber risk information between the United States government and the private sector to help individual organizations and industries as a whole better defend against attacks. Because of their position in the industry, regulators can be an important source of information on cyber threats, attacks, and trends. Information sharing and analysis organizations have made a resurgence and organizations can benefit by seeking their aid for insight on indicators of compromise during a data breach.

Regulatory investigations have the potential to represent a significant challenge in terms of money, time, resources, and distractions. Because regulators will have to be satisfied that the data breach has been completely resolved, organizations should engage with regulators as early as possible during the remediation process.

■ Notify insurance providers

After a data breach, organizations can expect to see significant costs arising from forensic investigations, outside counsel, crisis communications professionals, data breach notification expenses, regulatory investigations and fines, lawsuits, and remedial measures. Such costs can quickly reach tens of millions of dollars in a few weeks.

Once an incident is determined to be a breach, it's important to engage with the firm's insurance providers to evaluate the insurance coverage and determine which existing policies may cover the event; as well as identify the necessary reporting requirements.

One of the challenges with cyber insurance is the lack of standardization in terms of coverage. From a broad standpoint most policies cover the initial incident response and investigation. Few, however, cover remediation. Because the policies vary widely, general counsel and outside counsel have to understand the details of the policies to tailor an incident response approach that maximizes the coverage. Here, the outside forensics response team can also be invaluable in helping organizations to articulate and justify cyber insurance claims.

■ Conduct complete, focused digital forensics analysis

When a data breach occurs, organizations need answers fast: Who was involved? How did they do it? What data was compromised? What are the risks? Answers depend on the forensic analysis of digital evidence. Further, the proper preservation of digital evidence is crucial to demonstrate to regulators that reasonable security controls are in place or to prove wrongdoing in criminal prosecution. However, organizations all too often are thrown into panic. Hasty decisions are made and evidence is lost. Here, directors should look to outside counsel for guidance. Their experience and focus on minimizing legal liability make their advice about what should be considered evidence, and thus preserved, invaluable.

In the course of its forensics efforts, organizations typically encounter two challenges:

- **Limited scope of forensics.** Many times organizations fail to look beneath the surface in the hopes that a simple review will fix the problem. Alternatively, they may limit the scope of the investigation to mitigate the high cost of forensics. Such actions may fail to uncover the true cause and extent of the breach. By exploring all potentially compromised systems, organizations can reduce the risk of overlooking exposed system components.
- **Improper handling of evidence.** A company's internal IT staff may compromise the evidence even before forensic experts can preserve it. Organizations must ensure that the internal IT staff is mindful of proper evidence-handling protocol.

■ Focus on aggressive remediation

When an organization experiences a data breach, it is often difficult to determine the nature of the attack cycle and pathways of attack as hackers disperse their tools throughout the network. This is especially true in advanced persistent threat attacks, in which malware can remain dormant and undetected for months. The remediation phase is therefore critical to remove malware from infected hosts and prevent future reoccurrences of the same or similar breaches.

At one end of the remediation spectrum is sequential eradication. Here, incident responders work to eliminate malware as soon as it is discovered. This traditional approach has the benefit of lower costs and reducing the risk of data loss. However, the drawback is that the organization forfeits the opportunity to learn about the hacker's tactics and runs the risk of retaliation. Also, attackers may go quiet, making it more difficult to find their tools and requiring that forensic investigators shift their efforts to eradication.

At the other end of the spectrum is aggressive remediation, in which all remediation actions are executed simultaneously across the entire network. If executed properly, aggressive remediation precludes the hacker from detecting and reacting to the remediation actions. This approach is called for when an organization experiences repeated breaches by the same advanced attackers or a breach has gone undetected for weeks or months. Aggressive remediation provides a better understanding of the attacker's tools, tactics, targets, and motivations. Because this method fully removes all traces of the attacker's tools, threats, and vulnerabilities, including the attacker's ability to re-enter the network, it minimizes retaliatory risk.

This approach allows the attacker to remain active in the network during investigation. Should they become aware of forensic activities, they could move quickly to a destructive attack. Special forensic skills, extensive planning, and sophisticated execution therefore are required to avoid interfering with or alerting the attacker as to the forensic efforts underway, as well as to minimize the potential for damage and data loss.

Aggressive remediation outwits hacker mastermind

"Please don't lock the attacker out of the network." Not the request that any CEO wants to hear, let alone the leadership of a major retailer that was under attack by a hacker mastermind who was stealing 45,000 credit cards every three days. Yet here was the Secret Service explaining that it was the best live investigation in three years, and that if kept alive, they would be able to track and identify the hacker—with a good chance of getting a conviction.

Faced with the challenge of how to minimize the damage without alerting the attacker, the forensic team decided on the strategy of letting the attacker continue his efforts, but to change several digits of the credit card numbers the hacker was collecting. Other than actually trying to use the cards, the attacker would have no way of knowing he had stolen invalid card numbers. The ruse worked, allowing the team to keep the attacker alive in the network long enough to complete the forensic analysis and eradication. The attacker is now serving two 20-year jail terms.

■ The critical importance of network monitoring

If determined attackers want to get in, they will find a way. The real question is whether the organization will detect the breach. Unfortunately, the answer is, "Probably not." Advanced, targeted attacks focus on quiet reconnaissance and infiltration of their victims' network. Professional cyber criminals are so adept at cloaking their activities that they routinely go unnoticed for months, even years, without detection.

Although defense-in-depth has long been hailed as a best practice, organizations are now urged to improve their abilities to detect attacks that have succeeded. Robust network monitoring is a strategically important element in IT security and is crucial to determining if anything was stolen. By employing robust network monitoring organizations can maintain control, limit the damage, and plan for an appropriate response.

■ Summary

Organizations have reached a pivot point, realizing that it is no longer a question of if the firm has been hacked, but an assumption that it has. Faced with the new reality of operating the business while potentially executing incident response activities, organizations are placing a priority on robust network monitoring to detect the extraordinarily complicated threats hidden in the network. Once identified, these threats demand a host of remediation responses that include forensic preservation, containment, expulsion, and remediation. Responding to a major breach correctly requires a team of outside forensic and legal experts partnered with their internal incident response team. A well-defined incident response team includes key staff functions and line of business managers as well as C-level executives and corporate directors.

Experiencing a cyberattack is disruptive, and combating the malware behind large data breaches remains a constant challenge. Getting the right people involved and understanding the best way to efficiently use them is essential to properly investigating and remediating the event while managing costs and extent of business impact. Board directors and C-level leadership must ensure that their organizations are ready with a well thought out breach incident response plan to help minimize the organization's liability and exposure.

37

Lessons learned—containment and eradication

Rackspace Inc. – Brian Kelly, Chief Security Officer

Cyberattacks continue to proliferate and show no signs of stopping. Information security is a business risk issue, and concerns over how to manage data breaches have moved beyond IT security teams to the C-suite and the board. Recognizing that attacks happen to the best of organizations, board directors are asking, "What can be done to minimize the damage?" Based on the experience of senior information security leadership servicing some of the largest data breaches to date, here are ten lessons that offer guidance in successfully containing and eradicating cyberattacks.

■ Cast incident response in the context of business risk

Although the natural tendency has been to treat cyberattacks as a technical issue to be resolved by the security team, such attacks are serious business problems that can pose substantial risk to the business. Decisions made unilaterally by the security team without an appreciation for strategic initiatives can have significant implications for the corporation.

To correctly characterize the risk and make the appropriate decisions to limit the liability to the company, cyberattacks and incident response must be put in the context of business risk. For this to happen, discussions with the board must be two-way conversations. CISOs have to translate the event or incident into business terms, at which point the board and leadership team can provide a point of view or strategic focus that may be vital to the incident. For example, the incident response team may be unaware of such considerations as M&A activity, clinical trials, and new R&D efforts. Through board-level conversations the response team can gain the necessary insight into the motives of an attacker and make a connection that may alter the investigation.

■ Seek unity of command

Unity of command is vital to respond to a cyberattack. However, not every incident requires the same command and control structure. Careful planning should determine in advance the level of management required based on the severity of the event and identify those that require board attention and corporate officer leadership.

Similar to military operations, in which the general commands the day-to-day operations of the military during peacetime, a CISO oversees the day-to-day responsibilities and projects. During times of war, command shifts to the Joint Chiefs of Staff and designated war fighting commanders. The same holds true in a cyberattack. The incident response leader takes control and leads the team through the steps necessary to respond to the incident.

Effective command and control during these times of crisis is critical. However, when an incident is declared, people often come out of the woodwork to get involved. Because time is critical, nothing can be worse than senior executives trying to influence activity or wrestle control when an attack is in progress. Slow response and uncoordinated containment activities can provide attackers with the time necessary to move laterally in the network, creating an even more serious breach. It is therefore vital that command and control be clear, understood, disciplined, and followed with precision.

To increase leadership's understanding of the workings of command and control and provide insight into the protocols and procedures of incident response, it is imperative that organizations rehearse the incident response plan at least annually. Whether the activity is a mock tabletop exercise or a live-fire drill, the rehearsal gives company leadership and directors a baseline understanding of the criteria used to determine the severity of an event, the lifecycle of an attack and incident response, and the goals for each phase of the lifecycle.

The exercises also provide insights into the following:

- how and when to engage external partners
- what can potentially go wrong during the phases
- what types of communications are needed
- how to protect the incident response information flow that is for the response team's exclusive use
- how to bring other departments into the investigation.

Armed with such information, leadership and board directors are better enabled to formulate questions and act on the information to provide proper governance and oversight.

■ Retain incident response teams and outside counsel experienced in managing cybersecurity incidents

When it comes to containment and eradication, it is vital that internal security teams understand their strengths and weaknesses. Often internal teams assume they can handle the event and try to fix the problems themselves, only to make matters worse by accidentally destroying or tainting crucial evidence. Organizations are therefore turning to external counsel and forensic response teams that can step in on a moment's notice to respond to cyberattacks.

Selecting the right counsel and forensic team—especially those experienced in interactions with law enforcement—can be the difference between success and failure. In addition to benefiting from their expertise, involvement of an attorney allows organizations to maintain attorney-client privilege. Because different phases of the incident response lifecycle require different capabilities, such as evidence collection, forensic analysis, and malware reverse engineering, organizations should select teams that have broad expertise. Established relationships with several teams is wise because the scope and magnitude of an incident may require more than one forensics team. Having relationships with several partners provides a fallback.

The worst time to find a partner is during an incident. In addition to running the risk of no firm being available, the breached company is faced with paying rates that are non-negotiable and entering into a difficult relationship that often leads to protracted investigations. Selecting and vetting cyber response teams in advance allows the team an opportunity to learn about the firm's operational practices and environment. The forensics team can come up to speed quickly and hit the ground running. In addition to the qualitative advantage, selecting partners in advance provides a quantitative advantage in that you can pre-negotiate rates and terms that are acceptable to both parties and begin the relationship on a positive note.

Organizations also should look to engage a trusted advisor to provide independent advice to directors and officers regarding the security incident. Faced with pressure to deflect accusations or make things look better during an event, internal staff may report only what is necessary or skew information. An impartial trusted advisor knows how to interact with internal personnel, query the forensic investigators, analyze the findings, and provide the perspective that the board and senior management need for decision making. Many firms use outside counsel with experience in guiding incident response operations to perform this trusted advisor role.

■ **Employ good case management practices**
No one ever fully knows how an investigation will evolve. Even if it is unlikely that a security event will become public or that the investigation will end up in a court of law, directors should assume that it could and take the appropriate actions from day one. It is vital to follow good case management practices and do everything possible to preserve forensics evidence—from the first indication of the event through to the completion of the investigation.

Evidence is perishable and can be tainted. Organizations that are slow to engage the appropriate forensics partners run the risk of potentially destroying, tainting, or missing key evidence that could be crucial in the later stages of the investigation. By asking the question, "Should this go to court; what do we need to do from the moment we start

Make sure you have the right forensic team

Forensic services firms provide highly specialized resources that can cost tens of thousands of dollars. An inexperienced team, or one lacking the proper evidence collection, forensic analysis, and incident response skills, may not only cost an organization in terms of time and money but also jeopardize the success of mitigating the attack by inadvertently destroying or tainting evidence. It may be time to bring in a new team if the forensics team:
- is unable to put a big picture together that includes the scope of the breach as well as the sequence and path of movement
- has no clear plan for collection of evidence
- is unable to distinguish between evidence that is "need to have" and evidence that is "nice to have"
- takes a checklist approach to incident response
- is grasping at straws after the first couple of weeks
- is unable to scale efforts if needed
- is unable to provide guidance and stand firm in communications with clients, regulators, and other stakeholders
- fails to understand or exercise proper chain of custody.

this investigation to present a solid case?" organizations can limit their liability down the road and better position themselves for successful litigation.

■ Adopt an outcome-based approach

Some forensics organizations take a checklist approach to incident response. However, no two cyber events are the same, and incident response is not a scripted process. Security teams operate under the fog of cyberwar, and decisions will be made under conditions of stress, fatigue, and confusion in response to seemingly random events. What is needed is an outcome-based approach to incident response, recognition that there are multiple ways to achieve the outcome, and an understanding of what can go wrong. Normally, outcomes are based on a specific list of questions that must be answered by the incident response team based on initial attack indications and regulatory responsibility. The team should be focused on answering these questions during the investigation. Investigators who are experienced in outcome-based incident response are better able to focus on what matters, form hypotheses, take action based on the type of attack and observable facts, and pivot should something go wrong.

During the course of containment and eradication, it is expected that attackers will take new action based on the security team's efforts. One model that can be used to prevent enemies from gaining the upper hand is the "O-O-D-A Loop": Observe, Orient, Decide, and Act. This model provides a method for making informed decisions and acting based on feedback from various sources. Recognizing that attackers are doing the same, the key is to tighten and accelerate the OODA Loop, leveraging people, process, and technology to move faster than the adversaries.

■ Hire impartial, independent spokespersons for crisis communications

The stakes for immediate and effective crisis communications throughout an investigation have never been higher. During a cyber crisis, a company may need to notify customers, answer to the press, respond to regulators, and defend the company's conduct in parallel actions, such as a civil suit and a regulatory investigation.

A company's internal public relations team knows much about the organization but is not an expert in directing cyber breach communications. When multi-billion dollar payments and corporate reputations are at risk, board directors and senior management must take care to turn to independent, impartial crisis communications experts.

Cyberattacks are distressing events. Those involved often have an emotional attachment or are too close to the incident to be viewed as impartial in their communications. Independent experts provide the clear thinking and unbiased perspective that is required to assist the company in all dialogues and announcements—from initial notification to worst-case communications. Further, the external team will be able to ensure that once communications are initiated, such as notifying customers of a breach, follow-up communications occur on a timely schedule. Often overlooked is the need to manage negative nonverbal communications that may be sent to internal and external parties as a result of actions taken by the response team. For example, shutting down a website or requiring password changes sends a clear message that something has happened. The communications team must manage these types of communications as well. Finally, in addition to being able to articulate what is happening, it is vital that the crisis communications team stands firm in its mission to protect the company by advancing the facts in the face of unjustified assertions or incorrect accusations.

■ Be prepared for containment to affect business activities

Incident containment has two major components: stopping the spread of the attack and preventing further damage to hosts. During the containment effort, organizations should be prepared to shut down or block services, revoke privileges, increase controls, and place restrictions on network connectivity and Internet access. Such activities can affect business processes dramatically by restricting organizational functions and work flows; therefore, the decision to perform such actions should never be one sided. Because business activities are dynamic, the decision to implement controls during containment always should include a two-way discussion with business process owners and company leadership. It is vital that organizations have strategies and procedures in place for making containment-related decisions that reflect the level of acceptable risk to the organization.

■ Focus on people, process, and technology during eradication

Malware detection and eradication can be an expensive and time-consuming process, as malware can lie dormant in a system for months and then activate again. Although it is easy and tempting to apply a quick fix in the heat of the incident, attention must be given to finding and fixing the true root cause. Here, the natural tendency is to lead with a technology solution. With new security tools comes the belief that the problem is solved. The reality is that, without taking

people and processes into consideration, technology actually can create more complexity, consume more resources than it returns, and deliver only incremental value. In short, complexity is the enemy of security.

Organizations must take a holistic approach to eradicating and closing the security gaps. This may necessitate new processes and policies, new services and technologies, and additional personnel. Skimping on cybersecurity may result in much higher costs down the line. Board directors should be prepared to increase security budgets and can be firm but fair in maintaining their fiduciary responsibility by requiring the right justification from the security team.

■ Share information with others who can benefit

The fact that hackers have breached the computer systems is the kind of news that no organization wants to reveal. Corporate leadership worries about attrition of customers, negative press, and difficulties with partners that may occur if news of an incident leaks out. However, for the good of the industry, the sharing of incident details may

Attacker gains the upper hand—once

When the cyberattack happened, it caught everyone by surprise, but it shouldn't have. It was just a matter of time, because the organization had a high level of technology debt, the IT security lacked alignment with the business, the business unit failed to understand its level of risk and necessary controls, and the organization had given minimal attention to rehearsing incident response.

It took the organization more than 48 hours to detect the breach. Then, several days passed before they realized the event was bigger than what could be handled internally. The delay in detection and slow action to call in security experts allowed the attackers to move quickly through the network, expand their footprint, and ultimately affect more than twenty customer environments. The investigation and recovery lasted for about four months, with costs totaling in the millions.

Sensing easy prey, the attacker returned in several months. This time the organization was prepared. The technology debt had been paid, resulting in a stronger foundation and improved security monitoring. IT security was well aligned with the business, and the business unit understood and accepted its risk and controls. More important, the organization had rehearsed incident response scenarios. This time the attack was detected in minutes. The internal response team was able to shut the attack down in a matter of minutes with little cost and no risk to the business or customers.

be precisely what is needed. Cyberattacks are the new normal and security breaches no longer carry the stigma that they once did.

What is important to recognize is that cyber criminals use the same attacks over and over again. By using the same code with slight modifications, cyber criminals achieve efficiency in their efforts while driving their costs down. By sharing information with others who can benefit, such as other companies within the industry sector, the U.S. Computer Emergency Response Team, and cybersecurity researchers who may be able to assist, organizations can help protect others while driving up the adversary's costs.

■ Debrief following an event to capture lessons learned

What is worse than a big public breach? A second big public breach. Because the handling of cyberattacks can be extremely expensive, organizations may find it helpful to conduct a robust, non–finger-pointing assessment of lessons learned after major cyberattacks to prevent similar incidents from happening in the future. Capturing the lessons learned from the handling of such incidents should help an organization improve its incident handling capability. Questions to ask include the following:

- Why did this happen?
- What could have prevented it?
- Did we classify the event at the correct risk level?
- What were the indicators that drove the event classification?

- Are the risk definitions correct?
- Did we manage the command and control effectively?
- Did we bring the right people in at the right time?
- Did we think about everything properly from a risk perspective, business perspective, communications perspective, and customer perspective?

■ Summary

No matter what precautions are taken, no organization is immune to cyberattacks. Organizations must have a comprehensive incident response team that includes external incident response and forensic analysis, outside and in-house counsels, and public relations firms in place prior to any breach event. These partners provide incident response forensics, legal and crisis communications assistance; and will manage the incident in conjunction with the organization to mitigate the damage and return the business to full operational capacity as quickly as possible. Unfortunately, the worst time to figure out how to respond is during an actual incident. Making the plan up on the fly in the middle of a crisis only leads to mistakes that aggravate the situation. Lines of communication, roles, and identification of decision makers must be known before a breach occurs. Tabletop or similar exercises that include C-level management and board directors should be carried out to help organizations practice incident responses and stress-test their plans.

38

Cyber incident response

BakerHostetler – Theodore J. Kobus, Partner and Co-Leader, Privacy and Data Protection; Craig A. Hoffman, Partner; and F. Paul Pittman, Associate

Most security experts acknowledge that a dedicated and well-resourced attacker will eventually find a way to break into a company's network. Sophisticated attackers are not the only threat—financially or politically motivated individuals with less-than-average skills also have been able to compromise companies. Faced with an ever-increasing number of endpoints to guard, online access management issues related to cloud services and vendors, budgetary constraints, and the fact that systems are built and maintained by individuals (who are fallible), companies are recognizing at an increasing rate that a security incident involving the unauthorized access to its customer, employee, or sensitive business data is inevitable. How are companies responding? By taking a series of measures to become 'compromise ready,' including developing an incident response plan. Proper preparation for an incident enables a company to be better positioned to respond in a way that mitigates risk and preserves relationships. In addition, how a company responds influences whether the company experiences a drop in revenue or faces a regulatory investigation or consumer litigation. This response can significantly affect a company's reputation.

Officers and directors are tasked with ensuring that their company's incident response strategy is appropriate and adapts to the constantly changing threat landscape. They also have a role in overseeing the response to an incident. Incidents often arise just prior to an SEC reporting deadline, and companies that are caught unprepared may not be positioned well to withstand any subsequent scrutiny over their disclosure decision.

In this chapter we discuss the underlying state and federal notification obligations that are implicated by potential incidents along with best practices developed from our experience in helping companies respond to more than 1,000 potential events. Although these laws are a critical part of a response, responding to an incident is not just a legal issue. Being viewed as handling the incident well involves also an effective communications response.

■ Incident response best practices

A company's incident response should be guided by a plan that has been tailored to the company's industry and fine-tuned through mock breach exercises. The response plan is a critical element of the crisis management strategy—not because it provides a prescriptive, detailed list of action items, but because it has been refined and practiced through tabletop drills. A good plan outlines a flexible framework of the general steps that must be taken to prepare for, respond to, and recover from a security incident. An incident response plan must be flexible enough to adapt to the particular security incident the company is facing (e.g., network intrusion, denial of service, account takeovers, malware, phishing, loss of paper, employee data, security vulnerabilities detected by third parties, or theft of assets).

- *Identify the internal incident response team.* Identify team members from critical departments (e.g., IT, IS, legal, communications, internal audit, HR, risk management, business lines), describe their roles, and define how and when they will be activated when a potential incident is identified.
- *Identify who will lead the incident response team.* Companies approach this in different ways. For some, the IT and IS groups play a significant role. At highly regulated companies, legal and regulatory members will be integral to the response. Because some issues go beyond the technical response, being a good project manager is probably one of the key traits a company should look for when deciding who will lead the group. Practice drills also help

to ensure that the various team members understand their role and authority to make decisions.

- *Categorization.* Provide a simple structure for classifying events by severity (e.g., low, medium, high) and risk to "level set" the team regarding urgency, escalation to the C-suite, and level of engagement of the representative groups on the incident response team.
- *Response protocol.* Provide a flexible framework for executing the eight key steps of incident response: (1) preparation, (2) identification, (3) assessment, (4) communication, (5) containment, (6) eradication, (7) recovery, and (8) post-incident.
- *Third parties.* Identify key third parties that will assist the company, including external privacy counsel, forensics, crisis communications, mail and call center vendor, and credit monitoring.

Once the plan is created, test the plan for gaps and provide training for the incident response team. External privacy counsel often conducts these exercises, sometimes in conjunction with the primary forensic firm and crisis communications firm. Most companies choose to use a hypothetical scenario that they would consider to be the most likely catastrophic incident they may face (e.g., a payment card event for a retailer) followed by subsequent, periodic testing using different scenarios (e.g., service disruption, employee data).

No two incident scenarios are the same, so there is not a one-size-fits-all, turnkey solution to incident response. There are, however, critical factors that drive a successful response.

- *Notify and assemble incident response team members and begin the investigation.* Don't panic when a security incident arises. Be methodical, but swift, in your response. Assemble the incident response team members and notify them of the security incident. If a member of the C-suite is not on the team, there must be a direct connection to the C-suite so that decisions can be approved in a timely fashion and the response team can move forward with the investigation. It is useful to appoint a security incident manager; often this is someone with strong project management skills who can move the process forward in a productive way working alongside outside privacy counsel. Once the team is assembled, it should initiate an internal investigation into the security incident, and depending on the potential severity of the incident, daily progress calls should be scheduled.

- *Identify and fix the issue.* Conduct an initial analysis of the reported incident and focus on getting quickly to a point where the internal and/or external computer security firm can develop and implement an effective containment plan. If news of the incident is going to become public, at least the company will be in a position to say that it identified and blocked the attack from continuing. The company can then turn to identifying the full nature and extent of the attack. Working with internal resources, at least initially, is very common; however, consider bringing in external security firms when the company is facing capability, credibility, or capacity issues.

- *Gather the facts and let them drive the decision-making.* Resist the pressure to communicate about the incident too early or to be overly reassuring. Focus on the investigation. Institute a plan early on for collecting all available forensic data—hardware, devices, database activity, and system logs—and transfer it to a safe location for subsequent analysis. Create a timeline of events surrounding the security incident and the actions taken by the company. Structure additional investigation and response efforts based on the information gathered and the scope of the incident. Work to include any favorable findings in public communications; notification letters are often attached to class action complaints and therefore a company can rely on any

such helpful information when filing a motion to dismiss.

- *Determine any legal obligations and comply.* Experienced outside privacy counsel that is well versed in incident response can help the company quickly and accurately determine the state, federal, and international privacy and security laws and regulations that may be implicated by the security incident. Complying with these laws is sometimes a balancing act that requires a company to consider other factors. Engaging outside privacy counsel who understands how the regulators view these laws, as well as the challenges companies face in responding to these types of incidents, is critical. Outside privacy counsel must be a partner with the company in the response. There is no one-size-fits-all approach.

- *Communicate with the public and report to the incident response team.* During the course of the investigation and response, there should be constant communication among incident response team members. Periodic reporting meetings are useful. In addition, officers and directors should receive reports that provide essential facts and plans for responding to the security incident. It is critical to have outside counsel involved in the communications plan to preserve any privileges that may attach to communications. Further, develop a 'holding statement' for executives to use when communicating with the media, affected individuals, and shareholders. Also, consider creating a website and using a call center to keep affected individuals apprised of developments.

- *Eradicate remnants of the security incident and recover business operations.* When the security incident and any resulting damage have been contained, develop a plan to eliminate the vestiges of the security incident, restore the company's assets, and return your business to normal operations. Ensure that the threat created by the security incident is eradicated.

■ Potential legal issues and obligations

The issues caused by the 'patchwork quilt' of state breach notification laws in the United States receive a lot of attention and feed calls for a single federal law that pre-empts any inconsistent state laws. However, in most incidents, especially for incidents that affect individuals across the country, differences across state breach notification laws rarely make a difference in how the company responds. Complications do arise when only a few state laws are implicated, such as when one state does not have a "risk of harm" trigger that allows a company to determine that notification is not required but the other states do. There are no decisions from courts describing how to interpret and apply these laws. There are state attorneys general who have certain interpretations regarding the timing of notification and others who have well-known 'hot button' issues, neither of which are evident from reading the text of the notification law.

Notification

Typically, a security incident becomes a data breach when there is unauthorized access to unencrypted personally identifying information (PII), which is generally a person's name associated with his or her Social Security number, driver's license number, health and medical information, and financial information, depending on the state or federal law. When a data breach occurs, all states (except Alabama, New Mexico, and South Dakota) require that a company notify the affected individuals that their PII has been compromised. The breach notification laws of each state and the type of data that are considered PII vary between states and can create multiple and sometimes inconsistent obligations on the company required to provide notice. Most state laws require notice as soon as reasonably possible, whereas a few require notification within 30 or 45 days of discovery. Providing notification within 30 days of initial discovery is often a significant challenge.

In addition, certain federal laws such as the Health Insurance Portability and Accountability Act (HIPAA) and the Gramm-Leach Bliley Act (GLBA) require companies to notify affected individuals. Under HIPAA, notification is required within 60 days and a failure to provide timely notice will likely result in an investigation that may lead to a fine. Timely notification enables consumers to exercise self-help in monitoring their payment card, bank accounts, and credit reports to prevent fraud. By reducing the likelihood that consumers will be subject to fraud, a company can also reduce the likelihood of future suits based on the data breach.

Reporting

In addition to providing notification of a data breach to affected individuals, a company also may be required to report a data breach to other individuals and entities under certain state and federal laws and industry guidelines.

Law enforcement: Law enforcement can be helpful during an investigation, but it should be brought in at the appropriate time. Telecoms and financial institutions have specific guidelines regarding reporting to law enforcement, but most industries do not have similar regulations. Typically, companies engage either the Federal Bureau of Investigation (FBI) or the United States Secret Service (USSS), although local law enforcement can be helpful in certain situations. Your outside privacy counsel should have established relationships with law enforcement and understand when they should be contacted. Although law enforcement can be helpful with the investigation and communications with regulators, keep in mind that its goal is very different from the company's: law enforcement wants to catch the 'bad guy' and the company must figure out the appropriate way to respond to the incident.

Federal regulators: Certain industry-specific laws also require reporting of a breach to federal regulators. Under HIPAA, a company must report any data breach to the Secretary for the Department of Health and Human Services, although the timing of that reporting differs depending on whether the number of affected individuals exceeds 500. Under the GLBA, financial institutions must report a security incident to their primary federal regulator as soon as possible.

State attorneys general and agencies: Some state laws require a company to report a data breach to the state attorney general, depending on the number of affected individuals, which may range from 1,000 in some states to only one person in others. Other states require notification to state agencies, such as state consumer protection agencies, departments of health, or cybersecurity agencies. The form of the notice may also vary. Some states require simply that a copy of the breach notification letter that was sent to the affected individuals be filed with the state attorney general. Other states may require more, such as written notice identifying the nature of the breach, the number of affected individuals, any steps taken to investigate and prevent future breaches, and the content of the notice intended for the affected individuals. Working with regulators can be one of the most critical pieces of an incident response. Ensure that your outside privacy counsel has a working relationship with your regulators and can guide you on the timing and content of communications. In most cases, if this piece is handled appropriately, there is a greater chance of very little fallout.

Other entities: When payment card data are at risk, the response is governed by payment card network operating regulations that merchants have agreed to follow as part of the merchant services agreement with their acquiring bank and payment processor. The card network regulations define a specific security standard that merchants must comply with (PCI DSS). They also dictate the investigatory process and provide for the recovery of noncompliance fines and assessments to reimburse banks that issued cards

affected by the incident for their costs associated with fraudulent charges and the reissuing of cards. The liability assessments can be one of the largest financial consequences of an incident.

In certain circumstances, a company may be required to report a data breach to the media. Under state notification laws, if the company does not have sufficient contact information to mail notification letters to affected individuals, the company has to provide notice through substitute means, which involves posting a link in a conspicuous location on the company's website, issuing a press release to major statewide media, and sending an email to the individuals (if the company has their email addresses). HIPAA requires a press release if a data breach involves more than 500 affected individuals. In other circumstances, a company may have no legal obligation to report a security incident or data breach to the media but may feel compelled to do so in an effort to control the story and prevent inaccurate or misleading information from being conveyed to the public by the hacker, affected individuals, or other sources. Accordingly, careful thought should be given to developing a communications strategy as part of a company's incident response—one that considers not only the message but also the timing of the message and the medium in which it is distributed.

Board of directors: Although reporting a security incident to the board of directors is not required by any specific state or federal law, a director's duty to shareholders requires that the director be informed of important topics that significantly affect the overall business of the company. Consequently, directors may (and should) require that an incident response team member (preferably counsel) provide reports on any security incidents or data breach, and the progress of any incident response efforts. Some companies are establishing a special audit committee for cyber incidents and even engaging a "cyber advisor" to brief the board on these issues.

A company's response to a security incident or data breach can have significant legal and financial consequences beyond those associated with investigating and responding to an incident. Some state and federal laws allow for consumers affected by a data breach to assert a private right of action against companies. When the incident affects a large number of individuals, it is fairly common to see putative class actions filed in the hours or days after the incident becomes public. Regulators, such as the FTC, Department of Health and Human Services, and Federal Communications Commission may initiate investigations that may result in multimillion-dollar fines or the imposition of a consent order that imposes a lengthy obligation to implement a privacy and security compliance program and have it audited by a third party. Last, although not common, directors and officers may be named in shareholder lawsuits.

■ Role of external parties in a company's incident response

An incident response typically requires the involvement of several external parties who serve important roles in identifying and assessing the cause, extent, and impact of a security incident as well as crafting and disseminating a response to the affected individuals, the public, the media, law enforcement, and regulatory authorities. One step that may save a few days during an incident response is to engage and negotiate the master services agreements with these companies before an incident so that only a new statement of work has to be prepared when an incident arises.

■ *Privacy counsel.* An external law firm often serves as the 'quarterback' of the incident response. This role includes engaging other third parties to assist the firm in providing legal advice to the company, such as a forensics firm, which then serves as a foundation for establishing that attorney-client privilege. Work-product protection should apply to the communications with and findings of the forensic firm and others engaged in assisting the law firm. The external law firms also should provide guidance to other members of the incident response team on how to preserve privileges, such as through the use of an 'Attorney-Client Privileged Communication' stamp in emails and communications, for example. Outside counsel should collaborate with in-house counsel in determining whether there are any legal or contractual obligations to notify or report, or potential liability as a result of a data breach.

■ *Forensics firm.* An outside forensics firm is sometimes needed to conduct an examination of the available forensic data to determine whether there are signs of unauthorized access, and if so, determine the nature and extent of the issue and provide recommendations on short-term containment and longer-term measures to remediate and enhance security.

■ *Crisis communication firm.* Although public relations firms understand how to get a company into the news, crisis communications firms have to exercise a different skill set in guiding the communication strategy for companies facing security incidents. Those firms understand that there is often little, if any, good news to report, so they focus on communications designed to make it clear that the company is responding in a quick and transparent manner that is designed to protect affected individuals. They can also provide media training for the spokesperson and assist in responding to media inquiries in a consistent and measured manner.

■ *Breach response and notification firm.* Using a dedicated external call center and mailing vendor to notify and handle inquiries from affected individuals can greatly assist a company with the logistical challenges it faces during an incident response. The call center can answer calls from an approved FAQ sheet.

Regardless of the external parties retained to assist in an incident response, it is important to ensure that they are retained by outside counsel to enable the assertion of the attorney-client privilege and work-product doctrine to protect documents and communications generated in the investigation and during the response to a security incident.

■ Role of officers and directors in a company's incident response

The C-suite and boardroom play a small but important part in a company's actual incident response: they mainly ensure that critical executive-level decisions concerning impact to the business and expenditures are made promptly. This is best facilitated by having a C-suite representative serve as a member of the incident response team. It is also important for officers and directors to be engaged in the incident response process, because in the event that another security incident occurs, the officers and directors could be held accountable by consumers, shareholders, and regulators for any lack of familiarity with the company's cybersecurity program.

Given the potential liability and impact to a company's reputation posed by a data breach, directors should have procedures in place to ensure that they receive timely updates on any incident response. Communications with the board regarding the incident response and the findings of any investigation should be carefully crafted and limited to factual information if possible, because of the prospect of shareholder derivative suits. This is particularly important because communications to directors that are not made at the direction of, or by, counsel may not be privileged and could be discoverable in subsequent litigation.

Should a security incident or data breach be made public, executives should be prepared to comment on the incident. When necessary, a holding statement should be developed and vetted by counsel. Communications by officers or directors with the public should be accurate, complete, and truthful, but also simple, so as not to be misleading or admit liability. Any filings or disclosures with the federal regulators, such as the Securities and Exchange Commission, should be carefully vetted to ensure accuracy, which may prove difficult when the facts surrounding a security incident are being determined. This can be particularly problematic in quarterly (or periodic) earnings calls with analysts that may occur while investigation and response efforts are taking place.

■ Conclusion

In this 'cyber climate,' companies must be prepared for a security incident. Officers and directors cannot sit on the sideline; they must be aware of cyberthreats and engaged in developing and implementing an incident response plan to limit the amount of damage that can be caused by a data breach. An effective incident response can help preserve the company's reputation and limit its exposure, allowing it to continue and grow its business operations.

39

Communicating after a cyber incident

Sard Verbinnen & Co – Scott Lindlaw, Principal

Data security is the number one concern that keeps board members up at night, NYSE's annual *Law in the Boardroom* survey found. It's a rational nightmare for anyone running a company, given the explosion of data breaches and the havoc they can wreak. As recent shareholder derivative and securities lawsuits underscore, a director is not merely responsible for ensuring that a company's cyber defenses are robust. Rather, lawsuits against directors of Target Corp., the TJX Companies, and Heartland Payment Systems, Inc. have taught us that directors must also ensure that the company is prepared to manage the aftermath of a breach. To contain the damage, effective communications with a host of internal and external audiences are essential.

The two greatest harms inflicted by a breach are reputational damage and loss of customer loyalty, according to the Ponemon Institute, which compiles breach costs globally. To mitigate reputational damage, loss of customers, and related harms from a breach, it is critical that a company communicate clearly (and often simultaneously) with multiple audiences. The board's oversight of this aspect of cybersecurity should not start in the fog of a cyber crisis. It should begin well before an incident.

■ The director's duties and cybersecurity-related communications

A data breach can substantially diminish stock value, as several academic studies have found. The most recent study, involving 174 breaches, found "the cumulative change in net earnings including extraordinary items in the four quarters after a breach announcement is a 22.54% decrease, indicating deteriorated earnings performance." These findings by Kholekile L. Grebu, Jing Wang, and Wenjuan Xie of the University of New Hampshire Peter T. Paul College of Business and Economics do not always hold true. A study of several prominent data breaches by

Sard Verbinnen & Co. found that share price impact is hard to measure because of a multitude of factors affecting stocks. Still, a company should anticipate that revenue and profits may take a hit after a breach. A primary goal of a post-breach communications strategy should be to mitigate this impact as much as possible.

Because breaches can have a substantial effect on the bottom line, preparing for and responding to such incidents fall squarely in the director's fiduciary duties. As explained in Chapter 8, directors owe their companies certain obligations, such as the duties of care, good faith, and loyalty. In the context of cybersecurity incidents, these duties require directors to ensure the company develops a reasonable crisis-management plan for use in the event a breach occurs. This calls for board members to have at least a high-level understanding of communications strategies and tactics, for internal and external audiences.

For example, almost all states have laws requiring companies to notify customers when a breach compromises sensitive personal data. Directors and companies have been sued on the ground that they failed to take reasonable steps to notify consumers that a company's systems had been breached. When the law requires it, notifying customers about a breach is fundamentally a legal function but also a communications function. Plaintiffs will try to hold directors accountable for a perceived failure of notification. Likewise, regularly disseminating accurate information to shareholders may be a regulatory requirement but also requires effective communications. The Securities and Exchange Commission has put companies on notice as to the reputational harms of breaches and companies' disclosure obligations regarding cyber incidents. "Reputational damage adversely affecting customer or investor confidence" may cause an attacked company to sustain "substantial costs and suffer other negative consequences," the Commission wrote in disclosure guidance in 2011. The Ponemon Institute reported that in 2014, breach-related lost business costs, including the abnormal turnover of customers, increased customer acquisition activities, reputation losses, and diminished goodwill, cost the victimized companies an average of $3.72 million per incident.

Companies have an opportunity to mitigate each of these classes of loss through effective communications. This means following the law on all notifications required to consumers and investors, of course. However, a company should not stop there. Communicating about a cyber incident to customers and investors as required by law should be the bare minimum from a communications standpoint. To preserve goodwill and stanch reputational losses, companies must move beyond mere compliance and operate from a perspective of stewardship. They must demonstrate leadership, integrity, and responsibility through thoughtful communications. *To achieve that, these principles should guide any communications relating to a cyber incident*:

- **Preserve the company's credibility with all constituencies**, including consumers, customers, partners, regulators, employees, investors, journalists, and analysts.
- **Maintain control of the communications process** by establishing concise, agreed-upon messages so that the company speaks with one voice.
- **Provide pertinent, confirmed facts** without jeopardizing any internal or law enforcement investigations.
- **Coordinate all public communications with legal counsel** to (1) ensure accuracy; (2) avoid compromising any investigation or increasing legal exposure; and (3) preserve attorney-client privilege.
- **Prepare for potential negative legal, financial, and customer scenarios**.

These should be the tactical goals of communications responding to a cyber incident:

- Reassure all constituencies that you are taking steps to contain and fix the issue.
- Manage how the breach is portrayed in news and social media—where possible, position company as victim, not villain.

- Confine public comments to what you know. Do not speculate.
- Avoid prolonging news media coverage unnecessarily.
- Do and say nothing to heighten the interest of regulators.
- Provide no fodder to plaintiffs' attorneys.
- Minimize damage in the eyes of consumers, customers, and investors.
- Protect share price.

Companies must integrate these communications principles and goals into a coherent incident-response plan *before* a breach strikes. An effective plan will position the victimized company to communicate quickly and effectively in the event of a data breach or other security incident. Important decisions will have to be made in real time, but the tools and guidelines in a cyber incident response plan should ensure immediate engagement of the proper personnel, the proper process for obtaining and reviewing information needed to determine the appropriate communications response, and alignment on all appropriate steps to communicate to employees and external audiences.

A company's incident-response plan should identify members of several sub-teams, including legal, IT, and communications. Anyone who will be directly involved in making communications decisions or in the dissemination of internal and/or external communications must read and understand this plan. Press releases, key messages, question-and-answer documents, contact lists, and letters to stakeholders such as investors and employees should be prepared in advance, leaving blank spaces to fill in as facts emerge. The plan should contemplate the establishment of a dedicated website and whether the company's existing corporate blogs and social media presence may be useful communications instruments after a breach. The communications plan, and especially its contacts lists, should be treated as a living document. It should be kept up to date and reviewed and tested regularly.

Directors must make clear to management that they expect the company to be prepared to respond very quickly to any cyber incident and to communicate the company's position. As part of this, the board should review the company's budget for security risk management, ensuring the availability of the funds necessary to hire outside law firms, IT and forensics experts, remediation support services, and communications consultants.

■ Audiences to consider when responding to a breach

A company responding to a breach must communicate with myriad audiences. It must coordinate and calibrate its messaging with each while recognizing that messages aimed at investors may end up in news stories, that news stories will shape investors' perceptions, and that everything the company says could end up on Twitter.

- **Consumers, customers, and partners**: In addition to legally required notifications, the breached company must be prepared to communicate what it is doing to contain an incident; provide assurances, if applicable, regarding safety of customer information and recourse on future fraudulent activity; give front-line customer service representatives guidance on how to communicate with customers; provide a dedicated call center and/or website to handle customer inquiries; and provide third-party credit monitoring, if appropriate.
- **Journalists and social media communities**: It will not be sufficient to issue prepared public statements at the company's convenience. The victim company must be prepared to react to a deluge of media inquiries and be prepared for leaks. The company may also have to proactively engage reporters, including regional, national, and cybersecurity beat reporters. This requires developing a process for engaging the news media, including designating media spokespersons, preparing key executives for direct exposure to news media, correcting inaccurate reports,

and monitoring traditional and social media on an ongoing basis. The company must also prepare to use social media to distribute messages.

- **Investors and analysts**: The breached company must be prepared to answer questions about the impact of the incident on financial outlook and about the costs of response and security upgrades. It can expect to face such questions on its first earnings call after the incident, and thereafter. A Form 8-K may be required if shareholders would view the impact of the incident as material.
- **Internal audiences**: Employees need to hear from the company about what has transpired, and what changes in security policies and protocols are coming. They must be alert to future attacks and avoid talking publicly about the incident. Human resources should prepare to involve itself if employees had a possible role in causing the incident or failing to detect it.

In addition to the above audiences, the breached company must carefully weigh and coordinate each statement with a secondary set of audiences in mind. Plaintiffs' attorneys will be circling and will race to the courthouse to sue the company on behalf of purportedly aggrieved customers and shareholders. Banks and credit card companies who may have lost money on fraudulent transactions will expect to be made whole. Insurance companies will also be monitoring public statements if the victimized company has a cyber incident or other relevant policy and moves to file a claim.

■ Lawsuits against directors: communications issues

As if the breaches themselves weren't enough to keep directors up at night, board members have an additional and unique set of worries: shareholder derivative and securities lawsuits after an incident. Directors of Target, the TJX Companies, and Heartland Payment Systems, among others, have each seen these actions after breaches. These suits

typically comprise two main arguments. First, they allege directors failed to prevent the breach. Second, they contend directors covered it up and/or failed to notify investors and consumers. This latter class of arguments essentially alleges failures of communication. The cases against Target and Heartland show how the plaintiffs use derivative and securities suits to blame directors and officers for these alleged sins of communications, or lack thereof:

- **Target Corp**.: On December 18, 2013, the blog Krebs on Security broke the news of a major breach at the retailer. The next day the company confirmed it was investigating a security breach involving stolen credit card and debit card information of 40 million customers who shopped in its stores. A few weeks later, the company disclosed that the data theft was significantly more extensive and affected millions more shoppers than it had initially reported.

  Four sets of shareholders filed derivative lawsuits against Target officers and directors. Later these were consolidated into one derivative action. The plaintiffs alleged that directors breached their fiduciary duties by failing to "timely notify customers of the theft of their personal and financial information [and] to accurately notify customers regarding the scope and substance of the data breach." The amended complaint chronicled a series of statements in which Target provided shifting information. As a matter of media relations, this had the effect of continually adding fuel to the fire: each time the company updated the number of affected customers, the coverage spiked anew.

  The plaintiffs also pre-emptively argued that the directors' actions in managing the response did not constitute decisions under the business judgment rule, which would have protected them against such a lawsuit. "The Board caused Target to disseminate false and misleading public statements concerning, among other things, the true nature and extent of the data breach at the Company," the amended complaint stated. (A separate action brought by consumers similarly alleges that "Target failed to disclose and provide timely and accurate notice of the data breach to the public...")

- **Heartland Payment Systems, Inc.:** On December 26, 2007, hackers broke into Heartland's corporate computer network and stole about 130 million credit and debit card numbers and related card data. The SQL injection attack on its corporate network resulted in malware being placed on its payment processing system.

Plaintiffs brought a securities class action against the company after the U.S. Department of Justice indicted several individuals for what was reportedly then the largest data security breach in U.S. history. They accused CEO and Chairman of the Board Robert O. Carr and CFO Robert H.B. Baldwin of concealing the breach for more than a year—of "lying about the very existence of the breach." They also contended the defendants knowingly made false and misleading statements about the breach in a 10-K annual report to the SEC, during interviews with the media, in press releases, and in other public presentations and speeches. The plaintiffs alleged that Carr and Baldwin concealed the incident and made a series of materially false and misleading statements on an earnings call, "outright den[ying] that a security breach had even occurred at Heartland." The harm to

investors, the plaintiffs claimed, was that "Defendants' misrepresentations and omissions obfuscated the Company's true financial condition and future business prospects, artificially inflating the price of Heartland's common stock."

■ Conclusion

Cybersecurity is the number one fear keeping directors up at night, but they can rest a little easier by holding management accountable and requiring a current, useful preparedness plan before a crisis. Critical to any company's breach-response plan must be communications. A breached company cannot assume a defensive crouch and issue reactive statements at the times of its choosing. On the other hand, it should not say more than it is confident of, or more than is necessary to safeguard its interests and those of its customers and investors. An effective communications plan helps protect the company after a cyber incident by blunting the loss of reputation and customers and by keeping plaintiffs at bay.

Every breach starts with an event outside a company's control, and the Target and Sony Pictures attacks underscore how unfolding events can further buffet a company. However, with a communications plan that is carefully conceived and rehearsed, a company can meet its legal obligations to communicate and help limit the secondary harms of a cyber incident, such as loss of reputation and customers. It is incumbent on directors to ensure that the plan's communications components are ready to activate when the cyber crisis strikes.

VIII Cyber risk management investment decisions

40

Optimizing investment to minimize cyber exposure

Axio Global, LLC – Scott Kannry, CEO and David White, Chief Knowledge Officer

" We are living in the Dark Ages of security. We cling to outmoded world views and rely on tools and tactics from the past, and yet we are surprised to find ourselves living in an era of chaos and violence."

Amit Yoran, President of RSA;
2015 RSA Conference Keynote

Why begin a chapter about minimizing cyber exposure with a recent quote criticizing the security industry and raising a question about whether it is even possible to succeed? It underscores the importance of understanding the current climate, how it has evolved to the current state, and its inherent challenges. Ideally, one can then grasp that a new way of thinking about cybersecurity is critical to succeed and look to define a process and methodology that gives security leaders a better foundation to achieve that goal.

Let's start with where we've been. Our hope is that few, if any, security leaders still believe that impenetrability is achievable. We've been subject to a barrage of verbiage such as, "There are only two kinds of companies—those that know they have been hacked and those that don't yet know it," and hacked executives publicly expressing surprise that their organization was successfully victimized, despite investing in the best possible defense. However, that belief was prevalent for many years, and investment decisions during this "castle-wall" era were fairly easy to make: focus on buying technological controls to fortify the perimeter.

Thankfully, we have evolved from that era into one that we'll call the "defense-in-depth" era. The original premise was fairly simple: put up more castle walls, or perimeters, and hopefully the multiple layers will act in concert to create impenetrability, or at least something as close to it as possible. A more evolved premise is based on a mantra such as, "Operate as if the bad guys are already inside," which starts to balance perimeter controls with those that focus on behavioral monitoring, segmentation, and simulated internal environments. This trend is definitely one that is taking hold. Many firms still spend the majority of their security budgets on perimeter-focused controls, but spending is now being shared with internal and reactive controls.

However, despite the improved strategy, events over the past year and those that undoubtedly have happened since this chapter was written should easily debunk any notion that the defense-in-depth era has been substantially more successful than the castle-wall era. Arguably, it has gotten worse, in large part because of improvements and industrialization of the tools and techniques used by adversaries. This has led not only to calls for a rethinking of how security is approached but also to the practical reality that security leaders' jobs are more difficult than ever: their rate of success at protecting the enterprise seems to be precipitously declining, along with their job longevity.

Plus, the castle-wall and defense-in-depth eras exacerbated a problem central to security leader decision making; they facilitated a monumental buildup in the availability and use of technological controls. Evidence of this is apparent at the RSA conference, where a landscape of thousands of security providers displays their wares, each claiming to be the ultimate solution or silver bullet. Security leaders ask where to start. What should I spend my next dollar on? How can I justify this investment and intended return to the board? How can I keep my job when an event inevitably occurs? Welcome to the modern reality for security leaders.

We propose that it is time to evolve into what we'll call the cybersecurity enlightenment era. It's an era that focuses on risk management, not risk elimination, and where cybersecurity strategy is acknowledged as an investment challenge. It's also an era that highly values impact minimization because cyber events are inevitable and ultimately, the organization's resilience depends on having the financial resources to weather the storm. This point supports the relevance of the insurance industry, not only as a provider of financial certainty but also as an industry that can provide insight and data to support thoughtful cybersecurity investments. We'll now explain all of these elements and how this approach stands the greatest chance of minimizing exposure to the organization.

The approach is best evidenced by Figure 1, which depicts the relationship between cyber risk and cybersecurity capability. Organizations that have minimal cybersecurity capability face an extraordinary degree of risk. For these organizations, investments in basic controls will produce meaningful downward movement on the risk curve. It's also the reality that organizations on the far left side of the curve will be given harsh treatment by the insurance industry—premiums will be extraordinarily high or coverage may not be available at all—which is a signal that the organization must bolster its capability through traditional controls. At a certain point, however, the curve begins to flatten and the relative reduction in risk per dollar invested pales in comparison to that which was previously achieved. Beyond this point firms would be wise to invest more substantially in insurance because of its disproportionate effect on the risk curve. Unlike a traditional control, insurance actually reduces (or eliminates) the cost of an event and therefore shifts the entire risk curve downward. An organization that adopts this approach is one that is more thoughtfully protected and better able to withstand the impact of that inevitable event.

To better understand the elements, let's look at the risk calculus, which can be explained with the following equation:

$$Risk = \frac{Business\ Impact \times Likelihood}{Capability}$$

where business impact is a measure of impact to the enterprise from a cyber event, likelihood is an estimate of an event actually occurring, and capability is a measure of the organization's ability to detect, protect, respond, and recover from an event.

FIGURE

1

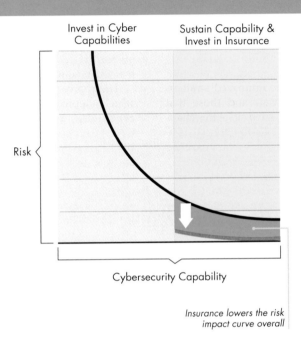

Invest in Cyber
Capabilities

Sustain Capability &
Invest in Insurance

Risk

Cybersecurity Capability

*Insurance lowers the risk
impact curve overall*

It is important to understand that organizations may have very little control over the numerator in this equation, as these elements are largely influenced by the constantly evolving threat climate, the capability and desire of adversaries to carry out an attack, and the ever-increasing complexity of the technologies controlling operations, which can fail unexpectedly in ways that result in damage. For example, various recent reports pegged the cause of a cargo plane crash on a failure in software configuration, evidencing the reality that cyber events aren't only those with malicious connotations. It's also important to recognize that neither business impact nor likelihood can ever equal zero, even for the most capable organizations.

Organizations can influence the denominator by implementing, sustaining, and maturing a capable cybersecurity program. This measure reflects the controls that an organization has in place to protect its cyber assets and to detect events. Many of these controls will be technological or administrative, but the human element is also critical and can't be overlooked, nor can the protocols surrounding third-party vendors, outsourced parties, and subcontractors. The denominator is also where the positive impact of insurance takes hold, because successfully responding to and recovering from an event depends not only on technical capabilities but also on the financial ability to cover the costs and losses involved.

How does an organization put actual numbers into the equation? Our recommendation is to start with developing and analyzing organization-specific cyber loss scenarios. Gather a group of individuals that represent key functions and insights into the organization—information technology and operational technology security, safety, risk management, treasury, and legal— and brainstorm about the likelihood and impact of cyber events across the critical functions of the organization. It's important to capture as much of the loss spectrum as possible—first- and third-party financial damages and first- and third-party tangible damages, the latter half being critically important for organizations that use industrial control systems.

In our experience, this type of exercise proves to be very fruitful. We've found that most of the informational insight actually resides within the organization—it's simply a matter of getting the right stakeholders at the table. In some instances, organizations are surprised at how much they already know and can bake into the calculations. For example, we've worked with energy firms that had already commissioned numerous loss engineering studies based on traditional perils such as earthquake, fire, or mechanical breakdown, each with fully developed impact estimates. All it took in this instance was confirmation from operational and cybersecurity leaders that a cyber event could produce many of the same outcomes, coupled with a technical discussion about the likelihood of such an event to very efficiently compile enough data for the numerator in the equation.

Using the loss scenario approach also helps inform the numbers in the denominator, because the technical part of the discussion helps determine the organization's capability to protect its operations from, detect signs of, and effectively respond to a particular scenario. For example, if we are working with a retailer and a scenario involving the theft of credit card information, we may start with the financial impact if the event occurs and then work backward to discuss where the information resides and how it is processed, and most critically, how each access point is or could be protected from known and conceivable threats. Here, it is useful to compare an organization's current capabilities against any applicable standards or regulatory frameworks, ensure that appropriate threat intelligence for that particular area of risk is being used, and continually monitor the performance of the organization's protective mechanisms in its own environment and the environment at large.

Benchmarking is also a critical and strongly recommended element of the capability factor. We recognize that many security leaders may be wary of supplying cyber program information for benchmarking purposes as to not create additional vulnerabilities by giving away the proverbial keys to the back door, but resources that do so in an entirely de-identified manner can provide powerful comparative insight that is otherwise unavailable. From a security leader's perspective, this information may actually be the most powerful, because it can provide justification for additional investment in controls and, in the worse case event of a breach, exculpability.

This is an appropriate place to introduce the final detail and insight for the denominator and right side of the risk curve—the importance of insurance coverage and relevance of the insurance industry to deploying an enlightened cybersecurity strategy. One of the roles that the industry can serve, and will increasingly serve, is a resource for benchmarking intelligence via the underwriting and premium pricing process. This capability is candidly in its infancy for a few reasons: the scope of coverage is evolving and therefore the depth of information required to underwrite is not truly comprehensive, many insurers are happy to deploy a nonintrusive approach as a competitive lever, and correlation information lacks in areas where claims or losses have not yet occurred. Despite this evolving capability, firms can find meaningful value in the process, because even an extraordinarily high premium or a denial of coverage does have informative value. Additionally, for areas in which cyber coverage is relatively more mature, top insurers do have enough data to provide a "risk engineering" benefit similar to other well-established areas of insured risk, and the industry is continually evolving to provide greater capabilities in this respect.

Another area of insurance industry relevance requires a more nuanced dive into coverage, but one that is important for its informative value and relevance to security investment decisions. Security leaders should familiarize themselves with their own firm's insurance portfolio as well as industry trends relating to coverage availability and pricing. The exercise should not be limited to cyber insurance, because despite what many in the insurance industry would profess, there is currently no such thing as an all-encompassing, all-risk cyber insurance policy. Cyber insurance, as it is commonly known, covers many first-party financial losses and resultant financial liabilities from a cyber event, but not tangible losses such as property damage and bodily injury. Therefore, firms also must be attentive to property, casualty, environmental, terrorism, and any other type of insurance that could provide coverage for losses resulting from a cyber event.

What type of actionable insight does this provide? On one hand, simply knowing what cyber exposures the insurance industry is willing to cover can help security leaders make investment decisions. For example, the insurance industry currently does not offer much, if any, coverage for losses attributable to the theft of intellectual property such as trade secrets and R&D. Knowing this may prompt overweight investment into controls and protocols protecting trade secrets, whereas investment into other areas of risk where coverage is readily available can be more balanced.

Beyond the continually evolving risk engineering capabilities of the insurance industry and the insight provided by simply understanding the complete insurance landscape for cyber exposures, the biggest benefit provided by insurance is the aforementioned ability to meaningfully reduce the risk curve. Here too it is critically important to understand the entire insurance landscape, because firms that purchase a single cyber insurance policy may be disappointed in how it performs. This point is not intended as criticism of the insurance industry—the industry does offer coverage for the vast majority of the cyber exposure spectrum—it's a point recognizing that comprehensive coverage for complex cyber events can involve multiple types of policies.

Ultimately, our hope is that this process and balanced approach provides a higher likelihood of minimizing cyber risk, especially in comparison to any of the legacy strategies deployed to date. If nothing else, it helps to more effectively minimize cyber risk through the effective deployment of insurance as a complementary control, but the process overall does produce defendable insight and a means by which security leaders can optimize investment while minimizing risk, thus allowing cybersecurity to start to evolve out of the dark ages.

41

Investment in cyber insurance

Lockton Companies Inc. – Ben Beeson, Senior Vice President, Cybersecurity Practice

A number of high-profile corporate data breaches, mainly in the US retail sector over the last two years, have led rapidly to a major change in enterprise cybersecurity strategy. Many chief information security officers (CISOs) now view risk avoidance as extremely challenging, if not impossible, and a traditional approach that builds layered defenses around the network perimeter as increasingly insufficient.

Accepting risk means adopting an approach that seeks to mitigate and build enterprise resilience. This approach now also must weigh the benefits of transferring residual severity risk from the balance sheet through cyber insurance. Here are 10 reasons to consider making the investment.

1. **Advanced persistent threats (APTs)**
   Targeted attacks, known as APTs, have become increasingly difficult to detect, let alone stop. The emergence of the nation-state as an adversary leaves the majority of organizations vulnerable regardless of the resources committed to defense.
2. **Governance and an enterprise-wide risk management strategy**
   The emergence of cybersecurity as a governance issue that must be addressed by the board of directors is redefining the role of cyber insurance as purely a financial instrument to transfer risk. Cybersecurity involves the entire enterprise, with numerous stakeholders, no longer only the domain of the IT department. Driving a culture of collaboration between these stakeholders is challenging for many organizations, but cyber insurance and, more importantly, the underwriting process can be the catalyst.
3. **Increasing regulatory risk**
   Liability to boards of directors is expected to increase and give added weight to a focus on governance. SEC guidance published in 2011 highlights how regulators see cyber insurance as part of a strong enterprise risk

management strategy. Many in the legal community see the launch in February 2014 of a federal cybersecurity framework (known as the NIST framework) as creating a standard of care to be used by plaintiff attorneys to allege negligence or worse.

4. **A financial incentive**
   Legislators are giving greater prominence to the role of cyber insurance. The failure to pass laws to drive stronger enterprise security has demonstrated the challenges in trying to enforce minimum standards. There is growing support for market-based incentives such as insurance that can reward strong cybersecurity through discounted premium or broader coverage. However, the insurance market for cyber risks is young, if not embryonic in some respects, and faces significant challenges if it is to continue to grow. Reversing the lack of actuarial data to model risk and an underwriting process that must change to meet ever-evolving threats sit at the top of the insurance industry's priorities.

5. **Vicarious risk to vendors and business associates**
   Adversaries are focusing increasingly on third parties that have access to sensitive information and other critical assets of the target enterprise. Professional service firms or cloud-based solution providers are examples of business associates whose security may be weaker than that of their client and consequently provide an easier back door for the attacker. Liability for a breach of personally identifiable information (PII) or protected health information (PHI) typically still rests with the enterprise data owner, even though a breach may have occurred to the vendor's network. Cyber insurance addresses costs of responding to a breach and possible privacy regulatory action or civil litigation.

6. **Insider threat**
   Attacks from the inside continue to be hard to prevent. Cyber insurance covers the employee as perpetrator as well as an attack by a third party. This will not extend to an act involving the board of directors or executive team.

7. **Security is not about compliance**
   Treating security as a compliance exercise only will result in failure. For example, many organizations that are compliant with payment card industry data security standards have been breached.

8. **Monetizing the cost of cybersecurity**
   One of the biggest challenges to the CISO is to quantify cybersecurity risk in dollar terms to the executive team. The premium charged by an insurance company can help solve this problem.

9. **Merger and acquisition activity**
   The difficulty in evaluating the cybersecurity posture in any acquisition target leaves the acquirer vulnerable.

10. **Operational technology**
    Industry sectors dependent on operational technology and industrial control systems are particularly vulnerable. Built primarily to be available 24/7 and to operate in isolation, these devices are increasingly being connected to the corporate information technology network and the Internet.

■ **The cyber insurance marketplace today**
It is estimated that more than 50 insurers domiciled mainly in the U.S. and London insurance market provide dedicated cyber products and solutions today. Buyers are concentrated overwhelmingly in the U.S. with little take up to date internationally, with low demand in the rest of the world. Annual premium spending at the end of 2014 was estimated to be in excess of $2 billion. Total capacity (the maximum amount of insurance available to any single buyer) is currently at about $300,000,000, although this is now contracting substantially in certain sectors such as retail and health care. Cyber insurance first emerged at the end of the 1990s, primarily seeking to address loss of revenue and data restoration costs from attacks to corporate networks. However, the underwriting process was seen as too

intrusive and the cost prohibitively expensive. It was not until 2003, and the passage of the world's first data breach notification law in California, that demand started to grow.

What does cyber insurance cover?

Insurers do not address all enterprise assets at risk. The majority of premium spent by buyers was intended to address increasing liability from handling personally identifiable information (PII) or protected health information (PHI) and the costs from either unauthorized disclosure (a data breach) or a violation of the data subject's privacy. Insurable costs range from data breach response expenses such as notification, forensics, and credit monitoring to defense costs, civil fines, and damages from a privacy regulatory action or civil litigation. Insurers also continue to address certain first party risks, including the impact on revenue from attacks on corporate networks, extortion demands, and the costs to restore compromised data.

Insurable assets include the following:

- PII and/or PHI of employees or consumers
  Data breach response costs to include the following:
  - Notification
  - Credit monitoring
  - IT forensics
  - Public relations
  - Defense costs and civil fines from a privacy regulatory action
  - Defense costs and damages from civil litigation
- Corporate confidential information
  Addresses defenses costs and damages incurred for a breach of third-party corporate confidential information. Certain insurers will extend to address misappropriation of a third party's trade secret, but first-party loss of intellectual property remains uninsurable.
- Corporate information technology network
  Addresses the loss of income as a consequence of network downtime.

Certain insurers will also extend coverage to downtime of vendors on whom a policyholder is reliant. This is commonly known as "contingent business interruption."
  Costs to restore compromised data
  Reimbursement for costs associated with an extortion threat
- Operational technology
  A few insurers have begun to extend coverage for the information technology network to also include operational technology such as industrial control systems.
- Physical assets
  Cybersecurity is no longer just about risks to information assets. A cyberattack can now cause property damage that also could lead to financial loss from business interruption as well as liability from bodily injury or pollution, for example. Understanding where coverage lies in a corporate insurance policy portfolio is challenging and at times ambiguous. An assumption that coverage should rest within a property or terrorism policy may not be accurate. Exclusionary language has begun to emerge and is expected to accelerate across the marketplace as losses occur. Dedicated products also have started to appear.
- Reputation and brand
  Insuring reputational risk from some form of cyber event remains out of the scope of the majority of insurers. At the time of writing, the London market has begun to innovate to address the financial loss after adverse media publicity. However, capacity remains constrained at $100,000,000 at best.

What does cyber insurance not cover?

- Intellectual property assets
  Theft of one's own corporate intellectual property (IP) still remains uninsurable today as insurers struggle to understand its intrinsic loss value once compromised. The increasing difficulty in simply detecting an attack and, unlike a breach of PII or PHI, the frequent lack of a legal obligation to

disclose, suggest that a solution is not in the immediate future.

◼ Leveraging cyber insurance as a risk management tool

Since 2009 the marketplace has evolved to also provide services to help buyers manage risk. Focused mainly on post-event response, turnkey products have emerged, which provide a panel of legal, forensics, and public relations specialists. Popular with smaller enterprises that lack the resources or relationships, this innovation has been a key component in increasing the relevance of cyber insurance and consequently its growth. Larger firms typically seek products based on breadth of coverage and the flexibility to use their own vendor network.

Services that help mitigate risk before an event occurs have started to emerge. Insurers likely will begin to incentivize buyers to adopt these services with rewards such as discounted premiums.

◼ How do insurers underwrite cyber risks?

Historically, underwriters have sought to understand the controls that enterprises leverage around their people, processes, and technology. However, the majority of assessments are "static," meaning a snapshot at a certain point in time through the completion of a written questionnaire, a phone call interview, or a presentation. A consensus is growing that this approach is increasingly redundant and that insurers will seek to partner with the security industry to use tools that can help predict and monitor the threat as part of the underwriting process to adopt a more threat intelligence led capability as part of the underwriting process. In fact, this already has started to happen, as certain insurers have started to use technology to underwrite vendor and M&A activity risks.

◼ How do insurers price risk?

Pricing cybersecurity risk remains a challenge. An insurance market that is only 15 years old has begun to build up a profile for frequency and severity of loss with regard to PII and PHI

assets. However, the ever-evolving nature of the threat, particularly the emergence of APTs, undermines the reliability of these statistics. Pricing risk to physical assets is a bigger problem because this has begun to emerge only since 2010, and actuarial data are extremely thin on the ground.

Fundamentally insurers continue to look for a strong security culture within the firm as a first step in risk triage. Additional factors such as industry, revenue size, and actual assets at risk also contribute to how risk is priced.

◼ How to engage the insurance market

Once a decision has been made to explore a suitable solution, the first step is to choose a broker. The lack of consistency in policy language from one insurer to the next means that a broker with dedicated expertise is vital for a successful outcome. First class brokers work with their clients to understand the assets at risk and how best to address them either under the existing insurance program or through a new dedicated product. An existing Directors and Officer's policy form (D&O) addressing management liability from a cyber event probably offers sufficient coverage. However, more often than not, liability to the enterprise requires a new dedicated product.

A broker should understand that insurers seek to understand the security culture of a firm and will work to position their clients as best as possible. For many larger organizations this does not involve completing a written questionnaire and staying divorced from the process. Rather, an investor-style presentation to the marketplace by key stakeholders in IT, legal, and risk management in particular, which involves questions and answers, ensures the best possible outcome. Top-tier underwriters appreciate that cybersecurity is not a tick-box exercise. They understand that the risk is dynamic and will not necessarily penalize a buyer today for shortcomings if a roadmap is spelled out as to how these shortcomings will be addressed in the next 12 months.

A broker must then negotiate competitive terms and conditions with competing insurers with a final recommendation as to whom their client should choose.

10 key coverage items to negotiate:

1. **Full prior acts coverage**
Insurers try to limit coverage to acts from the first day that the policy begins, known as the retroactive date. However, in the context of the challenges in detecting an attack, buyers should seek to remove this exclusion and avoid the risk of a claim denial.

2. **Restrict knowledge and notice of a circumstance to the executive team**
Again, an insurer should not be allowed to impute liability to the whole enterprise because detection has proven to be such a challenge.

3. **Security warranty**
Remove any language that tries to warrant that security is maintained to the same level as represented in the underwriting submission. The dynamic nature of the risk leaves this too open to insurer interpretation in the event of a loss.

4. **Operational technology**
The majority of insurance policies provide coverage only to the corporate IT network. If relevant, ensure that language is broadened to also address operational technology such as industrial control systems.

5. **Outside counsel**
Choice of counsel must be agreed upon up front. In the event of a security breach, a dedicated legal expert must take the response lead not least for attorney client privilege. Negotiating with an insurer during the event would be counterproductive.

6. **IT forensics**
In a similar vein to choice of counsel, the preferred forensics firm must be agreed upon up front. Forensics are not inexpensive and can form a significant part of the overall cost.

7. **Law enforcement**
Law enforcement typically is involved in a major security breach. In fact, many times the FBI, the agency leading cybersecurity corporate defense, notifies the enterprise before it becomes aware of the breach. A claim should not be excluded by an insurer for failure to disclose as soon as practicable if law enforcement had advised nondisclosure during the investigation.

8. **War and terrorism**
Many insurance policies exclude acts of war and terrorism which must be deleted with the emergence of the nation-state adversary in particular.

9. **Intentional act**
Ensure that coverage addresses the employee or insider as perpetrator acting in isolation of the executive team.

10. **Continuity of coverage**
When renewing the insurance policy with the same insurer, avoid signing a warranty regarding a circumstance or claim.

■ Conclusion

Cyber insurance has a broader role to play than simply reimbursing costs associated with a loss. Fundamentally, engaging in an underwriting process that forces collaboration from stakeholders across the enterprise can drive stronger cybersecurity resilience. Increasing regulator and shareholder scrutiny means that the case for investment will continue to grow. In addition, insurers will start to provide premium- and coverage-based incentives for adopting best practices such as the NIST framework and leveraging preferred technology tools.

IX Cyber risk and workforce development

42

Cyber education: A job never finished

NYSE Governance Services – Adam Sodowick, President

Whether it stems from a lack of education, a sense of ambivalence, or, in some cases, malice, nearly all cyber vulnerabilities begin and end with some degree of human error. In today's data-driven environment, companies must establish a culture of responsibility so that all levels of employees work together to maintain vigilant practices that mitigate cyber risk. Despite vast amounts of resources spent on countless firewalls, security systems, and algorithms to ferret out breaches, these complex efforts barely scratch the surface of the problem.

■ Overview

Cybercrime is one of the most prevalent economic crimes today according to PwC's Global Economic Crime Survey. The damages continue to grow with 24% of the more than 5,000 organizations represented in the 2014 PwC study reporting being a victim of cybercrime. A recent study by Verizon Enterprise Solutions points to another significant issue, noting that 66% of cybercrimes are not detected for at least six months.

The trajectory of costs continues to rise. According to the Ponemon's Cost of Cybercrime 2014 report, cyberattacks cost the average U.S. company more than $12.7 million. With some companies experiencing more than $61 million in losses, this average is an increase of more than 9% from the prior year.

Attacking the problem means understanding the source. As one of the top five most reported crimes against businesses, cybercrime is not merely a technology problem anymore. "It is a strategy problem, a human problem, and a process problem," according to the PwC report. The Online Trust Alliance's (OTA) 2015 Data Protection & Breach Readiness Guide reports that employees caused 29% of data breaches between January and June of 2014, proving that internal weaknesses are a significant area of vulnerability for every organization. The

OTA guide further reports that data leaks by employees who lost documents or used social engineering or fraud to access and leak information were caused by a lack of internal controls. Therefore, educating and cultivating true employee buy-in to a culture of responsibility is crucial to mitigating possible damaging breaches.

■ Types of insider threats

The genesis of insider threats is not always malicious; however, the malicious or politically driven acts tend to be the ones that make headlines. Media did not ignore instances such as Home Depot's former security architect who sabotaged his previous employer's computer network and the April 2015 case in which the Department of Justice indicted a Nuclear Regulatory Commission employee for attempting to deliver nuclear secrets to a foreign government via spearphishing tactics.

Although not intentionally malicious, a related form of insider abuse stems from a sense of privilege, when someone abuses the trust he or she is given to safeguard sensitive and valuable data. The 2014 Verizon Enterprise Solutions report found that in 55% of cases involving insider incidents, the primary motivator was privilege abuse; the primary motivator in 40% of cases was financial gain.

A 2012 survey of global employees by Boston-based data storage and information management company Iron Mountain found that workers often develop a feeling of personal ownership when they are involved with the collection of data. The study found that in Europe, for example, many office workers are likely to take data with them when they switch jobs, which, for certain subgroups, such as millennials, happens with more frequency than with previous generations. The study found that of those who did steal company information, 51% exited with confidential customer databases, 46% with presentations, 21% with company proposals, 18% with strategic plans, and another 18% with product/service road maps—all of which represent highly sensitive, valuable assets.

A vast number of cases are actually a result of error, employee ineptitude, or apathy. These situations can cause severe holes in the system and are cases for organizations to change behavior so that employees become a defensive tool against cyber risk.

The computer manufacturer Dell Inc., for example, boasts a "culture of security" that is fostered by the following four fundamental principles: security awareness training, proper access management, mobile security, and securing and monitoring the organization's networks, according to the company's white paper, *The Human Side of IT Security*.

Kevin Hanes, executive director, Security and Risk Consulting, Dell SecureWorks, describes how Dell's information security unit works with other organizations to deal with cybersecurity issues. "My view is organizations need to keep in mind that the bad actors are going to typically follow a path of least resistance, and often that path is the people," he notes. Dell's approach to imparting a cyber-aware culture at an organization begins at the top and involves consistent communication at all levels to ensure employees understand why the vigilance, inconvenient though it may be, is necessary in all aspects of what they do.

Interestingly, not all employees view the threats in the same light. In a June 2015 global study commissioned by Dell SecureWorks and the Ponemon Institute, 56% of the IT security/IT staff surveyed consider 'negligent insiders' a serious threat, whereas only 37% of the IT Security/IT corporate leaders surveyed considered such insiders a serious threat. This difference, the study's authors note, points to a need to listen more carefully to those in the "security trenches who are dealing with these threats."

■ Taking action

Once companies have better awareness of the root causes of insider threats, what steps can be taken? OTA recently reported that 90% of data breaches occurring in the first half of 2014 could have been prevented easily by adhering to commonly accepted best practices for data protection. For companies that are behind the curve, this means there is a lot of work to be done.

In addition to implementing stringent best practices and requiring employees to follow them, self-reporting is a key component. Each company should have a clear understanding about its reporting guidelines as well as what items or activities are suspicious.

Each organization's management and culture are unique, but looking to what works at other companies can help in understanding and making recommendations on sound starting places that help to benchmark practices and measure success of respective cybersecurity defense and mitigation programs.

■ Case study perspectives

Taking a look at a few case studies often can help pull blue sky ideals down to earth. At Teradata, a leading data analytics provider, Chief Compliance Officer Todd Carver says cyber awareness is viewed as a funnel, with new information continually feeding into the top and recirculating in the form of ongoing education to keep employees aware of the latest developments. Carver says his company's program spans from the board of directors to 11,000 employees in 43 countries. Protecting data and assets is one of the commitments in Teradata's code of conduct, and if anything isn't specifically covered in the training, or if employees come up with their own questions, Carver explains, there's also an ethics helpline so that employees can ask questions, request guidance, or say, "I screwed up. What do I do now?"

Annual ethics and compliance education covers a host of issues at Teradata, including cyber-related modules for intellectual property, privacy, phishing, and mobile-device awareness. The company also has policies in place regarding keeping a clean computer, password practices, and email usage, to name a few. In addition, Teradata uses role-specific training. It's all about getting employees truly engaged, Carver explains. "It's important to explain why we have these rules." Carver says his company has shared scenarios of attempted hacks to better help employees understand the need for the procedures.

Although Teradata works diligently to train employees and maintain awareness of cyber issues, Carver concedes the job is never finished. He continually takes the lessons learned and the new angles and feeds them back into the funnel, honing and sharpening the employee education program. Even with that level of attentiveness, Carver assumes his company will encounter a breach and is planning for that eventuality. He also feels it's important to help employees understand what to do if they think they've made a cyber-related error and how to report any questionable or erroneous activity.

Carver suggests three tips for chief compliance officers who are working to implement a more robust cyber awareness program. First, begin with including everybody. "It's all employees' job to assure data protection," he says. Second, it's an issue for all companies across all sectors and needs to be prioritized no matter what the industry. Finally, remember that what makes an organization vulnerable is the human aspect. "You could do everything [right] technology-wise, but could still be vulnerable because people are involved—employees, third-party vendors, customers, and the bad guys."

At Dell, Hanes' SecureWorks group handles security monitoring, consulting, and threat intelligence gathering for itself as well as its many clients. Although SecureWorks has the capacity to test "crazy amounts of malware samples" in a lab, according to Hanes, most companies can take steps on their own to mitigate risks from such activities as phishing and vishing (hacking attempts made via phone call). Creating, communicating, and monitoring protocols can go a long way toward keeping the human element in check, according to Hanes.

In his experience, Hanes says people generally have two mentalities: those who want to check a compliance box by doing annual training at their companies and those who want to transform employee behavior with programmatic changes. The former is much easier, but the latter has the potential to offer tangible results. Creating an organization with a cyber-aware culture requires an ongoing commitment, he explains, because even after years of training "check-the-box" employees, without a complete buy-in and understanding, there will still be those who click on a phishing email link.

■ Creating a cyber-aware culture
Proactive companies such as Teradata, Dell, and others understand that effective cyber awareness education can transform employees into a powerful force in the fight against cybercrime. Having a culture of awareness can help prevent breaches, keep data secure, and positively affect a company's bottom line. In fact, there's arguably no greater barrier to cyber risk than investing in and supporting the right employee culture.

Surprisingly, only 29% of companies surveyed by NYSE Governance Services and the Society of Corporate Compliance and Ethics train all their employees for cyber issues despite the fact that cyber was chosen one of the top three risk areas for employee education, according to the 2014 Compliance and Ethics Program Environment Report issued by the same two groups.

Companywide education often means elevating awareness for the board as well; especially because most board members say it's a difficult area for them to wrap their arms around. In the 2014 RSA/EY survey with *Corporate Board Member,* 83% of directors said that a significant impediment to their oversight of IT/cyber risk was the fact that it was constantly changing. A 2015 Cybersecurity in the Boardroom report published by NYSE Governance Services and Veracode notes that IT security matters are discussed in most or every meeting by 81% of director respondents. In a separate NYSE Governance Services' study with Spencer Stuart, the 2015 What

Directors Think Survey, 63% of director respondents said they are only somewhat confident that their board is adequately overseeing cyber risk; nearly a quarter of respondents said they are not confident about their board's oversight. In sum, there is clear indication that there is room for improvement at even the highest levels.

These findings build a strong case that board members, along with employees, would benefit from being included in the cyber awareness program at their organization to make better decisions and oversee cyber risk on an ongoing basis and help set the proper tone at the top. Roughly two thirds of companies appear committed to this idea. According to Ethisphere's 2015 World's Most Ethical Companies data set, 66% of respondents had offered their board formal training on information security/cybersecurity within the last two years.

■ Conclusion
There is no substitute for a sound, well-understood culture of responsibility and awareness with regard to cybersecurity, a pervasive risk that begins and ends with the human element. The bottom line is that unhappy and/or untrained employees can be a company's biggest threat, whereas a motivated, well-educated workforce can be its biggest defense. Proofpoint, a Sunnyvale, California, security service provider, warns that cyber criminals are continually adjusting to companies' employee education, so the cat-and-mouse game is never finished and constant vigilance is required.

Although the margin for human error will never be eradicated, with proper awareness education and follow through, companies can leverage their greatest asset to alleviate vulnerabilities and strengthen cybersecurity resistance.

43

Collaboration and communication between technical and nontechnical staff, business lines and executives

Wells Fargo & Company – Rich Baich, CISO

> " You can have brilliant ideas, but if you can't get them across, your ideas won't get you anywhere."
>
> *Lee Iacocca*

Delivering results is a key metric of success for any leader. Exceeding revenue goals, meeting hiring and retention goals, or ensuring operational budget goals are well known and understood results. These goals are clear, easily measurable, and most importantly all individuals understand their role in achieving these results. These goals often are established with limited collaboration and a single communication to the appropriate leaders with minimal tolerance associated with not achieving the goals. The language used when establishing these goals and publishing the results transcends technical and nontechnical executives. This information must be understood and actionable; regardless of the executives' background, having this information available allows them to make an informed decision. Leaders need the right information, at the right time to collaborate, communicate, and ultimately make the best decision. Information enables the executive to use a decision process or framework of reasoning to help rationalize the data and choose the best course of action. As the topic of cybersecurity rapidly moves to the top of every C-level executive's agenda, cyber leaders must embrace the importance of collaboration and communication while building bridges to ensure decisions are understood and actionable.

■ Establish a cyber risk decision framework

We live in a time of acute and persistent threats to our national security, our economy, and our global communities. The number of reported cyber incidents continues to grow. The threat of a cyber catastrophic event continues to lurk in the distance. New cyber vulnerabilities are reported each day and the frequency of zero-day threats is increasing. New victims make the headlines weekly. As a result, cyber leaders continue to be asked if their organizations are spending enough to address cyberthreats. To answer this question, cyber leadership must have the facts to establish a decision framework to guide them. Having a firewall, purchasing the latest technologies, growing the number of cyber professionals, and having information security policies do not adequately provide all the information needed to answer this question. Knowing what data to collect, demonstrating the ability to get the data in a timely fashion, operationalizing the data, and ensuring the data get to the right decision maker can provide an actionable framework. The following are a few examples of what information is needed to enable a framework:

- What risks will be mitigated if these additional funds are provided
- Specific cyberthreats are known, monitored, and integrated into the risk prioritization decision process.
- Vulnerabilities are identified, prioritized, remediated, and validated in a timely manner.
- Critical assets are well known, accountability is clear, and responsibility to ensure those assets meet defined protection criteria are met.
- The likelihood of a specific exploit, attack, or significant occurrence is understood and utilized in the cyber risk prioritization framework.

Having trustworthy data is the foundation to all cybersecurity decision frameworks. It is important to have a framework to help support the fundamental changes required to enhance cyber practices and enable communication.

Scenario: Cyber risk decision framework

Today, the media announces a new zero-day exploit that has been identified. Business executives want to know:

- What do they need to do to respond to the exploit?

- How vulnerable are their products and solutions to this exploit?
- Is there any potential for business impact to customers or suppliers?
- Do they need to contact their third parties to see if they are secure?
- Will this affect their ability to service their own third-party relationships?

Using the following framework formula to explain an approach could be helpful:

$$Risk = Vulnerability \times Threat \times Asset\ Value \times Probability\ of\ Occurrence$$

Having the trustworthy data readily available can allow cyber executives to quickly and confidently communicate throughout the organization and the third parties. For example, a quick query of the asset inventory indicates there are 50 instances of this exploit in the current infrastructure and five within the third-party ecosystem. Of those 50 internal instances, only three are external facing, and the remaining 47 are internal to the network. All the third-party instances are internal to the partner's network. The associated vendor to the zero-day exploit has provided a patch and recommended an immediate application of the patch. The internal cyberthreat team has reviewed the external intelligence, and there are already indications of potential miscreants scanning for the newly identified vulnerabilities. Additional intelligence and analysis suggest exploit code is already being crafted to take advantage of this new exploit. If successful, the exploit can be used to deliver malicious code throughout the organization providing kinetic and nonkinetic damage to an organization. Armed with this information, cyber leadership can quickly move to gain consensus, communicate recommendations, and influence the mitigation activities required to address the threat.

■ Defining your stakeholders
Trustworthy data are a key foundation to establishing cybersecurity creditability.

Performance of executives, regardless if they work in a line of business, in corporate staff, or in technology, is often measured by results. Achieving results in cybersecurity requires others taking action. Effective leaders can motivate groups of like-minded people to come together and rally behind a cause to achieve a goal. Finding those individuals in the organization is critical to success. Identifying individuals who will become stakeholders in the cybersecurity journey provide the support needed to drive change. The following is a list of potential stakeholders to consider:

- chief executive officer (CEO)
- chief financial officer (CFO)
- chief auditor
- chief administration officer (CAO)
- chief communication officer (CCO)
- chief risk officer (CRO)
- member(s) of the board of directors
- chief information officer
- line of business leader
- audit committee
- chief technology officer (CTO)
- line of business leaders, CIO, CTO, risk leaders

In addition to individual stakeholders, establishing a cybersecurity steering committee with cross-organizational representation can provide an additional platform for collaboration and communication. The purpose of the committee should be to promote cybersecurity awareness, provide a forum in which cybersecurity topics can be discussed, and to solicit cyber feedback to help evolve cyber practices and mature over time. In addition, the committee will seek to identify cybersecurity topics that may affect the broader applicable industry and the emerging trends that may affect the organization. The cybersecurity committee could:

1. review cybersecurity strategic direction and planned initiatives
2. discuss major milestones for cybersecurity initiatives that are in process of being deployed

3. assess business impact of material cybersecurity program changes
4. discuss lessons learned and situations in which program adjustment is prudent
5. identify potential areas of conflict and/or resource constraints between cybersecurity program and business priorities
6. discuss impacts from and/or to the larger applicable industry.

Stakeholders want the facts and reassurance that the information being reporting is trustworthy and actionable. Risk management is everyone's responsibility, and individuals take great pride when helping reduce risk. Proactively removing risk before the risk evolves in negative consequence is a significant measurement for success. Providing a stakeholder with the data that clearly demonstrate a risk was remediated before it was significant will win the trust of most individuals.

Scenario: Defining stakeholders
You have been asked by a line of business leader to provide information regarding a third party before a contract is signed. Due diligence is done for third parties before any contracts are signed; that is a leading industry practice. However, what if you and your cybersecurity team were able to provide cyber intelligence that suggests the potential third-party partner is on a top-five easiest-to-hack organization list being posted in credible underground forums? Having information without being able to make it actionable often results in a very heavy paper weight being created. In this scenario, having the cyber intelligence to provide the stakeholders helped provide transparency into cyber risks that can produce measured results. Maintaining a results-oriented mentality coupled with the right stakeholder group can help enable a cyber support culture.

◼ Delivering the message
Effective communication, especially during a time of change, requires frequent touchpoints. Having a communicator or a communication

team specifically aligned with the cybersecurity team can provide immense benefits. There is delicate balance associated with the frequency and content that is communicated to stakeholders. The fundamental goal is to tell the cybersecurity story throughout the organization through clear, concise, targeted communications through the most effective dissemination channels. Some will want more frequent communications, whereas others will desire less communication. Some will prefer "pull" communications and others will want the information pushed to them. Cultural appetite, tone from the top, and organizational commitment help drive the various required communication delivery techniques to ensure stakeholders are aware. Some examples include the following:

- publish monthly newsletters to various stakeholders
- create a robust intranet presence with tools and communications
- celebrate success stories of collaborative achievements
- provide platforms for cyber champion recognition
- track, measure, and report the effectiveness of the communications through a cyber communication dashboard

Having a venue into the corporate communications team provides cybersecurity the opportunity to align, influence, and enable the influx of cybersecurity into normal business communications. It is critical that the corporate crisis communication team be part of the cybersecurity incident response team because of the potential reputational impact associated with a significant cyber incident. During a time of crisis, concise and timely communications to key stakeholders and customers can often be the difference between an incident being managed and an incident being exaggerated.

Tactically positioning the cybersecurity story within the organization through effective education and awareness while addressing the latest trends in cybersecurity can

help build collaboration by demonstrating how individuals can partner with cybersecurity to address customer needs. Regardless of the industry, customers want to know their information is safe and the organization that has their data has a clear plan to achieve that goal. Adding cybersecurity reminders in existing individual customer communications begins to demonstrate that commitment to the customer. It takes a long time to earn trust, but it only takes a second to lose it.

This also holds true for internal stakeholders. Often the information and measurement of results reported by the cybersecurity team may not be perceived as positive news. For example, the cybersecurity team may implement new technology that provides an enhanced visibility into the health and hygiene of various technology assets. If these assets have never had this improved visibility, it is possible that the results may provide awareness of critical vulnerabilities or weakness associated with the platform. Consequently, when reporting these results, others may take offense to these perceived negative results. However, this is a great opportunity to educate leadership by explaining that it is far better to find these opportunities internally rather than be told about these vulnerability gaps from a law enforcement representative. Don't pass up the opportunity to build a champion; one champion can quickly lead to two, which, in turn, can often grow to thousands.

Conclusion
During times of conflict it is proven those countries that have aligned themselves with the right allies have prevailed and overcome grave challenges. These are challenging times; cyberthreats are real and present significant risks for most organizations. Communicating these risks to technical and nontechnical executives can often be a daunting task that requires additional background and context to successfully communicate the message. Executives are results driven and appreciate other executives who are proactive when dealing with risks. The ability to provide

trustworthy data and a cyber decision support framework enables cyber executives to translate a new language to other executives. These actions can positively enhance cybersecurity's internal reputation by strengthening trust and credibility across the organization. Taking the time to include, educate, and collaborate with stakeholders can build alliances. Having the right information is powerful, and those stakeholders who get accurate, timely, and meaningful data will have the opportunity to lead change.

44

Cybersecurity readiness through workforce development

Booz Allen Hamilton – Lori Zukin, Principal; Jamie Lopez, Senior Associate; Erin Weiss Kaya, Lead Associate; and Andrew Smallwood, Lead Associate

The demand for skilled cybersecurity professionals currently outweighs the supply. The growing sophistication of cyber adversaries, coupled with our increasingly networked enterprises, means that demand will only continue to grow. To compound this issue, traditional information technology (IT) roles are increasingly insufficient to address enterprise-wide cybersecurity risks. A broader skillset, including communication, change management, and leadership, is required in order to respond quickly and collaboratively to evolving cyber threats.

In light of these challenges, it is clear that a new approach to workforce planning and development is necessary. Yet what would that entail? This chapter covers five recommendations to improve your cybersecurity workforce, including: (1) rethink your approach to cybersecurity, (2) develop alternative talent management strategies, (3) empower your cybersecurity leadership, (4) connect your organization, and (5) invest in your cyber human capital.

■ Redefine cyber operations in your organization

Cyber operations are integral to every business function—a fundamental part of business management in which understanding your cyberthreat is key to your bottom line. Coupled with that is a recognition that the IT function and the cyber operations function are not one and the same. IT is an infrastructure enabler, whereas cyber operations are an organization-wide risk issue. A major cyber breach—one that involves sensitive corporate or customer data—poses more than a technical problem or a business continuity challenge. A major incident can create a multidimensional crisis that affects nearly all aspects of the company's business, as well as its customers, regulators, and other external stakeholders.

In addition, the talent management challenges for cyber operations are much more complex because there is a major crisis to backfill cyber talent. Even once your organizations recruits top cyber professionals, there is no guarantee you will retain them. As such, it is not enough for cybersecurity to be relegated to a subset of people, as with the IT function. Every employee in your organization faces cyberthreats, and talent management for IT and cyber operations should not be combined. By shifting this mindset and developing strategies that reflect these realities, your ability to develop an effective workforce will immediately improve.

■ Develop alternative talent management strategies

Most cybersecurity professionals are personified by their love for cutting-edge technology, casual work environments, and creative mindsets. These unique tendencies help them excel under the constantly changing cyber environment but differentiate them from the rest of your company in a number of ways—fundamentally, their atypical characteristics of (1) work environment, (2) work preferences, and (3) nontraditional career paths.

Recruiting, developing, and retaining this unique workforce requires alternative talent management strategies—strategies that are often connected to but distinct from those applied across the rest of your company.

Develop an appealing work environment

Not every business has a culture of prevalent ping-pong tables, free food, and a dress code involving flip-flops and jeans. However, there are environmental factors that companies must account for in attracting—and keeping—the necessary talent for accomplishing cyber work.

The nature of cyber work means that it is often executed in an environment that differs from that of its parent organization. Think of your cybersecurity practice as the fast moving, quickly adapting branch of your organization. Businesses that consider environmental factors for their cyber workforce are better prepared to adapt to changing threats.

Global business trends have shown successful cyber practices have five key traits: they are agile, multifunctional, dynamic, flexible, and informal.

Agile: *Cyber work requires agility. Employees act like chameleons shifting quickly and decisively as threat warrants change course and as a unit, the capability is alert to new circumstances.*

Multifunctional: *Cybersecurity is a team sport. A strong cyber practice is built of teams with diverse knowledge sets who can execute a variety of activities at once. Your employees do not have to be good multitaskers, but your overall capability does.*

Inquisitive: *Cyber professionals embrace learning and they will be curious; they will want to solve problems regardless of how hard it is to find the solution. Because threat actors across the globe are offering an array of new threats to consider, your cybersecurity work practice will change based on evolving information. By taking on new endeavors, your capability will be ready to solve new problems.*

Flexible: *Cyberthreats move fast. With constantly changing work requirements, your practice must be enabled to adapt to new areas of focus. Your cyber organization must be infused with a strategy that allows for employees to expand or change their roles to increase your capability's flexibility.*

Informal: *Cybersecurity professionals thrive in a nontraditional environment. Your recruits and team members will likely look for unconventional working hours and shifting duties. Creating this type of environment for your cybersecurity professionals allows your cyber organization to adjust quickly to tackle any challenge. Your cybersecurity practice may have different work locations, matrixed reporting lines, around-the-clock shifts, and a more relaxed dress code than the majority of your workforce. The budget process for your cyber organization may be centered around technological investments or on a different timeline to meet shifting threats. Given the work requirements, it is especially important that your cyber environment has leaders who not only share a competitive nature and passion for technology but also have success operating in dynamic, multifunctional environments.*

Understand work preferences

Like the work environment, your cybersecurity professionals also have unique work traits. These traits, or work preferences, make them the perfect candidates to tackle the daily challenges from threat actors around the globe but also can separate them from the rest of your organization. Recognizing these work preferences, for your capability as a whole as well as on an individual level, is critical to developing your cyber talent management strategies.

If your cybersecurity professional had a social media profile, it may look like this:

*Lover and early adopter of new technologies, as a cybersecurity professional my **passion for technology** fuels my curiosity to solve complex problems. I am a **systems thinker** with confidence in my ability to put things together and learn new techniques while using my **competitive** nature to fuel my work as well as engage in office competitions. As a natural **problem solver** and **abstract thinker**, I tend to look 'outside the box' and evaluate challenges from many different angles and perspectives before acting.*

As one method, try offering applicants an on-the-spot challenge while testing their ability to solve problems using senario-based challenges. Capitalize on your employees' problem solving skills by allowing them to be a part of strategy, offense, and defense and by fostering a culture that encourages every level of employee to suggest solutions. Reward your employees for forward thinking, provide them with constantly changing tasks with different levels of difficulty, and present opportunities to work with emerging technologies.

Create nontraditional career paths

Placing two cybersecurity resumes side by side can sometimes feel like you are comparing an apple to an orange. Cyber professionals have a variety of experiences, only some with an educational background in cyber and many with certifications to designate proficiency. Although it would be nice if cyber professionals could be 'cyber warriors,' or experts in all areas of cyber operations, your cybersecurity professional's diverse backgrounds more likely match the diversity of the cybersecurity field.

Booz Allen has found that instead of 'cyber warriors,' it is much more likely that your organization's cyber workforce will be composed of three types with many subsets in each: senior leadership, specialized experts, and generalist staff. Instead of imposing linear career paths on these cyber types, our work has shown that cybersecurity professionals work better under a 'build-your-own' career path option.

Senior leadership cyber professionals are a rare breed of combined expertise and leadership who can manage teams and operations. With specialized experts, their deep know-how within a specific group of cybersecurity capabilities often makes them the center of the talent war. Your generalist staff are early in their cyber careers or have chosen a broad role, making them equally high in demand but commonly part of a larger supply pool.

For most of your company, established career paths diagram career progression options through linear lines of technical experience or managerial ranks. However, attracting and retaining cyber professionals requires alternative pathways that reflect the diversity of positions within the field. For cybersecurity professionals, try providing a nonlinear career path—one that can be horizontal, vertical, and diagonal. Show cybersecurity professionals a set of attributes that describe how to progress using their experience, unconventional education, and industry certification.

This provides your cyber professionals with flexibility to put the pieces together using define career progression opportunities and opens up your ability to recruit talent who want to grow *with* your organization.

■ Give CISOs a 'seat at the table'
Although progress is being made in professionalizing and institutionalizing cybersecurity as a field, much remains to be done. In fact, less than half of Fortune 100 companies have a CISO. Organizations still struggle to build, recruit, and retain a cybersecurity workforce. There is no 'one-size-fits-all' for placement of the CISO within your organization. It depends on the industry, the type of organization, and what the organization is protecting. In some organizations, the CISO may report to the CIO. In others, with a different architecture, mission statement, and set of complex challenges, the CISO may report to the chief risk officer, or even directly to the COO or CEO.

No matter where the CISO sits in your organization, you need to give the CISO 'a seat at the table' during regular operations, for example, when discussing risk analysis, profit reductions, performance indicators, and other strategies in your organization's balanced scorecard. Elevating the level of your CISO during normal operations helps nurture leadership, management, and non-technical skills—skills that are critical during a cyber crisis. Further, by making the CISO a member of the C-suite leadership team, you will be able to raise the level of cyber awareness—and coordinated response— across your entire organization.

The CISO's role within the organization abruptly shifts to hands-on, crisis mode in a cyber breach. The CISO's foremost responsibility is to quickly address the crisis from a technical perspective. The CISO should be fully immersed in directing the cyber response, working with the computer incident response team or security operations experts to remediate and minimize damage, while delegating or outsourcing other roles/ issues such as policy implications, legal, and public relations.

Once relegated to the IT department, cybersecurity is now part of a company's core strategic planning and investment portfolio. That said, many CISOs currently don't have the appropriate skill set to deal with all the overall strategic implications of a major cyber breach. Although CISOs likely have the technical expertise required to fix the problem or at least manage it, they may not be prepared for the magnitude of other multidimensional challenges that surface during the crisis. In addition to technical know-how, CISOs have to be able to think on their feet, nimbly and calmly handling the internal and external nontechnical issues that may arise.

■ Connect your organization
The cyber-ready organization is a connected one. Ineffective collaboration between lines of business and the cyber function limits data sharing and effective change. However, before you can foster true collaboration between your lines of business, you must have appropriate cyber channels weaved throughout your organizational structure. Your organization needs effective processes in place to manage cyber-related communications and policies. This 'interconnectedness' comes to life when your central cyber unit is feeding information to key business leaders and those business leaders are implementing change throughout their lines of business and communicating information back to the core cyber unit. The cybersecurity function deserves to be placed at the center of your organization, to inform all of your business units.

Cybersecurity should be viewed as a central business function that informs other business units. See Figure 1.

You also will need strong leaders at the helm of each business unit who are bilingual in business and cyber operations. Cybersecurity is the new education leaders have to undergo to lead your organization effectively. In connecting the channels across your organization, all leaders must be on the same page, communicating the same message, implementing the same security measures, with the same vigor.

FIGURE

1

Cybersecurity as a central business function

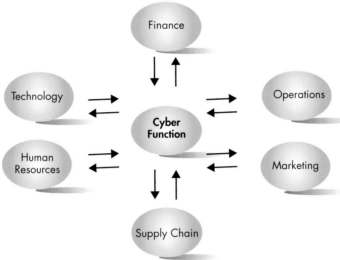

■ Finally, invest in cyber human capital

Most leaders in today's business world agree cybersecurity is important. However, when the meeting is over, will they truly buy in and embrace cybersecurity as a key priority for their divisions? This is the tough question CEOs, CIOs, and CSOs encounter. An organizational cybersecurity plan can only be as strong as the weakest commitment from any key leader. It doesn't matter how strong your security posture is for individual departments; if one division is vulnerable, your entire organization is at risk.

An effective way to improve the long-term security of your company is by investing in your cyber leaders and cyber workforce. Investments in technology and processes go unrealized unless your organization has strong cyber leaders along with a capable workforce to defend your networks and improve your security. Successful organizations will invest in their workforce, give their CISO a seat at the table, and foster integrated lines of communication for the sharing of cyber-related information.

45

Building a cyber-savvy board

Korn Ferry – Jamey Cummings, Senior Client Partner;
Joe Griesedieck, Vice Chairman and Co-Leader, Board and
CEO Services; and Aileen Alexander, Senior Client Partner

Given the growing magnitude and frequency of cyber-security breaches, which have the potential to shake major corporations to their core, cybersecurity has become an issue of enterprise-wide importance. These incidents have become commonplace events, and organizations that are targets may suffer lost or stolen intellectual property, damage or destruction of critical data or infrastructure, disruptions to critical operations, and loss of confidence among customers, investors, and employees. The longer-term damage to value and reputation is incalculable.

■ Startling statistics

PwC's Global State of Information Security Survey 2015 of more than 9,700 security, IT, and business executives found that the total number of security incidents detected by respondents climbed to 42.8 million this year, an increase of 48% over 2013. That is the equivalent of 117,339 incoming attacks per day, every day. The Identity Theft Resource Center reported a record high of 738 U.S. data breaches, a 28% year-over-year increase.

If you're thinking you can build a modern-day "moat" to keep the bad guys out, consider that the 2014 U.S. State of Cybercrime Survey, co-sponsored by PwC, CSO magazine, the CERT Division of the Software Engineering Institute at Carnegie Mellon University, and the U.S. Secret Service, found that almost one-third of respondents said insider crimes are more costly or damaging than incidents perpetrated by outsiders. In a virtual ecosystem that increasingly includes the Internet of Things (IoT), traditional firewalls do not ensure protection, as employees come and go each day with connected devices, such as smartphones and computers, which may wittingly or unwittingly introduce threats that can threaten the survival of the organization.

This greatly expanded cyberattack surface and resulting breaches add up to a huge price tag. The annual cost of cybercrime to the global economy is estimated to be between $375 billion and $575 billion, according to a June 2014 study by the Center for Strategic and International Studies; Gartner Inc. estimates that total spending will grow 8.2 percent in 2015 to reach $76.9 billion.

If that's not a wake-up call, we don't know what is. But, the challenge remains: translating awareness into an action plan. Although CEOs and boards are alert to the issue and the devastating, long-lasting effects of security breaches, there is surprisingly little knowledge of recommended practices to best position organizations defensively and enable quick and effective response when the inevitable occurs. Let's be blunt: There is no foolproof way of preventing security breaches, but a systematic, proven approach can make the difference between the survival and the demise of an enterprise.

■ **Alignment at the top**

Cybersecurity is an insidious threat, all the more so because breaches, including the most disastrous ones, often are not detected until the damage is done. One cybersecurity firm recently estimated that close to three quarters of security breaches go undetected. No board or management team can afford to become complacent. If you haven't yet fallen victim, you may have been smart, but most likely lucky. You should assume it's just a matter of time, perhaps there already has been a breach that has gone undetected, so plan accordingly.

In a relatively short time cybersecurity has gone from something that was compartmentalized and handled by the IT department to something that is regularly on the agenda at board meetings. At the same time "major threats" have been redefined, from identifying a Trojan horse and upgrading anti-virus software to threats that strike at the very heart of organizations and are capable of taking them down. The view and

importance of cybersecurity has shifted from something of marginal interest to the board to a high priority that resides within the board's risk management framework.

This is a new role for CEOs and directors, many of whom feel unequipped to deal with it because cybersecurity does not remotely relate to traditional areas of director expertise. Armed with a tested protocol to combat cyberthreats and the right resources, however, every board should be able to implement a preparedness and response plan that will give the board and management team, as well as investors, the reassurance that the company is as well positioned as reasonably possible to confront these ever-evolving challenges.

In practical, operational terms, what does all this mean for the C-suite and the board, and how can they get started on overseeing the many-headed beast that is cybersecurity? For one thing, it starts with ensuring everyone on the board is speaking the same language when it comes to cyberthreats. Because directors are generally business people, the common language should be the language of business.

■ **The right questions**

According to Melissa Hathaway, private sector cybersecurity expert and former cybersecurity "czar" under Presidents George W. Bush and Barack Obama, "Until cybersecurity is reflected in balance sheet terms, it's never going to be fully embraced by the board." She emphasizes that once cybersecurity has been identified as a critical risk, it must be managed with the same rigor and processes applied to other risks and remain visible on directors' dashboards with key, comprehensible metrics. "Tech speak," or any jargon that obfuscates the issues for directors, has no place in the boardroom.

The reality of boardrooms, however, is that the scale of that impact is often obscured or lost in translation. Unless directors can cut through the technical jargon in what are often massive amounts of information they receive, the size of the risk and the steps to mitigate it may not be clear. Companies depend on a functioning Internet, which was never invented with security in mind, and all that is linked to it. Therefore, related risks and costs must be made known to the board so that the cost of potential breaches can be calculated in capital and operational terms, rather than remaining hidden.

Among the questions directors should be asking regularly to ensure alignment as a team and a firm grasp on cybersecurity, says Hathaway, are the following:

- **Is cyber risk accounted for in our overall corporate planning process?** The board must be assured that cyber risk is an element of a broader risk framework and that exposures are recognized and planned for.
- **What is the process for evaluating security and measuring liabilities?** Boards should know not only what controls are in place but also how they are evaluated.
- **Do we have directors with relevant expertise?** Although boards may not require general technology expertise, it may be advisable to have one or more directors who understand IT and its associated risks, or have a security background.
- **Have we identified executive ownership of the issue?** The CEO should have controls in place that indicate how cybersecurity is being managed and the true costs to the business, which should be part of an internal and external audit.
- **What will we do in the event of a breach?** If and when a problem arises, a process should be in place for communicating effectively, internally and externally, and dealing with attendant costs.

Overseeing cyber risk

Boards are increasingly adding directors with cybersecurity backgrounds and, more generally, security expertise, but boards should not assume that they need to add a director with this specialized background. Much depends on company specifics and the industry in which it operates, so each board should decide on a case-by-case basis. Shortfalls in board experience often can be made up by retaining the appropriate additional expertise to advise on an as-needed basis; however, we are starting to see more demand for this specific sort of talent on boards.

Sometimes, as noted above, the board's most important role lies in asking the right questions, which may require business smarts and good old-fashioned common sense but not necessarily technical cybersecurity expertise.

As overseer-in-chief of the CEO and the business, the board has a responsibility for managing the company's risk portfolio, of which cybersecurity is now a key component. Proper oversight entails remaining at a high, supervisory level—not getting dragged down into the management weeds—and boards can properly perform their fiduciary duties by focusing on a few main areas.

The board must be reassured by the CEO that the most capable people are in the critical positions, and this extends to the leadership and team managing cybersecurity. With so much at stake, this is not a place to cut corners.

Directors should be kept abreast of main cybersecurity risks, as well as the remediation process and timeline for effectively dealing with them. Certainly no one expects directors to be technology wizards, but they should be inquiring about safeguards the company has in place to guard against intrusion and be satisfied by management that protection along with response and recovery capabilities are adequate. In addition, they will want to be informed about education for everyone throughout the organization, to ensure awareness of threats, and a step-by-step response plan to follow in the event of a breach.

The board at the nexus

Cybersecurity has expanded well beyond the confines of IT and emerged as a concern at the highest enterprise level, primarily because of the devastating potential effects on shareholder value, market share, reputation, and long-term survival. Cybersecurity is an issue that crosses all organizational silos and boundaries top to bottom, encompassing people, culture, and risk management and must bridge security, technology, privacy, and compliance. Cybersecurity is, therefore, taking its rightful place on a short list of the board's crucial responsibilities, which now include protecting a company's assets, particularly digital, as part of an organization's overall risk portfolio.

In fact, managing cyber risk doesn't differ significantly from managing more traditional forms of risk and must be managed in a similar way, remaining visible on directors' dashboards so that it is tracked and addressed regularly.

Those boards that do not have a cybersecurity expert as a member of their team should not assume they need a director with this experience, but they should seriously evaluate that potential need based on their situation and needs. Some boards have determined that they do require this expertise on their audit committee—where risk oversight generally lives—on a special cybersecurity subcommittee, or on a dedicated cybersecurity committee. While some boards have recruited this expertise, many have not and may not, accessing what they require to keep them informed and able to make key decisions either from internal technology experts or from external consultants to the board. These solutions are varied and tailored and continue to evolve.

CEOs and those who serve as directors on their boards are generally a smart group of people, and they don't have to be subject matter experts to provide oversight for the few crucial areas—including strategy formulation, succession planning, and risk management—in which they exercise their fiduciary duties. Cybersecurity is yet another form of risk, but it is a dynamic, still-emerging form that is new to most directors. We are likely years away from the point where boards as a whole consider managing cyber risk familiar terrain, so additional resources

can always be made available should directors need bolstering in this area.

In fact, directors owe it not only to their shareholders to ensure a comprehensive approach to monitoring and developing a proactive approach to tackling cybersecurity but also to themselves. With cybersecurity in the spotlight—where it is likely to remain—directors could also face personal risks, because D&O insurance may not be sufficient if boards don't take what are deemed appropriate actions. Boards should consider adding cyber insurance as part of a comprehensive approach to enterprise risk management if they are to continue to recruit the best directors. According to a recent post on the Harvard Law School Forum on Corporate Governance and Financial Regulation, "no company in the U.S. should forego buying cyber insurance to protect against the real, ever-present risk of a major cyber-attack and the massive costs associated with such a breach."

■ A framework to meet the cybersecurity challenge

Perhaps most important in properly meeting the cybersecurity challenge, ensuring preparedness and a ready response to any breaches, directors need a framework, which can be tailored to the needs of their organization, in which to operate. A deep dive into each area will link to additional responsibilities and timeframes, most of which will be the responsibility of management.

The baseline for board involvement in overseeing cybersecurity should comprise the six following components:

1. **Security strategy.** The board must ensure that the company has a strategic vision and a tactical road map that proactively protect assets and keep pace with escalating threats and evolving regulatory requirements.
2. **Policy and budget review.** Company security policies, and roles and responsibilities of all relevant leadership, should be evaluated, along with data

security and privacy budgets to ensure they are adequately funded.

3. **Security leadership.** The board must confirm that the organization has the credible leadership and talent to develop, communicate, and implement an enterprise-wide plan to manage cyber risk.

4. **Incident response plan.** The board should oversee the development of a comprehensive incident response plan that is widely understood, rehearsed, and stress tested.

5. **Ongoing assessment.** The board should periodically review a thorough assessment of the organization's information security capabilities, targeting internal vulnerabilities and external threats.

6. **Internal education.** The board should ensure that the company implements a strong communication and education program to create an environment in which all employees embrace responsibility for cybersecurity.

■ A cybersecurity strategy

Organizations must have a cybersecurity strategy, lest they simply be engaged in a game of whack-a-mole, reacting to one threat after another rather than having a comprehensive game plan. That is not to say that cyberthreats and breaches can be eliminated—clearly they cannot—but the resulting damage can be greatly minimized with significant planning and a quick response protocol.

In part, effectively managing cybersecurity starts at the top with the board recognizing what it must manage and how that will be done, including additional resources it may require. While the board may have ultimate responsibility for the war on cyberthreats, everyone, at every level of the organization, must understand his or her role on the front lines of this ongoing war, because threats can come from anywhere.

Moreover, in an increasingly robust regulatory environment with cybersecurity high on the SEC's agenda, adherence to best practices with a well-designed plan approved and monitored by the board should prove far preferable to regulations imposed from the outside. Given the current direction, in the near future it is likely that publicly owned companies will be required to disclose more information about their cybersecurity vulnerabilities, including data breaches.

Ultimately, boards should work with senior management to build a cybersecurity-aware culture if they are to truly protect their companies from this relatively new, continually morphing, and potentially devastating form of risk.

46

Evaluating and attracting your next CISO: More sophisticated approaches for a more sophisticated role

Egon Zehnder – Kal Bittianda, Selena Loh LaCroix, and Chris Patrick

The role of the chief information security officer (CISO) has changed dramatically in the last decade. No longer merely a digital sheriff called on to protect the firm's data valuables, the CISO is expected to act as a full strategic partner with the rest of the C-suite. The upgrading of the role is a natural response to the extensive technological, societal, economic, and geopolitical developments over the same time period. For many organizations, information—whether customer records, intellectual property, or strategic planning—is now their most valuable asset. As those assets have become more valuable, they have also become less secure because of the increase in the number and the sophistication of attackers, as well as the vulnerabilities inherent in an increasingly networked society.

The bottom line is that, although the CISO rarely reports directly to the chief executive officer, he or she must have the qualities expected at the CEO-1 level. Organizations endeavoring to fill the CISO role must ensure that their recruitment strategies and candidate evaluation processes keep pace with these greater expectations, lest those organizations increase their risk of unmet security goals, shorter CISO tenures, and the associated costs. This is in addition to the difficulty of maintaining a consistent security culture in the shadow of frequently changing information-security leaders.

■ Taking a holistic view of CISO candidates

Our observation at Egon Zehnder has been that when looking for their next CISO, organizations can benefit by taking a broader view of the required qualities and capabilities. Effective candidate evaluation can be achieved by dividing a candidate's career into its past, present, and future components and evaluating each element with the appropriate perspective. A consolidation of the three elements provides a holistic view of the CISO candidate that corresponds with the multi-faceted nature of the role today.

The past: What has the candidate done?

A candidate's credentials, work history, and track record have always been a central part of the evaluation process, and for good reason. This component includes examining the types of organizations in which the candidate has worked, their size and complexity, and which markets they served, and then seeing what the candidate accomplished in each role, what transformations the candidate has led, and the security record of the organizations under the candidate's watch. These findings provide the raw material, basic facts, and context for measuring the fit between the candidate and role. Although the CISO role has grown significantly beyond its technical roots, the technical expertise indicated by work history are essential "table stakes" for a candidate to warrant further consideration.

The present: What can the candidate do?

Until about a decade or so ago, exploring a candidate's work history generally constituted the bulk of the assessment process. Then the realization emerged that what a candidate had done so far is a mere subset of what a candidate could do, because one's work experience can never be so broad as to capture everything of which someone is capable. Looking at competencies is a way of taking an inventory of an executive's full leadership toolbox.

The key is to evaluate for the right competencies given the demands of the position. In our experience, five competencies are particularly important when evaluating CISO candidates. They are listed here in order from the most common to the most elusive:

1. **Results orientation:** The successful candidate must be able to move quickly to get the right things done. Audits are responded to in a timely fashion, the board of directors is clear on the impact of information security investments, and core data assets are well protected.

2. **Strategic orientation:** As mentioned earlier, the CISO must be a strategically oriented partner with critical thinking skills. He or she must process disparate information and generate valuable insight regarding external issues such as shifts in threats and countermeasures and internal matters such as business implications of information security policies and protocols.

3. **Transformational leadership:** Regardless of the context into which the new CISO is taking the helm—after a major breach, under the glare of heightened board scrutiny, or with an acquisition that must be integrated—he or she will need to transform systems to address current challenges, creating a vision others buy into and moving the organization forward while keeping day-to-day operations running smoothly.

4. **Relationship management:** The CISO must be able to lead in a matrixed environment, working diplomatically with a range of constituencies with different perspectives on information security, including the board, the CEO, the CFO, the COO, and general counsel. In addition to managing internal relationships, the CISO must also leverage external networks that include peers at other organizations, Internet service providers, third-party security solution vendors, and law enforcement and intelligence agencies. The CISO must have the gravitas and influence necessary to communicate effectively with each of these internal and external groups in a range of conditions, from off-site strategy sessions to emergency response.

5. **Team leadership:** Most organizations focus all their attention on filling the CISO position, leaving relatively little energy for establishing a pipeline of internal talent. This is understandable but

shortsighted. Identifying and developing internal information security leadership talent is critical to the long-term success of the function and should be considered part of the CISO's role.

The future: How will the candidate adapt to change and unforeseen developments?

Looking at competencies provides a more complete view of a candidate's abilities than examining just professional history. But competency-based assessment has its own limitations in that it assumes the future will be more or less like the past or present. It does not measure a person's ability to respond to fundamental changes such as those brought about by the current waves of digital transformation. Someone who looks highly qualified on paper and presents well thus can fall short of expectations as conditions become highly complex and ambiguous. Also, looking at only experience and competencies means the organization risks overlooking candidates who may seem underprepared today but with sufficient support would be best suited for the future.

In Egon Zehnder's examination of the assessments of thousands of senior executives, we discovered that those who flourished in the face of volatility, complexity, uncertainty, and ambiguity shared four traits, which collectively we call *potential*. The four elements of potential are the following:

1. **Curiosity:** A penchant for seeking out new experiences, knowledge, and candid feedback, as well as an openness to learning and change
2. **Insight:** The ability to gather and make sense of information to suggest previously unseen opportunities and threats
3. **Engagement:** A knack for using emotion and logic for communicating a persuasive vision and connecting with people
4. **Determination:** The resilience to fight for difficult goals despite challenges and to bounce back from adversity.

The elements of potential add an extra dimension to what is learned from a competency-based evaluation in the same way that examining competencies provides much more depth than merely looking at work history. None of these elements are sufficient on their own for identifying how a given candidate will respond to the unfolding challenges of the CISO role, but in combination they produce a vivid, and in our experience, highly accurate, portrait and predictor. These added dimensions are particularly important because of how much the CISO role has changed in the last several years. Few CISOs have established track records acting as the sort of strategic leaders—rather than technical managers—that the role requires today. The attributes of potential add another element to help identify who is likely to successfully navigate this leap.

But the above framework is only that—the quality of its output depends on the quality of the input. Without a concerted effort, reliable input can be difficult to obtain in CISO evaluations because of the tendency of data-security function to move quickly from crisis to crisis, leaving little concrete evidence of who did what when. The key to obtaining the needed level of detail is in-depth interviews with multiple informed references. Doing so requires the ability to tap an extensive professional network.

Because of the number of factors being weighed, it is important to not merely collect observations for each quality being examined but to place the candidate on a scale based on average performance in the industry. Some organizations also complement candidate and reference interviews with psychometric testing to provide another layer of objective input for the evaluation process.

■ Positioning the role

The market for top-tier CISOs is now highly competitive. Information security has become a high-profile corporate concern, and the bar has been raised on the pool of qualified candidates. By one estimate there were 2,700 CISO job openings in the United States in June 2015. So even if organizations are able to effectively evaluate candidates against current and future requirements, they must also be prepared from the start to actively sell the opportunity to an audience that is naturally skeptical.

In our experience, every CISO candidate asks four overarching questions when evaluating an opportunity:

1. **"Who is my sponsor and how much influence does he or she have?"** This is likely to be the first question on the CISO candidate's mind, and he or she is thinking about this issue in at least two specific ways. First, although the CISO is likely to have some interaction with the board and C-suite, there will still be many conversations that affect the information security function to which the CISO will not be privy. As a result, the CISO will have to rely his or her supervisor to act as an effective intermediary in advocating for resources and policy initiatives and in educating the board and CEO on information security issues as they unfold. Second, when the CISO needs to take an unpopular position to strengthen an organization's information security profile, he or she has to know there will be support in high places.

2. **"How deep is the organization's commitment to information security?"** This is more than a question of staff and budget allocation, although those elements are certainly important. The CISO wants to know that the C-suite and the board appreciate the complexity and uncertainty at the core of the information security function and the need for making everyone in the organization, top to bottom, responsible for security. For the CISO to be successful, he or she must be empowered to act and be armed with the necessary resources to deploy both in times of normalcy and crisis. Although the CISO expects organizations to have high standards, he or she will avoid enterprises who reflexively cycle through security teams.

3. **"What key performance indicators will I be measured against?"** Given that every large organization must assume that it is continually under cyberattack, it follows that security breaches are a matter of not "if" but "when." Therefore, it is not realistic for a company to hold its CISO to a "one strike and you're out" performance benchmark. The conversation about expectations is just as important as the ones about resources, reporting lines, and compensation.

4. **"Where will I be in five years?"** Those who lead the information security function are like other functional leaders in their range of career ambitions. For some, the opportunity to lead the function at a quality organization is the goal; others, however, are looking ahead to a CIO role or even a broader role in organizational leadership. It is important to understand each candidate's desires against what the organization can offer. Remember that the CISO's reporting relationship will be one factor that frames this issue in his or her mind.

Long gone are the days when an argument had to be made regarding the strategic importance of information security. In most organizations, the CISO role now has the weight and sophistication its responsibilities require. Organizations can assess the state of their CISO recruitment and assessment strategies by asking themselves the following four questions:

1. Have we identified the CISO's full range of strategic responsibilities and the competencies needed to be successful?
2. Do we have a consistent methodology for evaluating a candidate against those responsibilities?
3. Have we reviewed the CISO reporting relationship against the information security context of the organization to ensure that the CISO is adequately empowered to accomplish the organization's information security goals?

4. Do we have an adequate professional development program in place to support the CISO and his or her team to help them meet the standards demanded by the function's heightened importance?

From the answers to these questions, organizations can then begin to make the necessary adjustments to ensure they have the approach and tools to identify and attract the information security talent that can perform at the level the position now requires.

Contributor Profiles

New York Stock Exchange

11 Wall Street
New York, New York 10005
Tel +1 212 748 4000
Web www.nyse.com

TOM FARLEY
President, NYSE Group

Tom Farley is President of the NYSE Group, which includes the New York Stock Exchange and a diverse range of equity and equity options exchanges, all wholly owned subsidiaries of Intercontinental Exchange (NYSE/ICE). Mr. Farley joined the NYSE when ICE acquired NYSE Euronext in 2013, serving as Chief Operating Officer. He held previous roles at ICE, including SVP of Financial Markets and President and COO of ICE Futures U.S., formerly the New York Board of Trade.

Prior to joining ICE, Mr. Farley was President of SunGard Kiodex, a risk management technology provider to the derivatives markets. He has also held various positions in investment banking at Montgomery Securities and in private equity at Gryphon Investors. Mr. Farley holds a BA degree in Political Science from Georgetown University and is a Chartered Financial Analyst.

NYSE GOVERNANCE SERVICES

55 East 52nd St, 40th Floor
New York, New York 10005
Tel +1 212 323 8500

ADAM SODOWICK
President, NYSE Governance Services
Email Adam.Sodowick@nyse.com

Adam Sodowick is currently President of NYSE Governance Services after serving as Chief Operating Officer, where he was responsible for Product, Market Strategy, and Marketing.

Prior to NYSE Governance Services, Mr. Sodowick founded True Office in 2010 to solve a long-standing problem: the tedium and high cost of regulatory compliance training. Recognizing that humans are hardwired to learn via stories and play, True Office creates data-rich desktop and mobile compliance apps that help companies identify risk, save money, and educate employees on complex and risk-sensitive business issues in a fun way.

Since its launch, True Office has experienced a steep growth trajectory and has been adopted as the compliance training solution of choice for many Fortune 500 companies. True Office has won multiple awards across the GRC, Technology, and Innovation segments and has been featured prominently in many media outlets, including the BBC, the *Wall Street Journal, Forbes, Fortune*'s annual 500 Issue, and more.

Initially backed by Morgan Stanley Strategic Investments, The Partnership for New York City Fund and Rho Ventures, True Office was acquired by Intercontinental Exchange, parent company of the New York Stock Exchange in October 2014.

Prior to founding True Office, Mr. Sodowick was the co-founder and CEO of 50 Lessons. During this time, Mr. Sodowick pioneered the creation of the award-winning '50 Lessons Digital Business Library.'

Today, 50 Lessons is widely recognized as the world's pre-eminent collection of multimedia business insights from global business leaders. These assets are housed in a digital library and sold via various channels to more than 350 corporate customers and academic institutions globally.

Mr. Sodowick envisioned and led the publishing initiative behind the best-selling *Lessons Learned: Straight Talk From The World's Top Business Leaders*, a set of 24 books published by Harvard Business School Press. Initially backed by the BBC, 50 Lessons was acquired by Skillsoft in 2011.

Intercontinental Exchange

5660 New Northside Drive NW
3rd Floor
Atlanta, Georgia 30328
Tel +1 770 857 4700
Web www.intercontinentalexchange.com

JERRY PERULLO

Chief Information Security Officer
Email jerry.perullo@theice.com

Jerry Perullo has led the Information Security program at Intercontinental Exchange, Inc. (NYSE:ICE) since 2001. As Chief Information Security Officer, he is responsible for the security of ICE's heavily regulated exchanges and clearinghouses, including the New York Stock Exchange.

Mr. Perullo is an active participant in the Financial Services Sector Coordinating Council (FSSCC) and Financial Services Information Sharing and Analysis Center (FS-ISAC), where he serves as Chair of the Clearinghouse and Exchange Forum (CHEF). He also co-founded the Global Exchange Cyber Security (GLEX) working group under the World Federation of Exchanges and serves on several industry and customer advisory boards within the cybersecurity industry.

Prior to ICE, Mr. Perullo was a Principal Consultant at Digital Consulting and Software Services providing information security testing and consulting services to the health-care, energy, and data service industries and built an Internet Service Provider in the mid 1990s.

Mr. Perullo studied Computer Engineering at Clemson University and earned a BS degree in Legal Studies from the University of Maryland and an MBA from Georgia State University.

Palo Alto Networks Inc.

4401 Great America Parkway
Santa Clara, California 95054
Tel +1 408 753 4000
Web www.paloaltonetworks.com

MARK D. MCLAUGHLIN

Chairman, President, and CEO

Mark D. McLaughlin joined as president and CEO of Palo Alto Networks in August of 2011 and became Chairman of the Board in 2012. Previously Mr. McLaughlin served as President and CEO of Verisign. Prior to Verisign, he was the Vice President of Sales and Business Development for Signio and was instrumental in driving the acquisition of Signio by Verisign in 1999. Before joining Signio, he was the Vice President of Business Development for Gemplus, the world's leading smart-card company. Previous to Gemplus, he also served as General Counsel of Caere Corporation and practiced law as an attorney with Cooley Godward Kronish LLP. In 2014 President Obama appointed Mr. McLaughlin as the Chairman of the National Security Telecommunications Advisory Committee (NSTAC). He received his JD, *magna cum laude*, from Seattle University School of Law and his BS degree from the U.S. Military Academy at West Point.

DAVIS Y. HAKE
Director of Cybersecurity Strategy

As Director of Cybersecurity Strategy, Davis Y. Hake is responsible for building and sharing the company's strategy for cybersecurity thought leadership and delivering valuable information, insights, and instructional tools on all things related to cyberthreats and today's security landscape. Prior to joining Palo Alto Networks in 2015, Mr. Hake was a leader in U.S. government cybersecurity serving in the White House, at senior levels in the Department of Homeland Security, and as a policy expert for the U.S. Congress. Mr. Hake also drafted some of the first comprehensive cybersecurity legislation, for which he received a Federal 100 Award for leadership in the IT community. He is a graduate of the University of California–Davis, where he studied international relations and economics and received a Masters degree in Strategic Security Studies from the National Defense University.

Axio Global, LLC
77 Water Street, 8th Floor
New York, New York 10005
Tel +1 708 420 8611
Web www.axioglobal.com

SCOTT KANNRY
Chief Executive Officer
Email skannry@axioglobal.com

Scott Kannry is the Chief Executive Officer of Axio Global. Mr. Kannry's entire career has been in the commercial insurance industry with a focus on cyber and previously spent 10 years in the Financial Services Group at Aon. He works with clients in all industries but specializes in those with evolving cyber risks, such as energy, utility, transportation, and manufacturing. Mr. Kannry has been

awarded the Risk and Insurance Magazine "Power Broker" distinction and was named to Business Insurance Magazine's inaugural "Top 40 under 40" brokerage honor roll and 2014 Rising Star by *Reactions* magazine. Mr. Kannry received a BS and BA from Case Western Reserve University, a JD from the Northwestern School of Law, and his MBA from the Kellogg School of Management.

DAVID W. WHITE
Co-Founder and Chief Knowledge Officer
Email dwhite@axioglobal.com

David W. White is a founder and Chief Knowledge Officer at Axio Global. Axio is a cyber risk-engineering firm that helps organizations implement more comprehensive cyber risk management based on an approach that harmonizes cybersecurity technology/controls and cyber risk transfer. Mr. White works directly with Axio clients and is responsible for the frameworks and methods that guide Axio's services, including cybersecurity program evaluation and benchmarking, cyber loss scenario development and analysis, insurance program analysis, and data analytics.

Previously, Mr. White worked in the CERT Program at Carnegie Mellon's Software Engineering Institute, a cybersecurity research program primarily funded by the U.S. Department of Defense and the U.S. Department of Homeland Security. While there, he was responsible for technical leadership and research strategy for a portfolio of cybersecurity and resilience maturity models and frameworks and associated research, diagnostic methods, and training.

Mr. White served as chief architect for the Electricity Subsector Cybersecurity Capability Maturity Model (ES-C2M2) and served on the review team for the oil-and-natural-gas version (ONG-C2M2) and industry-agnostic version (C2M2). Mr. White co-authored the CERT Resilience Management Model (CERT-RMM) and served as the chief architect for the Smart Grid Maturity Model (SGMM).

Baker & McKenzie

**815 Connecticut Avenue, NW
Washington, DC 20006
Tel** +1 202 452 7000
Web www.bakermckenzie.com

DAVID C. LASHWAY

Partner
Email david.lashway@bakermckenzie.com

David C. Lashway leads Baker & McKenzie's global cybersecurity practice and is located in Washington, DC. He focuses his practice in the areas of crisis management, internal investigations, and complex criminal, civil and administrative litigation and has significant experience advising clients with respect to various aspects of cybersecurity-related matters. Mr. Lashway is a sought-after lawyer who advises the Fortune 100 on the full lifecycle of enterprise risks associated with information security, including before, during, and after a network breach, as well as federal regulatory and criminal matters. He regularly conducts global investigations around the theft or compromise of confidential data and is repeatedly called upon to litigate post-data breach issues. His clients include investment banks, publicly traded and private companies, trade associations, and individual managers, and his matters span the globe.

JOHN W. WOODS, JR.

Partner
Email john.woods@bakermckenzie.com

John W. Woods is a partner in Baker & McKenzie's Washington, DC, office. He co-leads the cybersecurity practice. His practice in the cybersecurity area focuses on internal investigations, data security compliance, privacy litigation, and information governance advice. He routinely counsels companies victimized by cybercriminals to investigate the underlying incident, coordinate with law enforcement, and manage consumer-related civil litigation and regulatory investigations. Mr. Woods has significant experience handling government investigations and business crimes, privacy litigation, class actions, information governance, and electronic discovery matters. He regularly oversees and advises on the intersection between data protection issues and data collection issues associated with internal investigations and litigations.

NADIA BANNO

Counsel, Dispute Resolution

Nadia Banno joined Baker & McKenzie's Dispute Resolution department in London as Of Counsel in September 2014. She previously held the position of Head of Litigation at the BBC, where she regularly advised the Executive Board and senior management on a wide range of high-value, high-profile disputes and investigations. Ms. Banno advises clients in the areas of regulatory and public law, defamation and media law, data protection, freedom of information, and commercial disputes. She also advises clients on the legal aspects of crisis and reputation management, including handling internal investigations and appearing before Parliamentary Select Committees.

BRANDON H. GRAVES

Associate
Email brandon.graves@bakermckenzie.com

Brandon H. Graves is a member of Baker & McKenzie's global cybersecurity practice and is located in Washington, DC. He has extensive experience in conducting investigations and advising clients before, during, and after cybersecurity incidents. He represents clients in a variety of industries on incident response matters and related disputes. Mr. Graves was formerly a law clerk for Judge J. L. Edmondson of the United States Court of Appeals for the Eleventh Circuit. Before graduating from the University of Virginia School of Law, he was an infantry officer in the 25th Infantry Division with service in Iraq. He holds a BS degree in Computer Science from the United States Military Academy at West Point.

BakerHostetler

BakerHostetler
45 Rockefeller Plaza
New York, New York 10111-0100
Tel +1 212 589 4200
Web www.bakerlaw.com

THEODORE J. KOBUS
Partner and Co-Leader, Privacy and Data Protection
Email tkobus@bakerlaw.com

Theodore J. Kobus is national leader of the BakerHostetler's Privacy and Data Protection team. Mr. Kobus focuses his practice in the area of privacy and data security. He advises clients, trade groups, and organizations regarding data security and privacy risks, including compliance, developing breach response strategies, defense of regulatory actions, and defense of class action litigation. Mr. Kobus counsels clients involved in breaches implicating domestic and international laws, as well as other regulations and requirements. Having led more than 800 data breach responses, Mr. Kobus has respected relationships with regulators involved in privacy concerns as well as deep experience to help clients confront privacy issues during the compliance risk management stages. He is invested in his client relationships and approaches engagements practically and thoughtfully. He is ranked in

Chambers USA and was one of only three attorneys named an MVP by Law360 for Privacy & Consumer Protection in 2013.

CRAIG A. HOFFMAN
Partner
Email cahoffman@bakerlaw.com

Craig A. Hoffman provides proactive counsel on the complex regulatory issues that arise from data collection and use, including customer communications, data analytics, emerging payments, cross border transfers, and security incident response preparedness. He uses his experience as a litigator and works with hundreds of companies who have faced security incidents to help clients develop a practical approach to meet their business goals in a way that minimizes regulatory risk. Mr. Hoffman conducts incident response workshops—built upon applicable notification laws and guidelines, "good" and "bad" examples from other incidents, and a tabletop exercise—to prepare companies to respond to security incidents quickly, efficiently, and in a manner that complies with applicable law while mitigating risk and preserving customer relationships. Mr. Hoffman also serves as the editor of BakerHostetler's Data Privacy Monitor blog, providing commentary on developments in data privacy, security, social media, and behavioral advertising.

F. PAUL PITTMAN
Associate
Email ppittman@bakerlaw.com

F. Paul Pittman provides guidance to clients in responding to data security incidents and data breaches, ensuring that they meet their response and notification obligations under state and federal data privacy laws. Mr. Pittman also advises clients on data privacy and security issues that may arise in their business and assists them with the development of data privacy notices and policies to ensure compliance with applicable laws and industry standards. In addition, he counsels clients on the permissible collection of data and usage in online advertising in compliance with online and mobile data standards. Mr. Pittman also offers his clients extensive experience defending against complex class action and state attorney general litigation.

Booz | Allen | Hamilton

Booz Allen Hamilton
8283 Greensboro Drive
Hamilton Building
McLean, Virginia 22102
Tel +1 703 902 5000
Web www.boozallen.com

WILLIAM (BILL) STEWART
Executive Vice President
Email Stewart_William@bah.com

William (Bill) Stewart currently leads the Commercial Cyber Business for Booz Allen Hamilton. In this role he leads teams that develop strategies and implement solutions for the most complex issues facing Private Sector Organizations. He has more than 25 years of professional experience building consulting and systems integration businesses.

Mr. Stewart is responsible for providing services that appropriately balance risk and resource expenditure. Current clients include C-suite executives as well as senior government officials. Mr. Stewart has extensive experience envisioning, designing, and deploying solutions that enhance business performance. He helps clients create cutting edge strategies that optimize and secure critical business systems.

Mr. Stewart and his team help clients develop state-of-the-art cyber solutions, including Threat Intelligence, Advanced Adversary Hunt, Incident Response, Insider Threat, and Identity and Access Control. Mr. Stewart also led Booz Allen Hamilton's Cyber Technology Center of Excellence (COE) with more than 3000 staff members, and he built a large Technology Consulting and Integration Business focused on the U.S. government.

Before joining Booz Allen, Mr. Stewart worked for a major electronics firm, where he developed communications security and key management devices. He also served as a Signal Officer, Battalion Commander, Brigade/Battalion S-3, and Company Commander in the U.S. Army.

He holds a BS degree in Engineering from Widener University and an MS degree in Electrical Engineering from Drexel University.

JASON ESCARAVAGE
Vice President
Email Escaravage_Jason@bah.com

Jason Escaravage is a leader in the Strategic Innovation Group for Booz Allen Hamilton. With a focus on Digital Services and Solutions, he drives the integration of Global Threat solutions for the firm's Predictive Intelligence division. He is an expert in the systems development lifecycle, software solution design and development, and intelligence support to real-world mission operations.

Mr. Escaravage is recognized for leading large-scale, complex information technology (IT) and analytical support programs supporting government and commercial clients and in multiple focus areas, including conventional operations, counter-terrorism, anti-money laundering, and cyberthreat analysis. He has led teams of global/cyberthreat intelligence analysts in support of U.S. government and commercial customers focused on collecting, processing, and fusing data to create actionable intelligence. He holds a degree in Military History and Computer Science from Rutgers University and is a certified Project Management Professional (PMP).

SEDAR LABARRE
Vice President
Email Labarre_Sedar@bah.com

Sedar LaBarre is a Vice President with Booz Allen Hamilton, where he leads the firm's commercial High-Tech Manufacturing Practice. He has more than 18 years of practical consulting experience—providing clients with unique advisory services equally balanced in strategy and functional expertise. Mr. Labarre leads a multi-disciplinary team focused on helping companies realize technology-enabled growth from advanced analytics, military grade cyber, and cutting-edge IT transformation.

Mr. Labarre is a recognized international expert in cybersecurity standards and was the chief architect of Booz Allen's CyberM³ reference model. He has worked extensively within all sectors of the U.S. government (cabinet-level agencies, all branches of the military, the intelligence community, as well as several small to micro government agencies); public sector clients in the United Kingdom, Europe, and the Middle East; and within the private sector areas of financial services, retail, telecommunications, consumer products, industrial manufacturing, and automotive.

LORI ZUKIN
Principal
Email Zukin_Lori@bah.com

Lori Zukin is a leader with Booz Allen Hamilton, where she leads People Innovations for the firm's Strategic Innovations Group. She has led engagements for clients in the public and private sectors and engaged with them to solve their toughest organizational challenges. She has directed several high-profile projects for federal and commercial organizations, providing talent management expertise to help them improve the bottom line.

Most recently, Ms. Zukin worked with a global pharmaceutical company to dramatically improve how a newly formed senior leadership team manages and measures performance while reducing risk during a period of significant growth. In other client engagements she has worked with large organizations to help them implement cutting edge solutions for cyber talent management and leadership development. She was also instrumental in developing Booz Allen's CyberSim tool, an immersive training and assessment tool used to select, train, and place cyber professionals.

Ms. Zukin holds a Doctorate degree in Organizational Psychology from George Mason University and a Master's degree in Organizational Psychology from Columbia University. She also holds a certificate in leadership coaching from Georgetown University. She is a certified executive coach through the International Coaching Federation. Ms. Zukin is on the faculty at Georgetown University's Institute for Transformational Leadership and served as a coach for the inaugural class of the Presidential Leadership Scholars Program created by former Presidents George W. Bush and Bill Clinton.

DENIS COSGROVE
Senior Associate
Email Cosgrove_Denis@bah.com

Denis Cosgrove is a leader in Booz Allen Hamilton's Commercial High-Tech Manufacturing business, where he is an advisor to senior clients and oversees project teams delivering strategy and analytical solutions. His recent client engagements include working with staff members of a major automaker to reimagine their approach to vehicle cybersecurity and partnering with them to build new capabilities. Within the firm, he drives thought leadership for branding and intellectual capital. Mr. Cosgrove previously worked with clients in the U.S. government national security market, developing new methods in risk analytics.

Prior to joining Booz Allen, he served as a Senior Associate Scholar at the Center for European Policy Analysis and taught undergraduate courses in philosophy. He earned graduate degrees studying political philosophy at the University of Chicago and international relations at Georgetown University. Mr. Cosgrove has published essays on foreign policy and presents an annual graduate-level lecture on strategy in Machiavelli's *The Prince* at Johns Hopkins University.

MATTHEW DOAN
Senior Associate
Email Doan_Matthew@bah.com

Matthew Doan leads Booz Allen's Commercial Cyber Strategy practice while also serving as a leader in the firm's High-Tech Manufacturing business. He specializes in driving innovative cybersecurity and risk management solutions, particularly for automotive, industrial, and consumer product companies. Mr. Doan provides fundamental knowledge in large-scale maturity assessments, enterprise risk management, strategic planning, organizational change management, and governance.

Mr. Doan has an array of experiences in consulting C-suites, boards, and other senior decision makers in driving important changes that effectively reduce business risk and capture new opportunity. Mr. Doan holds an MA in Security Studies from Georgetown University and a BBA in Computer Information Systems from James Madison University, as well as a Graduate Certificate in Applied Intelligence from Mercyhurst University.

TONY GAIDHANE
Senior Associate
Email Gaidhane_Tony@bah.com

Tony Gaidhane is a dynamic and innovative information security leader with a strong background in implementing IT security, compliance (including NIST and ISO), privacy, and risk management. His most recent experience includes diverse engagements such as leading the assessment of high-risk technology platforms for attack surface reduction for a large retailer, leading the build of a Cyber Incident Response Playbook for a large financial institution, and leading a supply chain cyber risk assessment for a large high-tech client. Mr. Gaidhane has more than 17 years of experience with cybersecurity, and his experience includes managing large Affordable Care Act implementations in multiple states for Accenture, as a senior leader in its Information Security Practice and as a Director of Information

Security for WellPoint, Inc. Mr. Gaidhane holds an MBA from Duke University's Fuqua School of Business and also BS and MS degrees in Computer Science from Nagpur University (India) and Texas Tech University, respectively. He also holds numerous certifications, such as the PMP, CISSP, CISM, CGEIT, CRISC, CISA, and CIPP/US in the fields of Information Security, Audit, Information Privacy, and Project Management.

JAMIE LOPEZ
Senior Associate
Email Lopez_Jamie@bah.com

Jamie Lopez is a leader with Booz Allen Hamilton's Strategic Innovation Group, where he provides thought leadership and talent solutions to his client base across the commercial and federal sector. He helps drive Booz Allen's TalentInsight™ Solutions focusing on Data Science and Cyber and Predictive Intelligence. In addition to his core consulting and advisory duties, Dr. Lopez serves as the Booz Allen Program Manager for a large human capital vehicle, where he leads a sizable team in the development of HR Shared Services, Competency Modeling, Talent Placement & Acquisition, Change Management, Promotional Systems, and Professional & Leadership Development.

Prior to joining Booz Allen Hamilton, Dr. Lopez was the Vice President of Lopez and Associates Inc., a thirty-year-old Industrial-Organizational psychology consulting company focusing on commercial clients in the financial services and utility sectors. In this capacity he specialized in talent management, individual assessment, and personnel selection.

Dr. Lopez completed his PhD in Industrial-Organizational Psychology at Hofstra University and MA degree with a Scholars Designation in I/O Psychology from New York University's Graduate School of Arts. He also holds an MBA in Finance with a specialization in Trading and Portfolio Management from the Fordham Graduate School of Business, a BA in

Psychology from the College of the Holy Cross, and an Advanced Graduate Certificate in Counterintelligence from Mercyhurst University.

JAMES PERRY
Senior Associate
Email Perry_James@bah.com

James Perry is a Chief Technologist in Booz Allen Hamilton's Strategic Innovation Group, where he leads the commercial cyber incident response planning, investigation, and remediation services offerings, including our National Security Cyber Assistance Program Certified Incident Response capability. Mr. Perry works with chief information security officers, security operations center directors, and incident response teams across finance, retail, energy, health, manufacturing, and public sectors. In this role, he helps organizations to design and implement Cyber Security Operations capabilities to protect from, detect, and respond to advanced cyberthreats. Mr. Perry leverages his experience supporting incident response investigations across multiple sectors to help these organizations prepare for and rapidly contain cyber incidents.

LAURA EISE
Lead Associate
Email Eise_Laura@bah.com

Laura Eise is a cybersecurity consultant in Booz Allen's commercial practice. In this role, she works with leaders across multiple industries in aligning cybersecurity programs to manage risk and meet the needs of the business. She specializes in programmatic assessment, incident response, enterprise risk management, strategy setting, and organizational design. Recently, she has led teams across the financial, retail, and manufacturing industries to create three-year strategy roadmaps to improve their cybersecurity programs. Ms. Eise is a co-author of the CyberM^3 maturity model and co-leads the firm's internal investment in the capability. She is also an Executive Coach and focuses on helping leaders and leadership

teams achieve significant organizational transformations. She is an Associate Business Continuity Manager with Disaster Recovery Institute International, a Certified Information Privacy Professional, and received a graduate certificate from University of Maryland in Cyber Security.

KATIE STEFANICH
Lead Associate
Email Stefanich_Katie@bah.com

Katie Stefanich is a management consultant that specializes in cyber incident management strategy, cyber education and outreach, and crisis communication. She has strong experience in authoring enterprise-wide cyber incident management strategies for retail, energy, and high-tech commercial organizations. Ms. Stefanich helps clients understand cybersecurity in terms of risk management, as well as identify and build cross-organization relationships for smooth incident response. She also has extensive experience providing strategic counsel to startups, entrepreneurs, and organizations interested in using lean startup methodology. Prior to her time at Booz Allen, Ms. Stefanich implemented integrated marketing campaigns for high-tech commercial organizations.

ERIN WEISS KAYA
Lead Associate
Email Weiss_Kaya_Erin@bah.com

Erin Weiss Kaya is a Lead Associate with Booz Allen Hamilton. She has more than 15 years of experience designing and managing strategic transformation programs, most recently serving as an external consultant on cybersecurity workforce and organization issues to the Department of Homeland Security and a number of large financial services institutions.

Ms. Weiss Kaya has served as an external consultant to Fortune 500 companies, state government agencies, and non-profits and as an internal strategic advisor and executive. She has led large projects for effective change implementations as well as cybersecurity human capital strategies, including the hiring, compensation, development, and allocation of cybersecurity workforce. She also manages Booz Allen's internal initiative in Cybersecurity Workforce and Organization, where she established a new service offering and designed a suite of tools to support clients in the development and maturation of their cybersecurity workforce capabilities. Ms. Weiss Kaya holds a BA from University of Maryland-College Park and a Masters degree from Columbia University.

CHRISTIAN PAREDES
Associate
Email Paredes_Christian@bah.com

Christian Paredes is an Associate on Booz Allen Hamilton's Predictive Intelligence team within the firm's Strategic Innovation's Group (SIG), where he focuses on cyberthreat intelligence (CTI) and CTI program development for commercial clients. Mr. Paredes has experience helping commercial clients to produce actionable threat intelligence for internal stakeholders at the operational and strategic levels. He has expertise in analytic tradecraft and production standards; technical threat intelligence; intelligence workflow integration with security operations; and threat intelligence program development. He has also worked with global organizations to assess their information security capabilities.

His emphasis on improving analytic quality by maximizing analyst time, resources, workflows, tools, and data sources has helped clients to realize value in their cyberthreat intelligence programs. Mr. Paredes holds an MS degree in International Affairs from Georgia Institute of Technology and a BA degree in Political Science from Georgia College & State University.

WAICHING WONG
Associate
Email Wong_Waiching@bah.com

Waiching Wong is part of Booz Allen Hamilton's high-tech manufacturing practice, providing strategy, competitive analysis, process improvement, organizational design, and project management support to commercial and government clients. Ms. Wong works with clients to seize business opportunities while navigating risks around connected products and the data used to power them. She holds a Masters degree in City and Regional Planning from Cornell University and a BA in Political Economy from the University of California, Berkeley.

BuckleySandler LLP
1250 24th Street NW, Suite 700
Washington, DC 20037
Tel +1 202 349 8000
Web www.buckleysandler.com

ELIZABETH E. MCGINN
Partner
Email emcginn@buckleysandler.com

Elizabeth E. McGinn is a partner in the Washington, DC, office of BuckleySandler LLP, where she assists clients in identifying, evaluating, and managing risks associated with privacy and information security practices of companies and third parties. Ms. McGinn advises clients on privacy and data security policies, identity theft red flags programs, privacy notices, safeguarding and disposal requirements, and information sharing limitations. She also has assisted clients in addressing data security incidents and complying with the myriad security breach notification laws and other U.S. state and federal privacy requirements. Ms. McGinn is a frequent speaker and author on a variety of topics, including privacy and data security, consumer financial services litigation, electronic discovery, and vendor management. Ms. McGinn received her JD, *cum laude*, from The American University, Washington College of Law in 2000, and received the Mooers Trial Practice Award. She received a BS from St. Lawrence University. Ms. McGinn has been recognized with the firm's Privacy, Cyber Risk, and Data Security practice group in Legal 500 (2013 and 2015).

RENA MEARS
Managing Director
Email rmears@buckleysandler.com

Rena Mears is a Managing Director at BuckleySandler LLP, where she focuses on data risk, cybersecurity, and privacy. She has more than 25 years' experience advising financial services, hospitality, technology, bio-tech, and consumer-focused companies and boards on effective methods for addressing data asset risks while operating in complex business and regulatory environments. Prior to joining BuckleySandler, Ms. Mears was a partner in a Big Four advisory firm's Enterprise Risk Services practice, where she founded and led the Global and U.S. Privacy and Data Protection practice. She has significant experience building and implementing multinational and enterprise data risk, privacy and security programs, performing compliance assessments, developing cybersecurity initiatives, and leading breach response teams. Ms. Mears has served on industry standards committees and company advisory boards for privacy and security. She regularly researches, speaks, and publishes on data risk, privacy, and cybersecurity and holds the CISSP, CIPP, CISA, and CITP certifications

STEPHEN (STEVE) M. RUCKMAN
Senior Associate
Email sruckman@buckleysandler.com

Stephen (Steve) M. Ruckman is a senior associate in the Washington, DC, office of BuckleySandler, where his practice focuses on privacy, cyber risk, mobile payments, and

data security, as well as federal and state investigations and enforcement actions.

Mr. Ruckman joined BuckleySandler from the Federal Communications Commission, where he served as Senior Policy Advisor to Commission's Enforcement Bureau Chief, advising him on enforcement strategies in the areas of privacy and data security.

Prior to his time at the FCC, Mr. Ruckman spent five years as an Assistant Attorney General at the Maryland Attorney General's office, where he was the first Director of the office's Internet Privacy Unit. The Unit played a leading role in several multistate investigations into practices that threatened consumers' online privacy and security, including the largest privacy settlement in AG history.

Mr. Ruckman is a graduate of Yale Law School and Yale Divinity School.

TIHOMIR YANKOV
Associate
Email tyankov@buckleysandler.com

Tihomir Yankov is an associate in the Washington, DC, office of BuckleySandler LLP. Mr. Yankov represents clients in a wide range of litigation matters, including class actions and complex civil litigation, as well as government enforcement matters.

His government enforcement experience includes representing clients before the Consumer Financial Protection Bureau (CFPB), the New York Department of Financial Services (DFS), and various state regulators and attorneys general, as well as in cases involving unfair, deceptive, and abusive acts and practices (UDAAP).

Mr. Yankov also counsels clients on electronic discovery issues, including matters related to document and data retention, data assessment, data extraction strategies, and pre-litigation discovery planning.

Mr. Yankov received his JD from American University (*cum laude*) and his BA from the University of Virginia.

The Chertoff Group

1399 New York Avenue, NW
Suite 900
Washington, DC 20005
Tel +1 202 552 5280
Web www.chertoffgroup.com

MICHAEL CHERTOFF
Co-Founder and Executive Chairman
Email Emily.Dumont@chertoffgroup.com
(assistant)

Michael Chertoff is Co-Founder and Executive Chairman of The Chertoff Group, a premier global advisory firm that focuses exclusively on the security and risk management sector by providing consulting, mergers and acquisitions (M&A), and risk management services to clients seeking to secure and grow their enterprises. In this role, Mr. Chertoff provides high-level strategic counsel to corporate and government leaders on a broad range of security issues, from risk identification and prevention to preparedness, response, and recovery.

From 2005 to 2009, Mr. Chertoff served as Secretary of the U.S. Department of Homeland Security (DHS), where he led the federal government's efforts to protect our nation from a wide range of security threats, including blocking potential terrorists from crossing the United States border or allowing implementation of their plans on U.S. soil. Before leading DHS, Mr. Chertoff served as a federal judge on the U.S. Court of Appeals for the Third Circuit and earlier headed the U.S. Department of Justice's Criminal Division. In this role he investigated and prosecuted cases of political corruption, organized crime, and corporate fraud and terrorism—including the investigation of the 9/11 terrorist attacks.

JIM PFLAGING
Principal
Email jim.pflaging@chertoffgroup.com

Jim Pflaging is the global lead for The Chertoff Group's business strategy practice. Based in Menlo Park, California, Mr. Pflaging works closely with leading technology companies, private equity investors, and system integrators to identify, diligence, acquire and build, exciting companies. Based on dozens of successful client engagements, Mr. Pflaging has become a trusted advisor on technology and security to many in the U.S. Government and private industry. Mr. Pflaging has more than 25 years of Silicon Valley experience including 15 years as chief executive officer of cybersecurity and data management companies. He serves on the board of several security companies and is a frequent speaker on technology and security issues.

MARK WEATHERFORD
Principal
Email mark.weatherford@chertoffgroup.com
or andrea.katzer@chertoffgroup.com
(assistant)

Mark Weatherford is a Principal at The Chertoff Group, where he advises clients on a broad array of cybersecurity services. As one of the nation's leading experts on cybersecurity, Mr. Weatherford works with organizations around the world to effectively manage today's cyberthreats by creating comprehensive security strategies that can be incorporated into core business operations and objectives.

Prior to joining The Chertoff Group, Mr. Weatherford served as the U.S. Department of Homeland Security's first Deputy Under Secretary for Cybersecurity. In this position, he worked with all critical infrastructure sectors as well as across the federal government to create more secure network operations and thwart advanced persistent cyber threats. He previously served as the Chief Information Security Officer for the states of Colorado and California and as Vice President and Chief Security Officer for the North American Electric Reliability Corporation (NERC).

Coalfire

361 Centennial Parkway, Suite 150
Louisville, Colorado 80027
Tel +1 303 554 6333
Web www.coalfire.com

RICK DAKIN

Chief Executive Officer (2001-2015)

Rick Dakin provided strategic management IT security program guidance for Coalfire and its clients. After serving in the U.S. Army after graduation from the U.S. Military Academy at West Point, Mr. Dakin began his management career at United Technology Corporation. Prior to co-founding Coalfire, he was President of Centera Information Systems, a leading eCommerce and systems integration firm. He was a past president of the FBI's InfraGard program, Denver chapter, and a member of a committee hosted by the U.S. Secret Service and organized by the Joint Council on Information Age Crime.

Mr. Dakin passed away June 20, 2015.

LARRY JONES

Chief Executive Officer
Email Larry.Jones@Coalfire.com

Larry Jones has served as Chairman of the Board of Coalfire since 2012 and became CEO in 2015. He has more than 25 years of experience building, operating, and growing public and private companies in the business process outsourcing, marketing services, enterprise software, smart-grid, information, and IT services industries. He has a proven track record as the CEO of six companies and has served as director of 13 private equity, public, and VC-backed companies and executive chairman of two others. Prior to his leadership role with Coalfire, from 2007 to 2011, Mr. Jones was CEO of Denver-based StarTek, Inc. (NYSE: SRT), a provider of global outsourced call center and customer support services. He has also served as CEO of Activant Solutions, an enterprise software company; chairman of WebClients, an internet affiliate marketing firm; CEO of Interelate, Inc., a marketing services firm; CEO of MessageMedia (NASD: MESG), an email marketing services company; CEO of Neodata Services, Inc., a direct marketing services firm; and was founding CEO of GovPX, a provider of government securities data. Mr. Jones also was a senior vice president at Automatic Data Processing and held various positions at Wang Laboratories between 1977 and 1987.

Mr. Jones currently also serves as a director of Diligent Corporation (NZX: DIL) and Essential Power, LLC. He is also active member and Fellow in the National Association of Corporate Directors (NACD). Over the past 10 years, Mr. Jones has served as director of numerous public and private companies including Work Options Group, StarTek, Exabyte, Activant Solutions, Realm Solutions, SARCOM, WebClients, DIMAC, and Fulcrum Analytics. Mr. Jones graduated from Worcester Polytechnic Institute with a degree in computer sciences in 1975 and earned his MBA from Boston University in 1980.

COVINGTON

Covington & Burling LLP
One City Center
850 Tenth Street, NW
Washington, DC 20001-4956
Tel +1 202 662 6000
Web www.cov.com

DAVID N. FAGAN
Partner
Email dfagan@cov.com

David N. Fagan, a partner in Covington's global privacy and data security and international practice groups, counsels clients on preparing for and responding to cyber-based attacks on their networks and information, developing and implementing information security programs, and complying with federal and state regulatory requirements. Mr. Fagan has been lead investigative and response counsel to companies in a range of cyber- and data security incidents, including matters involving millions of affected consumers.

KURT WIMMER
Partner
Email kwimmer@cov.com

Kurt Wimmer is a Washington partner and U.S. chair of Covington's privacy and data security practice. Mr. Wimmer advises national and multinational companies on privacy, data security, and digital technology issues before the FTC, the FCC, Congress, the European Commission, and state attorneys general, as well as on strategic advice, data breach counseling and remediation, and privacy assessments and policies. He is chair of the Privacy and Information Security Committee of the ABA Antitrust Section and is a past managing partner of Covington's London office.

NIGEL L. HOWARD
Partner
Email nhoward@cov.com

Nigel L. Howard, a partner in Covington's New York office, helps clients execute their most innovative and complex transactions involving technology, intellectual property, and data. Mr. Howard has been at the forefront of initiatives to protect data assets for his clients, helping them achieve a competitive advantage or fend off a competitive threat. He advises clients on their proprietary rights to data and global strategies for protecting these assets. He has represented companies in transactions covering the full spectrum of data-related activities, including data capture and storage, business and operational intelligence, analytics and visualization, personalized merchandizing, and the related cloud computing services, such as Data as a Service and Analytics Infrastructure as a Service.

ELIZABETH H. CANTER
Associate
Email ecanter@cov.com

Elizabeth H. Canter is an associate in the Washington, DC, office of Covington. She represents and advises technology companies, financial institutions, and other clients on data collection, use, and disclosure practices, including privacy-by-design strategies and email marketing and telemarketing strategies. This regularly includes advising clients on privacy and data security issues relating to third-party risk management. Ms. Canter also has extensive experience advising clients on incident preparedness and in responding to data security breaches.

PATRICK REDMON
Summer Associate
Email PatrickRedmon@gmail.com

Patrick Redmon will graduate from the University of North Carolina School of Law in 2016. He graduated from Fordham University in 2007 with a BA in Philosophy and Economics and in 2013 was awarded an MA in Liberal Arts from St. John's College in Annapolis, Maryland. Mr. Redmon is the Managing Editor of the *North Carolina Law Review*.

Dell SecureWorks
One Concourse Pkwy NE
#500
Atlanta, Georgia 30328
Tel +1 404 929 1795
Web www.secureworks.com

MICHAEL R. COTE
Chief Executive Officer
Email info@secureworks.com

Michael (Mike) R. Cote became chairman and CEO of SecureWorks in February of 2002 and led the company through an acquisition by Dell in February of 2011. Under his leadership Dell SecureWorks has become a recognized global leader in information security services, helping organizations of all sizes protect their IT assets, reduce costs, and stay one step ahead of the threats. Previously Mr. Cote held executive positions with Talus Solutions, a pricing and revenue management software firm acquired by Manugistics in 2000. He joined Talus from MSI Solutions, where he was Chief Operating Officer, and his early career included international assignments with KPMG. He

was the Ernst & Young Entrepreneur of the Year Regional winner for Alabama/Georgia/Tennessee in 2011 and was awarded The Deal of the Year by The Association of Corporate Growth (ACG) and The IndUS Entrepreneurs (TiE). Mr. Cote's leadership style is punctuated by high integrity and a client-centric philosophy.

Delta Risk LLC
4600 N Fairfax Dr., Suite 906
Arlington, Virginia 22203
Tel +1 571 483 0504
Web www.delta-risk.net

THOMAS FUHRMAN
President

Thomas Fuhrman is President of Delta Risk. In this capacity he is a practicing cybersecurity consultant and the leader of the Delta Risk business.

Prior to joining Delta Risk, Mr. Fuhrman was the founder and president of 3tau LLC, a specialized consulting firm providing information security and technology advisory, analysis, and strategy services to senior clients in commercial industry and government, in the United States and internationally. He is a former Partner at Booz Allen Hamilton, where he led a $100 million consulting practice in cybersecurity and science and technology serving Department of Defense clients.

Mr. Fuhrman has more than 35 years of military and government experience and has expertise in many areas including cybersecurity strategy, policy, and governance; cybersecurity controls and technology; and risk management.

Mr. Fuhrman has degrees in electrical engineering, mechanical engineering, and mathematics and is a Certified Information Systems Security Professional (CISSP).

EgonZehnder

Egon Zehnder
350 Park Avenue, 8th Floor
New York, New York 10022
Tel +1 212 519 6000
Web www.egonzehnder.com

KAL BITTIANDA

Email kal.bittianda@egonzehnder.com

Kal Bittianda is a consultant at Egon Zehnder, a global executive search and assessment firm. Based in the firm's New York office, Mr. Bittianda advises and recruits senior executives in technology, telecommunications, and fintech, with a special focus on emerging technologies. He also leads the firm's Cybersecurity Practice.

Prior to joining Egon Zehnder, Mr. Bittianda served in leadership positions at several privately held technology-enabled businesses. He built teams and led growth in North America for Kyriba, an enterprise cloud solutions provider, for EXL, a knowledge and business process outsourcing firm, and for Inductis, an analytics consulting and services firm. He was previously an Engagement Manager at the Mitchell Madison Group. Mr. Bittianda started his career in technology and leadership roles at Unisys and International Paper.

Mr. Bittianda earned a BTech in Naval Architecture at the Indian Institute of Technology, MA in Industrial Engineering from Purdue University, and an MBA from Harvard Business School.

SELENA LOH LACROIX

Email selena.lacroix@egonzehnder.com

Selena Loh LaCroix is a consultant at Egon Zehnder, a global executive search and assessment firm. Based in the firm's Dallas office, she is global leader of the Legal, Regulatory and Compliance Practice and of the Global Semiconductor Practice. She recruits senior legal and technology executives for Fortune 500 and private-equity owned portfolio companies and consults to boards of directors on a range of issues.

Prior to joining Egon Zehnder, Ms. LaCroix was a senior international attorney with major international law firms as well as serving in house at Texas Instruments and Honeywell International, where she was Asia Pacific General Counsel. Ms. LaCroix began her career as an attorney in private practice at Gray Cary Ware & Freidenrich (now DLA Piper) in California and in Singapore, focusing on mergers and acquisitions, intellectual property, and admiralty law.

Ms. LaCroix completed the Graduate Program in American Law at the University of California at Berkeley and Davis. She holds an LLB from the National University of Singapore and is admitted to practice law in Singapore, California, and the United Kingdom.

CHRIS PATRICK

Email chris.patrick@egonzehnder.com

Chris Patrick is a consultant at Egon Zehnder, a global executive search and assessment firm. Based in the firm's Dallas office, he is a trusted advisor for CIO and C-suite talent strategy and development for global companies across a diverse set of industries, including retail/consumer products, IT services, industrial, financial services, and digital. As the global leader for Egon Zehnder's Chief Information Officer Practice, Mr. Patrick advises some of the world's leading corporations on talent development and assessment at the board level and across the executive suite.

Prior to joining Egon Zehnder, Mr. Patrick was CIO/Vice President of Mergers and Acquisitions with Chatham Technologies, a start-up telecommunications systems manufacturer/integrator. Previously, he was a Senior Manager with Ernst & Young Consulting and MD80 Project Manager for McDonnell Douglas in Los Angeles.

Fidelis Cybersecurity

4416 East West Highway
Suite 310
Bethesda, Maryland 20814
Tel 1 800 652 4020 *or* +1 617 275 8800
Web www.fidelissecurity.com

JIM JAEGER

Chief Cyber Strategist
Email jim.jaeger@fidelissecurity.com

Jim Jaeger serves as Chief Cyber Strategist for Fidelis Cybersecurity, responsible for developing and evolving the company's cyber services strategy while synchronizing it with product strategy. Mr. Jaeger previously managed the Network Defense and Forensics business area at Fidelis, including the Digital Forensics Lab. He also held leadership roles for a wide range of cyber programs, including General Dynamics' support for the DoD Cyber Crime Center, the Defense Computer Forensics Lab, and the Defense Cyber Crime Institute.

Mr. Jaeger is a former Brigadier General in the United States Air Force. His military service includes stints as Director of Intelligence for the U.S. Atlantic Command, Assistant Deputy Director of Operations at the National Security Agency, and Commander of the Air Force Technical Applications Center. Mr. Jaeger frequently advises organizations on strategies to mitigate damage caused by network breaches and prevent their reoccurrence. He also presents on Large Scale Breach "Lessons Learned" at cyber symposiums worldwide.

RYAN VELA

Regional Director, Northeastern North America
Email rvela@fidelissecurity.com

Ryan Vela brings expertise in large-scale breach incident response management to Fidelis Cybersecurity. He has 15 years' experience in conducting investigations and digital forensic analysis and has served as Director, Lead Investigator, Quality Assurance Manager, and Forensic Examiner. For the past 12 years he has led large-scale breach incident responses for the private and public sectors, specializing in organizational strategies, incident response, network security, computer forensics, malware analysis, and security assessments. He facilitates liaison with legal counsels, regulators, auditors, vendors, and law enforcement. Also during this time Mr. Vela served as a Strategic Planner at the Defense Computer Forensics Laboratory (DCFL) and Defense Cyber Crime Institute (DCCI), where he established operational improvements and laboratory accreditation. Mr. Vela earned his MBA from Johns Hopkins University and bachelor's degree from Georgetown University.

Fish & Richardson P.C.

One Marina Park Drive
Boston, Massachusetts 02210-1878
Tel +1 617 521 7033
Web www.fr.com

GUS P. COLDEBELLA

Principal
Email coldebella@fr.com

Gus P. Coldebella is a principal at the law firm of Fish & Richardson concentrating on cybersecurity, litigation, and government investigations. From 2005 to 2009, he was the deputy general counsel, then the acting general counsel, of the U.S. Department of Homeland Security, focusing on all major security issues confronting the nation. As the department's top lawyer, Mr. Coldebella helped lead implementation of President Bush's Comprehensive National Cybersecurity Initiative, designed to shore up the government's civilian networks from attack and to promote information sharing and cooperation between the public and private sector.

At Fish & Richardson, he focuses on helping companies plan for and respond to cyberattacks. As a securities litigator, he is well positioned to advise public companies on SEC disclosures regarding cybersecurity and boards of directors' corporate governance responsibilities to oversee and manage this important enterprise risk.

Mr. Coldebella is a graduate of Colgate University, where he currently serves as audit committee chair on its Board of Trustees; he received his JD, *magna cum laude*, from Cornell. He is on Twitter at @g_co.

CAROLINE K. SIMONS
Associate
Email simons@fr.com

Caroline K. Simons is a litigation associate at Fish & Richardson P.C. Her practice focuses on white collar defense, cybersecurity and trade secret theft, internal investigations, and complex commercial litigation, including significant state and federal appellate experience. In 2013 Ms. Simons was selected by the Boston Bar Association to participate in the Public Interest Leadership Program. Ms. Simons is a graduate of Harvard College and Columbia Law School.

Georgia Tech | Institute for Information Security & Privacy

Georgia Institute of Technology
North Ave NW
Atlanta, Georgia 30332
Tel +1 404 894 2000
Web www.gatech.edu

JODY R. WESTBY, ESQ.
Adjunct Professor
Email westby@globalcyberrisk.com

Jody R. Westby is CEO of Global Cyber Risk and provides consulting services in the areas of privacy, security, cybercrime, and cyber governance. She is a professional blogger for *Forbes* and also serves as Adjunct Professor at Georgia Institute of Technology's School of Computer Science.

Previously, Ms. Westby launched In-Q-Tel, was senior managing director at PricewaterhouseCoopers, was senior fellow and director of IT Studies for the Progress and Freedom Foundation, and was director of domestic policy for the U.S. Chamber of Commerce. Ms. Westby practiced law at Shearman & Sterling and Paul, Weiss, Rifkind, Wharton & Garrison.

She is co-chair of the American Bar Association's Privacy & Computer Crime Committee (Science & Technology Law Section) and co-chair of the Cybercrime Committee (Criminal Justice Section) and served three terms on the ABA President's Cybersecurity Task Force. Ms. Westby speaks globally and is the author of several books and articles on privacy, security, cybercrime, and enterprise security programs. She has special expertise in the governance of privacy and security and responsibilities of boards and senior executives. She is author of the 2008, 2010, 2012, and 2015 *Governance of Enterprise Security Reports* and was lead author of Carnegie Mellon University's *Governing for Enterprise Security Implementation Guide*. She graduated *magna cum laude* from Georgetown University Law School and *summa cum laude* from the University of Tulsa and is a member of the Order of the Coif, American Bar Foundation, and Cosmos Club.

Institutional Shareholder Services Inc.
702 King Farm Boulevard
Suite 400
Rockville, Maryland 20850
Tel +1 646 680 6350
Web www.issgovernance.com

MARTHA CARTER
Head of Global Research
Email martha.carter@issgovernance.com

Martha Carter is the head of global research for ISS. In this role, she directs proxy voting research for the firm, leading a research team that analyzes companies in more than 110 markets around the world, provides institutional investors with customized research, and produces studies and white papers on issues and topics in corporate governance. In addition, Ms. Carter serves as the head of the ISS Global Policy Board, which develops the ISS Global Proxy Voting Policies. Named for five years in a row to the National Association of Corporate Directors' Directorship 100 list of the most influential people in the boardroom community (2008–2012), Ms. Carter has been quoted in media around the world and is a frequent speaker for corporate governance events globally. Ms. Carter holds a PhD in finance from George Washington University and an MBA in finance from the Wharton School, University of Pennsylvania.

PATRICK MCGURN

Executive Director and Special Counsel
Email patrick.mcgurn@issgovernance.com

Patrick McGurn is executive director and special counsel at ISS. Considered by industry constituents to be one of the leading experts on corporate governance issues, he is active on the U.S. speaking circuit and plays an integral role in ISS's policy development. Prior to joining ISS in 1996, Mr. McGurn was director of the Corporate Governance Service at the Investor Responsibility Research Center, a not-for-profit firm that provided governance research to investors. He also served as a private attorney, a congressional staff member, and a department head at the Republican National Committee. He is a graduate of Duke University and the Georgetown University Law Center. He is a member of the bar in California, the District of Columbia, Maryland, and the U.S. Virgin Islands. Mr. McGurn serves on the Advisory Board of the National Association of

Corporate Directors. He was named to the 2011 National Association of Corporate Directors' Directorship 100 list.

INTERNET
SECURITY
ALLIANCE

Internet Security Alliance
2500 Wilson Boulevard
Arlington, Virginia 22201
Tel +1 703 907 7090
Web www.isalliance.org

LARRY CLINTON

President
Email lclinton@isalliance.org

Larry Clinton is President of the Internet Security Alliance (ISA). He is the primary author of ISA's "Cyber Social Contract," which articulates a market-based approach to securing cyber space. In 2011 the House leadership GOP Task Force on cybersecurity embraced this approach. In 2012 President Obama abandoned his previous regulatory-based approach in favor of the ISA Social Contract model. The ISA document is the first and most often referenced source in the President's "The Cyber Space Policy Review." He is also the primary author of the Cyber Security Handbook for corporate boards published by the National Association of Corporate Directors (NACD) in 2014. In 2015 Mr. Clinton was named one of the nation's 100 most influential persons in the field of corporate governance by NACD. He has published widely on various cybersecurity topics and testifies regularly before Congress and other government agencies including the NATO Center for Cyber Excellence.

K&L GATES

K&L Gates LLP
**K&L Gates Center
210 Sixth Avenue
Pittsburgh, Pennsylvania 15222-2613
Tel** +1 412 355 6500
Web www.klgates.com

ROBERTA D. ANDERSON
Partner
Email roberta.anderson@klgates.com

Roberta D. Anderson is a partner of K&L Gates LLP. A co-founder of the firm's global Cybersecurity, Privacy and Data Protection practice group and a member of the firm's global Insurance Coverage practice group, Ms. Anderson concentrates her practice in insurance coverage litigation and counseling and emerging cybersecurity and data privacy-related issues. She has represented clients in connection with a broad spectrum of insurance issues arising under almost every kind of business insurance coverage. A recognized national authority in insurance coverage, cybersecurity, and data privacy–related issues, Ms. Anderson frequently lectures and publishes extensively on these subjects. In addition to helping clients successfully pursue contested claims, Ms. Anderson counsels clients on complex underwriting and risk management issues. She has substantial experience in the drafting and negotiation of "cyber"/privacy liability, D&O, professional liability, and other insurance placements. Ms. Anderson received her JD, *magna cum laude*, from the University of Pittsburgh School of Law and her BA from Carnegie Mellon University.

KAYE|SCHOLER

Kaye Scholer LLP
**The McPherson Building
901 Fifteenth Street NW
Washington, DC 20005-2327
Tel** +1 202 682 3500
Web www.kayescholer.com

ADAM GOLODNER
Partner
Email adam.golodner@kayescholer.com

Adam Golodner is a partner and the Leader of the Global Cybersecurity & Privacy Practice Group at Kaye Scholer LLP, a leading global law firm. Mr. Golodner represents companies on cyber and national security matters globally—including public policy, litigation, corporate governance, and transactions.

Prior to joining Kaye Scholer, he spent ten years as an executive at Cisco Systems, Inc., where he led cyber policy globally. Before Cisco, Mr. Golodner was Associate Director of the Institute for Security, Technology and Society, Dartmouth College; Chief of Staff of the Antitrust Division, United States Department of Justice: Deputy Administrator of the Rural Utilities Service, USDA; and Search Manager, The White House Office of Presidential Personnel (on leave from law firm).

Mr. Golodner is also a Senior Advisor at The Chertoff Group, a member of Business Executives for National Security (BENS), and a Fellow at the Tuck School of Business.

Korn Ferry
2101 Cedar Springs Road
Suite 1450
Dallas, Texas 75201
Tel +1 214 954 1834
Web www.kornferry.com

AILEEN ALEXANDER
Senior Client Partner
Email aileen.alexander@kornferry.com

Aileen Alexander is a Senior Client Partner and co-leads Korn Ferry's Cybersecurity Practice. Based in the firm's Washington, D.C., office, she has led senior executive searches across the security domain. She also partners with the firm's Board & CEO Services practice.

In a previous position with another international executive search firm, Ms. Alexander served clients in the aerospace and defense and professional services sectors.

Prior to the talent management profession, Ms. Alexander was a Professional Staff Member on the Committee of Armed Services in the U.S. House of Representatives. Previously, she was a Presidential Management Fellow in the Office of the Secretary of Defense and served as a Captain in the U.S. Army.

Ms. Alexander holds a master's degree in public policy from Harvard University's Kennedy School of Government and earned a Bachelor of Arts degree from The Johns Hopkins University.

JAMEY CUMMINGS
Senior Client Partner
Email jamey.cummings@kornferry.com

Jamey Cummings is a Senior Client Partner in Korn Ferry's Global Technology and Information Officers Practices, and he co-leads the firm's Global Cybersecurity Practice. Based in the firm's Dallas office, he is also a member of the firm's Aviation, Aerospace & Defense Practice.

Prior to Korn Ferry, Mr. Cummings served as an associate principal in the industrial, supply chain, and transportation and logistics practices of another leading executive search firm, where he executed executive search assignments for public and private equity-backed companies.

Earlier in his career, Mr. Cummings was a consultant with The Boston Consulting Group in Dallas and, before that, he served nine years with distinction as an officer in the U.S. Navy's SEAL teams.

He earned a master's degree in business administration from Stanford University and graduated with merit with a bachelor of science in aeronautical engineering from The United States Naval Academy.

JOE GRIESEDIECK
Vice Chairman & Co-Leader, Board & CEO Services
Email joe.griesedieck@kornferry.com

Joe Griesedieck is Vice Chairman and Co-Leader, Board and CEO Services at Korn Ferry. He focuses primarily on engagements for board director searches across multiple industries, as well as working with boards of directors on succession planning and other related senior talent management solutions.

Mr. Griesedieck's prior experience includes two terms as global chief executive officer of another international search firm. He also served as co-head of the firm's strategic leadership services practice in North America.

Prior to entering the executive search profession, Mr. Griesedieck was a group vice president with Alexander & Baldwin, Inc., and spent a number of years with the Falstaff Brewing Corporation, concluding his tenure as president and chief operating officer and as a director of this NYSE company.

Mr. Griesedieck has been named by The National Association of Corporate Directors (NACD) to the Directorship 100, recognizing the most influential people in corporate governance and the boardroom.

Mr. Griesedieck is a graduate of Brown University.

LATHAM&WATKINS LLP

Latham & Watkins LLP
555 Eleventh Street NW
Suite 1000
Washington, DC 20004-1304
Tel +1 202 637 2205
Web www.lw.com

JENNIFER ARCHIE
Partner
Email jennifer.archie@lw.com

Jennifer Archie is a litigation partner in the Washington, DC, office of Latham & Watkins with extensive experience investigating and responding to major cybersecurity and hacking events, advising clients from emerging companies to global enterprises across all market sectors in matters involving computer fraud and cybercrime, privacy/data security compliance and program management, advertising and marketing practices, information governance, consumer fraud, and trade secrets. Ms. Archie regularly supports Latham & Watkins' leading national and global M&A, private equity, and capital markets practices in identifying, evaluating and mitigating deal or company privacy and data security risks.

Littler Mendelson P.C.
1900 Sixteenth Street
Suite 800
Denver, Colorado 80202
Tel +1 303 629 6200
Web www.littler.com

PHILIP L. GORDON, ESQ.
Co-Chair, Privacy and Background Checks Practice Group
Email pgordon@littler.com

Philip L. Gordon chairs the Privacy and Background Check Practice Group of Littler Mendelson, the nation's largest law firm representing only management in employment law matters. He counsels employers on the full range of workplace privacy and data protection issues, including background checks; monitoring employees' electronic communications; regulating employees' social media; developing "bring-your-own-device" programs; compliance with HIPAA and other federal, state, and international data protection laws; and security incident preparedness and response. Mr. Gordon sits on the Advisory Board of BNA's *Privacy and Security Law Report* and Georgetown University Law Center's Cybersecurity Law Institute. Mr. Gordon was named to *Best Lawyers in America* in 2014 and 2015 and a *Colorado Super Lawyer* annually since 2006. He received his undergraduate degree from Princeton University and his law degree from the New York University School of Law. He served as a law clerk on the United States Court of Appeals for the Tenth Circuit.

Lockton Companies Inc.
1801 K Street, NW, Suite 200
Washington, DC 20006
Tel +1 202 414 2653
Web www.lockton.com

BEN BEESON
Senior Vice President, Cybersecurity Practice
Email bbeeson@lockton.com

Ben Beeson advises organizations on how best to mitigate emerging cyber risks to mission critical assets that align with the business strategy. As insurance continues to take a greater role in a comprehensive enterprise cyber risk management program, he also designs and places customized insurance solutions to fit an organization's specific needs.

Mr. Beeson is also engaged in the development of Cybersecurity Policy in the U.S. and U.K.. In March 2015 he testified before the Senate Commerce Committee on the evolving cyber insurance marketplace.

A frequent public speaker, in April 2015 Mr. Beeson was one of the first panelists to present on the topic of Cyber Insurance at the world's largest Cyber Security Conference, RSA, San Francisco.

Prior to moving to Washington, DC, Mr. Beeson was based in Lockton's London office for seven years, where he cofounded and built one of the leading cybersecurity teams within the Lloyd's of London marketplace.

Mr. Beeson holds a BA (Hons) degree in modern languages from the University of Durham, U.K., and a certification in Cyber Security Strategy from Georgetown University, Washington, DC.

National Association of Corporate Directors

2001 Pennsylvania Ave. NW
Suite 500
Washington, DC 20006
Tel +1 202 775 0509
Web www.nacdonline.org

KEN DALY

Chief Executive Officer

Ken Daly is the Chief Executive Officer of the National Association of Corporate Directors (NACD). As head of the nation's largest member-based organization for board directors, Mr. Daly is a recognized expert on corporate governance and board transformation. Prior to NACD, Mr. Daly was an audit partner at KPMG, where he also served as the partner-in-charge of the national risk management practice. After retiring from the firm, he assumed the role of executive director of KPMG's Audit Committee Institute. He routinely lends his regulatory expertise to counsel audit committees in critical areas, and he has extensive experience as an auditor and consulting with companies in the banking and insurance industries. Mr. Daly is a frequent speaker and writer on many issues confronting today's corporate board, including executive compensation. He regularly appears in media and has been quoted in the *Wall Street Journal*, the *New York Times*, and Fox News Radio, among others.

ORRICK

Orrick, Herrington & Sutcliffe LLP

51 West 52nd Street
New York, New York 10019-6142
Tel +1 212 506 5000

ANTONY KIM

Partner
Email akim@orrick.com

Antony Kim is a partner in the Washington, DC, office of Orrick, Herrington & Sutcliffe and serves as Global Co-Chair of its Cybersecurity and Data Privacy practice. Mr. Kim represents clients in federal and state regulatory investigations, private actions, and crisis-response engagements across an array of cybersecurity, data privacy, sales and marketing, and consumer protection matters, on behalf of private and public companies.

ARAVIND SWAMINATHAN

Partner
Email aswaminathan@orrick.com

Aravind Swaminathan is a partner the Seattle office of Orrick Herrington & Sutcliffe LLP and serves as the Global Co-Chair of its Cybersecurity and Data Privacy practice. Mr. Swaminathan advises clients in proactive assessment and management of internal and external cybersecurity risks, breach incident response planning, and corporate governance responsibilities related to cybersecurity and has directed dozens of data breach investigations and cybersecurity incident response efforts, including incidents with national security implications. A former Cybercrime Hacking and Intellectual Property Section federal prosecutor, Mr. Swaminathan also represents companies and organizations facing cybersecurity and privacy-oriented class action litigation that can often follow a breach.

DANIEL DUNNE
Partner
Email ddunne@orrick.com

Dan Dunne, a partner in the Seattle office of Orrick, Herrington & Sutcliffe LLP, represents corporations, financial institutions, accountants, directors, and officers in complex litigation in federal and state courts. Mr. Dunne defends directors and officers in shareholder derivative suits, securities class actions, SEC, and other state and federal regulatory matters.

pillsbury

Pillsbury Winthrop Shaw Pittman LLP
1200 Seventeenth Street, NW
Washington, DC 20036
Tel +1 202 663 8062
Web www.pillsburylaw.com

BRIAN FINCH
Partner
Email brian.finch@pillsburylaw.com

Brian Finch is a partner in the Washington, DC, office of Pillsbury Winthrop Shaw Pittman LLP. He has been named by *Law360* as one of its "Rising Stars" in Privacy Law in 2014 and a "Rising Star" by *National Law Journal D.C.* He is a recognized authority on

cyber and physical security matters, focusing his practice on providing proactive liability mitigation advice to clients.

Mr. Finch is also a leading authority on the SAFETY Act, a federal statute that can provide liability protection to companies following a terrorist or cyberattack.

He is a senior advisor to the Homeland Security and Defense Business Council, serves on the National Center for Spectator Sports Safety and Security's advisory board, and is an adjunct professor at The George Washington University Law School.

Mr. Finch regularly speaks and writes on security issues and has written articles for the *Wall Street Journal, Politico, The Hill,* and other publications.

Rackspace Inc.
1 Fanatical Place
City of Windcrest
San Antonio, Texas 78218
Tel +1 860 869 3905
Web www.rackspace.com

BRIAN KELLY
Chief Security Officer
Email brian.kelly@rackspace.com

Brian Kelly brings three decades of leadership in security, special operations, investigations and intelligence to Rackspace.

In the Air Force, Mr. Kelly rose to the rank of lieutenant colonel. He led teams involved in satellite surveillance, cybersecurity, and special operations; as a Department of Defense Senior Service Fellow, advised the Joint Chiefs of Staff and the Secretary of Defense; and received a Department of Defense meritorious service medal.

In the private sector, Mr. Kelly held the positions of vice president with Trident Data Systems, principal (select) at Deloitte, and CEO of iDefense. He led the Giuliani Advanced Security Center and served as executive director of IT risk transformation for Ernst and Young. Mr. Kelly is the author of *From Stone to Silicon: a Revolution in Information Technology and Implications for Military Command and Control.*

Mr. Kelly holds a degree in management from the U.S. Air Force Academy, an MBA from Rensselaer Polytechnic Institute, and an MS degree from the Air Force Institute of Technology.

Sard Verbinnen & Co

475 Sansome St. #1750
San Francisco, California 94111
Tel +1 415 618 8750
Web www.sardverb.com

SCOTT LINDLAW
Principal
Email slindlaw@sardverb.com

Scott Lindlaw is a Principal at Sard Verbinnen & Co, a strategic communications firm that helps clients manage overall positioning and specific events affecting reputation and market value. He counsels companies on how best to prepare for and respond to data breaches, as well as how to effectively communicate in a wide range of other special situations and transactions. Before joining Sard Verbinnen, Mr. Lindlaw practiced cybersecurity and intellectual property law at the law firm Orrick, Herrington & Sutcliffe LLP. In addition to litigating IP cases, several of which went to trial, he wrote extensively about developments in data-breach litigation. Prior to his legal career, Mr. Lindlaw was a reporter for The Associated Press, including a four-year posting as an AP White House correspondent, covering President George W. Bush.

STROZ FRIEDBERG

Stroz Friedberg LLC
2101 Cedar Springs Rd #1250
Dallas, Texas 75201
Tel: +1 214 377 4556
Web www.strozfriedberg.com

ERIN NEALY COX
Executive Managing Director
Email enealycox@strozfriedberg.com

Erin Nealy Cox is an Executive Managing Director at Stroz Friedberg, a global leader in investigations, intelligence, and risk management. In this capacity, she leads the Incident Response Unit for Stroz Friedberg. Ms. Nealy Cox is responsible for the overall operations of the global incident response group, including supervising first responders, threat intelligence analysts, and malware specialists. These responders are deployed to assist corporate clients affected by cyberattacks, state-sponsored espionage, and data breach cases in sectors, including retail, hospitality, energy, biomedical and health, and critical infrastructure. Ms. Nealy Cox also maintains a full docket of corporate client assignments in the areas of cybercrime investigations, data breach response, digital forensics, and electronic discovery processing. She is a trusted advisor to top executives, in-house lawyers, and outside counsel.

Prior to Stroz Friedberg, Ms. Nealy Cox served as an Assistant U.S. Attorney, leading major cybercrime prosecutions nationwide while also handling complex cases of white-collar fraud, public corruption, and intellectual property theft. Additionally, she served as Chief of Staff and Senior Counsel for the Office of Legal Policy at the Department of Justice in Washington, DC, during the Bush Administration.

Treliant
RISK ADVISORS

Treliant Risk Advisors LLC
1255 23rd Street NW
Suite 500
Washington, DC 20037
Tel +1 202 249 7950
Web www.treliant.com

DANIEL J. GOLDSTEIN
Senior Director
Email dgoldstein@treliant.com

Daniel J. Goldstein is a Senior Director with Treliant Risk Advisors. He advises clients operating in complex business and regulatory environments on data risk mitigation strategies and solutions. His career has centered on guiding U.S. and multinational clients through complex international data protection requirements to provide business solutions that can be implemented across large organizations.

Prior to joining Treliant, Mr. Goldstein was the Director of International Data Privacy for Amgen GmbH in Switzerland. At Amgen, he initiated and led privacy and data protection efforts across Amgen's global affiliates, while managing an international privacy office and a network of data protection officers.

Mr. Goldstein is a graduate of the UCLA and the Golden Gate University School of Law and a member of the State Bar of California. He is a Certified Information Systems Security Professional (CISSP) and a Certified Information Privacy Professional (CIPP–US and Europe).

U.S. Department of Justice

Cybersecurity Unit
1301 New York Ave NW
Suite 600
Washington, DC 20530
Tel +1 202 514 1026
Web www.justice.gov
Email cybersecurity.ccips@usdoj.gov

In December 2014 the Criminal Division created the Cybersecurity Unit within the Computer Crime and Intellectual Property Section to serve as a central hub for expert advice and legal guidance regarding how the criminal electronic surveillance and computer fraud and abuse statutes impact cybersecurity. Among the unit's goals is to ensure that the powerful law enforcement authorities are used effectively to bring perpetrators to justice while also protecting the privacy of every day Americans. In pursuing that goal, the unit is helping to shape cybersecurity legislation to protect our nation's computer networks and individual victims from cyberattacks. The unit also engages in extensive outreach to the private sector to promote lawful cybersecurity practices.

VISA

Visa Inc.
900 Metro Center Boulevard
Foster City, California 94404
Tel +1 415 932 2100
Web usa.visa.com

CHARLES W. SCHARF

Chief Executive Officer
Email OfficeoftheCEO@visa.com

Prior to joining Visa Inc., Charles W. Scharf spent nine years at JPMorgan Chase & Co. as the chief executive officer of Retail Financial Services, one of JPMorgan Chase's six lines of business and a major issuer of Visa-branded cards. He was a member of the firm's Operating Committee and its Executive Committee. Mr. Scharf was previously managing director at One Equity Partners, which manages $10 billion of investments and commitments for JPMorgan Chase.

From 2002 through 2004, he led Bank One's consumer banking business, helping to rebuild the brand, expand the branch and ATM network, and develop senior talent. He was appointed Chief Financial Officer of Bank One in 2000, leading the company's effort to fortify its balance sheet, improve financial discipline, and strengthen management reporting. Mr. Scharf spent 13 years at Citigroup and its predecessor companies, serving as chief financial officer for Citigroup's Global Corporate and Investment Bank prior to joining Bank One. He was chief financial officer of Salomon Smith Barney when its parent company—Travelers Group—merged with Citicorp in 1998 to create the nation's largest financial institution. Mr. Scharf became CFO of Smith Barney in 1995, after serving in a number of senior finance roles at Travelers companies, including Smith Barney, Primerica and Commercial Credit Corporation. He previously served on the Board of Visa U.S.A. from 2003 to 2007 and the Visa Inc. Board from 2007 to January 2011. He was also previously director of Travelers Insurance.

He holds a Bachelor of Arts degree from Johns Hopkins University and an MBA degree from New York University. He is currently on the Executive Council for UCSF Health, the Board of Trustees for Johns Hopkins University, the Board of Directors for the Financial Services Roundtable, and the Board of Directors for Microsoft Corp.

Wells Fargo & Company
420 Montgomery Street
San Francisco, California 94104
Tel +1 800 869 3557
Web www.wellsfargo.com

RICH BAICH

Chief Information Security Officer
Rich Baich is Wells Fargo's Chief Information Security Officer. Prior to joining Wells Fargo, he was a Principal at Deloitte & Touche, where he led the Global Cyber Threat and Vulnerability Management practice. Mr. Baich's security leadership roles include retired Naval Information Warfare Officer, Senior Director for Professional Services at Network Associates (now McAfee) and after 9/11, as Special Assistant to the Deputy Director for the National Infrastructure Protection Center (NIPC) at the Federal Bureau of Investigation (FBI). He recently retired after 20+ years of military service serving in various roles such as a Commander in the Information Operations Directorate at NORAD/Northern Command Headquarters; Commanding Officer Navy Information Operations Center (NIOC), Denver, Colorado; Special Assistant at the National Reconnaissance Office (NRO),

Real Time Military Analysis Center, the Reserve Armed Forces Threat Center, the Center for Information Dominance, and the Information Operations Technology Center (IOTC) within the National Security Agency (NSA). Mr. Baich was also selected as an advisor for the 44th President's Commission on Cybersecurity.

Wilson Elser Moskowitz Edelman & Dicker LLP

**55 West Monroe Street
Suite 3800
Chicago, Illinois 60603
Tel** +1 312 821 6105
Web www.wilsonelser.com

MELISSA VENTRONE
Partner
Email melissa.ventrone@wilsonelser.com

Melissa Ventrone, chair of Wilson Elser's Data Privacy & Security practice, focuses privacy breach response (pre- and post-event), including assisting clients with identifying, evaluating, and managing first- and third-party data privacy and security risks. Ms. Ventrone frequently advises clients on compliance with state, federal, and international laws and regulations. She has assisted numerous clients with identifying and mitigating cybersecurity risks, including incident response.

A member of the Marine Corps Reserve for more than 20 years, she uses her strong organizational skills to manage Wilson Elser's breach response team, quickly bringing lawyers, clients, and forensic and breach response vendors together to optimize response time and effectiveness. Ms. Ventrone has handled numerous breaches for small and large entities, including merchants, financial institutions, medical providers, and educational institutions, successfully reducing public and regulatory scrutiny and protecting clients' reputations.

LINDSAY NICKLE
Partner
Email lindsay.nickle@wilsonelser.com

Lindsay Nickle is experienced in assisting clients with the development and implementation of risk management processes and data security measures related to the receipt and use of confidential, private, and highly sensitive data. As part of the firm's breach response team, Ms. Nickle assists clients in developing an efficient and prompt response to the loss or compromise of sensitive and protected data. She has assisted numerous clients with responding to data security incidents, and she is experienced with standards and issues unique to consumer protection, as well as the payment card industry. She also has provided guidance and advice regarding regulatory compliance within the financial industry.

Ms. Nickle is an experienced civil litigator with a background in general civil litigation and creditors' rights. In her years of representing financial institutions, she has handled litigation and arbitrations involving fraud and identity theft issues related to financial accounts. Ms. Nickle has extensive courtroom experience, including successfully handling more than one hundred bench and jury trials.

World Economic Forum

World Economic Forum
**91-93 route de la Capite,
CH-1223 Cologny/Geneva
SWITZERLAND
Tel** +41 (0) 22 869 1212
Web www.weforum.org

DANIL KERIMI
Director, Center for Global Industries

Danil Kerimi is currently leading the World Economic Forum's work on Internet governance, evidence-based policy-making, digital economy, and industrial policy. In addition, he manages Global Agenda Council on Cybersecurity. Previously, Mr. Kerimi led

Forum's engagement with governments and business leaders in Europe and Central Asia, was in charge of developing the Forum's global public sector outreach strategy on various projects on cyberspace, including cyberresilience, data, digital ecosystem, ICT and competitiveness, and hyperconnectivity. Before joining the Forum, Mr. Kerimi worked with the United Nations Office on Drugs and Crime/Terrorism Prevention Branch, the Organization for Security and Cooperation in Europe, the International Organization for Migration, and other international and regional organizations.

ELENA KVOCHKO
Cyber Security Strategist

Elena Kvochko is currently head of global information security strategy and implementation in the financial services industry. Previously, she was Manager in Information Technology Industry at World Economic Forum, where she led global partnership programs on cyber resilience and the Internet of Things and was responsible for developing relationships with top information technology industry partners. Prior to her position at the Forum, she worked as Information and Communication Technology specialist at the World Bank. Ms. Kvochko focused on a portfolio of projects aimed at leveraging ICT for economic growth and transparency in emerging economies.

Ms. Kvochko is an author of numerous publications and reports and has contributed to *Forbes*, the *New York Times*, and *Harvard Business Review*.

Individual Contributor

ROBERT (BOB) F. BRESE
Former Chief Information Officer, U.S. Department of Energy
Email rfbrese@gmail.com

Robert (Bob) F. Brese is a Vice President and Executive Partner with Gartner, Inc., the world's leading information technology research and advisory company. He brings his recent, real-world Federal CIO experience to provide IT leaders with insight on their most pressing issues and their most thrilling business opportunities. Most recently, Mr. Brese was the Chief Information Officer (CIO) for the U.S. Department of Energy (DOE), whose national laboratories, production facilities, and environmental cleanup site missions span open science to nuclear security. Mr. Brese led DOE's policy, governance, and oversight of more than $1.5 billion in annual IT investments, as well as DOE's key initiatives in open data, cloud computing, and energy-efficient IT strategies. Mr. Brese also served as the Department's Senior Agency Official for Privacy and for Information Sharing and Safeguarding. A leader in the U.S. Government's cybersecurity community, Mr. Brese was a key contributor to the Administration's efforts in cyber legislation; policy; cybersecurity technology research, development and deployment; and in the cybersecurity protection of the country's critical infrastructure.